DISCARDED
W9-BKA-139

LOSE YOUR BROKER, NOT YOUR MONEY

LOSE YOUR BROKER, NOT YOUR MONEY

by Dan Calandro

Lose Your Broker LLC

Lose Your Broker LLC
PO Box 3608
Newtown, CT 06470

ISBN 978-0-9836613-0-6
Library of Congress Control Number: 2011930545

Printed in United States of America

To the U.S. military and America's first responders,
the great protectors of the free market.
Thank you!

ACKNOWLEDGMENTS

There is no place to start but at the beginning. To my mother, Tootsie, the greatest financial manager I've ever known. Thank you for everything, especially for not giving up. To my wife, Charlene, and daughters, Jenna and Jamie, thank you for sacrificing a piece of your husband and father so that I could pursue this passion of mine. You inspire me!

To my right arm in life, Justin T. Gill, know how grateful I am and that I treasure our partnership. I could not have done this without you. To my lawyer, Robert V. Gaulin, I cannot thank you enough for believing in me from the start and for everything you've done for me since. Know that I appreciate it all. And to Scott Griggs, thank you for your investment in this project.

To two people I know only through email: Michael Wilde, who referred me to Linda Carbone, and Linda Carbone, who referred me to my magnificent and extremely tenacious editor, Ellen Neuborne. Ellen, you are exactly what I was looking for. I am blessed to have found you and extremely grateful that you took me on. From the bottom of my heart, thank you!

To my other partners in life, Dave, Bob, and Chris, with a special thanks to Chris who helped out with the tagline for the book. I value our relationship. To David Wilk, thanks for making my dream come true. To all those who had to listen to the endless stories of my trials and tribulations with this book, but most specifically Mat, Debbie, and Chrissie; Uncles Ralph and Eddie; Pelle, Sean, LT, and Geoff. A special thanks to Al and Marie for always being there. And let me not forget the great Rico Bonzinni, a very dear friend.

Thanks to you all. We did it!

CONTENTS

PREFACE

The Road to Here

I was a senior in college when Black Monday hit, driving the Dow Jones Industrial Average down 508 points and planting the seed for what would eventually become my business, my mission, and this book.

That day the Dow lost 23% of its value and lit up my finance professors like Christmas trees. They couldn't have been more delighted to be teaching what they were teaching in such exciting times. And yet they could not agree on what had just happened or on what we should do next.

One professor thought it was 1929 all over again. His advice was to steady the market by buying mutual funds. Another believed it was nothing more than a blip on the radar. He also advocated buying mutual funds. And this big swoon we'd just witnessed? No big deal. But a third instructor thought it was exactly that: a Big Deal. I remember him skipping into class on that dark Monday night with a huge smile on his face. "Everything is on sale," he said. "It's like going to Wal-Mart."

It was the first time I'd ever heard of Wal-Mart, as the discount retailer had not yet entered my local market in the American northeast. Before I could inquire, he rattled off the names of many other companies, one right after the other. "Buy them all," he said. "But if you can only afford one, buy Wal-Mart."[1]

"What about mutual funds?" I asked.

"They stink, " he said. His tone was calm, cool, and confident.

I didn't really ponder the stink factor of mutual funds again until I'd embarked on my career. While working in corporate finance, I decided to go back to graduate school at night. Near the end of my studies, I was given a project in a marketing class that resurrected my Black Monday experience. The assignment was to create a viable product, then write a complete plan to launch it to market. I recalled the Black Monday professors' wide deviation in attitude toward mutual funds.

The disparity in their opinions gave me an idea: if mutual funds did in fact stink, then there was room in the market for a better type of fund. I set out to create a super mutual fund, one that would outperform all the rest. That was when I discovered the scam called mutual funds—that they're overpriced for the performance they deliver. I also discovered that Wall Street brokers purposely overcomplicate the investment task. They do this to feed their own gluttonous desires, not because investment is hard to do or understand. It was then that I began to develop the investing process you'll read about in *Lose Your Broker, Not Your Money*.

The method outlined in this book has evolved over time. The model has been fine-tuned, the scope expanded, and the message refined. The results are dramatic. They prove that you don't need to be an "expert" to be successful with investment. All you need is common sense, basic math skills, your life experiences, and a mechanism to transform those elements into successful investment techniques. That's what I'm here to deliver. And I can do it.

1 Since that time, Wal-Mart has produced an amazing 1,451% return on investment.

For the past fifteen years, I've spent my career at the grassroots of investment—raising private equity capital, launching new products, revitalizing brands through leveraged buyouts and operational turnarounds, and consulting to high-net-worth individuals and their family businesses. One of my roles in life is to transform complex financial matters into language nonfinancial people can understand. My business is built around it. This book is one of the ways I've chosen to get the word out.

You can understand this! Everything you need to invest successfully on your own is here. My method is guaranteed to produce the high-octane results you've always dreamed of. It's all based on fact and mathematics, and has proven itself over the long term. Take each chapter slowly, step by step, and soon you will have the courage to lose your broker, not your money.

CHAPTER 1

Lose Your Broker: Step One in the Investment Process

Over time, because of their costs, approximately 80% of mutual funds will underperform the stock market's returns.

—The Motley Fool (Fool.com), April 3, 2006

It's a bold step, I know. You think you can't do it, that you can't invest on your own and be successful. You think investing is *too hard, too complicated*, and therefore *beyond your capabilities*. You think you're not smart enough, that you need a broker to have a chance at investment success. Of course, that's exactly how brokers want you to think. This kind of inferiority complex doesn't appear out of thin air, it doesn't happen by chance, and it's not uncommon. It's there for a reason. And as the old saying goes, it's not personal—it's just business.

Wall Street is a place where business and investment have become so synonymous that it's hard to tell the difference between the basic act of investing and the business of investment. The Wall Street establishment, a.k.a. the Business of Investment, is in the business of connecting those who need capital with those who have capital to invest. They "broker" the transaction of stocks, bonds, and other investment products. They do it to make money. That's their business. That's the Business of Investment.

The goal of all business is to earn profits; more and more every year. Business therefore is about growth. In order for the Business of Investment to grow, either more people must invest more money, or more people must pay more money to invest, or both. And what's the easiest way for the Wall Street establishment to do that? By performing a function you simply cannot comprehend. And how do they do that? They overcomplicate everything so you *can't* understand it. That's marketing. That's the Business of Investment.

Not investment itself.

Investment follows basic logic and common sense. It's not hard to do or understand. For instance, the best products are supplied to markets by the best businesses, which in turn produce the best investment results. This concept is quite easy to grasp, and success is no harder to achieve. Successful investment requires nothing more than basic math skills, common sense, and the experiences of your life. Once these are combined with the tools and techniques provided in this book, building and managing a successful portfolio is embarrassingly easy to do.

Want some proof? Here's a sample of what you can expect from the rest of this book.

DEFINE YOUR OBJECTIVES: OUTPERFORMING THE PROS

The easiest way to achieve success is to begin by clearly defining your objectives. For example, it's no secret that the vast majority of mutual funds fail to achieve "market returns." This well-known fact makes it appear that beating "the market" is a particularly hard thing to do, perhaps even impossible. This is an illusion. But since most professional fund managers fail to achieve this high-water mark, success to us will always mean the creation of investment portfolios that beat "the market" over a long period of time.

Just two steps are required to beat "the market" consistently. Define what it is, then build a better mousetrap.

Step 1: Defining "the market"

The definition of "the market" is a topic of much debate on Wall Street. Though most people commonly refer to the Dow Jones Industrial Average (DJIA) as "the market," there is a large contingent on Wall Street that touts the Standard & Poors 500 (S&P 500) as the superior market indicator. Let's settle that dispute right now.

During the modern era, which I define as the twenty-eight-year period from 1980 to 2008, the DJIA outperformed the S&P 500 by 245% points (810% versus 565%, respectively), or 8.8% per year. A comparative chart (fig. 1.1) looks like this.[2]

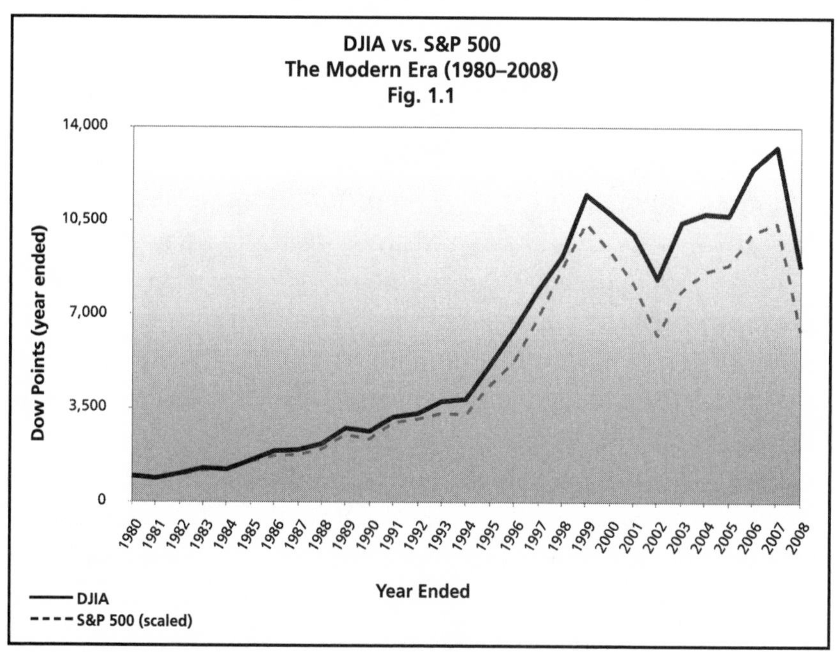

2 The DJIA and S&P 500 are indexed on two different scales. Scaling is a technique used to place those indices on the same scale. To do this, one item is scaled to the other at the starting point. It is then allowed to move according to its own performance, but on the same scale. This technique draws a more vivid comparison. The item scaled is noted.

That's a pretty telling view, don't you think? The DJIA clearly outperforms the S&P 500 over a very long period of time. No doubt about it. This makes you wonder how there can be so many people on Wall Street who tout the S&P 500 as the "superior" market indicator. They do so to establish it as their benchmark for success because it's easier to reach.

We'll aim higher. To us, success will be defined by outperforming the Dow Jones Industrial Average, a.k.a. "the market," because it's the highest benchmark for success. To outperform it is to outperform most professional fund managers.

Since short-term success can easily be called a fluke, we'll prove performance over a long period of time, viewing results through three different time frames. The first viewpoint is the thirteen-year period from 1995 to 2008. I know thirteen years is an odd block of time to review, but it's perfect. Think about it. The period begins with President Bill Clinton and the tech boom, followed by a recession, then the tech bust, a change in administration to President G. W. Bush, September 11, war, recovery, another war, the housing boom, recession, the housing bust, ending with the collapse of the financial markets. It's a potpourri of volatility and a perfect proving ground for our method.

Fig. 1.2, on the next page, shows the trend line of the DJIA and S&P 500 during this thirteen-year benchmark period, signified as 13YBM-08, or simply 13YBM. During the 13YBM, the DJIA outperformed the S&P 500 by twenty-five percentage points (72% versus 47%, respectively). Along the trend line, the DJIA experienced less volatility and rebounded faster after down periods, eventually outperforming the S&P 500.

But the trend line in this chart looks different than it does in the twenty-eight-year chart. There, the S&P 500 trend line never crosses over the DJIA as it does here. That's because of scaling. This chart was scaled in 1995 and the twenty-eight-year chart was scaled in 1980. The performance trend shown in fig. 1.2 is what actually happened during this thirteen-year time span, but it starts from a different point and has fewer years of

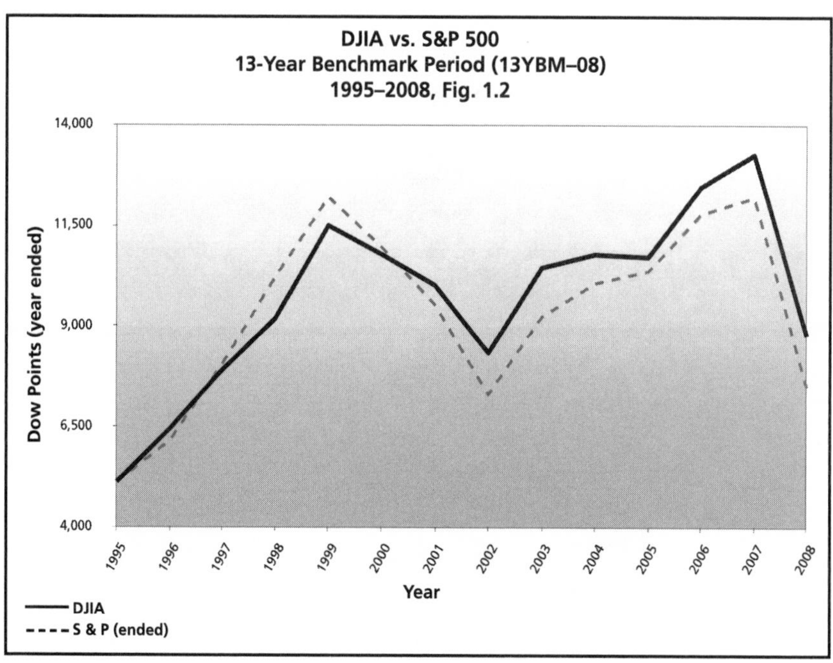

experience, thus producing a different trend line. That's why multiple viewpoints are helpful when assessing performance.

The S&P 500 rose above the Dow during this 13YBM because of the Internet-driven tech boom, which transformed all businesses into global entities overnight. As a result, more stocks participated in the run-up during this period. It was after all "irrational exuberance." So when the bubble burst, more stocks had to participate in the run-down, which explains why the S&P 500 suffered a greater decline during the sell-off. It makes total sense.

The next two charts (figs. 1.3 and 1.4, on the next page) are ten-year perspectives, the best block of time to view. Ten years provide enough time and enough market dynamic to accurately assess the trend of "the market." Both ten-year benchmark periods are confined within the 13YBM. The first block of time is the beginning ten years of the 13YBM, or 1995–2005, signified as 10YBM-05; the second is the last decade of the 13YBM, or 1998–2008, signified as the 10YBM-08.

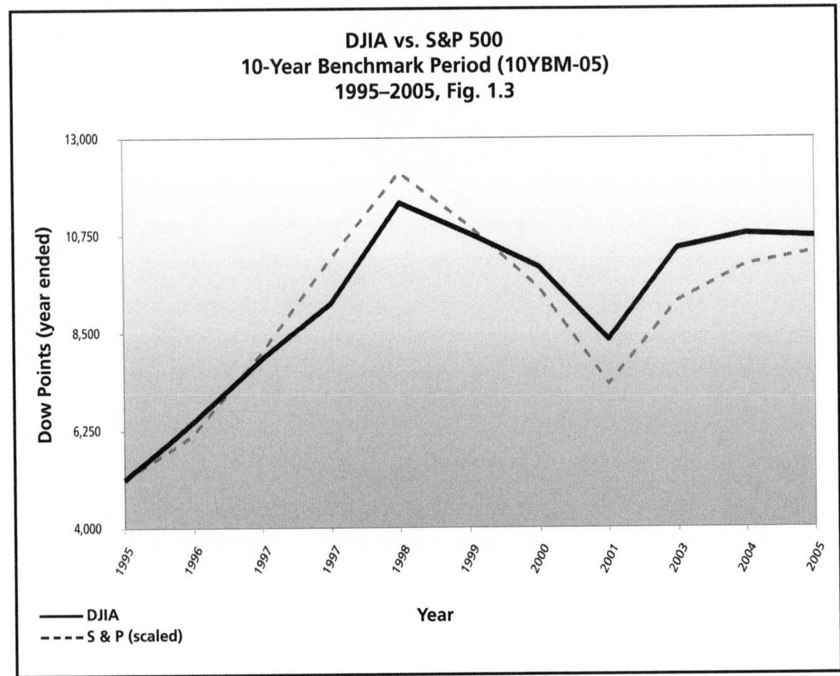

DJIA vs. S&P 500
10-Year Benchmark Period (10YBM-05)
1995–2005, Fig. 1.3

DJIA vs. S&P 500
10-Year Benchmark Period (10YBM-08)
1998–2008, Fig. 1.4

14,000
11,500
9,000
6,500
4,000
Dow Points (year ended)
1998
1999
2000
2001
2002
2003
2004
2005
2006
2007
2008
Year
DJIA
S & P (scaled)

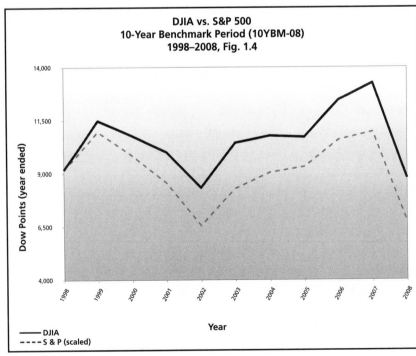

What a difference three years make! In the 10YBM-08 chart, the tech boom was replaced with the "financial crisis" of 2008, and it shows. Never once did the S&P 500 trend line cross over the Dow's during this volatile downward period. And even though both portfolios lost ground during the 10YBM-08, which would you rather own?

Look at the table in fig. 1.5, which compares the returns of the three benchmark periods.

Return on Investment
Fig. 1.5

	13YBM-08	10YBM-05	10YBM-08
DJIA	72%	109%	-4%
S&P 500	47%	103%	-27%

Besides setting low expectations, those who tout the S&P 500 as superior to the DJIA are also too smart for their own good. They are quick to point out that the S&P 500 is bigger than the Dow and therefore better than the Dow. This is where logic and treachery collide.

Consider this anecdote. Major league baseball is a sport where statistics provide a basis of comparison for players spanning generations. It's also a sport where a 70% failure rate over the course of a long career can easily land a player in the Hall of Fame. For instance, the late great Ted Williams was considered one of the best hitters the game ever saw. Ted ended his career with a .344 batting average (a .656 failure rate) and was the last player to hit above the coveted .400 mark for a season. Actually, Ted ended a season with an average better than .400 three times, in 1941, 1952, and 1953. But no one ever talks about Ted doing it three times. It's always just the one: 1941. Why?

In baseball, a player is required to accumulate a certain number of at-bats to be eligible for the season batting title. In 1952

Ted had only ten at-bats and in 1953 he had just ninety-one plate appearances, well short of the four hundred at-bats required to qualify for the season title. So why would the league have such a requirement?

Because it's easier to outperform with smaller numbers!

This is true not only in baseball, but in anything else where large numbers exist. The stock market is no exception. The S&P 500 contains a much larger sampling of stocks than the DJIA, with almost seventeen times the number of stocks (five hundred versus thirty, respectively). The Dow moves more swiftly, rebounds faster, and incurs less damage on the downside because it's smaller, with its strong companies closer in number to its weak companies. Not true with the S&P 500, which has a larger number of weak companies than the Dow; this forces the average to fall. And even though the S&P 500 average is comprised and calculated differently than the Dow, it's still harder to raise the performance level of a much larger section of the stock market when compared to the much smaller and much more agile Dow.

This brings up the old risk-versus-reward debate. Some believe that portfolios must be comprised of a vast number of stocks in order to "minimize risk." This is one of the great contradictions of the Wall Street mantra. How exactly do you assume less risk by owning more stocks? It doesn't make any sense in theory and in practice it doesn't prove true.

Wall Street sells diversification to "smooth out" the peaks and valleys of the stock market's movements, to thus provide less volatility. But the opposite is actually true. With 470 more stocks than the DJIA, the S&P 500 experienced higher highs and lower lows in the 10YBM-05. In other words, more volatility. In the 10YBM-08, the S&P 500 experienced lower highs and lower lows, and in both time periods underperformed the DJIA. Which portfolio has more risk? Which has more reward?

More is always better in business, which makes bigger better. That's business, not investment. Investment is about performance.

Knowing that our ongoing objective is to consistently outperform the DJIA over the long term, let's assume that we're not confident in our ability to select quality stocks, that we don't know how and where to find them, and that we don't know how to assemble them in a manner that will achieve above-average results. What to do?

Let Dow Jones select and assemble your stocks for you.

Step 2: Building a Better Mousetrap

Current DJIA components are made public on the Dow Jones website (www.djaverages.com). To outperform it, simply own a tighter sample of "the market." In other words, why own "the market" when you can simply own the highest-performing pieces of it, say, twenty-eight, twenty-one, or even fifteen of the Dow's thirty stocks. Doing so, and eliminating stocks by the lowest weight first,[3] these three smaller "market portfolios" outperform the DJIA by double-digit percentages over the long term, while Wall Street's unreachable benchmark, the S&P 500, is the only underperformer in the bunch. Look at the results in the table, fig. 1.6, below, and chart, fig. 1.7, on the next page.

Fig 1.6

	Market Exposure[4]	13YBM ROI	+/- DJIA
DJIA	100%	72%	0%
Dow 15	50%	126%	+54%
Dow 21	70%	113%	+42%
Dow 28	93%	106%	+35%
S&P 500	1667%	47%	-25%

3 DJIA weightings as of February 2, 2006, the day I began building data for this book.
4 As defined by the DJIA.

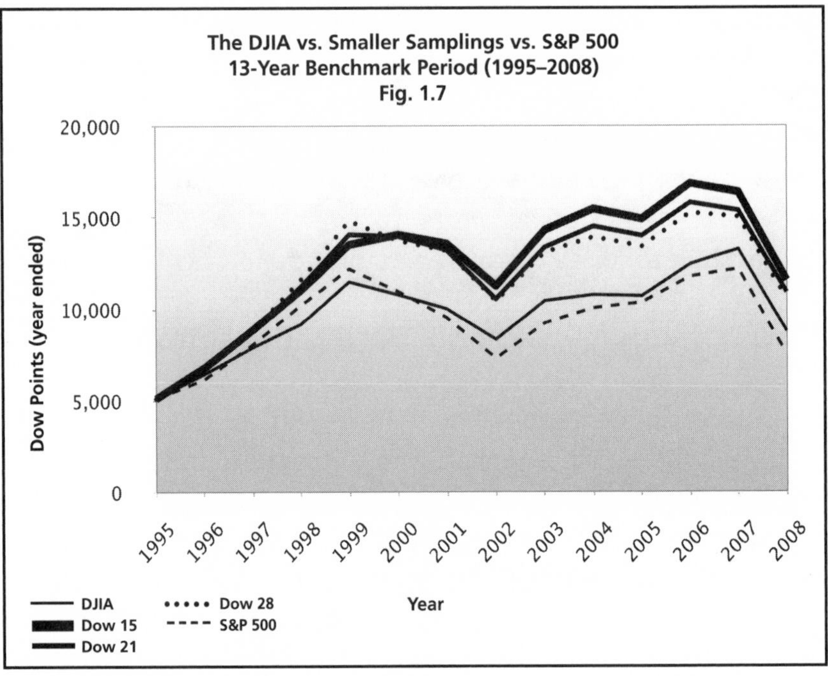

Look at the trend line of the fifteen-stock portfolio! It's less volatile, experiences higher lows (the preferred dynamic), recovers faster after downturns, and retains more upside than any other portfolio size. It has half the risk and produces 54% points more return. Why?

Because it's easier to outperform with smaller numbers.

The reason most mutual funds "underperform the stock market's returns" has nothing to do with "costs," as the Motley Fool suggests. *It's because they're not built to beat "the market."* The average mutual fund owns more than a thousand stocks. How the heck are they supposed to outperform a thirty-stock average? It's damn near impossible. That's why mutual funds aren't sold for performance, but for diversification. Which is why you need more of it—not just one mutual fund, but a basket of them. Yet despite mutual funds' lackluster performance, market penetration for them continues at astounding rates.

In 2008, 92 million individuals in 52.5 million U.S. households owned, on average, four mutual funds.[5] Let's face it, if investing successfully on your own were easy to do and simple to understand, a third of all Americans wouldn't pay someone else to do it for them—and in such poor style. That's why Wall Street makes investing seem so complicated.

Mutual funds are Wall Street's answer to the "complicated" world of investment it has created. Mutual funds are managed by experts, make diversification easy, and appear to be cost effective. Whether or not they're a frugal way to invest doesn't matter. Their performance stinks, which makes them expensive.

The reason Wall Street brokers love mutual funds so much is that they make a lot of money from them. After all, Wall Street is in the business of stock trading, and mutual funds are a great way to sell a thousand stocks in a single clip. Remember, bigger is better, and more is better in big business. Mutual funds are great for big business.

But how are they working for you?

It's time for something different: a new and simple recipe for investment success. Success is well within your reach and no harder to achieve than beating "the market." But in order to be successful, you must be comfortable investing. And the only way to begin achieving that comfort is to understand why you feel you can't succeed.

Understanding Why You Feel the Way You Do

The reason you lack the confidence to invest on your own is because the establishment has drilled a false sense of incompetency into your head. Wall Street spends a lot of time, money, and effort convincing you that it's crazy—even financial suicide—to lose your broker and invest on your own. Perhaps you've even heard horror stories about some poor soul who

5 2009 Investment Company Factbook, Investment Company Institute, www.icifactbook.org.

tried to go it alone and lost their shirt, like so many day traders did during the dot-com implosion. Since then, those kinds of stories have been enough to convince most people that they are safer, *and even smarter*, to relinquish control of their financial assets and place them in the "hands of professionals."

But how far has that gotten you?

Portfolios holding the oft-touted basket of mutual funds got clobbered during the most recent financial collapse; accounts down 60% to 70% were commonplace. But none of the pros on Wall Street saw it coming, and in the midst of calamity none of them had any palatable explanations or measure of the situation. Then to top it all off they sidestepped disaster with multimillion-dollar bonus payouts and taxpayer-funded bailouts.

How did they get away with it?

Understanding the Strategy of Overcomplication

It begins with the commercials that pop into your evening news, your ballgame, or your favorite sitcom. "Making sense of investing." "Profit from our experience." "Timely in an untimely world." What's the collective message? You need Wall Street. You need their experience, their knowledge, and their precise execution because *you can't do it*. Hey, an Edward Jones ad actually had the audacity to end with "investing on your own isn't so smart either." Are they kidding? That's a nice way to say, "Hey, stupid, give me your money. You're not smart enough to know what to do with it." What nerve. But that's all you hear, so over time you begin to believe it. That's called classical conditioning, and it's a tactic Wall Street uses to keep its party going.

By creating a complicated world, the Wall Street establishment maintains the fiction that you're not smart enough to invest successfully on your own, so you need them to do it for you. They use the strategy of overcomplication to cause a level of confusion so great that it produces investor dependence.

Investors dependent on financial guidance are most prone to buy more investments than they logically need. That's how Wall Street makes the most money it can.

But they're not the only ones using this tactic. The U.S. government has also adopted the practice. After all, look at what it's done to the nation's retirement account, Social Security. To this day it is the only underfunded and overborrowed retirement plan that is legal to exist. It is bankrupt by any reasonable account, a disaster waiting to happen.

And how does the government get away with it?

The same way Wall Street gets away with taking your money year after year while producing poor results. It maintains that running Social Security is difficult, complicated, and damn near impossible to do successfully. As a consequence, it endorses the notion that viable retirement planning is impossible for the ordinary American to perform. Otherwise we might rise up and reclaim the process, by demanding back more of our tax dollars to invest on our own.

To put it plainly, overcomplication that causes confusion is a tactic used to gain power, control, and money at your expense. This is why no one can understand their elected politician's reasoning for the failure of Social Security or their broker's explanation of basic market dynamics. If you can't understand it, then you need them to do it for you, and you have no way of holding them accountable when they do it poorly.

I know that in a perfect world Wall Street would make record profits, Social Security would be solvent, and you would consistently exceed your financial objectives. But in an imperfect world like the one we live in, if one of these three must suffer—their business profitability, their political success, or your financial objectives—which do you think will lose out?

This is why you must take control of your investment assets. I can say quite confidently that no one cares more about your financial well-being than you do, and that's why no one will do a better job of managing it than you will. The only reason you think you can't do it is because you have been fooled into believing you can't. It doesn't get any more complicated than that.

In fact, it is absurd to think that a person with the skills to earn enough money to invest does not also have the skills to invest that money successfully. Investment requires effort, not hard labor. It requires common sense, basic math skills, and your life experiences, not a sophisticated degree. Your problem isn't that you don't have the ability to invest successfully, it's that you don't know you have it. The only things you've been missing are the tools, techniques, and confidence to perform the task successfully.

That's what I'm here to deliver.

You can do this!

THE LOSE YOUR BROKER METHOD: A ROAD MAP TO SUCCESS

Success begins with a clear definition of your objectives. Know up front that it's impossible to establish real, legitimate investment goals without understanding how everything works. So you might not be able to establish your objectives until you finish reading this book. And that's okay. Everything you need is here. But take your time with it. Investing is a multiple-step process and therefore complex by definition.

Markets are also complex. And because they're comprised of multiple parts, they can be viewed from various perspectives. The next chapter covers the many meanings of the word "market." It also provides a thorough but easy to understand explanation of basic market dynamics, as well as effective tools and techniques to monitor and assess those dynamics. This is essential reading. Markets are where investment begins and performs. To understand markets is to understand investment. After you finish reading chapter 2, you will never look at "the market" in the same way again. And that's a good thing.

Let me caution you about skipping ahead to the chapter on stock picking. Poor portfolio construction is the number one reason most investors fail to achieve their investment objectives. Chapter 3, "Assembling Your Investments," unveils a stock allocation model of my own creation. It's easy to understand, simple to use, and produces superior performance results. An allocation model is useful for many reasons, but perhaps the most endearing element of a model is that it serves as a blueprint for construction, thus highlighting the components (stocks) required for building a winning portfolio. Trust me when I tell you, stocks are much easier to select when you know what you're looking for.

Of course, a collection of poor stocks, assembled any which way, will ultimately produce poor investment results. Stock selection too has been portrayed as something much more scientific than it really is. In a nutshell, the best products are delivered to markets by the best businesses, which in turn produce the best investment results. How could it be any other way? Chapter 4 provides effective techniques for building a list of quality investments.

Once you have a robust stock selection list, it's time to narrow it down to the best ones. Chapter 5 is dedicated to enhancing your stock selections through a fundamental analysis (the financial statistics of a business). Don't let this scare you off. The language is straightforward, the math is basic, and the overcomplication has been completely removed. It does require effort, but it's well worth it. As you'll see, a fundamental review has a powerful impact on performance.

By the time you're through with the first five chapters, you'll know how to build a winning stock portfolio. But investment goes beyond that. Portfolios comprised of stocks alone are at the mercy of stock market movements, which as we know can be quite unnerving. There are two surefire ways to mitigate that risk. *Expand a portfolio to multiple asset classes* and *implement an effective buy low, sell high strategy to lock in profits and rebalance risk*.

Chapters 6 and 7 demonstrate the most effective strategies to hedge stock market risk while answering the age-old mysteries of when, why, and how to buy, sell, or hold. Investment is an active sport. As such, there's no room for a set-it-and-forget-it mentality. Adjustments must be made, and these chapters show you how.

Chapter 8 contains a few parting thoughts and my personal guarantee: you can outperform that portfolio your broker sold you, and you can be comfortable doing it.

THE INVESTMENT BEFORE YOU

My objective for this book is that it be the best investment you've ever made, in both time and money. If I succeed in this mission, then it will also be the best investment I ever made, in both time and money. That's the way investment works.

But why should you listen to me? Why should you invest in this book? After all, I'm a virtual unknown. I've never worked a day on Wall Street, never run a billion-dollar hedge fund, and I'm not a college professor. What gives me the authority to write such a book, and with such boldness?

To begin with, I know how easy it is. I know that you don't need a sophisticated degree to understand investment, that there is plenty of time in the day to stay on top of your investments, and that you have everything required to do so successfully. I'm certain. I'll also bet that you're fed up with getting blindsided by the stock market, tired of being confused by its complicated rhetoric, and frustrated by lackluster performance results. I know you're looking for something you can understand and comfortably perform. I know you're looking for results.

My method produces them consistently over the long term. There is much proof in this pudding. Perhaps that's where my confidence stems from. Only someone like me, completely outside the Wall Street bubble, could write such a book in such a way. I don't know anyone on Wall Street and I'm not looking to join a fraternity. My only commitment is to you, the reader. And for my investment to succeed, you must be successful at investing. Our successes are tied together. I'm good with that.

I think there are many people who can't understand why they consistently underperform average stock market returns and who don't know where to turn for an understandable explanation. I think that many people feel hustled, and that Wall Street is an insider's game. This has led me to believe that there are many people looking for something completely different.

That's me.

Lose Your Broker is a guide to investment from the grassroots, not the Ivy League–filled towers on and around Wall Street. So if you're looking to invest in advice from yet another Wall Street mogul or stuffed-shirt college professor, this isn't the book for you. Put it down and move on. No hard feelings.

But if you're looking for a blueprint to investment success that you can understand and comfortably perform—that is guaranteed to produce the high-powered investment results you always dreamed of—then you've come to the right place. That's my objective.

Are you ready to get started? I'll see you on the next page.

CHAPTER 2

The Many Meanings of "Market" and Why They're Important

Remember the fall of 2008? It was a season that affected everyone, from the very rich to the very poor. Financial events made headlines everywhere, and the country was abuzz. Homes were lost. Retirement savings evaporated. Careers ended. Some Wall Street firms teetered on the brink of catastrophe, while other iconic institutions fell into legendary ruin. It was termed a "financial crisis," or a "subprime mortgage crisis." But what actually happened? And how did it happen?

The reason most people don't know the answers to these questions is that they don't know what a Market is, how they are constructed, or what makes them move. Wall Street has created mass confusion around basic market dynamics. It does so because Markets are where investment begins, performs, and earns profit. To understand Markets is to understand investment, and then the events that occurred in the fall of 2008 make total sense.

We'll cover all of that in this chapter, but not in the usual way. For instance, you may be wondering why I used a capital "M" when the word Market clearly appeared in the middle of a sentence. It's not because I flunked eighth-grade English; I promise you that. It's because I've learned that the word "market" means so many different things to so many people that the best way to clarify its meaning is through a combination of definitions and visual cues. We'll use these techniques to differentiate the Market (what it actually is) from the Dow Jones Industrial Average (what most people refer to when they use the term "the market").

This chapter should therefore look different, sound different, and feel different. My purpose is to eliminate the confusion Wall Street has put into "the market." Confusion surrounding it will serve as nothing short of a roadblock to your individual investment success. To be confused about the Market is to be confused about investment, the stock market, and the Dow Jones Industrial Average. When that is the case, there is no way to invest successfully. That is Wall Street's aim.

Not mine.

Markets are easy to understand and assess, but it is a process. Markets are comprised of multiple parts and can therefore be viewed from multiple perspectives. That's why this chapter is broken down into three sections: The Market and How It Crashed, The Stock Market, and The Dow Jones Industrial Average. This is essential reading. Markets are where investment begins, performs, and earns profit. Yes, I know I said that before. And I promise it won't be the last time you read it. It is *that* important.

Once you understand the Market, you will completely understand how it can reach crisis conditions and ultimately collapse. Without such market clarity, the "financial crisis" will remain impossible to understand, and "the market" will continue to be the inexplicable, irrational, and unpredictable adversary that raided your retirement account the last time. There is simply no reason to live in that condition. Your patience and effort here will pay huge dividends once we get to the fun stuff of building high-powered portfolios that blow away market returns, with consistency and predictability. That's our aim. And it all starts right here, at the Market level.

THE MARKET AND HOW IT CRASHED

Perhaps the most confusing aspect of "the market" is the term. It's used to refer to a host of different things: the stock market, the New York Stock Exchange, the Dow Industrial Average, and the economy to name a few. Perhaps that's the most confusing thing about investment in general—lots of terms are used to describe the same thing. This can be used to cause confusion.

As I've said from the beginning: Wall Street has transformed basic market dynamics into a complicated science not because it's impossible to understand, but because there's more money in it. Complication is a business strategy used to keep you in the dark. To reverse this situation, I will use a series of capital letters, quotation marks, and italics to distinguish like words from each other. This is a strategic move to clear the confusion. That's the Lose Your Broker way.

Okay, here we go.

In its simplest form, a market is a place of trade where buyers meet sellers to exchange goods for cash. Markets therefore facilitate trade. Trade, also defined as the exchange of goods for cash, can also be called business activity. So market activity is business activity, sometimes called "business" for short. See that—lots of terms all meaning the same thing.

In order for a market to profit, consumers must be willing and able to purchase goods they want and/or need; and enterprise must be willing and able to supply those products to markets at a profit. These are basic concepts we all can fathom. Your grocery store, for example, is a market. It's a place where you go to purchase groceries for cash. For that market to exist, investors had to place capital at risk to construct the building, stock the shelves, and employ the staff. They did so in hopes that the business it conducted would earn a profit, so investors could earn a return on their investment.

This highlights the basic purpose of all markets: they're about making money. They exist for the very purpose of profit. Profits represent return on investment, which is why investors invest. In a nutshell, markets are about money, profit, and return on investment. That's their reason for being.

Markets are not complete and cannot exist without consumers. Without them, there is no one to pay the price of goods. Consumers determine demand for products supplied to markets by enterprise. It can be said then, that all Markets are comprised of three parts—business, investment, and consumers—because there is no business without investment, no investment without business, and no business without consumers. This can be shown mathematically as follows:

Market = Business + Investment + Consumer

Which can be narrowed down to:

Market = Enterprise + Consumer

Or also:

Market = Supply + Demand

All markets are constructed with these same three parts. This is Market construction. So when you see "market" spelled with a capital letter—the Market—I'm specifically referring to it from a construction perspective: the combination of consumers, business, and investment. A Market can also be described as a marketplace, an architecture in which business, investment, and consumer meet to conduct market activity. So it can be a grocery store, an industry, or a country. The Market refers to the structure in which the activities happen. When you see Market, think marketplace.

And because all markets have three parts (business, investment, and consumer) and two sides (supply and demand), they are complex by definition. Complex is easily made complicated, as Wall Street is so adept at doing. Yet markets are anything but that. They follow basic logic. For instance, markets crash when all three market components fail to conduct market activity; that is, when they cease to do business. In this case Business and Investment fail to supply markets in a responsible and profitable way, and Consumers are either not willing or are unable to purchase goods for cash. It's a complete and utter breakdown of market dynamics. They crash.

That's what happened in the fall of 2008. Banks ran out of money, their product of trade. Investors would not invest in them, though many had the money to do so, and consumers were tapped out. They either didn't have money, couldn't get it, or wouldn't spend it. In the fall of 2008, the Money Market crashed. It ceased to function and conduct market activity.

Picture the same thing happening to your grocery store and you'll find it makes perfect sense. If the store is deteriorating, the parking lot is always nearly empty, and the few customers who do shop there leave with just an item or two, then common sense dictates that the store will soon fail. How do we know? Well, investors are not investing in the building, business activity is light, and the consumer base has dwindled to an unprofitable level. To drive by this market one day and see an OUT OF BUSINESS sign on the door will be no surprise at all; indications of failure were apparent all along.

Acts of war can be surprises. Market failures rarely are.

How Are Markets Measured?

Markets are measured by the amount of activity they conduct; that is, the amount of cash exchanged for goods, a process also known as spending. Your grocery store's activity is measured by the amount of money consumers spend, calculated by a simple tally of all cash register receipts. But your grocery store is just one market. Add together the activity of all the grocery stores in the country and what you end up with is *the grocery market:* the total of all grocery market activity.

But the grocery market is just one kind of market. There are many, many different kinds of markets: the clothes market, the automobile market, the computer market, etc. Add together all the spending activity of all markets within a country and you have total market activity, or *the market*. When you see the market formatted in italics—*the market*—I'm referring to it specifically in terms of market activity; that is, in terms of spending.

Another way to express spending is GDP. Gross Domestic Product is the universal measurement of market activity; it is defined as the total value of final goods and services[1] produced within a country's borders within a year, shown mathematically below.

GDP = private consumption + business investment
+ government spending + net exports

And where:

GDP = *the market*

In other words, GDP categorizes market activity by spending class: consumer, business, government, and foreign. Of the four GDP spending classes, consumer spending accounts for approximately two-thirds, or 66%, of *the market* (GDP) in the United States. That leaves just one-third of total market activity for the other three spending classes: business, government, and foreign—an average of just 11% each.

This tells us something extremely important about markets: consumers are the primary driver. Without them there is no purpose for business and no need for investment. No consumers, no market. As the consumer goes, so goes *the market* (GDP). *Consumers are market*—and that's true for all Markets.

The reason most people don't understand "the market" (as indicated by the DJIA) is that they fail to see themselves as active participants in *the market* (GDP). Markets are not the mystical

1 Final goods and services are those sold to end users, so as not to double-count market activity used in the construction of goods.

objects Wall Street would have us believe. Markets are about people—people making products, people selling products, and people buying products. As such, markets act like people. They are complex and imperfect. They have good days and bad days. Sometimes they appear irrational, and sometimes they are. But the unexpected ends there.

If people (consumers) are generally doing well, then business and investment are doing well. And that means Markets (marketplaces) are doing well. Like people, markets do well when they're making money (when they're profitable). Markets want to grow, markets want prosperity, and markets want stability, just like people do.

The average person has thousands of market experiences each day, with access to a vast network of information that includes friends, relatives, and coworkers—consumers one and all. To know the consumer is to know the market. And no one understands this better than Wall Street. It spends millions of dollars each year to find out what you the consumer are doing, what your status in life is, and how current market conditions affect you. But you have access to this information already. This puts you one step ahead.

So, really, the only requirement to understanding *the Market*[2] (a.k.a. the economy) is the ability to understand the consumer. If you are a consumer, then you are market. If conditions are good for you, then they are good for business and investment and thus good for the marketplace and market activity. That's the way market logic works.

Investment logic is no different. The best investments are found in the best markets because the best markets have the best consumers, which attract the best businesses, which in turn produce the best investment results. How could it be any other way? Limit your investments to the best markets and your

2 *The Market* is a complete view of the Market's Construction and Activity, shown mathematically as: *the Market* = the Market + *the market*
the Market = the economy

chances of success increase dramatically. It's important then to be able to distinguish a good market from a bad one.

What Kinds of Markets Are There?

Markets come in three basic forms: free, state controlled, and socially controlled. The best markets are free markets, because people would rather be free than controlled by government. Consumers prefer freedom, businesses prefer freedom, and investors prefer freedom. Why? Because freedom is a better investment than government.

Free markets minimize government's role in *the Market* (the economy). Consequently, they maximize the individual consumer by encouraging private ownership of property and allowing income and other assets to redistribute naturally through the free market system. Free markets encourage entrepreneurs (not government) to innovate, solicit, and invest private (non-government) capital. In this way enterprise (not government) supplies products to free markets, where consumers of their own free will demand them.

Capitalism is the government ideology that embraces the free market system through the minimization of government's role in the marketplace, thus allowing for more spending freedom in *the market* (GDP).

The opposite of a free market is a state-controlled market. In this case, government owns and controls 100% of supply (a.k.a. business and investment), thereby employing every working citizen and controlling demand (consumer). A state-controlled market is one in which government owns and controls both sides of the marketplace; both supply and demand.

Communism is the government ideology that strives for a classless society through common ownership of all property and enterprise. This is an impossible feat. There are always two classes of people: the rich and the poor, the governors and the governed. In any event, this "common ownership" is under the stewardship of the government, usually comprised of a single authoritarian party. Since everything is "community owned" there is no possibility of individual, organizational, or private ownership. This minimizes the consumer and maximizes government's role in *the Market* (the economy), transforming basic market dynamics from supply and demand into give and take. Needless to say, this is a constraining force to market activity and investment.

The socially controlled market holds that the redistribution of income and property should be subject to social control, shared by popular collectives (like labor unions) and the government. Under this system, unions control the labor force (thereby exercising control over consumers and demand) and the government controls supply through regulatory powers and partial ownership of enterprise. The result is that these two groups control *the Market* (the economy). As such, they are not free markets; they are markets controlled by social organizations with the goal of social fairness. Socialism is the ideology that embraces socially controlled markets.

Policy dedicated to social "fairness" sounds like a good thing, but in practice it's a major market problem, for two reasons. First, by minimizing the consumer there is no choice but to minimize *the market* (GDP). Second, large bureaucratic organizations and governments can never distribute cash and other assets as efficiently and effectively as free markets instinctively do. This limits market potential.

The market here in America is often referred to as a free market, which is not entirely correct. The United States is an extremely regulated and controlled market, in some cases to excessive proportions. The energy and banking markets come quickly to mind. The United States also has a progressive tax code whereby government redistributes wealth to social programs such as Social Security and unemployment benefits. Finally, through the use of a central bank, the U.S. government controls the supply of money and the availability of credit through the regulation of interest rates.

Ultimately the lesson you need to take away from this section is that markets can be defined by the amount of freedom residing within them. You must first determine what type of market you're planning to invest in. Otherwise you might be looking for free market investment returns in a state-controlled market, which to the say the least is an unreasonable expectation. Defining market type is a key element to establishing reasonable and achievable investment goals.

Market freedom can be quickly ascertained by viewing the highest tax rate (that's the force that limits consumer spending and business investment), which defines the extent of government's role in *the market* (GDP). The table in fig. 2.1 provides a basic framework for defining markets.

Fig. 2.1

Market Type	Highest Tax Rate	Government Spending % of GDP	Consumer Spending % of GDP
Free Market	< 25%	< 25%	66% >
Socially Controlled Market	50% +/-	50% +/-	50% +/-
State-Controlled Market	66% >	66% >	< 25%

Most world markets are hybrids of these three basic market forms. Each market has its own unique blend, as each market has its own governing body and ideology. For example, the U.S. market can be defined as a socially controlled free market: a free market with extensive social controls. It is considered to be a free market because it has traditionally been the freest market in the world.

For that reason it should be no surprise that the U.S. market leads the world with a $14 trillion GDP. Japan, a much more controlled market than the United States, ranked a distant second with a $4.8 trillion GDP. China, with a billion-plus more people than Japan, ranks third with $4.2 trillion[3]. Fig. 2.2 shows a table of the top ten world markets.

Fig. 2.2

Rank	Market	(Trillion) GDP	%	(000) Population	GDP $/ person
1	United States	$ 14.33	23.0%	306,188	$46,801
2	Japan	$ 4.84	7.8%	127,630	$37,953
3	China	$ 4.22	6.8%	1,335,962	$3,160
4	Germany	$ 3.82	6.1%	82,062	$46,526
5	France	$ 2.98	4.8%	65,073	$45,764
6	United Kingdom	$ 2.79	4.5%	61,612	$45,234
7	Italy	$ 2.40	3.9%	60,090	$39,923
8	Russia	$ 1.76	2.8%	141,850	$12,386
9	Spain	$ 1.68	2.7%	45,853	$36,704
10	Brazil	$ 1.67	2.7%	191,004	$8,717
	Subtotal (Top 10)	$ 40.48	65.0%		
	All others (203 countries)	$ 21.77	35.0%		
	Gross World Product	$ 62.25	100.0%		

3 The World Factbook, U.S. Central Intelligence Agency (2008 estimates).

All markets move in accordance to free market principals. Conditions good for free markets are good for investment, good for business, and good for consumers because freedom is a better investment than government control. Government control under the guise of social fairness comes at the expense of free market activity, thereby reducing it. State-controlled or socially controlled markets can never outperform a free market *because they are not free to do so*. The more markets are controlled by government, the more government is involved in it, the less room there is for free market activity. That's bad for business, bad for investment, and bad for consumers.

Furthermore, governments are cesspools of waste and short-sightedness. They focus their spending efforts on need rather than want. Need maintains a market; want drives it. Markets that are controlled to service need, and need alone, fail to satisfy wants and desires. This limits *the Market* (economy). That's bad for business, bad for investment, and bad for consumers.

Markets: Their Controlling Force

Some people blame the crash of 2008 solely, or at least primarily, on the free market system, or free market principals. This is utter nonsense. I don't know a free market bank in the world that would lend money to someone it didn't know a thing about. Yet adjustable rate mortgages (ARMs) with bargain-basement teaser rates and down payments of less than five 5% were routinely issued to people without income and employment verification, and who had credit ratings of less than six hundred points. Taking on such a blind risk is not a natural occurrence in a free market. The marketplace therefore had to be coerced into such behavior.

So who held the proverbial gun to the market's head? Who else? The government.

Governments control markets. That's their purpose and reason for existence. A government's goals in all cases is market stability and steady growth. It pursues these goals in three main ways:

- Controlling behavior by imposing and enforcing laws and regulations
- Controlling the amount of currency in circulation (often referred to as money supply) and the availability of credit through regulation of interest rates
- Controlling the amount of money markets have to spend through taxation

When markets fail, government has failed in its core mission to provide market stability. Markets do not crash on a whim; threatening conditions exist long before collapse. These conditions generally follow an extended period of overheated growth that produces a wide-scale and rapid rise in prices: a.k.a. inflation. These conditions exist for a reason. Either government allowed them to exist, encouraged them to exist, or both.

To be clear, *market crashes are a failure of government first and foremost because government controls the Market* (the economy). It's important then to be able to identify changes in a market's condition.

Critical Indicators of a Market's Condition

Times change. Things change. And markets change. They can go from good to bad, bad to good, or bad to worse. The key is to identify changes in market conditions so you can make timely adjustments to your investment portfolio. Luckily most market indicators are easy to spot. The same factors that affect you the consumer negatively also affect business and investment negatively. This makes them easy to monitor. There are five key indicators that signify changing market conditions:

- Taxes
- Unemployment
- Inflation
- Interest rates
- Laws and regulations

Let's go through these indicators one by one to illustrate how they affect markets and what you can do to monitor them.

Taxes

Taxes represent the government's ownership percentage of your earnings. If your tax rate is 20% you work one day per week for the government. Taxes reduce the amount of money you have to spend in markets and therefore reduce free market spending. That's bad for you, bad for business, and bad for investment.

Perhaps it is appropriate to point out that *businesses do not pay taxes*—they collect them. Whatever they might owe the government in taxes they collect first from you, via their pricing structure. Here's the mathematical definition of price.

Price = Cost + Taxes + Profit

Corporate taxes increase prices and limit capital resources to pay employees and expand operations. That's bad for business, bad for investment, and bad for employees (a.k.a. consumers). And when taxes on investment go up, investors have less money to invest. That's bad for businesses looking to start or expand, which is bad for the unemployed, as well as employees looking to expand their careers or wage bases. Tax changes signal a change in market condition, and the stock market will react. Taxes restrict free market activity and are thus bad for business and investment.

Markets and investments grow during times of expansion and shrink during recessions. Changing tax rates is a tactic the government uses to expand or contract *the market* (GDP). Raising taxes during a recession is equivalent to pouring gasoline on a fire because it shrinks an already shrinking market. When *the Market* (the economy) needs spending energy, lowering taxes is the best medicine because it provides additional cash to markets instantaneously.

Unemployment

The unemployment rate represents the percentage of consumers who are not working. When you're unemployed you have less money to spend in markets. That's bad for you, bad for business, and bad for investment. Rising unemployment signals that business is shrinking. Businesses cut jobs either because there is nothing for those workers to do or the business cannot afford to pay them. That's bad for investment. The table below (Fig. 2.3.a) gives a guideline for interpreting the unemployment rate.

Fig. 2.3.a

	Dangerously Low	Desired	Warning	Dangerously High
Unemployment	0%–2%	3%–5%	6%–9%	10%+

Dangerously low or zero unemployment is a no-growth market condition; businesses cannot expand labor and thus cannot expand operations. This is not good for business or investment. It is also extremely rare.

Inflation

Inflation is defined as the general rise in prices; it is the cost of money. Inflation limits purchasing power because more money is required to purchase the same amount of goods. And when prices increase faster than wages, consumers lose money year after year because the price of goods is rising faster than their ability to earn. As a consequence, consumers purchase fewer goods. That's bad for markets and investment. Fig. 2.3.b provides a guideline to inflation.

Fig. 2.3.b

	Desired	Warning	Dangerous
Inflation	1%–3%	4%–6%	7%+

The opposite of inflation is deflation, a general decrease in prices. This condition, believe it or not, is worse than inflation. Deflation on a national level is bad because it signifies a shrinking *Market* (economy) and needless to say is a bad thing for enterprise, employees, and markets.

Interest Rates

Interest rates represent the cost of borrowing. And since the government establishes key interest rates through the Federal Reserve, it thus controls the availability of credit to the marketplace. When the Fed raises interest rates it does so to discourage borrowing; in other words, to discourage the Market from spending beyond its means. But markets need debt to operate and grow. High interest rates increase the cost of operation and growth. That's bad for business, bad for investment, and bad for consumers. Fig. 2.3.c shows the guideline.

Fig. 2.3.c

	Dangerously Low	Desired	Warning	Dangerously High
Interest Rates*	0%–1%	2%–5%	6%–9%	10%+

* Fed funds rate

Interest rates of 0% are dangerous for many reasons, but mostly because the government loses one of its major tools to spur on market activity, as it cannot encourage borrowing beyond 0% interest rates.

Monitoring Market Indicators

Changes in these four market indicators are easy to identify. Taxes change only after a long public debate in the United States and therefore should come as no surprise once enacted. National data for inflation, interest rates, and unemployment are plastered all over the news media—radio, TV, print, and the Web —once reported. So keep your eyes on the current news, in one venue or another.

But you should also monitor these items in your own life, with your own experiences. Watch the deductions listed on your paycheck and compare your year-end tax payments to those of prior years. Become a smart shopper by monitoring the prices you pay for goods in markets. Also notice the activity in those markets, or their parking lots as you drive by. (Men, women are a great asset when assessing all facets of market activity. They are generally the smartest and most active shoppers.) Especially monitor the price of gasoline; since all goods must travel to markets it thus affects the price of all goods. Interest rates are posted in every bank and are easily found on the Internet. Unemployment can be assessed by the percentage of people you know who have lost their jobs or are in jeopardy of losing their jobs.

The best way to assess business is to talk to the personnel in local enterprises. Besides a nice conversation piece, most local retailers are more than willing to tell you how their business is doing. Wherever I go I ask waiters, cashiers, and shop owners how business is, in what direction costs are heading, and how they've been impacted by recent government regulations. The information they provide is always spot on and extremely insightful.

Work these conversations into the chores of daily life and sample as many people from as many different walks of life as you can. And don't forget about your network of family, friends, and coworkers. This is how you assess market activity. Once you've collected your market research, compare it to national data when it's reported. Remember, the U.S. *market* (GDP) is $14 trillion. As such, market stimuli is felt at the grassroots level long before it appears in national data. So don't be surprised if you're way ahead of the national picture. (I'm generally eighteen to twenty-four months ahead of national data.)

Now it's time to get to the fifth and final market indicator on my list. It's different from the rest and not as easily identified, assessed, or explained. For these reasons I've set it apart for special treatment.

Laws and Regulations

Laws and regulations are a different kind of beast than any other market indicator. Much in the same way that Wall Street overcomplicates everything about investment, the government overcomplicates its regulatory action. Legislative poison is usually contained in the fine print of a thousand-page bill, its perils often not revealed until many years after the law was passed. You need to know what your government is doing. Government policy changes are changes in Market (marketplace) conditions! Investors must take note.

Markets can be expanded or contracted through legislative action. When the government contracts the Market (marketplace) through regulation, it shrinks *the market* (GDP). Needless to say this is not a positive sign for business, investment, or consumers. But when government uses regulation to expand markets, it does so to encourage markets to conduct activity beyond their natural and self-imposed limits. This coercion has no choice but to put stress on the Market (marketplace), which is forced to act against its basic instinct. There is no better example of this than the 2008 crash. That's where we go next.

Putting It All Together to Understand the Crash of 2008: An Exposé

Knowing what we now know about the market, its makeup, motivating factors, and controlling force, let us examine the crash of 2008 from the complete market perspective: construction, activity, and governmental action. This story, stretching back decades, evolved over time. But since markets begin and end with the consumer, that's where we'll start.

To begin we must acknowledge that there is always a thirst and hunger for American land. The private ownership of land is a basic tenet of liberty and independence. It is central to the American Dream. A piece of it, regardless of location, and even with punitive subprime mortgage contracts attached, is a piece of land in the best market in the world: the $14 trillion U.S. market. It is impossible to fault anyone who stretches out their arms to attain it.

To cause a market crash is a crime indeed, but that crime is not attributable to the consumers at the forefront of collapse. The government encouraged the huge commitment of buying a piece of real property to a vulnerable consumer base with an irresponsible frivolity advertised as "fair" and "easy." This fatal error in judgment, the ultimate culprit in the collapse, was made by the government. It was the government that allowed and encouraged the Market (marketplace) to assume more debt than it could pay back. Not the consumer.

But who are these consumers tagged as "irresponsible" by the U.S. government? How and why did they become irresponsible? Were they irresponsible before they obtained loans? And if so, how did they get a mortgage in the first place?

Well, we know that subprime mortgage consumers were at the point of impact. Subprime mortgages come in many varieties, most commonly the adjustable rate mortgage (ARM). ARMs have low introductory rates that can adjust after a certain amount of time, usually two or three years. Subprime mortgages are a mechanism used to provide loans to individuals with low credit ratings (often below six hundred). Unlike a conventional ARM, the subprime ARM adds a premium to the adjusting interest rate in order to compensate the lender for the higher risk associated with the consumer.

This might make sense using conventional risk-reward theories, but in practice it makes none. If someone with poor credit is having trouble paying their bills, then logic dictates that they will have more trouble paying higher interest rates. Am I wrong here? But by operating in this fashion, banks transformed high-risk loans into higher-risk propositions.

Why would they do this?

The Community Reinvestment Act (CRA), originally signed in 1977, sought to reverse the deteriorating conditions in lower-income neighborhoods by encouraging banks to lend money to the people who lived there (lower-income consumers), so they could reinvest in their neighborhoods and make them nicer. Since the government could not force banks to assume these higher-risk loans, this legislation aimed to encourage banks into doing so by mandating them to be evaluated for CRA compliance. However, in classic governmental style the law failed to clearly define "compliance." But here's the best part: no penalties were assessed for noncompliance.

Huh?

You see, the government could not force banks to make these higher-risk loans, nor could it financially penalize banks for not assuming higher risk. This kind of pressure is unconstitutional. Instead lawmakers attempted to encourage banks into doing so, by making the same federal agencies in charge of CRA compliance evaluations also responsible for approving new bank branches, mergers, and acquisitions. In other words, if banks wanted to grow they had to make more high-risk loans.

Despite this political maneuver the CRA got off to a slow start, with banks often citing the legislation's "safe and sound" standard to restrain their market exposure to lower-income borrowers. Unable to leave well enough alone, Congress amended the CRA various times during the next several decades to get the program moving. In each instance the goal was to expand the mortgage market to lower-income consumers.

For example, an amendment in the 1980s made CRA ratings available to the public. The goal was to increase demand for subprime mortgages, while encouraging communities to organize and protest bank practices. In other words, to pressure banks into supplying more loans to lower-income consumers. This is an example of the government encouraging market expansion through legislative and regulatory action.

The CRA was again modified a series of times in the 1990s. Most significantly, CRA ratings were simplified to one-word assessments (outstanding, satisfactory, or noncompliant), making them easier to read, assess, and protest; CRA ratings were posted on the Internet, facilitating public protests by community organizations, *which now counted against bank CRA ratings.*

These legislative changes emboldened community organizations like ACORN, which now, with the ability to block bank expansions, mergers, and acquisitions, were empowered to extort banks into dedicating more of their lending power to affordable housing. This kind of power also created the opportunity for banks to move closer to community organizations by offering payoffs, bribes, and backroom deals to stifle protests. These actions corrupt market activity.

These regulatory moves occurred during the tech boom of the late 1990s, which created all sorts of new wealth in the marketplace. At that time *the market* (GDP) was growing at a robust pace, inflation and unemployment were low and stable, and spirits were high. The world market was connected by the Internet, giving local mom-and-pop stores access to global consumers. Money was flowing, and banks were popping up all over the place.

CRA compliance became essential to their expansion.

Also at this time CRA amendments provided expanded scope, power, and resources to the Federal National Mortgage Association (Fannie Mae) and the Federal Home Loan Mortgage Corporation (Freddie Mac). Fannie Mae was established in 1938 to create a secondary market for mortgage debt. Fannie would either purchase or guarantee a certain amount of mortgage debt from banks in order to facilitate a bank's ability to balance risk levels in their debt portfolios. This too was a government effort to expand the mortgage market. In 1970 Freddie Mac was established to compete with Fannie Mae, thus expanding the mortgage market even more. These two entities were government-sponsored enterprises (GSEs): public-private partnerships in enterprise. It's a scary thing anytime the government is part of enterprise, but it's even scarier when the government starts another business to compete against itself. That's twice the trouble.

In the 1990s resources to Fannie and Freddie were increased dramatically. They also received a congressional mandate to increase their purchases of lower-income consumer mortgages that went so far as to establish a target. In other words, the government told Fannie and Freddie how much high-risk debt to take on. That target increased to 52% in 2005, with 22% of those loans dedicated to a "special" section of the market: consumers "with income less than 60% of their area's median income."[4] This kind of high-risk loan-making is well beyond the norm of free market boundaries.

Remember, the purpose of the CRA and its amendments was to encourage banks into this kind of high-risk behavior. As such, banks often found themselves beyond the "safe and sound" standard in the CRA. Fannie and Freddie were then deployed to relieve the banking system of mortgage debt, by either purchasing debt or guaranteeing it. This made room for banks to make more loans, which they had to do if they wanted to remain CRA

4 Russell Roberts, "How the Government Stoked the Mania," *Wall Street Journal* online, October 3, 2008, http://online.wsj.com/article/SB122298982558700341.html.

compliant and thus grow during the heyday of the tech boom.

Back then everything was hunky-dory: there was plenty of money and plenty of growth to offset the higher risks associated with subprime mortgage portfolios. Remember, the goal of all business is to grow. Indeed, these loans were high risk, but Fannie Mae and Freddie Mac were active in the marketplace, purchasing debt and guaranteeing more against default. This made it easier for banks to take on the additional risk. And it also made subprime mortgage paper a lucrative commodity.

Enter: Wall Street.

In 1997 Bear Stearns and First Union were the first companies to "securitize" subprime mortgage debt. Securitization is the process of bundling mortgage paper into a fund, which, much like a mutual fund, is then traded as a security. Once bundled, the securities were called asset-backed securities or mortgage-backed securities.

Asset-backed securities were a unique Wall Street creation. They were backed by an asset, U.S. real estate, which was enjoying a full-fledged housing boom. Higher housing prices meant higher valuations for asset-backed securities, which came along with interest rates much higher than the market norm (thanks to the add-on premium for subprime mortgages). And because they were endorsed by GSEs, they carried an implied U.S. government guarantee. In short, asset-backed securities provided high income, high growth, and minimal investment risk.

And the world bought in.

Demand for asset-backed securities skyrocketed. This provided Fannie Mae and Freddie Mac with a mechanism to sell mortgage debt and thus clear it from their books. It also afforded them the opportunity to purchase more mortgage debt from banks, which in turn cleared more room for banks to make more high-risk loans.

Can you see the house of cards being built here?

And because Fannie and Freddie were now both buyers and sellers of mortgage paper, they had effectively turned themselves into a hedge fund financed by taxpayer dollars. The U.S. government has absolutely no constitutional authority to conduct this kind of business activity. In fact, government should never enter business because it has an unfair advantage over all other enterprise: it can guarantee the full faith and support of the American people, for generations to come!

The U.S. government has unlimited resources to go along with an unreliable management team driven by political success rather than return on investment. This awful combination produces reckless activity and dreaded outcomes, as seen in the fall of 2008. For instance, due to the government's bold and aggressive expansion of the mortgage debt market, housing prices continued to rise at a blistering pace, causing asset-backed securities to experience huge capital appreciation. Many firms borrowed money against their rising asset-backed securities to buy more asset-backed securities. This pushed demand even higher, and well beyond free market limits.

In the critical years leading up to the 2008 crash the Federal Reserve was expanding the money supply, meaning it was adding more dollars to circulate in the economy. Call that Easy Money. At the same time the Fed was aggressively lowering short-term interest rates. In fact, interest rates averaged just 1.5% from October 2001 to June 2004, about half the rate of inflation. In this case the borrower did not pay interest, but rather gained purchasing power from taking on more debt, because interest rates were lower than inflation. Call that Cheap Money. Add them together and they make a Cheap and Easy Money Policy.

The purpose of Cheap and Easy Money is to encourage borrowing, or in other words, to encourage spending beyond one's means. This is how government changes market behavior by using monetary policy such as interest rates and money supply to increase market activity. This added fuel to the fire and forced housing prices to explosive heights. It also provided first-time homeowners with something they never realized before: capital gains. Refinancing one's home became a routine tactic to pay off those tapped-out credit cards, pull out some cash for spending, and perhaps buy a new car. Some refinanced their homes multiple times; others "flipped" their homes to cash out or parlay the profits into another, perhaps better, home—also leveraged to the hilt. For the first-time homebuyer it was like printing money, with seemingly no end in sight. It was irrational exuberance all over again.

And then the proverbial shit hit the fan.

To slow this overheated growth, the government began raising interest rates in 2003; by midyear 2006 the federal funds rate had increased 425% (from 1% to 5.25%). These rates directly affected ARMs, which were adjusting to higher rates (tack on the premiums for the subprime borrower). Also during this time national gasoline prices more than doubled, rising 108%. The chart in fig. 2.3 compares the movements of average gasoline prices and short-term interest rates, as depicted by the federal funds rate.

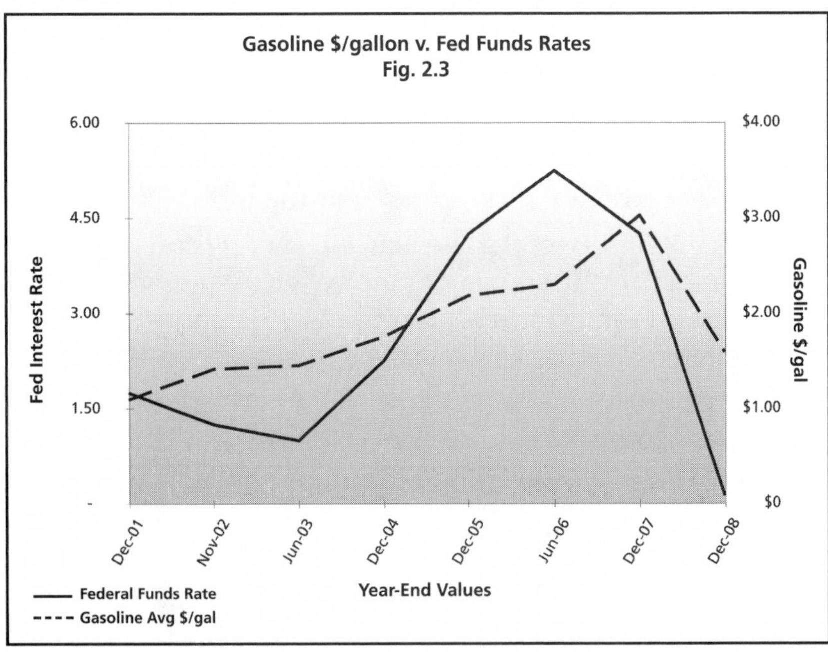

Imagine the consumer whose mortgage payment adjusted in 2006, when gasoline prices shot up over $4 a gallon in some markets. Inexperienced homeowners never had a chance. Until this point, owning a home was easy—no harder than the next refinance. They thought it would always be that easy. But this misconception was not their fault. It was all they knew. And let's face it, the government made it that easy with Cheap and Easy Money Policy and an irresponsible overexpansion of the debt market.

When the bubble burst it crashed the banking system. But the damage did not end there. Many of these high-risk loans and asset-backed securities were insured. When subprime borrowers began to default, note holders filed claim for relief. This brought AIG, the world's largest insurance company, to its knees. Hard to imagine, I know, as insuring against catastrophic loss is its business. It's what they do. But AIG didn't have the money to pay the claims.

Why?

Well, perhaps it bit off more than it could chew. But most probably it chose not to fully fund loss reserves because the government guaranteed many of the high-risk loans and asset-backed securities by way of the Fannie and Freddie relationship. By participating in *the Market* (economy) this way, the government gave AIG no reason to prudently fund loss reserves. Government's presence in the marketplace caused it to do things it normally wouldn't do, which made business practices more risky.

For instance, insurance companies invest heavily in bond and debt portfolios as a common practice to service their insurance products. For the reasons already stated, asset-backed securities became a favorite. Insurance companies like AIG therefore also morphed into a quasi hedge fund by insuring against the default of high-risk subprime mortgages, while making investments in the same. They got hit with a double whammy. And as the disaster spread throughout the entire industry, banks, insurers, and investment companies all scrambled to raise capital. But the well was dry. The market was a mess, and there was no incentive to invest. So capital stood on the sidelines.

Enter: Government.

In unprecedented fashion, President G. W. Bush authorized a massive bailout of the financial industry, making one of the most ridiculous statements ever uttered by a sitting president: "I've abandoned free-market principals to save the free-market system." Really. That's like a captain saying, "I've abandoned ship to save the ship." It's an oxymoron.

Bailouts are a bandage. They do not address the systemic causes of collapse. So what should the government have done to correct the problem?

Instead of taking control of business, the government should have honored its central banking role and acted as the lender of last resort. Bridge loans should have been established to all financial institutions in trouble while they reorganized, restructured, and raised capital under new operating plans. Of course, only the best management would have been able to raise new capital. The others would have ended up in bankruptcy.

Good.

Failure is a part of freedom and the free market system. It's a healthy thing; a required element to the cleansing process and quite necessary. We all can't be winners all the time. And let's face it, some companies belong out of business.

When markets crash they cease to conduct market activity. Consumers are not willing and/or able to spend, investors are not willing to invest, and businesses cannot supply markets. In 2008 banks ran out of money and borrowing power, investors did not heed the call for capital, and consumers were tapped out. *The Market* (the economy) was in dire need of capital. The most efficient and effective solution to this dilemma would have been Market tax cuts.

If the U.S. government had cut personal tax rates in the fall of 2008, consumers would have had more money to pay their bills: their credit cards and mortgages, for instance. That would have helped consumers—and banks. If capital gains taxes on investment had been cut from 15% to 5%, investors would have had greater incentive to invest during such a high-risk time. And if business taxes had been cut from 35% to 15%, companies would have returned to profitability faster, which would have stymied unemployment, provided greater price stability in the marketplace, and paved the way for better investment results. Had these measures been taken, the free market would have had the ability to bail itself out, which would have left innocent taxpayers to be exactly what they should have remained: innocent bystanders.

Once taxes were cut, the next thing the government should have done was throw out all the bogus legislation enacted during the last meltdown of major corporations. The Sarbanes-Oxley Act, another massive piece of government regulation, was implemented after the collapse of megacorporations WorldCom and Enron (also during the Bush era), with the sole purpose of ensuring companies "too big to fail" wouldn't fail again. Clearly, it doesn't work and should have been thrown out as a matter of course.

Yet when President Bush advised bailing out the financial industry in October of 2008, he found virtually no opposition in Washington, DC. Presidential candidates Obama *and* McCain both endorsed the plan, leaving the government to once again fail the American taxpayer. That failure continues to this very day, as U.S. government policy is no different now than it was during the run-up to the housing bust: Cheap and Easy Money Policy and a massive expansion in debt and government spending. The last crash was ugly. The next one will make it seem like child's play. The answer to solving an overspent and overleveraged market is not more debt and more spending. It's fiscal restraint and lower taxes. Presidents Reagan, Kennedy, and Coolidge have proven this. Why haven't we learned?

How did the stock market react to all this? That's our next topic.

THE STOCK MARKET

The birth of the Stock Market can be traced back to 1792, when a small group of entrepreneurs gathered underneath a buttonwood tree in New York City to organize a formal system of stock trading. This Buttonwood Agreement, as it became known, was not the creation of a business, but rather a way to organize business activity (specifically stock trading) to make it more efficient. Let it be no surprise then that these entrepreneurs were in fact stock brokers.

Who would've thought?

It took twenty-five more years for the group to establish a business, which they did in 1817. Also at the time, they opened the doors to a brand new, centrally located trading floor. It was the first of its kind and cost more than $4 million, which as they say was a lot of money back then. That institution became what we now know as the New York Stock Exchange (NYSE). The NYSE, listed under the symbol NYX on its namesake exchange, has a market value of $9 billion. That's a 74,900% return on initial investment, or 390% per year for 192 years!

Why am I giving this history lesson? Because I want you to know that the Stock Market was created and is run by brokers —and brokers really know how to make a lot of money for themselves. Keep that in the back of your mind as we move along.

The NYSE is a place where investors (buyers) go to exchange their money for shares of corporate ownership, a.k.a. stock. It's a place where business owners (sellers) go to raise capital by selling their stake in ownership for cash. It's a market for stock trading. NASDAQ, founded in 1971, is another market for stock trading. Together, NYSE and NASDAQ make up the Stock Market (the marketplace for stock trading).

The Stock Market is the combination of all stock markets. Like all other markets it is measured by its activity of trade. Trade is calculated by the amount of business it conducts, referred to as *the stock market. The stock market* is total stock market activity: the trade of all listed stocks. Since the DJIA is comprised of just thirty stocks and the S&P has only five hundred stocks, they are not *the stock market,* but instead are an indicator of the activity that occurs on it. They are a sample of stock market activity, not the total of it. They're stock market indicators. That too is an important point to remember.

Though all markets have the same parts, they don't all operate the same way. The Stock Market, for instance, is a restricted market, meaning it's a members-only place of trade. For a stock to be eligible for trade on the Stock Market floor, corporations must meet certain requirements and pay the Stock Market a listing fee. This is the price of admission for access to investor capital.

And because individual investors cannot participate on the Stock Market floor, they must pay someone to "broker" transactions on their behalf. The closed nature of the Stock Market is to keep stock trading as efficient as possible, to promote high volume and stock market growth. (Remember, they really know how to make a lot of money for themselves.) Wall Street firms pay the Stock Market fees to be allowed to conduct market activity on its floor. They recapture these fees by charging commissions or managerial fees to individual investors.

In other words, Wall Street firms are the official middlemen of investment transactions that take place in the Stock Market. They are Stock Market participants, making money by representing both buyers and sellers in investment transactions. For their businesses to grow, Wall Street firms must create demand for investments and investment products. To do so, they overcomplicate everything, and portray themselves as unbiased facilitators of trade who are simply connecting buyers and sellers to do business. But this neutrality is impossible to achieve.

In addition to representing both buyers and sellers of the same stocks, Wall Street firms raise capital for corporations, many times retaining a portion of stock as compensation for their efforts in making the deal. They provide investment advice to investors by telling them which stocks to buy, sell, or hold, while at the same time actively trading stocks on their own account, possibly in contrary fashion. And they create arms-length investment products like mutual funds, which can easily be used to support the stocks they underwrite and bring to market. In a nutshell, Wall Street firms have their hands in too many cookie jars not to be self-serving.

So if you're calling your broker for unbiased advice, plan on getting what their boss told them to say. Brokers are regular people, working folk just like you and me. They do what the company demands in exchange for a paycheck. Independence and objectivity are not part of their job description. They can't be.

Okay, let's recap. The Stock Market is in the business of stock trading, and the more the merrier. It was created by brokers and is run by brokers. Wall Street firms are its participants—those who broker stock market activity—and they know how to make a lot of money for themselves. The Dow Jones Industrial Average and the S&P 500 are not *the stock market*, but indicators of its general direction.

Are you with me so far? Okay, let's move on.

What Makes the Stock Market Move?

Ah yes, there is much confusion about this too. With twenty-four-hour cable news programming, media outlets compete for ratings by transforming current news into the most important news. As such, it's no surprise that during earnings season, earnings drive the market, and when economic news is due to report, the economy drives the market. But neither of these is true.

If earnings drove the stock market, then stock market performance would resemble the change in earnings. But price-to-earnings ratios expand and contract all the time. If we're to believe that earnings drive the stock market, then a 10%

increase in earnings would drive stock prices up 10%. But that hardly ever happens. And if the economy drove the stock market, then stock prices would generate returns in proportion to the change in GDP. But this doesn't happen either, as illustrated clearly by the chart in fig. 2.4.

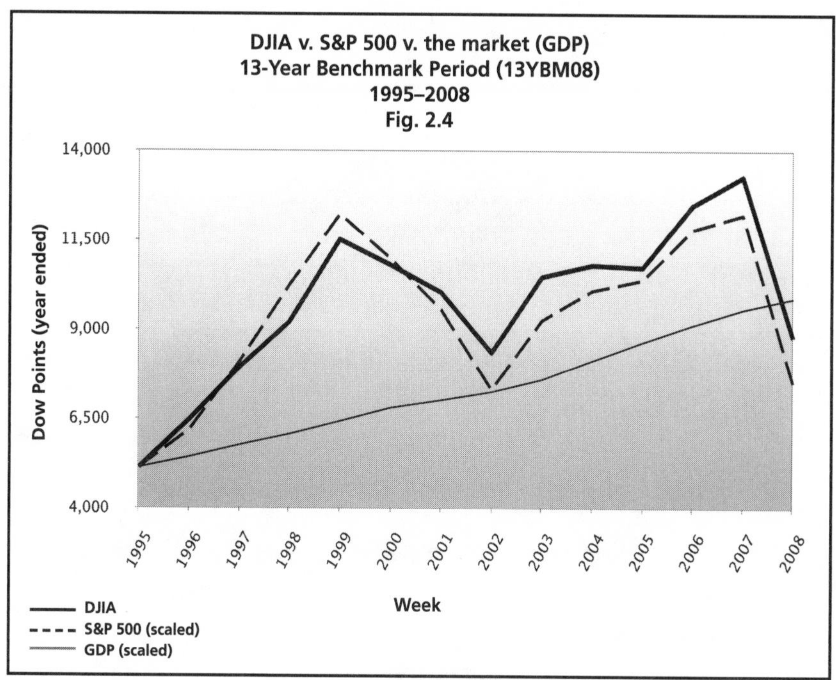

You see, the stock market doesn't move on earnings; it moves on earnings' potential. It doesn't move on the economy; it moves on economic potential. Earnings and economic activity are concrete. They're fact. Potential is subjective; it's speculative.

Speculation is the driving force behind the stock market's movements.

Yes, speculation. Think about it. During the tech boom, every dot-com under the sun was immediately driven to a hundred bucks a share. This in the face of prospectuses declaring that the organizations wouldn't be profitable for ten years or better. What warranted such billion-dollar valuations?

Speculation.

Also during this time, companies like General Electric (GE) traded at price-to-earnings (P/E) ratios[5] eight to twelve times their growth rate. Why? Because GE was going to start selling jet engines on eBay?

No, of course not.

Speculation about how much GE was going to capitalize in this "new paradigm" of enterprise is what drove its valuation to unsustainable heights. Remember, at the time Wall Street was drunk on speculative euphoria, fed by the unknown limits of this new kind of global commerce—and what the Internet meant for business expansion and profits. To one and all, the sky was the limit. It was after all "irrational exuberance": a.k.a. speculation on steroids.

Speculation causes stock market volatility and both will forever be a part of life with public investment. Consider it a healthy sign of life, like a pulse is to a human being. Markets are about people and thus have a human rhythm. The stock market is no different and will act according to human nature. Consider that the U.S. Stock Market represents the capital market for capitalism. Capital markets are run by—who else?—capitalists. Stock market activity will therefore be extremely sensitive to any encroachment on the free market system. It will swiftly and punitively trade down on such news. That's common sense.

Also consider the Stock Market to be filled with impulse shoppers looking to satisfy their own gluttonous desires first and foremost. The Wall Street establishment is too close to the situation and way too involved in the action not to get jittery. As a consequence, the stock market overreacts to everything, good news or bad.

That brings us to the most important rule about speculation: it is impossible to predict the level of speculation that will find

5 P/E ratios are explained thoroughly in chapter 5.

its way into *the stock market.* Sorry folks, that's the truth. There are millions of investors located all over the world, and they all have different motives. Attempting to pinpoint the stock market's movements is a fruitless endeavor. Luckily, this capability, endowed by no one, is not required to invest successfully.

Instead, successful investment requires the ability to be comfortable with stock market behavior and an understanding of where we are in the cycle. Realize that the same stimulus that causes *the Market* (the economy) to move also causes *the Stock Market* to move, and in the same direction. Anything that negatively affects *the market* (GDP) will also negatively affect *the stock market* (as indicated by the DJIA). Their only difference is in character: GDP is reported by the government in arrears. It is actual and finite, while *the stock market* is priced daily via free market activity, which makes it subjective by nature, and free to run wild with speculation. So it does.

And what are they speculating about?

You.

Remember, consumers are two-thirds of *the market* (GDP) in the United States. As such, most of the speculation is about how current market conditions affect them: how much money they will have and how and where they will spend it. Because on the other end of that consumer spending is a business that produced the goods that are in demand, and an investment that stands to profit from it.

And because speculation always factors into stock market movements, price corrections are an inherent part of the stock market game. Expect them. Plan for them. And capitalize on them. The key is to base your investment decisions on market conditions, not stock market conditions. If you do this you will always be ahead of the stock market game.

Don't believe me?

Let's put these concepts into practice. The Dow Jones Industrial Average (a.k.a. "the market") began 2007 at 12,463. In February 2007, a full eight months before "the market" peaked,

HSBC, the Bank of China, announced larger than expected loan defaults stemming from subprime mortgages in America. It was the first time most of us heard the term "subprime mortgage." In the days and weeks to follow, several mortgage companies failed and/or announced emergency conditions. In response to this news the DJIA dropped more than seven hundred points in March 2007, shredding 5.8% from its early year high point.

Call this the first tea leaf spelling disaster: a flare, if you will.

The news in April and May 2007 wasn't getting any better, as several other mortgage companies filed for bankruptcy. Yet the situation was billed by some financial pundits as "just a few isolated instances" and "nothing much to worry about," so the stock market rallied on the positive opinion. The Dow increased 13.1% from its March low point, not because the subprime problem went away, but because the stock market speculated that things weren't that bad.

All kinds of financial institutions started to fail and/or show major signs of distress in June, July, and August 2007, including Bear Stearns, UBS, Credit Suisse, Alliance Bancorp, and Countrywide Financial, once again citing subprime mortgage concerns. The disease wouldn't go away. And the stock market shook once again, giving back almost all of its yearly gains.

But "things were not as bad as some said," economic data was providing "mixed signals," and "the world was not falling apart." So the stock market speculated one more time on the positive dream. The Dow rose swiftly, hitting its all-time high in early October 2007, rising above the 14,000 mark and up nearly 14% for the year, yet bank after bank continued to fail.

Pure speculation drove the stock market to this record high.

Soon after hitting this high-water mark, two failed Bear Stearns hedge funds were tied to other Wall Street firms. Red flares lit up the sky as CEOs from iconic financial institutions Merrill Lynch and Citigroup resigned after reporting multibillion-dollar losses (never a good a sign for investment), and the stock market swiftly sold off. The DJIA ended the year at 13,265, up 6.3% for the year, but down 6.4% from its peak. Fig. 2.5 shows the 2007 chart.

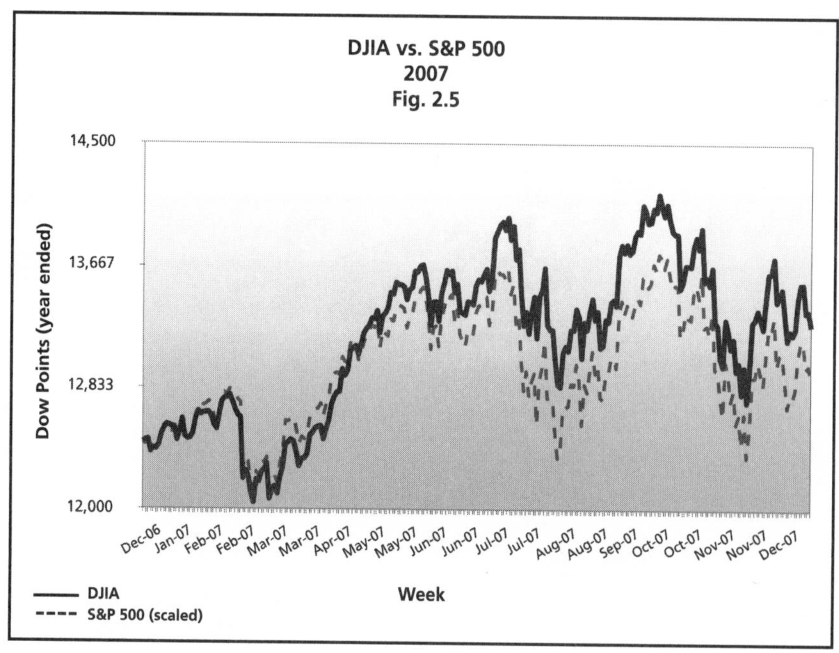

News of the subprime mortgage "crisis" appeared all over the airwaves in 2007. The stock market knew it was there, and knew it was a problem. This is evident by the amount of volatility in the chart, which depicts an indecisive investor base speculating on the strength of the marketplace and whether or not it could withstand the subprime firestorm. But no one really knew.

Speculation driven by uncertainty causes this kind of volatility.

The tea leaves kept appearing in 2008, with financial institutions failing almost daily. Bear Stearns fell in March; notorious no-income-verification lender IndyMac went under in July; government-sponsored enterprises Fannie Mae and Freddie Mac failed in September; and then after more than a hundred years in business, Lehman Brothers shut their doors for good.

On October 10, 2008, eighteen months after the initial signs of trouble and twelve months after "the market" hit its all-time high, the crash of 2008 was now in full swing. The DJIA got hammered, ending the year at 8,776, down 34%. Fig. 2.6 shows the chart.

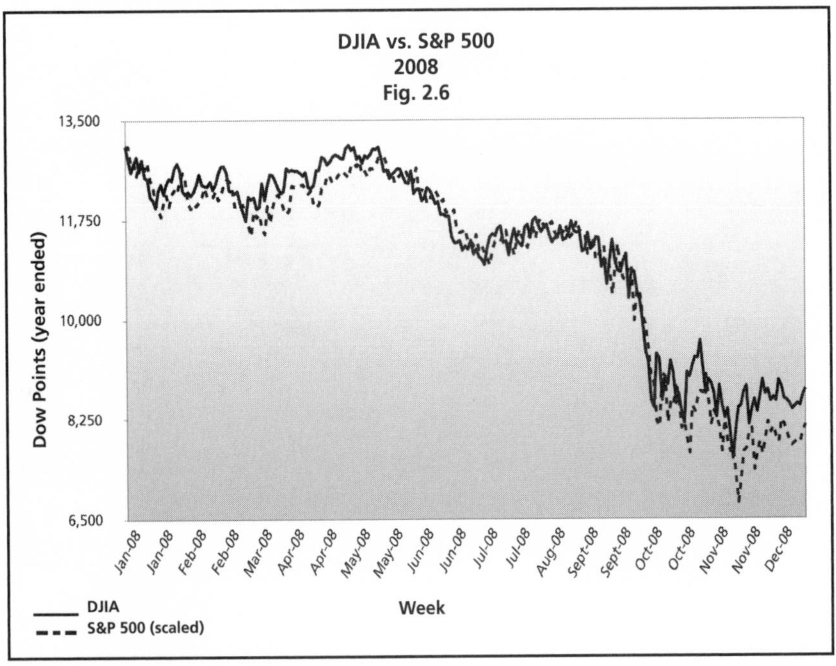

There was a long time and plenty of opportunities to make adjustments to investment portfolios before the bottom fell out of the stock market in late 2008—if investors had been taking their cues from *the Market* (economy). (Remember, the Dow was around 12,500 when HSBC fired the first salvo in February 2007.)

Now that we know everything that was going on in the Market (marketplace), *the stock market's* movements make perfect sense. There was too much debt built on the backs of a fragile consumer base: the low-income, first-time home buyer.

When the stock market starts acting crazy, as it did in February 2007, that's the time to begin planning your next investment move. You don't have to move. But you need to plan your next move. Why? Because the market displayed a sign of change—

larger defaults on subprime loans—and *the stock market* shook, as indicated by the DJIA. That's a signal to act. Remember, it's buy low, sell high, not the greedy interpretation buy at the lowest, sell at the highest. What to do with your portfolio and why to do it is the topic of another chapter. The point to take away here is to notice signals of change in *the Market* (the economy) and take your investment cues from that, not *the Stock Market.*

The best tool to indicate stock market activity is the Dow Jones Industrial Average, if for no other reasons than it is reliable and easy to understand. It's also a magnificent piece of work. That's where we go next.

The Dow Jones Industrial Average (DJIA)

Dow Jones & Company was in the news and information business from the very beginning. Namesakes Charles Dow and Edward Jones began their enterprise in 1882 by selling daily news sheets called "flimsies" to local subscribers in the Wall Street area. In 1889 they launched the *Wall Street Journal.* Seven years later, in 1896, the Dow Jones Industrial Average made its first appearance in the *Wall Street Journal*.

Why is this significant?

According to Dow Jones, "One hundred years ago, even people on Wall Street found it difficult to discern from the daily jumble of up-a-quarter and down-an-eighth; whether stocks were generally rising, falling, or treading water. Charles Dow devised his stock average to make sense out of this confusion."[6]

Who were the customers of the *Wall Street Journal*? Investors who wanted to know which way the stock market was going before making their investment decisions, and stock brokers who needed this information to sell more stocks. Charles Dow knew that if he could satisfy this demand by providing stock market indication he would sell more newspapers. That

6 Dow Jones Indexes, www.djaverages.com/?view=industrial&page=overview.

was his goal of course. The Industrial Average was simply a means to that end.

Indeed there were less publicly traded stocks back then, but there were still a lot. I don't know what a calculator looked like over a hundred years ago, but I do know it didn't look like a laptop. Just as I know a printing press didn't look like today's digital laser printers. Yet there were still just twenty-four hours in a day. For this reason, Mr. Dow's market portfolio had to be efficient in construction and easy to calculate to meet nineteenth-century operational deadlines.

Goals often dictate strategies required for success.

As such, Mr. Dow strategically selected only a small number of stocks. The first composition of the Dow Jones Industrial Average included just twelve, exclusively industrial, stocks. It began as a truly "industrial average," designed and constructed to measure industry, not necessarily *the Market* (the economy). The original twelve Dow components were:

American Cotton Oil
American Sugar
American Tobacco
Chicago Gas
Distilling & Cattle Feeding
General Electric
Laclede Gas
National Lead
North American
Tennessee Coal & Iron
U.S. Leather preferred
U.S. Rubber

That about sums up early American industry, wouldn't you say? Industry was certainly less complex a hundred years ago than it is today. But even in its earliest form the DJIA was a model of diversification, covering all the major industrial markets: food, energy, and basic materials, to be specific. In addition, industry was sampled from all over 1896 America, with gas from Chicago, coal from Tennessee, electric power from the Northeast, and cattle, cotton, and tobacco from the southern states. This kind of diversification by location enabled the DJIA to gauge the condition of national employment.

The Dow Jones Industrial Average was smart from the start.

Most impressive is the DJIA's ability to produce reliable market indication for as long as it has. This kind of consistency and reliability can only come through change, because markets change. The DJIA was expanded to twenty stocks in 1916 and then to thirty stocks in 1928. Also during this time, the DIJA changed its mission from indicating industry to indicating *the Market* (the economy). The reason it stayed put at thirty stocks is that there hasn't been a need to increase it: as *the Market* grew larger and more complex, so did corporate America. So when it comes to diversification, the number of stocks selected isn't nearly as important as the makeup of the companies selected. Dow Jones has proven this for more than a century.

And though the Dow has gone almost a hundred years without being expanded, its components have been modified numerous times. Most recently changes were made in late 2008 and early 2009 to eliminate failed automaker General Motors in favor of Cisco Systems; failed bank Citigroup was replaced with Travelers Insurance; failed insurance giant AIG was replaced with Kraft Foods; and Bank of America and Chevron replaced Altria (a.k.a. Philip Morris) and Honeywell to reflect changes that occurred in *the Market* (the economy) in the wake of the 2008 crash.

However, since every analysis performed in this book is back-tested and compared to the DJIA over the course of the thirteen-year benchmark period (1995–2008), we will use only the Dow components reflective of that period of time. This will provide a truer analytical comparison. Fig. 2.7, on the next page, shows those thirty Dow stocks, listed in alphabetical order.

Dow Jones Industrial Average
Fig. 2.7

1. 3M Co. (NYSE: MMM) (conglomerate, manufacturing)
2. ALCOA Inc. (NYSE: AA) (aluminum)
3. Altria Group Inc. (NYSE: MO) (tobacco, food)
4. American Express Co. (NYSE: AXP) (credit services)
5. American International Group Inc. (NYSE: AIG) (insurance)
6. AT&T Inc. (NYSE: T) (telecom)
7. Boeing Co. (NYSE: BA) (aerospace/defense)
8. Caterpillar Inc. (NYSE: CAT) (farm and construction equipment)
9. Citigroup Inc. (NYSE: C) (money center banks)
10. Coca-Cola Co. (NYSE: KO) (beverages)
11. E.I. du Pont de Nemours & Co. (NYSE: DD) (chemicals)
12. Exxon Mobil Corp. (NYSE: XOM) (major integrated oil and gas)
13. General Electric Co. (NYSE: GE) (conglomerate, media)
14. General Motors Corp. (NYSE: GM) (auto manufacturer)
15. Hewlett-Packard Co. (NYSE: HPQ) (diversified computer systems)
16. Home Depot Inc. (NYSE: HD) (home improvement stores)
17. Honeywell International Inc. (NYSE: HON) (conglomerate)
18. Intel Corp. (NASDAQ: INTC) (semiconductors)
19. International Business Machines Corp. (NYSE: IBM) (computer, various)
20. Johnson & Johnson (NYSE: JNJ) (consumer products conglomerate)
21. JPMorgan Chase & Co. (NYSE: JPM) (money center banks)
22. McDonald's Corp. (NYSE: MCD) (restaurant franchise)
23. Merck & Co. Inc. (NYSE: MRK) (drug manufacturer)
24. Microsoft Corp. (NASDAQ: MSFT) (software)
25. Pfizer Inc. (NYSE: PFE) (drug manufacturer)
26. Procter & Gamble Co. (NYSE: PG) (consumer goods)
27. United Technologies Corp. (NYSE: UTX) (conglomerate)
28. Verizon Communications Inc. (NYSE: VZ) (telecom)
29. Wal-Mart Stores Inc. (NYSE: WMT) (discount, variety stores)
30. Walt Disney Co. (NYSE: DIS) (entertainment)

The Dow vividly paints a picture of almost every facet of American culture. It's an amazing piece of work and the perennial model of efficient market diversification, with just thirty stocks.

So how does the Dow do it? How does it reliably indicate the market average, so much so that it is often referred to as "the market" when it isn't even *a* market? First, there isn't a better way to achieve the market average than by owning as much of it as possible. With this goal in mind the Dow selects only large, well-diversified companies that service many, many market segments.

Second, it selects its components so that they mimic GDP spending patterns. Most of the Dow's components generate revenue primarily from consumers, plus a select few that trade primarily with businesses and government. All conduct trade with foreign markets (imports and exports).

And third, the Dow selects stocks with varying performance levels within their respective industries. In other words, it selects some high industry performers, like IBM, and low industry performers, like General Motors. It then combines them with consistent performers like Johnson & Johnson and Procter & Gamble. Together they produce average, which of course is the Dow's goal.

The DJIA is a collection of stocks designed to mimic *the Market* (the economy) using just a small number of publicly traded stocks with varying performance levels, aimed to produce average performance results. That's the Dow in a nutshell.

Breaking Down "the Market" (a.k.a. the Dow Jones Industrial Average)

As we know, *the Market* (the economy) is the total of many, many markets. Major markets are called industries. There are seven major industries within which all businesses, operating in any market segment, can be categorized. They are:

Basic
Consumer services
Consumer staples
Energy
Financial
Industrial/Conglomerates
Technology

As mentioned, the DJIA diversifies its investments throughout these industries in a manner that reflects GDP. But you need not invest in them all, nor should that be your aim. That will only produce *average* results. Your goal should always be above average. However, the important thing to learn right now is how the DJIA (a.k.a. "the market") is diversified. Once you understand this it's easy to build a better mousetrap: a portfolio that yields above-average results. That's always our goal.

Let's go through the industries one by one, using the Dow's components as a guide to understanding.

The *basic industry* is comprised of companies that deliver goods that are "basic" in nature. They may also be goods used to serve a basic purpose of culture. The DJIA accesses this industry in the following way (fig. 2.8.a).

Dow Components: BASIC
Fig. 2.8.a

Company	Market/Symbol	Market Segment
ALCOA Inc.	NYSE: AA	aluminum
Caterpillar Inc.	NYSE: CAT	farm and construction equipment
E.I. du Pont de Nemours & Co.	NYSE: DD	chemicals
General Motors Corp.	NYSE: GM	auto manufacturers

By way of example, Alcoa procures a basic raw material (aluminum) that General Motors uses to make automotive vehicles. Those vehicles travel on roads built by machinery made by Caterpillar. Dupont makes chemicals used to produce the materials utilized in the manufacture of cars, heavy equipment, and many other goods. All are a "basic" need of culture, or serve a "basic" function.

The *consumer services industry* is made up of companies that provide a service. Services are intangible products; that is, they are used or purchased without accumulating an asset. The Dow components for this industry can be seen in fig. 2.8.b.

Dow Components: CONSUMER SERVICES
Fig. 2.8.b

Company	Market/Symbol	Market Segment
AT&T Inc.	NYSE: T	telecom
Home Depot Inc.	NYSE: HD	home improvement stores
McDonald's Corp.	NYSE: MCD	restaurant franchise
Verizon	NYSE: VZ	telecom
Wal-Mart Stores Inc.	NYSE: WMT	discount, variety stores
Walt Disney Co.	NYSE: DIS	entertainment

Wal-Mart and Home Depot are large retailers. Retailers are markets, venues for trade. Retailers do not make products; they buy them at a wholesale price and resell them at a retail price. They're resellers. Reselling is a service. Wal-Mart indicates the spending pattern of the average consumer and Home Depot gauges the health of home improvement/construction consumers. Telephone service is an intangible product, meaning you can't touch it or acquire it. AT&T and Verizon provide access to the communications market. McDonald's is a restaurant, a retail establishment for prepared food. Even though goods are purchased and consumed, it's a food service. Disney is a media and entertainment company. It services the enjoyment desires of consumers, providing a glimpse into the status of consumer disposable income.

The *consumer staples industry* is comprised of companies that deliver products that are "staples" to current life and culture. These are products consumers purchase in all kinds of economic conditions. They satisfy need more than want. Fig. 2.8.c shows the Dow components for consumer staples.

Dow Components: CONSUMER STAPLES
Fig. 2.8.c

Company	Market/Symbol	Market Segment
Altria Group Inc.	NYSE: MO	tobacco, food
Coca-Cola Co.	NYSE: KO	beverages
Johnson & Johnson	NYSE: JNJ	consumer products conglomerate
Merck & Co. Inc.	NYSE: MRK	drug manufacturer
Pfizer Inc.	NYSE: PFE	drug manufacturer
Procter & Gamble Co.	NYSE: PG	consumer goods

Food, beverages, and hygiene products are standard products in American life: they're staples. If there's any gray area in this grouping, Merck and Pfizer are it. Both companies have huge pharmaceutical development units and as such can easily be included in the technology industry (developing drugs is called biotechnology). However, for most of the thirteen-year benchmark period both companies operated substantial consumer products divisions, selling well-known items such as Listerine and Pepcid AC; hence their inclusion in the consumer staples industry.

The *energy industry* is composed of companies that procure and/or distribute any form of energy, including oil, gas, coal, and electricity. The Dow accesses this industry with just one component (fig. 2.8.d, on the next page).

Dow Components: ENERGY
Fig. 2.8.d

Company	Market/Symbol	Market Segment
ExxonMobil Corp.	NYSE: XOM	major integrated oil and gas

It is important to note that although ExxonMobil may own and operate retail gas stations, its core business is to procure oil, refine it to gasoline, and distribute it to many independently owned gas stations. ExxonMobil's main business is wholesale trade and therefore not a service.

The *financial industry* is comprised of companies using money, credit, risk of loss, or investment products as their main product of trade. These are banks, credit card companies, insurance, and the notorious business of investment, as represented in fig. 2.8.e by the following Dow components.

Dow Components: FINANCIAL
Fig. 2.8.e

Company	Market/Symbol	Market Segment
American Express Co.	NYSE: AXP	credit services
American International Group Inc.	NYSE: AIG	insurance
Citigroup Inc.	NYSE: C	money center banks
JPMorgan Chase & Co.	NYSE: JPM	money center banks

The *industrial/conglomerate industry* is made up of companies that provide products used in industry, or that are so big and diverse they're impossible to fit into any other industry. The Dow covers these markets with the following stocks (fig. 2.8.f, on the next page).

Dow Components: INDUSTRIAL/CONGLOMERATES
Fig 2.8.f

Company	Market/Symbol	Market Segment
3M Co.	NYSE: MMM	conglomerate, manufacturing
General Electric Co.	NYSE: GE	conglomerate, media
Honeywell International Inc.	NYSE: HON	conglomerate

Though all three of these companies sell to consumers, the bulk of their trade is to industry. For instance, GE makes jet engines used for the construction of airplanes (technology); it also makes sophisticated medical equipment, sold to the health care market (consumer service); it also has a huge financial arm that extends credit to consumers and enterprise (financial); and it still sells lightbulbs (consumer staples). Honeywell manufactures products for transportation like turbo units for cars (basic) and parts for aerospace (technology). And 3M, among other things, is the adhesive specialist, supplying glues to almost every industry, including Scotch tape to consumers.

The *technology industry* is all about innovation. It's about enhancing current products and creating new markets by creating new products. Technology is about the future and tomorrow's products. The Dow represents this industry with the following stocks (fig. 2.8.g, on the next page).

Microsoft and Intel were the first two NASDAQ stocks to be included in the Dow. They were added to the DJIA in November 1999, after the tech boom was essentially over. Clearly, Dow Jones didn't want its average to be driven by lofty tech-boom valuations. Dow Jones waited for market penetration of the personal computer to approach maturation before inclusion. (They are so smart.) Before that, IBM was the Dow's stalwart computer component, and it used preeminent computer printer maker Hewlett-Packard to round out the segment.

Dow Components: TECHNOLOGY
Fig 2.8.g

Company	Market/Symbol	Market Segment
Boeing Co.	NYSE: BA	aerospace/defense
Hewlett-Packard Co.	NYSE: HPQ	diversified computer systems
Intel Corp.	NASDAQ: INTC	semiconductors
International Business Machines Corp.	NYSE: IBM	computers, various
Microsoft Corp.	NASDAQ: MSFT	software
United Technologies Corp.	NYSE: UTX	conglomerate

Technology is another major industry the Dow uses to boost its exposure to business and government GDP spending classes. It uses Boeing and United Technologies, which sell exclusively to business and government.

Okay, that's all seven industries. In summary, the DJIA (a.k.a. "the market") looks like this (fig. 2.9).

DJIA – Diversification by Industry (Ranked by Weight)
Fig. 2.9

Rank	Industry	No. of Stocks	% of Total Stocks	% by Weight
1	Technology	6	20%	22%
2	Consumer staples	6	20%	21%
3	Consumer services	6	20%	15%
4	Financial	4	13%	15%
5	Basic	4	13%	12%
6	Industrial	3	10%	11%
7	Energy	1	3%	5%
	Total	**30**	**100%**	**100%**

That's "market diversification" by industry. Fig. 2.10.a shows the same portfolio using a horizontal view.

DJIA Allocation Model
Fig. 2.10.a

Priority	Highest	→	→	→	→	→	Lowest	
Industry Rank	1	2	3	4	5	6	7	
Industry	Technology	Consumer Staples	Consumer Services	Financial	Basic	Industrial	Energy	Total
No. of Stocks	6	6	6	4	4	3	1	30
% of Stocks	20%	20%	20%	13%	13%	10%	3%	100%
% by Weight	22%	21%	15%	15%	12%	11%	5%	100%

Fig. 2.10.b

Priority	Stock Ranking	Technology	Consumer Staples	Consumer Services	Financial	Basic	Industrial	Energy
Highest	1	IBM	Altria	Wal-Mart	AIG	Caterpillar	3M	Exxon Mobil
↓	2	Boeing	P&G	Home Depot	American Express	Dupont	Honeywell	
↓	3	UTC	JnJ	McDonald's	Citigroup	Alcoa	GE	
↓	4	Hewlett-Packard	Coca-Cola	Verizon	JPM Chase	GM		
↓	5	Microsoft	Merck	AT&T				
Lowest	6	Intel	Pfizer	Walt Disney				

And fig. 2.10.b, on the previous page, shows how the Dow components lay out by industry, in priority order by weight as of the snapshot date.[7]

This is "the market." It is "market diversification" with just thirty stocks. Remember, the goal of this portfolio is to be average. It is designed to be average, inspired by *the Market* (the economy) and market dynamics. "Market returns" therefore represent average returns, which makes the DJIA an average portfolio. That's its goal.

Our objective is to be above average.

There are two guaranteed ways to outperform "the market" (the Dow) over the long term. Build a better portfolio using *superior construction* and *superior components.* Superior construction is the next chapter. Now the fun begins.

7 The snapshot date is February 2, 2006, which represents the day I began building data for this book.

CHAPTER 3

Assembling Your Investments: A Road Map to Success

Building a portfolio is like building anything else. In order to be efficient you need assembly instructions before you begin building: a blueprint, if you will. In investment these blueprints are called models. That's what this chapter is about. It's not about stock picking. That's next. But don't skip ahead. A poorly constructed portfolio is the number one reason many investors consistently fail to achieve their objectives.

Far too many people think investment begins and ends with stock picking, and who could blame them. The bookshelves are littered with books focusing on the "science" of stock picking. And let us not forget those cable news shows mad about identifying the next highfliers yet to take flight. Although stock selection is important, it's only a small piece of the investment process. That process begins with an understanding of *the Market* (economy) and how it relates to stock market activity and the Dow Jones Industrial Average. The next step is to build a better portfolio. That begins with modeling, not stock picking.

The real reason most people don't know where to begin with picking stocks is that they don't know what they're building and therefore have no clue what materials they need to complete construction. No blueprint, no clue. With an investment model, on the other hand, quality stocks are much easier to find because you know exactly what you're looking for.

Modeling also removes one of the greatest frustrations plaguing average investors, they hate getting blindsided by their investments. To understand how your portfolio is constructed is to know how it will act under any market condition. This kind of familiarity breeds confidence and increases your comfort level.

So an allocation model is your blueprint. And it is also your concrete. Even quality stocks have bad days and bad stretches of time. Ask Toyota about that. It happens. But as you will see, solid portfolio construction can overcome the ill effects of many poor stock performances or poor stock selections. Trust me, stocks become much easier to pick when you know you don't have to be perfect. (An allocation model is also an extremely useful tool when making portfolio adjustments, but that's the topic of a later chapter.) Nothing will give you more personal assurance and more confidence in your investments than knowing how they're assembled.

Consider stocks to be the wood used in building a house. Sure, a hardwood like oak would be best for sturdy construction. But how durable would that house be if it was built on a foundation of hay? Modeling is the foundation of your portfolio. It's the primary source of your portfolio's strength and an extremely important step in the investment process.

When modeling a portfolio you begin by thinking not in terms of individual stocks, but of where you want your money distributed in *the Market* (economy). Think of it this way: stocks represent businesses that supply products to markets. The products those companies deliver to markets determine their market segment and their industry of operation. Modeling is the process of allocating your investment dollars throughout the various marketplaces, to diversify them and thus eliminate overexposure to any particular industry, market segment, or GDP spending class.

For example, General Motors is a well-known stock. GM makes cars. Transportation is a basic need of culture and thus part of the basic industry, in this case serving the automobile market. The purpose of an allocation model is to make sure you don't have too many stocks serving the same industry (basic) or market segment (the automobile market). If a portfolio is overloaded in any one industry or market segment, its performance becomes reliant on that market, and that's not good. Imagine your portfolio being reliant on General Motors, which lost 93% during the 13YBM. That's a scary thought. The purpose of an allocation model is to eliminate the possibility of that kind of reliance, and that kind of fright.

We'll begin our modeling discussion with none other than the Dow Jones Industrial Average. Since the DJIA is built to indicate "the market" and does so reliably, by definition it indicates full market diversification. This can be expressed as follows:

Industries	**Stocks**		**Market Coverage**
7	30	=	100%

I took a snapshot of the Dow to use as my baseline for demonstrating how construction works. As mentioned in the previous chapter: things change, times change, markets change, and the DJIA also changes. That's okay. If you can beat the DJIA as of the snapshot date, you can beat "the market" today. No worries. What's important right now is to understand how the DJIA is constructed because then it's easy to beat. As shown in fig. 3.1, on the next page, here is how the Dow allocates its investments throughout *the Market* (economy).

Like most portfolios, the DJIA is top heavy, allocating approximately 60% of its investment dollars to its top three industries; the fourth- and fifth-ranked industries account for approximately 25% of the portfolio, while the final two industries account for just around 15%.

DJIA: Diversification by Industry (Ranked by Weight)
Fig. 3.

Rank	Industry	No. of Stocks	No. of Total Stocks	% by Weight
1	Technology	6	20%	22%
2	Consumer Staples	6	20%	21%
3	Consumer Services	6	20%	15%
4	Financial	4	13%	15%
5	Basic	4	13%	12%
6	Industrial	3	10%	11%
7	Energy	1	3%	5%
	Total	30	100%	100%

Using actual weights[1] as the tiebreaker, the technology industry ranked highest in Dow priority among all industries, with six stocks and 22% of weight. Consumer staples was right behind in second place, also with six stocks but with 21% of weight. Consumer services also accounted for 20% of the stocks (six) but only 15% of the weight. With four stocks, financial takes the fourth-ranked industry spot, edging out basic by weight; 15% versus 12%, respectively. With three stocks, the industrial/conglomerate industry ranks sixth in Dow priority. Finally, the energy industry's one stock component ranks seventh and last in priority.

That's market construction during much of the 13YBM, and it makes total sense. America is a technology-driven market; staples and services are right behind that, then financial,

1 The Dow is a weighted average that uses a special divisor and current pricing to calculate. As such, its priority rankings can change based on the price performance trend of its components. The Dow's weightings listed here are as of the snapshot date.

industrials, and energy. Yep. That about sums up the American market, which is the Dow's goal.

Always remember that the Dow's objective is to indicate the average direction of stocks. Its structure therefore defines average construction. Replicating it can do nothing but replicate its performance. That's not our goal.

Let's begin the construction process by reaffirming our objective: to build well-diversified stock portfolios that prove to consistently beat "the market" (a.k.a. the DJIA) over the long term.

We'll do that in this chapter only by means of construction. In other words, we're going to limit our stock selections in this chapter to those of the Dow thirty. The only difference will be how those Dow stocks are assembled. The difference in performance then will be due solely to the method of construction.

In addition all portfolios will begin with an initial investment of $5,117, which represents the DJIA's starting point at the beginning of my designated thirteen-year benchmark period (end of year 1995). This way the charts won't have to be scaled.

Okay, here we go.

Instead of using market construction we'll use something better to build our portfolios. I've developed an allocation model designed to be above average in construction. Generically called the 1X-X1 Allocation Model, it comes in three main variations: 15-51 (fifteen stocks), 16-61 (twenty-one stocks), and 17-71 (twenty-eight stocks). All three models use the same logic and work the same way. To understand the logic of one is to understand them all. But as seen in chapter one, a fifteen-stock portfolio significantly outperforms thirty-, twenty-eight-, or even twenty-one-stock portfolios. For that reason the fifteen-stock portfolio will be the emphasis of this chapter.

In its base form the 15-51 allocation model accesses five of the seven possible industries, spreading fifteen stocks across those five industries. The model first ranks industries in priority order from 1 through 5, with 1 being the highest in priority. The number one industry is allocated five stocks. Each subsequent industry receives one less stock, until finally reaching the number five industry, which receives just one stock.

In a nutshell, the 15-51 model ranks industries 1 through 5, with the first industry receiving 5 stocks and the last receiving 1. That's how I came up with the name 15-51. It looks like this (fig. 3.2).

The 15-51 Allocation Model (in DJIA priority)
Fig. 3.2

Priority	Highest	→		→	Lowest	
Industry Rank	**1**	2	3	4	**5**	$5,117
Industry Name	Technology	Consumer Staples	Consumer Services	Financial	Basic	Total
No. of Stocks	**5**	4	3	2	**1**	15
% of Portfolio	33%	27%	20%	13%	7%	100%
Investment $	$1,706	$1,365	$1,023	$682	$341	$5,117

As you can see, the number one industry receives the largest investment allocation (33%). This allocation is derived by dividing the number of stocks allocated to that industry (5) by the total number of stocks (15). To arrive at the investment dollar allocation for an industry, simple multiply the allocation target (in this case 33%) by the total amount of investment dollars ($5,117), which provides a $1,706 investment allocation for the number one industry.

The second-ranked industry receives a 27% allocation, which is 4 industry stocks divided by the total of 15 (and $1,365); the third-ranked industry gets 20% (3 stocks divided by 15), and right on down the line. A comparison between 15-51 construction and "the market" (DJIA) follows in fig. 3.3.

DJIA: Diversification by Rank vs. 15-51 Model
Fig. 3.3

DJIA: Diversification by Rank					15-51 Model		
Rank	Industry	No. of Stocks	No. of Total Stocks	% by Weight	No. of Stocks	% of Total Stocks	+/- DJIA
1	Technology	6	20%	22%	5	33%	12%
2	Consumer Staples	6	20%	21%	4	27%	5%
3	Consumer Services	6	20%	15%	3	20%	5%
4	Financial	4	13%	15%	2	13%	-2%
5	Basic	4	13%	12%	1	7%	-5%
6	Industrial	3	10%	11%	0	0%	-11%
7	Energy	1	3%	5%	0	0%	-5%
	Total	**30**	**100%**	**100%**	**15**	**100%**	

This table highlights the first structural difference between the Dow (a.k.a. "the market") and 15-51. 15-51 overweights in high-priority industries and underweights in the lowest. What does that mean?

A portfolio allocated in the same manner as "the market" is considered to be "balanced." In other words, if "the market" has 20% in technology and your portfolio has 30% in technology, your portfolio is overweighted in technology by 10%. In this case 15-51 places 33% of its investment dollars in the number one–ranked industry (technology) where the Dow allocates just 20% of its leading industry (also technology).

The logic behind 15-51 is to place more investment dollars where you are most comfortable and most optimistic. In this example 15-51 places more investment dollars in the largest parts of "the market" (DJIA) with its top three industries accounting for 80% of the portfolio compared to 60% for the Dow. To make this kind of overweighting possible, 15-51 underweights in the lowest-priority industries (industrial and energy) by eliminating them completely from the portfolio.

In short, the 15-51 model utilizes a smaller sample of stocks than the DJIA, overweights in its highest-priority industries, and underweights in the lowest. These two features begin the foundation of an above-average portfolio.

The next step in modeling is to determine stock allocations within those industries. Before we dive into placing those allocations in the 15-51 model, let's take another look (fig. 3.4, next page) at a detailed blueprint of the DJIA and how it prioritizes stocks within industries, as of the snapshot date.

In all the portfolios to follow in this chapter, we will use these same stocks, prioritized in this same manner. In other words, IBM will always be the highest-priority technology stock, just as Pfizer will always be the lowest-priority consumer staple. Once again, the only difference in performance of the portfolios shown in this chapter will be due to changes in construction —and construction alone. The stocks and their priority rankings will remain true to the DJIA as of the snapshot date.

Okay, let's keep going with the model.

To determine stock allocations within each industry slot, 15-51 uses the same logic to prioritize stocks as it does with industry rankings: it overweights in highest-priority stocks and underweights in the lowest-priority ones. We do this by attaching a "weighting" to each stock within each industry. To arrive at the stock weighting, simply reverse the stock ranking for that industry.

DJIA Allocation Model
Fig 3.4

Priority	Highest	→					Lowest	
Industry Rank	1	2	3	4	5	6	7	
Industry	Technology	Consumer Staples	Consumer Services	Financial	Basic	Industrial	Energy	Total
No. of Stocks	6	6	6	4	4	3	1	30
% of Stocks	20%	20%	20%	13%	13%	10%	3%	100%
% by Weight	22%	21%	15%	15%	12%	11%	5%	100%

Priority	Stock Ranking	Technology	Consumer Staples	Consumer Services	Financial	Basic	Industrial	Energy
Highest	1	IBM	Altria	Wal-Mart	AIG	Caterpil-lar	3M	Exxon Mobil
↓	2	Boeing	P&G	Home Depot	Amex	Dupont	Honey-well	
	3	UTC	JnJ	McDon-ald's	Citigroup	Alcoa	GE	
	4	Hewlett Packard	Coke	Verizon	JPM Chase	GM		
	5	Micro-soft	Merck	AT&T				
Lowest	6	Intel	Pfizer	Disney				

For example, the stock allocation for Industry 1 looks like this (fig. 3.5).

Fig. 3.5

Industry 1				
Stock Rank	Weighting	% of Cat.	$	% of Total
1	5	33%	$569	11.1%
2	4	27%	$455	8.9%
3	3	20%	$341	6.7%
4	2	13%	$227	4.4%
5	1	7%	$114	2.2%
5	15	100%	**$1,706**	33.3%

In this industry, the number one stock received a 5 weighting because Industry 1 is comprised of five stocks. This places the heaviest weight allocation on the highest-priority stock. Again, it's the stock you're most optimistic about. The investment allocation is derived by dividing the stock's weighting by the total industry weight. In this case the number one stock would receive a 33% allocation (5 ÷ 15). The number two stock gets the second-highest weighting (4) and receives a 27% allocation (because 4 ÷ 15 = 27%); the number three–ranked stock gets 20% (3 ÷ 15); and so on.

To determine the investment dollars per stock, simply multiply its stock allocation by the investment allocation for the industry. In this case the number one stock receives $569 investment dollars (33% x $1,706). The second-ranked stock receives $455 (27% x $1,706) and so on.

To make navigation throughout the 15-51 model simple, we will refer to stock components and their location in the industry-stock position format. It looks like this: IS position: 1-3, which means

Industry 1, Stock 3; or, IS: 4-2, which refers to Industry 4, Stock 2.

Okay, the number two industry in the 15-51 model looks like this (fig. 3.6).

Fig. 3.6

Industry 2				
Stock Rank	**Weighting**	**%**	**$**	**% of Total**
1	4	40%	$546	10.7%
2	3	30%	$409	8.0%
3	2	20%	$273	5.3%
4	1	10%	$136	2.7%
4	**10**	**100%**	**$1,365**	**26.7%**

Here the industry weighting adds up to 10, and because there are only four stocks, IS position: 2-1 receives a 4 weighting and a 40% investment allocation for this industry (4 ÷ 10 = 40%.) IS: 2-2 gets a 3 weighting and a 30% allocation, and so on and so on.

The other three industries of the 15-51 model look like this (fig. 3.7).

Fig. 3.7

Industry 3				
Stock Rank	**Weighting**	**%**	**$**	**% of Total**
1	3	50%	$512	10.0%
2	2	33%	$341	6.7%
3	1	17%	$171	3.3%
3	6	100%	**$1,023**	20.0%

Industry 4				
Stock Rank	**Weighting**	**%**	**$**	**% of Total**
1	2	67%	$455	8.9%
2	1	33%	$227	4.4%
2	3	100%	**$682**	13.3%

Fig. 3.7, continued

Industry 5				
Stock Rank	Weighting	%	$	% of Total
1	1	100%	$341	6.7%
1	1	100%	**$341**	6.7%

That's above-average 15-51 construction.[2]

Next we're going to stuff the thirty Dow components into my 15-51 allocation model. To get you comfortable with the construction process and variations that can be made to the base model, we'll go through several examples. In every case, however, the two constants that won't change will be that we eliminate fifteen, or 50%, of the Dow's stock components; and we'll use 15-51 construction. And we won't always end up with the best fifteen stock components. That'd be no fun. It's too easy to beat the Dow when all your stocks are above-average performers (as you'll see in the next chapter). Right now it's about making a better pie from the same bunch of apples.

We'll start the demonstrations by performing eliminations based simply on their Dow priority rankings as of the snapshot date; the lowest-ranked stocks and/or industries will be dropped from the 15-51 portfolio completely. That blueprint looks like Fig. 3.8, on the next page.

Okay, those are the stocks we ended up with and how we allocated them. Before moving on let's quickly talk about what's missing in this 15-51 portfolio as compared to the Dow. Remember, the DJIA returned 72% over the course of the 13YBM.

First off, the bottom two industries are gone: number six–ranked industrial/conglomerates and number seven in priority energy have been completely removed from this portfolio.

2 See appendix for additional views of the 15-51 model layout.

The 15-51 Allocation Model: DJIA Components
1X-X1 Allocation Model, X = 5 Format
Fig. 3.8

Priority	Highest	———	———	———→	Lowest	
Industry Rank	1	2	3	4	5	**$5,117**
Industry	**Technology**	**Consumer Staples**	**Consumer Services**	**Financial**	**Basic**	**TOTAL**
No. of Stocks	5	4	3	2	1	**15**
% of Portfolio	33%	27%	20%	13%	7%	**100%**
Investment Dollars	$1,706	$1,365	$1,023	$682	$341	**$5,117**
Stock Rank						
1	IBM	Altria	Wal-Mart	AIG	Caterpillar	
2	Boeing	P&G	Home Depot	Amex		
3	UTC	JnJ	McDonald's			
4	Hewlett-Packard	Coca-Cola				
5	Microsoft					

Four stocks have been eliminated from these industries, including Exxon (+303%), 3M (+78%), Honeywell (+46%), and GE (+42%). Together these four stocks averaged a 117% return, a clear 45% points better than Dow's 13YBM return.

In addition to those depletions, number one industry technology lost Intel (+114%), and second-ranked staples lost Merck (-6%) and Pfizer (+74%); third-highest Dow priority industry, consumer services, lost three dogs: Verizon (+4%), AT&T (+3%), and Disney (+22%); fourth-ranked financials lost Citigroup (-32%) and JPMorgan Chase (+60%); and fifth-ranked basic lost a disastrous trio: Dupont (-25%), Alcoa (-8%), and pitiful GM (-93%).

In other words, we threw out some good and a lot of bad. In the end the group we lost can be defined nothing more than below average, which left 15-51 with nothing less than above average. Funny how that works.

So this by any definition is an above-average portfolio, but it is just one. Remember, there is no one right way to invest successfully. The key is to find the best way for you. That will still take some time to figure out. But don't worry. By the time you're finished reading this book, you'll be able to draw that ideal blueprint. That too is part of my guarantee.

Now on to the results.

This first 15-51 portfolio outperformed the Dow Jones Industrial Average by 100% over the course of the thirteen-year benchmark period, doubling the Dow's output 144% versus 72%, with just 50% of the risk. The initial $5,117 investment was worth $12,491 at the end of 2008, *after* the Market crashed. Fig. 3.9, on the next page, shows the chart.

Yep. A picture is worth a thousand words.

The 15-51 portfolio is above average in construction and above average consistently beats average over the long term—always. The 15-51 portfolio has a smaller number of stocks, overweights in highest-priority industries and stocks, which in

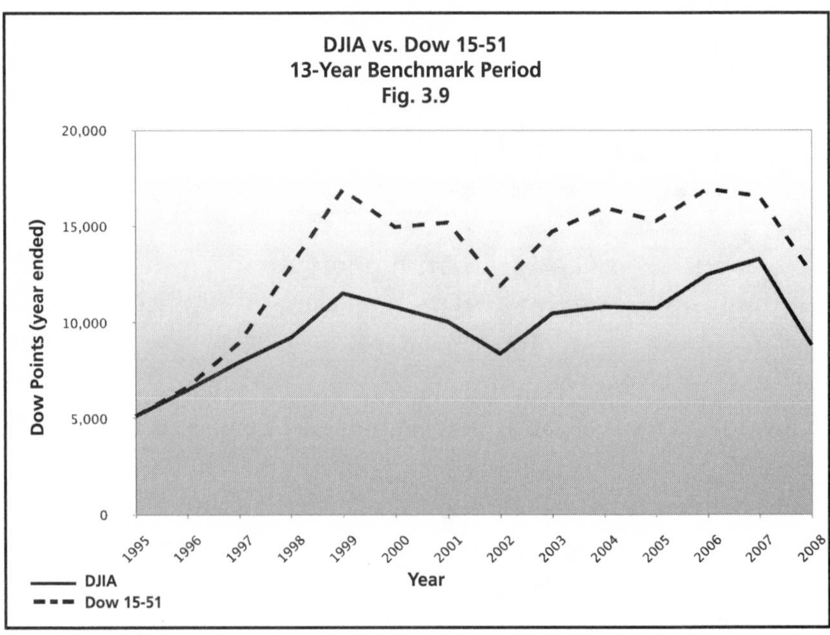

turn produces above-average investment results. That's its goal and mission, and its purpose for existence.

This chart should also dispel any false belief that your above-average stock portfolio won't go down when the stock market sells off. It will. That's what happens. But as this picture shows, the 15-51 portfolio experiences higher highs, higher lows, and faster and more potent recoveries after downside corrections. That's what you want. And let's be fair, this 15-51 portfolio produces superior results not because of superior stock selection, but because of superior construction.

That's the point of this chapter.

Don't mind me if I repeat myself. I do so to stress the most important focal points to successful investment. I understand how easy it is to get lost with investment. It's complex. I get it. Take it slowly and reread a section if you get lost. You'll get the hang of it. I'll do my best to keep you focused by reinforcing the most important points.

Once again, the Dow's goal is to be average. And we know

what average looks like. (If not, go back and look at fig. 3.4.) The goal of all 15-51 portfolios is to be above average, which begins with above-average 15-51 construction. Its possibilities are limitless.

Perhaps this is a good time to point out that portfolio construction can help define you as an investor. We can learn a lot about the Dow by looking at its makeup. For instance, the DJIA ranks technology first in industry priority as of the snapshot. Anytime technology is in the top spot, the portfolio must be considered "aggressive." Why? Because technology is about innovation: creating new products and new markets. Technology is about aggressive growth. There is more risk in aggressive growth because it's harder to achieve. Also know that higher risk generally produces more price volatility. It's part of the beast.

But the Dow doesn't have much choice in this priority. America is a technology-driven market, and its goal is to indicate "the market." It must have a representative allocation. But you don't have to. You could own more or less, depending on your goals and objectives.

There's one more point I'd like to make clear before we move on. If your goal was to be average, like the DJIA, you'd need to include dogs like AT&T, Verizon, and Disney to drag down the exemplary performances of fellow consumer service members Wal-Mart (+ 420%, not a typo), Home Depot (+127%), and a surprisingly strong McDonald's (+183%). That's another way the Dow achieves its goal of average. That's them.

Our goal is above average, which with 15-51 construction can easily be had without constructing the portfolio in an "aggressive" manner. Perhaps the best attributes of the 15-51 model are its flexibility, durability, and consistency of performance under almost any makeup. Follow me through a few more examples and you'll begin to see why I fell in love with the 15-51 model the moment I created it.

Perhaps this first 15-51 example was a bit unfair. After all,

Microsoft wasn't added to the DJIA until 1999, and it appeared in the 15-51 portfolio from 1995. As a consequence, the 15-51 portfolio enjoyed Microsoft's explosive performance contribution during the Internet boom, rising a robust 271% over the course of the 13YBM. So in this next example we'll take it out.

Microsoft resides in IS: 1-5. To remove it we'll slide technology down to the number two industry spot, which will cause the software giant to naturally fall off the bottom. To put this portfolio on a less aggressive footing, consumer staples will get promoted to the top industry spot. Holding all other Dow Jones priorities true, the 15-51 portfolio blueprint looks like this (fig. 3.10).

The 15-51 Model: DJIA Components
1X-X1, X = 5 Format
Fig. 3.10

Industry Rank	1	2	3	4	5	**$5,117**
Industry	Consumer Staples	Technology	Consumer Services	Financial	Basic	**TOTAL**
No. of Stocks	5	4	3	2	1	**15**
% of Portfolio	33%	27%	20%	13%	7%	**100%**
Investment Dollars	$1,706	$1,365	$1,023	$682	$341	**$5,117**
Stock Rank						
1	Altria	IBM	Wal-Mart	AIG	Caterpillar	
2	P&G	Boeing	Home Depot	Amex		
3	JnJ	UTC	McDonald's			
4	Coca-Cola	Hewlett-Packard				
5	Merck					

This portfolio replaces Microsoft with Merck at IS: 1-5. Merck returned -6% over the course of the 13YBM. That's a 277% swing in stock performance. You would think such a move would dramatically affect the portfolio's performance in the negative sense. But actually, this 15-51 portfolio returned 138% over the course of the 13YBM, 67% points better than the DJIA and just 5% off the portfolio with Microsoft included. See the chart in fig. 3.11.

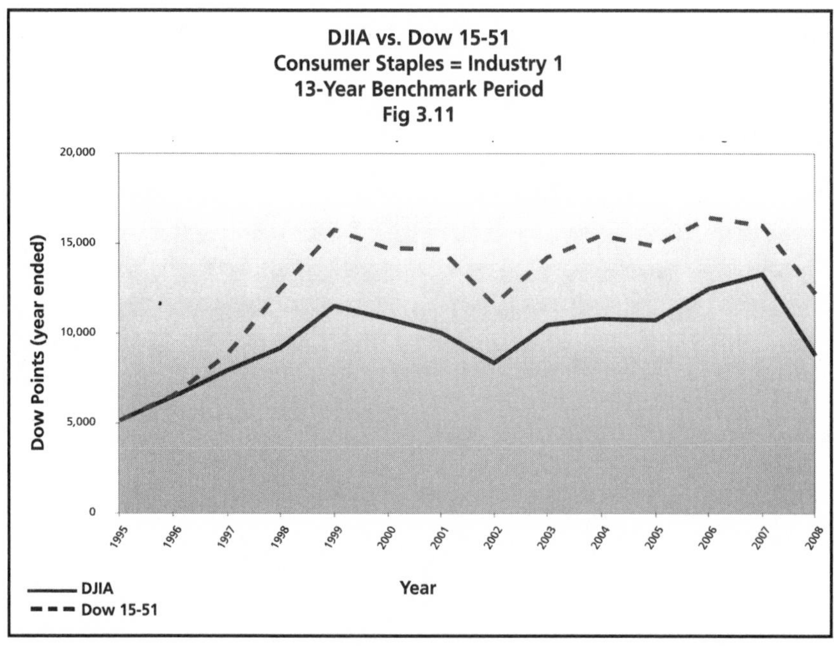

How can that be?

Superior construction.

The 15-51 model is extremely durable. Though it overweights as compared to market construction, it's still extremely balanced. At IS: 1-5, Microsoft was allocated just 7% of the total technology industry allocation and just 2.2% of the total portfolio. Again, the purpose of an allocation model is to minimize reliance on any particular stock, market segment, or industry. The 15-51 model does this superbly.

Consider your portfolio a team of stocks. Each one has a job to do and role to serve. It's not about getting lucky with a few hot stocks to make money. It's about a finely tuned cohesive team that will outperform the average over the long distance. I know, I know. You're concerned about picking the right stocks. Relax. We'll get to that. For now, keep your eye on the construction ball. It'll make everything easier later on.

Don't quite trust me yet?

In the next example we'll bring in the two industries eliminated from the previous portfolios (industrial and energy) and purposely restructure the portfolio to include a large number of big losers, like AIG -93%, GM also down -93%, and Citigroup -32%. Perhaps this will calm your nerves about stock picking. But to make this example even more challenging, we'll eliminate the highflying industries of technology and consumer service, and the robust returns of the likes of IBM and Wal-Mart. In fact, of the fifteen stocks in this portfolio only six beat "the market." That means nine, or 60%, of this 15-51 portfolio's components failed to outperform the Dow. Fig. 3.12, on the next page, shows us the blueprint.

The 15-51 Model: DJIA Components
1X-X1, X=5 Format
Fig. 3.12

Industry Rank	1	2	3	4	5	**$5,117**
Industry	**Consumer Staples**	**Basic**	**Financial**	**Industrial**	**Energy**	**TOTAL**
No. of Stocks	5	4	3	2	1	**15**
% of Portfolio	33%	27%	20%	13%	7%	**100%**
Investment Dollars	$1,706	$1,365	$1,023	$682	$341	**$5,117**
Stock Rank						
1	Altria	Caterpillar	AIG	3M	Exxon Mobil	
2	P&G	Dupont	Amex	Honeywell		
3	JnJ	Alcoa	Citigroup			
4	Coca-Cola	General Motors				
5	Merck					

Yuck. The chart (fig. 3.13) appears on the following page.

This portfolio outperformed the DJIA by 12% points over the course of the 13YBM, 84% versus 72%, respectively, despite the government taking control of 20% of the portfolio's holdings (AIG, Citigroup, and GM), despite no technology allocation, and despite 60% of its components failing to beat the market average. Yet it still did something that the vast majority of mutual funds fail to do: it beat "the market" (DJIA) over the long term. How?

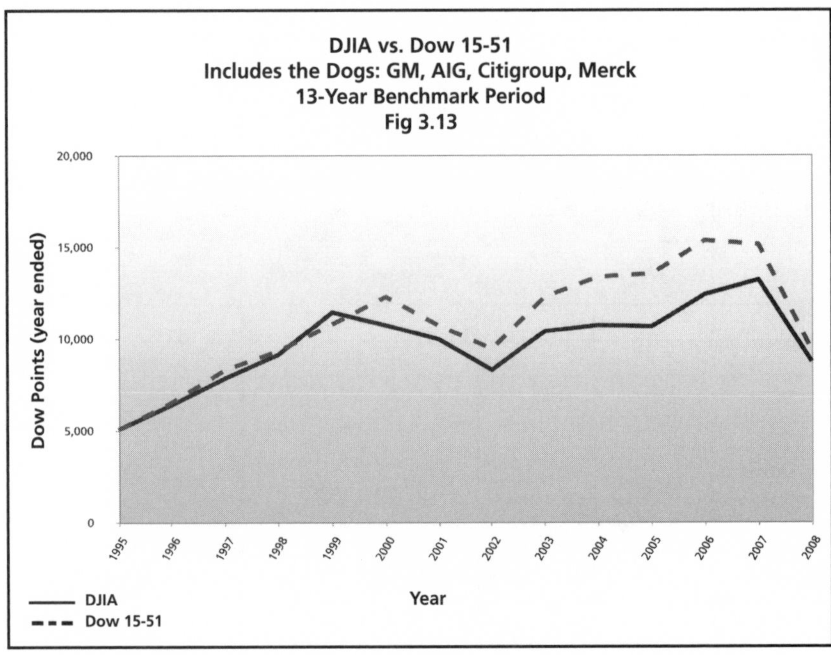

Superior construction. The 15-51 Allocation Model is a better mousetrap.

Again, there is no one right way to achieve success. The key is to find a method that makes you comfortable. Superior construction goes a long way in achieving that success. There are limitless possibilities with the 1X-X1 models. Many will be demonstrated in the following chapters. There are so many more it's impossible to mention them all.

Up to this point we have maintained consistency within each individual industry. Let us assume for the moment that you want to own a modestly aggressive portfolio with 15-51 construction, but you also want access to every industry, thus elevating the 15-51 portfolio's potential market coverage to 50%.[3] To do so two industry slots must be utilized to serve two different industries.

3 50% Market Coverage = 7 Industries Accessed ÷ (7 Total) + 15 Stocks ÷ (30 Required).

In this next portfolio, Industries 1 and 3 will be used to serve two different market allocations. Consumer staples and services will share the Industry 1 spot, and appear in rotating fashion, still according to Dow Jones priorities. For instance, IS: 1-1 will be Altria (Staple number one priority), followed by Wal-Mart (Service number one priority) at IS:1-2, followed by P&G (Staple number two priority), etc. Industry 3 is shared by basic and industrials, and will be rotated accordingly. The blueprint for that portfolio is shown in fig. 3.14, below.

The 15-51 Model: DJIA Components
1X-X1, X=5 Format
Fig. 3.14

Industry Rank	1	2	3	4	5	**$5,117**
Industry	Consumer Staple/ Service	Technology	Basic/ Industrial	Financial	Energy	**TOTAL**
No. of Stocks	5	4	3	2	1	**15**
% of Portfolio	33%	27%	20%	13%	7%	**100%**
Investment Dollars	$1,706	$1,365	$1,023	$682	$341	**$5,117**
Stock Rank						
1	Altria	IBM	Caterpillar	AIG	Exxon Mobil	
2	Wal-Mart	Boeing	3M	Amex		
3	P&G	UTC	Dupont			
4	Home Depot	Hewlett-Packard				
5	JnJ					

This 15-51 portfolio, though less aggressive than the DJIA and with half the risk, almost doubled the DJIA's output over the course of the 13YBM, earning 143% versus the Dow's 72% —after the Market crashed in 2008. The chart looks like fig. 3.15, below.

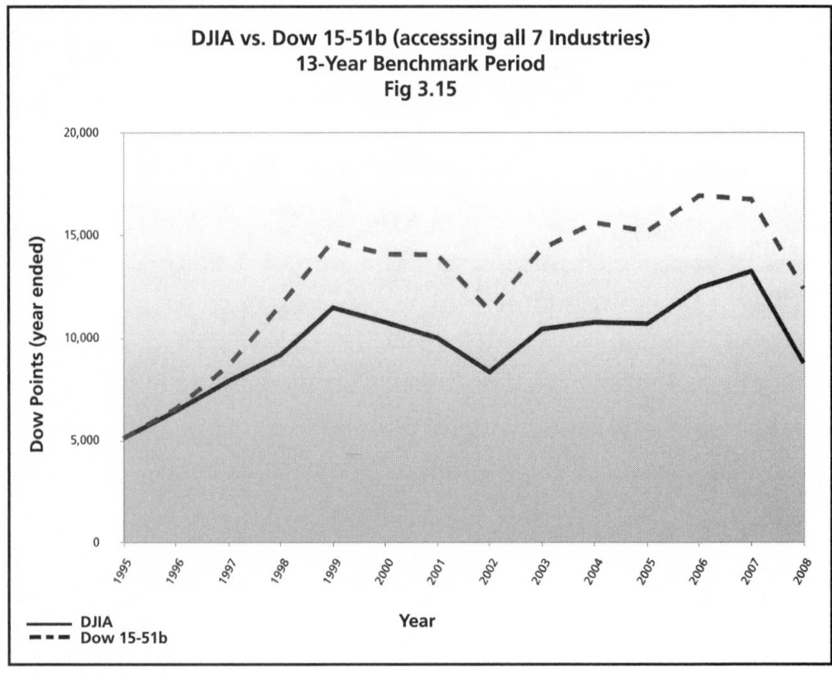

This portfolio will serve as our base portfolio going forward. Our goal will be to improve it. After all, superior construction is only half the battle. Superior components only make performance better.

But quickly, before we move on: I mentioned the 1X-X1 allocation model comes in two other variations: 16-61 and 17-71. The 16-61 model spreads investments across six industries, with the number one industry receiving six stocks and the number six industry receiving one stock. It is a twenty-one-stock

stock model. The 17-71 model spreads stocks across all seven industries, with Industry 1 receiving seven stocks, and Industry 7 getting one, totaling twenty-eight stocks. These models are detailed in the appendix. But their performance is exactly what you would expect. They beat the Dow but produce more average results, because they consist of more stocks and therefore more of the market average.

Fifteen stocks are easily found, easily monitored, and easily managed. The 15-51 model outperforms every other makeup. It's the best!

And it's even better with better stock components. That's next.

CHAPTER 4
Identifying Quality Investments

The reason most people view stock picking as a scientific process is because Wall Street has turned it into one. When stocks appear as something mysterious, they become impossible to understand, predict, and distinguish from other stocks. That's why Wall Street convinces us that picking good stocks requires the best education, the right kind of experience, and a seat at the table when executive managers speak. Without such credentials, they say, you'd be crazy to go it alone.

I say Lose Your Broker—you have all it takes.

Stocks are shares of corporate ownership. They represent businesses that deliver goods to markets. The kinds of products these companies deliver to markets determine their market segment and industry of operation.

Also recall that markets are where investment begins, performs, and earns profit (a.k.a. return on investment) and that consumers are market.

By definition, consumers produce more than two-thirds of total return on investment (ROI). Knowing this, it's easy to figure that companies (stocks) that satisfy consumer demand the most—and do so most profitably—turn out to be the best investments. It's really quite logical.

The only matter left to address is what satisfies consumers the most. And the answer to that is Value. Value can be defined as a quality product sold at a fair price, shown mathematically as follows:

Value = Quality Product + Fair Price

Companies that consistently supply Value to markets draw mass-market appeal (a.k.a. lots of consumers), which is required to achieve large-scale profits. Businesses that grow large-scale profits most quickly also return the best investments results. This isn't a leap of faith.

There is a wise old saying in investment: "You buy stock, but you invest in people." This is so very true. Stocks are just stocks—faceless images that appear on parchment paper with gold foil stamping and red ribbons. But once you begin to see Stocks in a different light, that they represent Businesses (companies) that provide goods to Markets (marketplaces), they become more real. When you view Stocks (businesses) in this mindset, they no longer seem the mysterious objects they are portrayed to be. That's what you're looking for.

You see, investing is an extremely personal process. It's not about picking the "best stocks." It's about selecting the right investments for you. That's the only way you can be comfortable with them.

This chapter provides you with all the techniques required to build a robust stock selection worksheet. We'll use these techniques to improve the stock list of the 15-51 Base portfolio outlined at the end of the previous chapter. Later I'll show you that list again to refresh your memory. But for right now it's all about identifying quality investments. And the best way to do that is to follow your money.

THE FOLLOW YOUR MONEY METHOD OF STOCK SELECTION

Since consumers fuel corporate profits, the best way to find great investments is to pinpoint the quality products that are part of your everyday life. Behind each and every one of them is a potential opportunity for investment. The same is true for me. So to improve the stocks of the 15-51 Base portfolio, we'll use my consumer experiences to locate quality investments. To do that we'll start at my favorite place: music.

Wherever I am and wherever I go, if the music's not on it's always close by. I love all kinds, from all eras, in almost every genre. For the music lover, Apple's nifty iPod is the best invention since the 8-track cassette player made your favorite music portable.

The iPod provides easy access to tons of music, with instant playlists, music sorting, and digital sound—all in a unit slightly thicker than a credit card. It's an amazing piece of modern technology. Now that I have an iPod I never want to live without one. But I did have one small problem with the iPod. It made my old stereo obsolete—it wasn't "iPod ready."

That's when I found Bose.

As all music lovers know, the music is only as good as it sounds. And Bose makes great sound products. It also makes a great example for assessing investment quality. In fact, dare I say, you can learn everything you need to know about investment from Bose. I say this knowing full well that I can't "prove" my Bose assessment. After all, Bose is a privately held company and as such it is impossible to get any kind of data, financial statements, or analyst reports about the ROI earned by Bose investors. Nor do I know anyone who has ever worked there so there is no "inside information" to speak of. My credentials to discuss Bose begin and end with my consumer experience, which allows me to say quite confidently that Bose is a damn good investment.

Bose makes a docking station specifically designed for the iPod. No larger than a two-slice kitchen toaster, its sound is crisp, pure, and free from distortion at any volume. And priced at a few hundred bucks, it's well worth it, especially to a music fanatic like me. That's value.

Shortly after listening to the Bose for the first time, I quickly searched the Internet for a stock symbol, but there was none. Again, Bose is a privately held company. This happens sometimes. But dead-end roads like this shouldn't deter you from constantly searching the marketplace for quality investments. Investing takes practice, like anything else. The more you do it, the better you'll get at it. We'll go through several examples in this chapter so you can get a feel for the process. But let's stay where we are for another moment.

What I like most about Bose is that it knows what good music sounds like and relies on the artist to define it. Its goal is to stay true to the artist who created the music, by producing sound as close to the original recording as possible. People like me appreciate that dedication. You see, I am Bose's target market (the consumer it is looking to satisfy); it must please me in order to succeed. And it did. That's a good investment.

For further proof, below is a letter included with the warranty information of my Bose docking station. It's what separates it from the competition.

> ***Our Commitment to You***
>
> *We take great pride in designing our products with the goal of providing the highest accuracy musical performance possible in the price range of that product. We strive to reproduce the musical sounds as closely to the original performance. And we strive to avoid flashy sounds such as those associated with accentuated bass and/or treble frequencies. While those sounds may be initially attractive to the novice, they are not real and are not enduring. In addition, we use only the highest quality parts and the*

latest assembly and quality control techniques to ensure the reliability and long life of our products.

Our reputation rests on our steadfast pursuit of this policy in sound systems for the home, the automobile, and businesses.

At Bose we reinvest 100% of our earnings back into the company. This enables us to support research that continually gives rise to new technologies for improving sound reproduction.

When you purchase any product from Bose, we encourage you to compare it, as we do, to competitive products for musical accuracy. We believe that this process will enhance your appreciation of the product you select.

With best wishes from all of us at Bose for many years of enjoyable listening.

I love that kind of bravado. Bose consistently produces great products and knows it. It's their goal. And it put its money where its slogan is "Better sound through research." That's commitment. That's good management. That's a good investment.

And there is no one on Wall Street that can tell me differently just because I don't know who the CEO is and never saw a financial statement. Let this Bose example serve as proof positive that these items are not required to identify quality investments. Proof of investment quality isn't found in tables, charts, and inside information; it's found in the quality of products sold and the manner in which management conducts business in the marketplace. As a result, let the following equation serve as your single most important guiding principal to selecting quality investments.

Quality Investment = Quality Management + Quality Products

Some organizations have quality ingrained into their culture. Honda and Toyota are two that come quickly to mind, despite Toyota's recent troubles. We'll get to that in a moment. But again, I draw this conclusion from the most important investment criteria I can use: my own consumer experience.

I live in the American northeast, an area where Mother Nature can be quite difficult. We get extreme weather conditions during all four seasons and as the old saying goes, "If you don't like the weather here, wait ten minutes and it'll change." You have to be ready for anything, at any time. Here, reliability is worth a premium.

That's why I own my share of Honda equipment, from snow blowers to power washers, to generators. They always start easily, with just a single pull, and require little maintenance. Honda also produces quality motorcycles, marine engines, and quads, not to mention their highly rated automobiles. Reliability, efficiency, and performance—priced right: that's Honda. That's value.

Value proves investment worth and managerial proficiency where it counts: in the marketplace. Stick to companies that demonstrate this competence and you will never be sorry. Ignore this basic trait, however, and you will live to regret it. I've been there and done that. Here's a valuable learning experience.

My hobby is bass fishing. When my Toyota Tacoma proved incapable of hauling my boat, I searched for a full-size pickup truck. Deciding to give the American automaker a shot, I accepted the Chevrolet "friends and family" deal before it was in vogue and acquired a 2004 Silverado—at a whopping $15,000 discount compared to the price of a new Toyota Tundra.

And I regret it.

Sad to say, the 2004 Chevy Silverado is like driving an antique from the 1970s. It gets awful fuel mileage, and though it was "tight" when I drove it off the lot, it didn't take long for it to "loosen up." About six months in it began to rattle, shimmy, and shake over every little bump I found, and I seemed to find them all. When I recently had the brakes replaced, the mechanic advised me that the truck would only last for another few years: rust was spreading like a cancer throughout the frame. That was hard for me to take because I opted for the much ballyhooed undercoating to protect against such a case.

I made a huge mistake investing in the Silverado: I compromised one of my core investment values for the sake of price. That's always a setup for failure. But what bothers me most is that I knew GM was a disaster long before I bought the Silverado.

There is much debate over what caused the debacle in the U.S. auto industry; whether management or unions are responsible. There is plenty of blame to go around. But let's be fair. Management engineers the vehicles, designs the plants, procures the components, markets the brands, and signs the contracts with labor unions. Even knowing that the unions are not innocent in all of this, I can't pin the blame on them.

GM's managerial blunders are plastered all over everyday life. I cringe every time I see a commercial for the GMC Sierra because it's the same exact vehicle as the Chevy Silverado. For some reason GM sees economies of scale in the tactic of competing against itself. From advertising to production, GM must spend time, effort, and money to differentiate the Sierra from the Silverado (as well as many other models). What an overlapping waste of time and money. That's a sign of bad management. Unfortunately the signs don't end there.

The redesigned Chevy Camaro came along far too late, and when it finally arrived to market, it was impossible to find in advertising. Ditto for Pontiac's below-average relaunch of the GTO. These were costly mistakes to make when Ford was launching the new Mustang and Shelby models, and Chrysler was introducing an interesting revision of the Charger. When you're last to the race, you have to bust out of the gate like a thoroughbred trying to win a Triple Crown race. And where is the Trans Am? The price of the Chevy Corvette has escalated beyond the means of many muscle-car enthusiasts. The Trans Am could easily fill this void. But no, GM's management would rather figure out ways to compete against the Silverado using another GM logo.

Everywhere you turn, GM fails to produce quality. Its components—switches, wipers, radio, ventilation, seating—are inferior to its competition's. Handling and pedal response is slow and sloppy, and their doors lack that tight, vacuum-sealed fit so commonly found in finely engineered Asian and European models. GM's management team is asleep at the wheel. That's bad management. That's a bad investment.

These factors are all the more reason not to have bailed them out. Let's face it, some businesses belong out of business. Sadly, GM is one of them. It hasn't been competitive in the marketplace for a long time, which is indicative of its stock price trend. Take a look at the chart in fig. 4.1 that compares GM to Honda, Toyota, and the Dow.

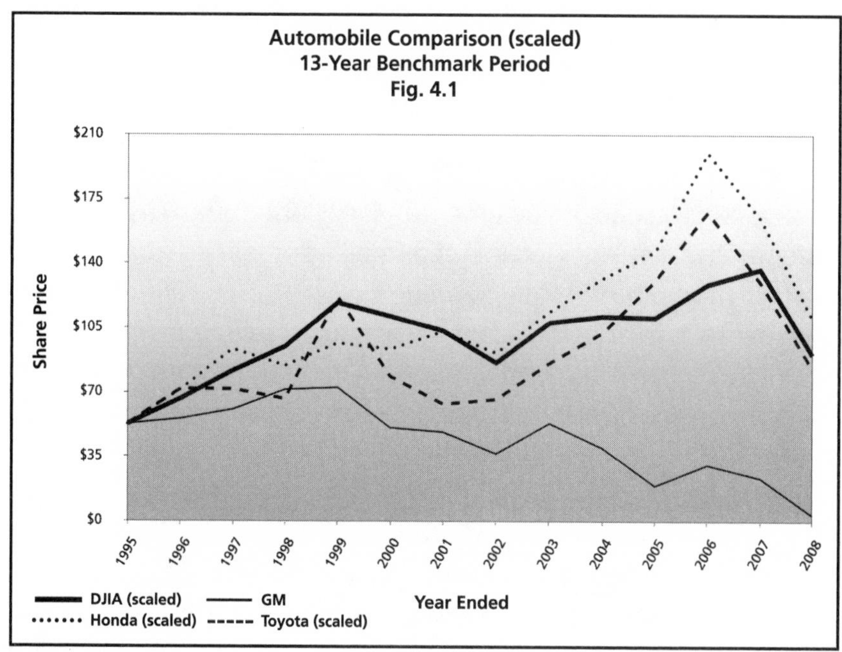

First things first: it's always a major warning when a stock trends down while "the market" trends up. The Dow Jones Industrial Average represents "the market" standard and thus establishes the line of average in every chart in which it appears. GM is a Dow component and thus part of the Average. It is clearly a below-average contributor to the portfolio and a below-average performer.

Honda and Toyota are GM's competitors; they compete for my automotive spending dollars. This chart says it all. Even at a steeply discounted price, GM was a bad investment. It wasn't competitive either in the marketplace or in the stock market. This despite increased revenues from military sales made in response to 9/11, proving once again that governments don't contribute much to market profit. Consumers drive investment success, not government. And price discounts don't get it done in the long term. Quality is the driver of long-term stock value. And GM displays little.

This is not the case with Honda and Toyota. Their brands are fresh, clean, and appeal to almost any consumer. Both have superior reliability and performance track records. I say this knowing full well about Toyota's recent problems, and we're going to get to that, but right now let's continue to make sense of the stock trends shown in fig. 4.1. Honda and Toyota took completely different roads to the same approximate destination, and each one makes total sense.

Toyota is purely an automobile maker, selling three lines of cars—Scion, Toyota, and Lexus—to three different markets: economy, midvalue, and luxury. Its results will therefore mimic those of the automobile market, which are extremely sensitive to consumer credit and spending patterns. As you would expect, Toyota's stock price felt a lift when the tech boom was creating all sorts of new wealth. When it busted and recession kicked in, Toyota's stock price declined sharply because consumers had less money to spend on cars. During recovery people bought more cars and Toyota's stock price went up. When the market crashed in 2008 and credit dried up, Toyota's stock price fell off the cliff —exactly as you would expect.

Honda, on the other hand, is much more diversified than Toyota and thus drew a different trend line than the automobile market (using Toyota as an indicator to that market). Honda serves multiple market segments: cars, motorcycles, marine, home and yard, etc. This kind of diversification gives Honda its different trend line.

Remember, diversification is more about which Stocks (companies) you select than the number of stocks you own. The purpose of diversification is to eliminate overexposure to any one particular market segment. This can be done by investing in companies that service multiple market segments. So when car sales slump during a recession, perhaps the homeowner eliminates the landscaping service and purchases a new lawn mower. Honda then loses revenue in cars but picks up revenue from homeowners purchasing yard equipment.

This is not to say that Honda is right for all portfolios and Toyota is wrong. If one-dimensional companies like Toyota find their way into your portfolio, look to diversify them with companies that service many market segments. A collection of single-market companies will produce a more volatile trend line, because fewer markets are covered.

Just because Toyota is more volatile than Honda doesn't make it a bad investment or its management bad for not diversifying. Toyota sticks to its core competency, auto making. It will therefore always be reflective of the car market and extremely sensitive to consumer-borrowing patterns. Understanding your stocks and their market characteristics will help you construct a portfolio that will produce a trend line that makes you comfortable.

Toyota consistently produces quality products and, until that changes, will always be a worthwhile investment. But as much as I like Toyota products, it must be said that it is largely a below-average performer, as it rarely outperforms the Dow. Yes, it goes up when it's supposed to go up and, yes, it is just as predictable on the downside. But still, it's a below-average performer.

It is time now to address Toyota's recent problems, where certain models experienced unintended and uncontrollable acceleration. The problem was initially thought to be a sticky gas pedal, or a floor mat that became wedged to the gas pedal, causing the car to speed without control. Fatalities occurred and lawsuits were filed. This is regrettable and most unfortunate.

Keep in mind that no automotive company is perfect. They've all had many recalls and no doubt will have more in the future. And some of them are serious. This is an unfortunate normal occurrence in this industry. Know this when you invest in it.

That said, I hated the way Toyota handled the situation. I understand that it's a Japanese company operating in a foreign market (America) and it wanted to tread lightly with what it said in the public forum. But let's be fair, its management handled the situation like a bunch of doves. From the onset Toyota's public message should have been strongly behind its record of quality and success, yet shown the willingness and open mindedness to investigate and resolve all valid claims. Innocent until proven guilty.

Moving ahead several months after the incidents occurred, and after extensive research and analysis, the problem surrounding these cases was determined to be driver error. But then several months *after* that research was revealed, Toyota settled a multi-million-dollar lawsuit for deaths caused by unintentional acceleration. Needless to say, it's hard to know what really happened.

What we do know is that the economy was in shambles when the accusations were made. Also at this time, the U.S. government (GM's ownership) was railroading a competing automaker with public castigations, hearings, fines, and threat of lawsuits (that's another reason government should stay away from enterprise). Remember, this was in the aftermath of the "financial crisis" when automakers were competing for dollars from a dwindling consumer base. This kind of market chaos gave some desperate consumers a venue to levy false claims, and some did. I suspect a business decision was made to quickly settle all critical claims out of court to make the matter go away. Fair enough.

We'll talk more about when to buy or sell an investment in a later chapter, but to follow the point to its logical end, a problem like Toyota's will cause you to lose faith in your investment. That's normal. But it doesn't mean that it's time to automatically liquidate your investment. It might be a good time to buy low. In any event, the key to making your decision is how the company handles the crisis. Keep your eyes and ears open and monitor what it's doing to regain your trust. If it repeatedly falters and is unable to recover your confidence, then it's time to sell. Monitoring the actions of publically traded companies is easy, with major events plastered all over TV, radio, and the Internet. Investing requires this kind of effort. Besides, the more you know about your investments the more comfortable you will be with them.

That said, you must learn to trust yourself, your belief system, and your common sense. They will always serve you well.

Okay, we've discussed several investments and we still haven't dropped any big managerial names. As I've said, quality products are a reflection of quality management. This is not to say that well-known business leaders like Jack Welch or Donald Trump don't matter. These titans can add positive value to an organization from the moment they step foot in the door. To illustrate this point, we'll shift our attention to the technology industry and assess the impact of two iconic corporate leaders: Apple's Steve Jobs and Microsoft's Bill Gates.

But before we dive in you should know that both companies performed well above average over the course of the 13YBM. Microsoft returned 271%, which looks flat compared to Apple's trend line, which boasted an impressive 441% gain in spite of the market meltdown in 2008. Recall what was said in the last chapter about aggressive growth: it's harder to achieve and therefore brings about more volatility. That volatility looks like this (fig. 4.2, on the next page).

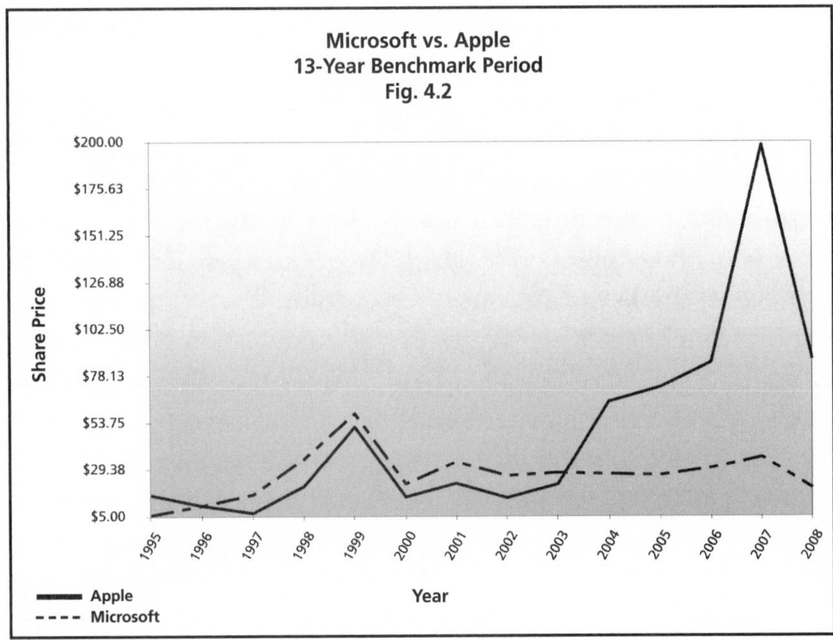

Here are some key points to consider before we start our discussion. Having left the company in 1985, cofounder Steve Jobs returned to Apple in 1997 and soon after replaced Gil Amelio, who did a terrible job as CEO. In January 2000 Bill Gates stepped down as CEO of Microsoft. The first iPod was delivered to market in 2001; that market was dramatically expanded in 2003 when iTunes was made available to Microsoft Windows consumers.

I don't know about you, but the first thing I thought of when I saw the iPod was "Where the heck was Microsoft?" With its billions of dollars in cash, the only thing Microsoft offered during this time was new software versions of Windows and Office that were less stable and less functional than previous versions. Technology is about innovation. And that's not it.

In a nutshell, Bill Gates stepped down because he knew he was done; he had lost his vision and his technological edge. His replacement apparently never had it; as to this day, Microsoft has failed to produce any kind of innovative product to catch the market by storm. For no other reason than this, its stock has failed to move in any significant way since the tech-boom correction.

By contrast, Steve Jobs reinvigorated the Apple brand by reengineering its desktop and laptop personal computers. The new products are microthin and space efficient, powerful, sport fantastic graphics capabilities, and as with all Apple products are reliably easy to use. After the successful launch of the iPod, Jobs and company extended that success into an "iFamily" including the iPhone, iTouch, and now the new iPad. Quality products one and all. That's innovation.

Apple outperformed Microsoft during the 13YBM because it had better management that was delivering better products to markets. Steve Jobs outcompeted, outdeveloped, and outinnovated the powerhouse that Bill Gates was, and the stock chart proves it.

I'm not suggesting that one person can do the job alone. It requires a team of people to achieve large-scale success. But if you're going to assess management, then there's only one person to consider: the CEO. Every organization takes on the personality of its chief executive officer because he or she establishes the vision, sets the agenda, and builds the team to carry out the mission. For public companies, the Internet makes it easy to research CEOs.

So, yes, big names matter. And, yes, it helps to know who's responsible for your investment dollars. But it is not required. Regardless of the names associated with a company, quality products are the best reflection of managerial competence.

Another way to find potential investments is to look at competitors of the Stocks (companies) you already know. Retail stores are part of the consumer service industry and, as you might have gathered, I'm a "do-it yourselfer" in and around the home. In the 15-51 Base portfolio, Home Depot was positioned at IS: 1-4.

Home Depot was the first to mass market construction and

home improvement materials to the consumer in a price club type format. The company's original pitch was that its sales representatives were trade professionals and could therefore help the consumer select the right materials and also provide technical tips to perform the task successfully. It was a great idea. But as Home Depot stores grew in number, the company relaxed its operational standards. The stores became sloppy and cluttered, and the help became less than helpful.

Then Lowe's stores started to pop up.

Lowe's does everything that Home Depot doesn't, and does it all better. Its stores are neat, clean, well stocked, and the staff is not only helpful but extremely courteous. To figure out which is the better investment is as easy as being a consumer who has experienced both retail establishments. That's it. Fig. 4.3 shows the comparative chart

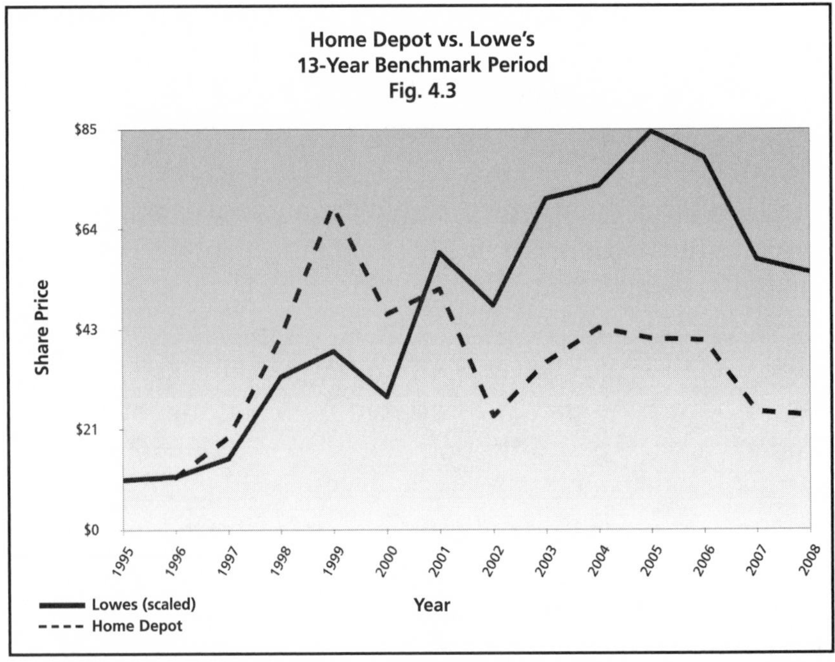

Over the course of the 13YBM, Home Depot returned a respectable 127%, but Lowe's returned a whopping 414%. Why? Because Lowe's management team is committed to doing a

better job at retail than Home Depot, and it's reflected in the stock price. It doesn't get any more complicated than that.

This same philosophy can be applied to Dow component Wal-Mart and its Target rival. Both are discount retailers. Wal-Mart may be the world's largest, but Target stores in my area are neater, cleaner, and the staff is more helpful than Wal-Mart's. In my wife's opinion, Target's products are of higher quality than Wal-Mart's, so combined with the better shopping experience Target provides, its products are worth the slightly higher price. A comparative chart follows in fig. 4.4.

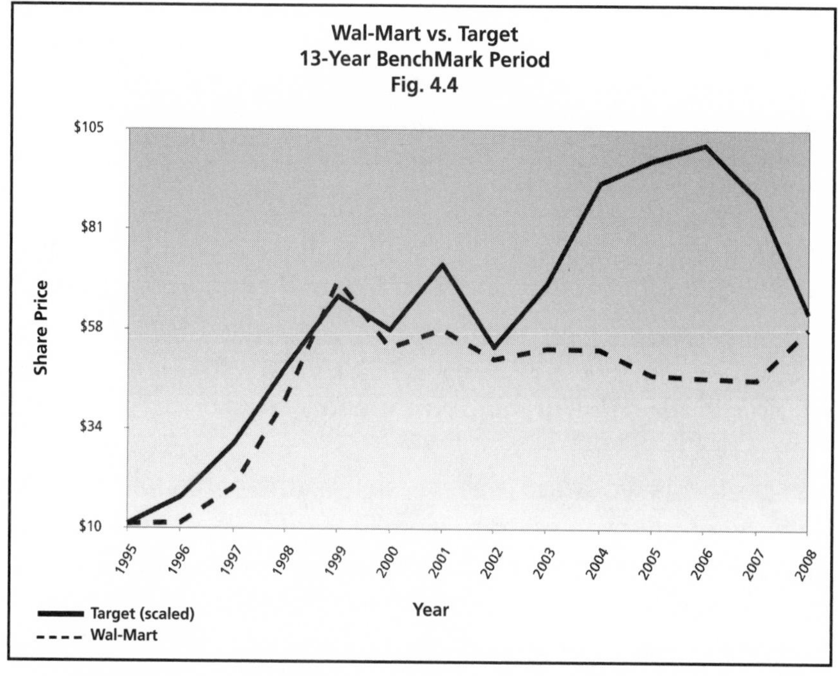

These stocks traveled completely different paths to nearly the same endpoint. Both are well-above-average performers. In the end Target outperformed Wal-Mart by 32% points, 452% versus 420%, respectively. Again, there is no right or wrong here. It's about being comfortable with the investments you select and selecting them for the right reasons.

Comfort with investing comes most easily when you understand why your investments are moving as they do. For instance, Target didn't do anything wrong at the end of the 13YBM; the Market fell apart. Accordingly, investors gravitated toward Wal-Mart's position of market dominance and its key positioning statement, "Always Low Prices,"[1] heading into a recession that some feared would become a depression. But Target is still my choice because I think it does it better than Wal-Mart does. That's me.

You're you. The best investments for you will be different from the best investments for me, because we're different and we have different life experiences. That's okay. It's what makes the world go around. Right and wrong can only be determined by whether or not you are comfortably achieving your objectives and maintaining your investment discipline.

Think of it this way: the Follow Your Money Method is not a discipline, but rather a tactic used to identify quality investments. Investing in Value is a discipline. In order to define value for yourself, determine what you like and what your priorities are, then stay true to them. Otherwise you'll spend your life looking for the next best stock. Once this becomes the case you will constantly chase higher returns and lose all discipline. That's dangerous territory.

The 15-51 Allocation Model is an investment discipline established to protect against this scenario. It confines you to a certain number of stocks, allocated throughout the marketplace in a specific manner. Think of your portfolio as a Navy SEAL team for investment: there's no room for the ordinary. When you only have space for fifteen stocks, each one should represent some element of your belief system or be special in its own way. This makes buying low in volatile markets much easier. Belief is a mechanism to that end.

For example, Altria Group is located at IS position 1-1, at the

1 After nineteen years, in 2007 Wal-Mart changed its slogan to "Save Money. Live Better."

top of the 15-51 Base portfolio. Formerly known as Philip Morris, Altria is a huge tobacco conglomerate. In my opinion, tobacco is a "yesterday's" product. It's heavily taxed, extremely regulated, and, truth be told, it can't be considered a positive element to culture. Regardless of income or profit potential, there's no room for it in my portfolio. That's me. And you should stay true to you.

But continuing with me, ditto for a company that does something you vehemently disagree with, like when news surfaced that General Electric was doing business with an enemy (Iran) of the United States. In my book, that's all the reason required to immediately liquidate all holdings. There is no reason to be tolerant or politically correct when it comes to your investments. Investment is about performance and staying true to your core values.

Think of investing as the act of handing your money over to a company's management team so that they invest it for you. Because it is actually the company that is responsible for earning you returns on investment, not the Wall Street establishment. They're just middlemen. They cannot create profit (return on investment). Businesses (stocks) do that.

Stocks create profit by delivering quality products to markets. If a company conducts business activity contrary to your belief system, penalize it for the behavior: do not purchase its products and do not invest in its operations. That's how the free market works. Besides, quality investments surround you; they are easily found in your household cupboards and your garage. You'll be surprised at what you come up with.

That's how I found Church & Dwight, which delivers Arm & Hammer baking soda to the market—which is in a whole lot of cupboards across the U.S.A. It also distributes a host of other quality products, including my favorite toothpaste, Mentadent. Take a look at the chart in fig. 4.5, on the next page, comparing Church & Dwight to Dow components Procter & Gamble and Johnson & Johnson.

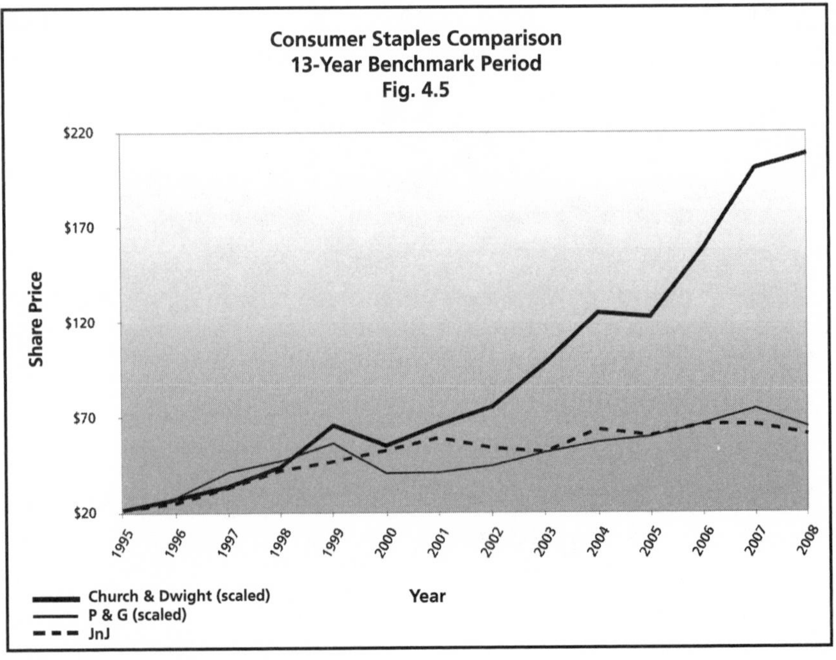

Though it's hard to tell, all three stocks performed well above average during the 13YBM. Johnson & Johnson returned 184% and Procter & Gamble gained 203%, but their trend lines look flat compared to Church & Dwight's amazing 874% gain. It's an extremely well-managed company (a thirteen-year stock trend cannot be called a fluke) that gets very little press. It's one of my favorites, and I found it in my cupboard.

More often than not, quality that appears in the marketplace also appears as quality in the stock market. Again, this follows basic logic. Can you imagine a world where poor products translated into great stock performance? There'd be no sense to it. Thankfully, reality doesn't work that way. Good products produce good investments. Great products manufacture great investment returns. Bad products translate to bad investments. More times than not.

Products and services that you know and love, those closest to you, will be the best investments for you because they are part of your life. This makes them easier to monitor, which provides insight to their future stock market performance and makes them easier to buy low during hostile markets.

On top of all that, the Follow Your Money Method is also smarter financially. Think about it. If you invest in the companies you patronize, you essentially pay yourself a dividend for purchasing the products you enjoy most. You own a piece of the company that produced them and therefore a portion of their profits. In other words, you pay yourself back for purchasing products you already buy. It's a win-win and makes total financial sense.

Here's another way to approach the process.

Never diminish the value of tapping into your network of friends and family for potential investments. I have a cousin who works for Wells Fargo and know a friend's wife who has been there for more than a decade. I also know a few others who have friends who work there. They all love it. They like the way Fargo trains and treats its workforce, and they believe in the company's commitment to high-quality banking. That's a huge testament to managerial competence, as employees aren't always the easiest to satisfy. This is market research at its finest.

As we know, Wells Fargo is a bank and all banks sell the same product: money. And they all get it from the same place: the government. Management therefore is the only difference among banks. So it was no surprise to me that Wells Fargo was a buyer when banks were failing left and right during the recent crash, purchasing troubled Wachovia Bank at a deep discount. Remember, it's buy low. Wells Fargo knew that, and took advantage of the weakness. That's what you like to see in an investment. Take a look at fig. 4.6, on the next page, to see how Wells Fargo compared to Dow components JPMorgan Chase and Citigroup over the course of the 13YBM.

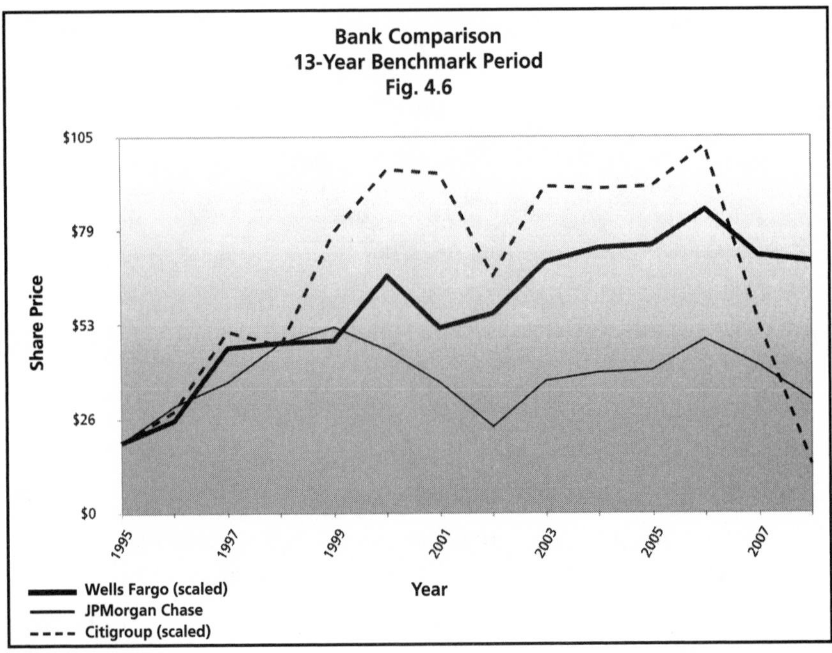

Wells Fargo produced an ROI of 257% over the course of the 13YBM and stood tall in the face of a collapsing market, on the sturdy legs and strong back of a well-trained and dedicated workforce. That's quality management. That's a quality investment.

During this same time, JPMorgan Chase returned a below-average 60% and Citigroup produced a pitiful -32%. I don't know anybody who works for Chase, but I do know some who work for Citigroup—and they hate it. No shock there. After all, when Citi was being bailed out by the U.S. taxpayer in the fall of 2008, and cutting its workforce, its management team decided not to withdraw its multimillion-dollar naming sponsorship of the new ballpark for the New York Mets. What a joke. The bank didn't have enough money to honor loan commitments, but they somehow justified spending millions to see their name on a new baseball field. Yeah, that makes sense. Advertise about the business you have no intention of conducting. That's ego-driven managerial incompetence. That's a bad investment, just like the chart suggests.

But if you were in Citigroup and liked how they did things before the meltdown, that's no problem. Learn from it. As we've seen, one bad apple can't spoil the entire bunch when using superior 15-51 construction. The point to grab on to here is how helpful your friends and relatives can be in identifying quality investments. Quality surrounds them too.

Another great place to find potential investment opportunities is in what some people call "junk mail." Junk is what you end up with after you've used something. If you don't know what it is, you don't know that it's junk. The same goes with mail. After you look at it, junk mail is transformed into something useful called: market research. You get an idea of what kinds of businesses (and how many) are trying to contact you, what they're selling, and how they're marketing their products. They are competing for your spending dollars, which tells you something about current market conditions and the value being offered in it.

For instance, there was a time when I was getting five to ten pieces of advertisements per week from banks and credit card companies. They were throwing money at me. But when the shoe dropped in the fall of 2008, only a few of their mailings continued.

Capital One, with its catchy slogan, "What's in your wallet?" was steady all along. I had to take a look and see what they were all about. Here's a chart (fig. 4.7, on the next page) comparing them to Dow component American Express.

Capital One jumped all over its premium rival from the beginning and gained 330% during the 13YBM, compared to just 40% for Amex. There can be little argument that Capital One was seeking growth more aggressively than Amex was. It was scattered all over television and the U.S. postal system. American Express, although active, pursued growth more tepidly.

That brings me to another point: *the Market* (economy) is an extremely competitive place, and all businesses compete in different ways. Sprinters look for speed out of the blocks; for

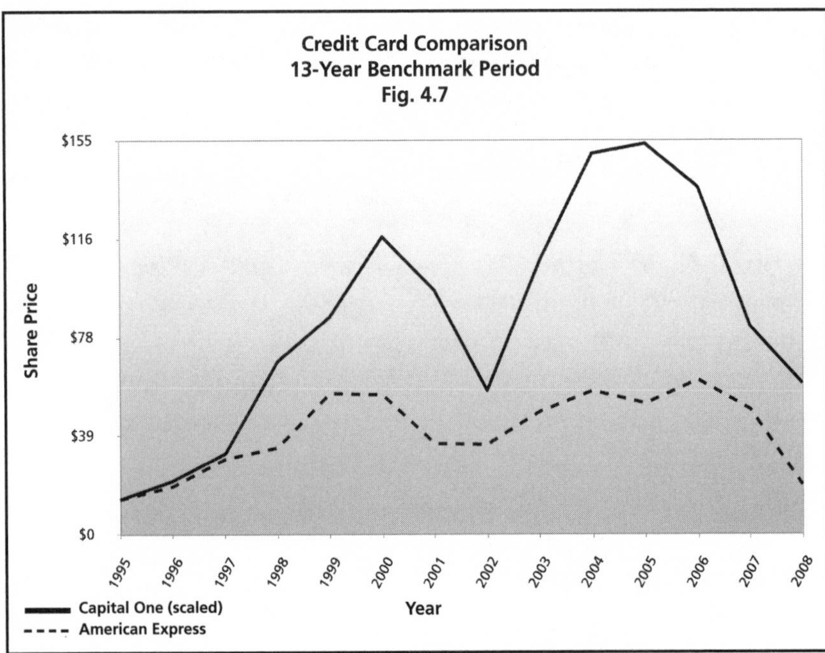

marathoners it's all about pace. Stocks have different personalities too. They are of course operated by different people, with different missions, priorities, and tactics. So to an extent, all businesses are different.

However, all credit card companies will be extremely sensitive to consumer spending patterns because that's where the bulk of their activity comes from. During market expansions like the tech boom, consumers spent more money and borrowed more money. Because of this, credit card companies made more profit and their stocks went up. During market contractions (a.k.a. recessions) they get clobbered because consumers spend less and default more. As a consequence, credit card companies make less profit and their stocks decline.

Aggressive growth will bring about increased volatility. Capital One was seeking that. Amex, not so much. Again, the movements of the stocks you select should make sense for their industry, their standing within it, the conditions of *the Market* (economy), and how they conduct business in the marketplace. It all should make sense.

Okay, so far in this chapter we've identified a lot of quality investments. Remember, our goal from the previous chapter was to improve the stock listing of the 15-51 Base portfolio and its fifteen Dow components. Here's the blueprint for that portfolio again (fig. 4.8).

The 15-51 Base Portfolio: DJIA Components
1X-X1, X = 5 Format
Fig. 4.8

Industry Rank	1	2	3	4	5
Industry	**Consumer Staples/ Service**	**Technology**	**Basic/ Industrial**	**Financial**	**Energy**
Stock Rank					
1	Altria	IBM	Caterpillar	AIG	Exxon Mobil
2	Wal-Mart	Boeing	3M	Amex	
3	P&G	UTC	Dupont		
4	Home Depot	Hewlett-Packard			
5	JnJ				

As we saw, this portfolio almost doubled the DJIA's output over the course of the 13YBM, gaining 143% versus 72% for the Dow. It's time now to fine-tune our definition of success for the portfolio we are building.

Instead of trying to create just another portfolio, let's try to do something special. Let's try to fill a void in "the market" and create a new kind of market indicator. We'll call it the 15-51 Indicator (the Indicator, or 15-51i, for short). Its objective will be to indicate how the "strength of the market" is performing, not "the average." The portfolio will achieve this by using above-average 15-51 construction and above-average components. We'll continue to honor market diversification allocations similar to that of the DJIA and GDP. By doing so the 15-51i will indicate above-average performance results, while the Dow will continue to measure the average.

Remember, you need not construct your portfolio in this manner. That's up to you. The point is to achieve your objectives. My goal here is to indicate strength and above-average returns through superior market construction. To construct this portfolio, we'll begin with the 15-51 Base portfolio and make a few changes based on my consumer experiences. Here they are.

We'll remove Altria Group in favor of Church & Dwight, replace Home Depot with Lowe's, and discard Wal-Mart in favor of Target. We'll drop Hewlett-Packard and add Apple, replace Dupont in the basic industry with Honda, and revamp the financials by replacing Amex and AIG with Capital One and Wells Fargo.

In a nutshell, this portfolio replaces seven of the fifteen Dow components with some of my favorites. Because it is not ranked in priority order, it represents the stock selection worksheet of the 15-51 Indicator portfolio (fig. 4.9, on the next page).

Let's talk about the Indicator from a wider perspective.

Thus far we haven't mentioned anything about broad-scale investments in popular asset classes, such as emerging markets or international investments. Of course, most if not all of the Stocks (companies) in the 15-51 Indicator sell to foreign customers, so the portfolio already has "international" exposure. And let us not forget about the inclusion of Japanese original, Honda. The portfolio also has coverage in emerging markets via the included stocks that invest in those venues. In that arena those are the right companies in which to invest your money, not high-risk mutual funds.

In my opinion, mutual funds dedicated to international and

The 15-51 Indicator—Not Ranked, Not Final in Alphabetical Order
Fig. 4.9

Industry Rank	1	2	3	4	5
Industry	**Consumer Staples / Service**	**Technology**	**Basic / Industrial**	**Financial**	**Energy**
NOT RANKED					
1	*Church & Dwight	*Apple	3M	*Capital One	Exxon Mobil
2	JnJ	Boeing	Caterpillar	*Wells Fargo	
3	*Lowe's	IBM	*Honda		
4	P&G	UTC			
5	*Target				

* New (non-Dow components)

emerging market investments offered to the average investor are the biggest scam advertised on Wall Street. Let the rich people gamble in these high-risk environments. Superior 15-51 construction is all you need to achieve your objectives. Besides, if you can't invest successfully in your own Market then you can't succeed in someone else's. The odds are stacked too high against you. So stay away from any broker recommending these kinds of investments to augment lackluster portfolio performance.

I'd like to close this chapter by rebuking another recurring theme to the Wall Street mantra that "past performances are not indicative of future results." Just as the Dow consistently outperforms the S&P 500 over the very long term and will continue to do so in the future, the 15-51 Indicator will consistently outperform them all, and for the very same reasons. The Dow outperforms the S&P 500 because of better construction and components. The 15-51 Indicator is superior to them both—past, present, and future.

You see, when you produce below-average results like Wall Street does, you need disclaimers for future actions. But above-average construction always produces above-average results. Then again, the only thing I have to sell you is this book. Wall Street has about twenty thousand stocks.

It's time to lose your broker, not your money. You can do better by sticking to your home market and keeping your tactics simple. Let the 15-51 Indicator be your guide to above-average investment results and your new benchmark for success.

In order to show you what above-average looks like via the 15-51 Indicator, its stocks must be ranked in priority order. To do that, we'll use Fundamentals (the financial statistics of an organization) as the deciding factor. Don't worry; it won't be so bad. And trust me, it's well worth the effort.

The fundamentals of Fundamentals is next.

CHAPTER 5

The Fundamentals of Fundamentals: Using Statistics to Assess Value

Can mathematics tell us everything we need to know about investment? No, they can't. Numbers can't determine the absolute "best" stocks to own, nor can they indicate the "perfect" time to buy or sell your investments. But they can give you something extremely important: insight.

Poor management has victimized many quality products over the years. In other words, quality does not always produce profit. A fundamental review is a mechanism used to assess an organization's profitability, solvency, and operational efficiency. It is the numerical report card of managerial competence and should be consistent with the products a company delivers to markets. A company's "fundamentals" should validate your market experiences. Nothing generates more comfort and confidence in your investments than seeing this to be true.

Fundamentals are also an extremely useful tool when ranking your stocks in priority order. Remember, the goal of portfolio construction is to overweight your investment allocations in the highest-quality Stocks (companies). A fundamental review can easily separate the men from the boys and facilitate the task of assembling your stocks into the 15-51 model.

Fundamentals can also be used to weed out the marginal, or below-average, stocks that find their way onto your stock selection worksheet. When space is precious, as with 15-51 methodology, you should have little tolerance for stocks with poor fundamentals. They have no choice but to produce poor long-term results. To expect the contrary is nothing short of a gamble.

In a nutshell, above-average market returns are most easily obtained with a collection of above-average investments. Selecting companies with high-quality fundamentals is a means to that end.

Indeed, there are a multitude of numbers, multiples, and ratios used to evaluate investments. So many in fact that you'd fry your brain if you tried to learn them all, let alone assess each and every one of them. But even if you did take them all on, you'd end up more confused than when you started. The purpose of this book is to eliminate that kind of confusion, not create it. That's Wall Street's thing. Not mine.

In this chapter we'll review the fundamentals of Fundamentals, the basics of financial numbers: which ones are most important, where they come from, how they're calculated, what they mean, and how they should be used when evaluating your stock selections. Be forewarned, this is another long chapter, broken down into several sections for easy reading. But stay with it. There is a huge payoff to a fundamental review, as you will soon see.

But before we dive into it, I must caution you not to get overzealous with "the numbers." This can easily happen once you become proficient with them. Guard against it. Numbers appear definite, firm, and reliable. Not true. They can and will mislead you if you let them. For proof positive of this, consider the anecdote of the missing dollar.

Three men walk into a motel and ask the desk clerk for a room for the night. The clerk tells them that the rate for a single room is $30. Each man pulls a $10 bill out of his pocket and hands it to the clerk, who then gives them a key. Shortly after the men retire to their quarters, the motel owner comes out of his office and tells the clerk that occupancies of more than two people per room receive a discounted rate of $25. The clerk opens the cash register and pulls out five $1 bills and proceeds to the three men's room. Once there, he tells them about the discount, handing each of them $1. But when he realizes that he can't split the remaining $2 evenly among the three, he slides the two extra bills into his pocket and leaves.

To do the math out loud: each man paid $10 (for a total of $30) and then received $1 back as a discount, which nets to $9 per man—multiplied by 3 men equals $27—plus the $2 in the clerk's pocket adds up to $29. Where's the dollar that would make a total of $30?

Answer: It's missing. It's the missing dollar, proving that numbers aren't perfect!

In fact, numbers are impersonal, meaningless, and quite misleading all by themselves. Let's take $50 million, for example. Is that a good number or a bad one? It's a big number; definite, firm, and finite. But what does it mean, and what does it reveal?

The biggest problem with numbers is that they can't tell the whole story, regardless of their size. They can change completely with just a single word, say, "loss," "debt," or "blunder." This is why fundamentals—numbers, statistics, and financial formulas—should never be used as the primary reason to make an investment. A fundamental review is just a piece of the investment process, not the entire procedure. Its purpose is to confirm or reject your market experiences and to shed new light on a prospective investment than you would otherwise not see. That's it.

What scares most people away from fundamental reviews is that many are derived from the financial statements of their respective organizations, and there's a lot of math involved. Don't let this scare you away. The math is basic. And the notion that one must be an accountant or finance professional in order to understand the financial statements—the income statement, balance sheet, and cash flow statement—is not true at all. What you need is a basic understanding of how everything works, and that's all in here.

A large section of this chapter is a tutorial providing you with thorough explanations of the basics. Sure, some of it may be a bit dry and a little boring. But gut it out. The knowledge will serve you well. I say this, and have spent the time and effort preparing this chapter, knowing full well that many fundamentals are provided free of charge on websites like MSN and Yahoo! In my opinion, it's best to know how to arrive at these answers yourself. This way you're not dependent on someone else. That's the Lose Your Broker way.

Fundamental No. 1: Stock Price

Stock price is the only statistic not found in or calculated from a company's financial statements. Instead, stock price is determined by free market activity, where buyers and sellers agree to trade corporate ownership (stock) for a certain amount of cash. The price paid represents the market value of one share of stock.

Stock price conveys two important things: what investors think about a company and what a company thinks of itself. Some companies use their stock price as an element to build their corporate identity. They do this to create a certain image, to attract a certain kind of investor, or to attract a certain number of investors (a.k.a. demand).

Let's take, for example, the stock price of famed investor Warren Buffet's Berkshire Hathaway, which closed 2008 at $96,600 for a single share, off an eye-popping high of $150,000 per share before the market crashed. The only reason for a stock price to be this high is that the company wants it to be that high. Clearly, Buffet is trying to attract a certain kind of investor, and create a certain image for his business: rich, premium, and selective. That's the image factor.

The same is true for Google, which closed 2008 at $303, but was as high as $715 before the crash. Google, representing the new wave of technology, opened at $100 per share on August 19, 2004, and hasn't split since. Google adds to its corporate identity—bigger, stronger, and better than the average technology company—through its stock price. Image: there's simply no other reason for the price to be that high.

Stock splits can easily be issued to bring a share price down to lower levels. Many companies do this to make their stock more affordable to more people. Their hope is to create attention and demand, thereby pushing their stock price higher. Stock splits are a tactic employed to increase demand.

But not all stocks can split. At the bottom of this class are the so-called penny stocks. Some people think this term refers to stocks that trade for less than a buck. To me, anything trading for less than $10 is a penny stock. The reason these stocks won't split is that a cheaper price won't attract more investors; it won't push the stock price higher.

Consider a penny stock to be as reliable as a dollar item you purchase in a five-and-dime. They're disposable. Some people incorrectly believe it's easier to earn higher rates of return with stocks that trade at lower prices because a $1 stock only has to move ten cents to achieve a 10% return. The theory here is that a ten-cent return is more easily had than a $10 return for a $100 stock (also a 10% return). That's pure speculation and totally bogus.

You invest in businesses, not stock prices.

As mentioned, investing is more of a discipline than anything else. Stock price is a good place to set an initial standard. For instance, I don't recommend that the average investor consider stocks under $15, because they're just not reliable enough. There's plenty of quality out there and thus no reason to bottom feed. If a company can't hold a $15 stock price, move on. That's my recommendation. But if you decide to swim in these dangerous waters, here's one bit of additional advice: if you like a stock at $15, you'd better love it at $5 because it can easily get there. So if you don't love it at $5, don't date it at $15. That's my two cents on the matter.

That said, perhaps it is appropriate to address the most

important rule of all in fundamentals: any single number, all by itself, means very little. And stock price is no exception. To invest in a stock solely because it has a low price is a major error in judgment. Share price by itself is perhaps the least revealing fundamental of all. The long-term stock price trend, on the other hand, is perhaps the most revealing.

In my opinion, stock price trends (not simply stock price) are where fundamental analysis begins. They reflect the heartbeat of an organization. And when you compare it to the Dow Jones Industrial Average, you get a good gauge of how a stock performs against the baseline average. This trend line can help you to quickly eliminate poor performers (a.k.a. poor investments); or it can provide a glimpse into their future movements.

Let's return to our automaker example from the previous chapter. Fig. 5.1 shows a chart without Toyota included.

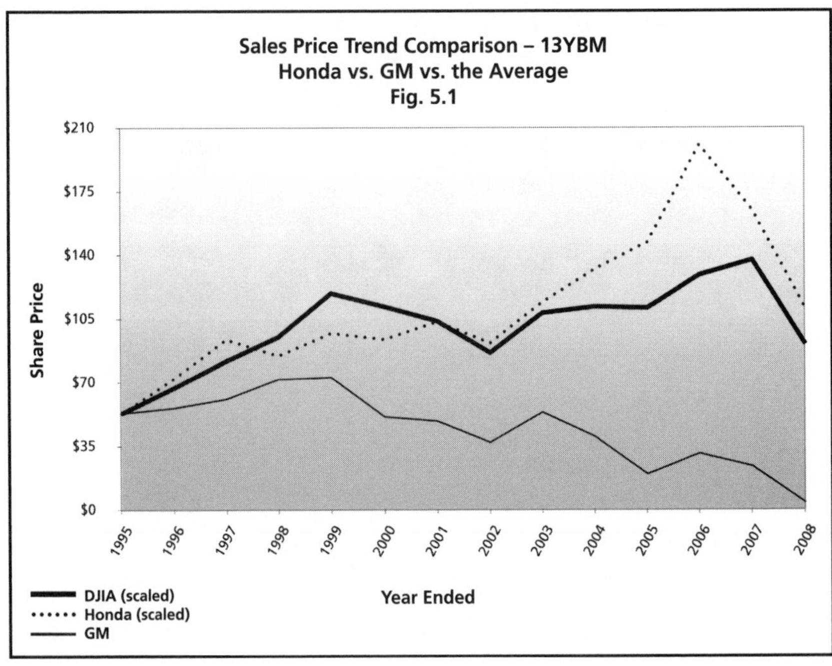

Here's an important question about using stock price, and stock price alone, as a fundamental basis for investment. At what point in GM's trend line is the price "cheap"? That is, at what entrance point is it "easier" to earn a 10% return from its starting point?

Compare that to Honda.

According to my experience, Honda's stock price trend is as reliable as its products, and so are GM's. They validate my market research.

So when Honda's stock price goes down, it's not a bad thing—it's on sale! Why? Because Honda consistently delivers value to the marketplace; when market conditions turn around, so will its stock price. Remember, market forces are more powerful than any single investment or collection of investments. Even quality investments go down in poor markets. That's the time for long-term investors to buy them low.

Though it is true that one fundamental shouldn't talk you into an investment, a bad one can certainly talk you out of an investment. A trend line like GM's makes the investment decision easy, as there is simply no reason to pursue it any further. But if you still love the company and you can live with the trend line, don't make your investment decision yet. Move onto the next fundamental.

Each of the other fundamentals is in some way derived through the three types of financial statements. We'll take each type individually, highlighting key fundamentals along the way.

Financial Statement No. 1: The Profit and Loss Statement

All three financial statements begin or end with the earnings number. For that reason, we begin with the profit and loss statement (P&L), commonly referred to as the income statement. This is the financial statement that calculates earnings, perhaps the most quoted number in all investment. And why not; earnings (a.k.a. profit) represent return on investment (ROI). It is the goal and purpose of all enterprise.

In its most basic form, earnings is defined as revenue less expenses, shown mathematically as follows:

Earnings = Revenues – Expenses

On the P&L, expenses (a.k.a. costs) are broken down into two categories: variable and fixed. Variable costs are those directly associated with the products sold, generally referred to as cost of goods sold. Fixed costs are those that do not vary based on the level of production (like rent, administrative staff, selling and marketing efforts); they are grouped together and labeled overhead, sometimes called selling, general, and administrative (S, G, & A.) Fig. 5.2 shows what a standard profit and loss statement (P&L) looks like.

Fig. 5.2

		Example	
Math	**Profit and Loss Statement**	**$**	**%**
+	Revenues (a.k.a. Sales)	$20	100%
-	Cost of Goods Sold	$10	50%
=	Gross Margin	$10	50%
-	Overhead (S, G, & A)	$7	35%
=	Earnings (a.k.a. Profit ÷ Loss)	$3	15%

Earnings is the amount of money left over after all expenses (variable and fixed) have been deducted from revenue; it is the "the bottom line" of a company's operation. Companies that lose money on the bottom line are inherently more risky than those with positive earnings. That's common sense.

The P&L is a handy statement not only because profit and loss are easy to spot, but also because it highlights certain elements of profitability. For instance, gross margin (GM) can be defined as the sales dollars generated from products sold, less the direct costs to deliver those products to markets. Gross margin represents product profitability. This is measured effectively in percentage form by dividing costs by sales, shown mathematically as follows:

Gross Margin % = Cost of Sales ÷ Sales

(50% = $10 ÷ $20, as seen in fig. 5.2)

Companies with higher gross margin percentages earn profit more efficiently than companies with low ones. In our example, the gross margin percentage (GM%) is 50% ($10 in costs divided by $20 in sales). Though you can't always get it, I like companies with a GM% of 50% or better.

The same goes for net income. By dividing net income (a.k.a. earnings) by sales, you can assess how efficiently a company generates bottom-line profit, calculated as follows:

Net Income % = Earnings ÷ Sales

(15% = $3 ÷ $20, as seen in fig. 5.2)

For example, a company with a 15% net income percentage earns money more efficiently than a company with a 1% earnings percentage because it will take less sales to generate the same amount of net income. I like companies with a net income percentage (NI%) greater than 10%, though you can't always get that either.

But why can't you always get it?

Because different market segments operate under different circumstances and thus have different operating norms. Some industries rely heavily on debt; others don't. Some market segments are famous for high margins; others are notorious for low ones. The best way to determine if a stock has "good" fundamentals is to compare it with competitors serving the same general market segments, which we'll review shortly.

Earnings are often quoted on a per-share basis, called earnings per share (EPS). EPS is derived by dividing earnings by the number of shares outstanding, shown mathematically as:

$$\text{Earnings} \div \text{Shares Outstanding} = \text{Earnings Per Share}$$

Besides operational activity, EPS is also dependent on the number of shares outstanding. Many companies actively purchase and sell stock in their own company. They sell their stock to raise capital and buy it back because they perceive it as the best investment for their capital expenditure. Consequently, earnings growth and EPS growth can tell two completely different stories. This can be seen quite clearly in the example below (fig. 5.3).

Fig. 5.3

Company A	Year 1	Year 2	Change
Earnings	$25,000	$27,500	$2,500
Earnings Growth		10.0%	
Shares Outstanding	5,000	4,500	(500)
EPS	$5.00	$6.11	$1.11
EPS Growth		22.2%	

When companies buy back their own stock they limit the amount of shares available for trade in the stock market. By limiting supply, Company A raises its earnings per share to 22%

in Year 2, even though earnings grew at just 10%. It's always good to know what's driving the change in EPS (operations or stock buybacks), because EPS is used to calculate the P/E ratio.

Fundamental No. 2: Price-to-Earnings Ratio (P/E)

Besides stock price and earnings, the price-to-earnings ratio is probably the most often mentioned fundamental. Also called the P/E multiple, or simply the multiple, it's defined as the share price divided by earnings per share, shown mathematically as follows:

$$\text{Share Price} \div \text{Earnings Per Share (EPS)} = \text{P/E Ratio}$$

For example, a $50 stock price for a company with $5 in earnings per share renders a P/E ratio of 10. The reason P/E is also called "the multiple" is because it's the number that earnings must be multiplied by to arrive at the current share price. In this case, $5 (EPS) must be multiplied by 10 (P/E) to arrive at the current price of $50.

So what justifies a 10 multiple for one company versus a 50 for another?

Growth.

High premiums are paid for consistent growth on Wall Street. The companies that grow their revenues and earnings the fastest will be will be rewarded the highest P/E multiples. These highfliers are usually Wall Street's darlings, and the speculation surrounding them often runs amuck. This increased attention fuels demand and overreaction, which causes wild swings in price and P/E multiples. Once again, here's how that volatility looks in a comparison between Microsoft and Apple (fig. 5.4, on the next page).

Like all other fundamentals, the P/E ratio means very little on its own. But when connected to a company's growth rate, it provides an extremely useful pricing gauge. As a general rule,

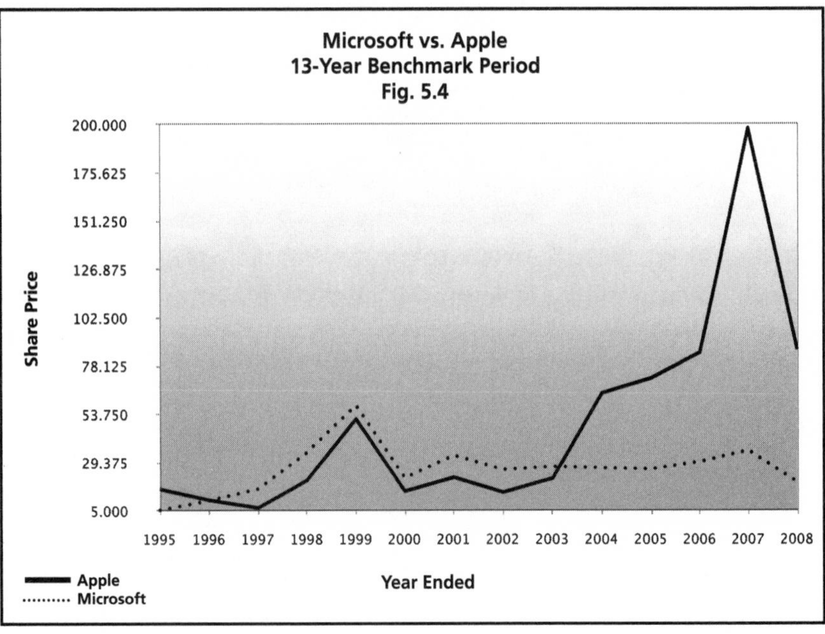

the closer the multiple is to its long-term growth rate the less price volatility you can expect. Before investing, compare the current P/E to its conventional trading range and its growth rate. This will give you an idea of the immediate price volatility you can expect from a stock. This makes it easier to handle a several-point drop in price shortly after you invest. It's hard to believe how often that happens. In any event, momentary changes in stock prices matter much less if you're investing in a company for the right reasons (see chapter 4).

Going back to our example, during the last three years of the 13YBM, Apple's revenues were growing an average of 30%, and its earnings averaged 57% growth. As a result, it wasn't uncommon to see Apple's P/E at around 35 before the market crashed. Also at this time Microsoft had growth rates of 17% and 19% (revenues and earnings respectively), while its P/E was at around 15, slightly below its growth rates.

After the crash the P/Es for both companies contracted

significantly. Apple's P/E ended at 17, losing eighteen multiple points (just above 50%); and Microsoft's P/E dropped to 10, losing five multiple points (about 33%). Apple's multiple contracted more than Microsoft's because it had more room to give.

Remember, at this time the stock market was speculating about how much the economy would shrink because of the crash. When the market shrinks, growth slows, and PE multiples contract. As a result, those companies that enjoyed inflated multiples on the way up had to correct more severely on the way down. That's the way it goes.

The P/E multiple is a pricing gauge—that's it—and just one more piece to the fundamental puzzle.

Financial Statement No. 2: The Balance Sheet

The balance sheet is a listing of a company's assets, liabilities, and equity. It is called the balance sheet because there are two sides to the statement—debit and credit—and both sides must equal, or "balance." Assets appear on one side (debit), and the total of liabilities and equity appear on the other side (credit). The balance sheet formula looks like this.

Assets = Liabilities + Equity

Assets are what the company owns, liabilities are what it owes (a.k.a. debt), and equity is comprised of two parts: capital invested by shareholders and the accumulated earnings or loss for all years of operation, called retained earnings. Equity, also called net worth, is the difference between what is owned and what it is owed, shown mathematically as follows:

Assets – Liabilities = Net Worth (a.k.a. Equity)

An ordinary balance sheet looks like this (fig. 5.6).

BALANCE SHEET
Fig. 5.6

Assets:		Liabilities:	
Current Assets:		Current Liabilities:	
Cash	$5	Accounts Payable	$3
Accounts Receivable	$3	Accrued Expenses	$7
Inventory	$2	Total Current Liabilities	$10
Total Current Assets	$10		
		Long-Term Liabilities	$20
		Total Liabilities	**$30**
Fixed Assets:			
Property	$5	Stockholders' Equity:	
Plant	$25	Paid in Capital	$5
Equipment	$10	Retained Earnings/(Loss)	$15
Total Fixed Assets	**$40**	**Total Stockholder's Equity**	**$20**
Total Assets	**$50**	**Total Liabilities & Equity**	**$50**

As you can see, each side totals to $50: they balance. And because both sides must always balance, the balance sheet formula can be twisted and turned several different ways. For instance:

Assets = Liabilities + Equity

Then:

Assets – Liabilities = Equity

And also:

Assets – Equity = Liabilities

As you will soon see, these relationships will assist us in determining how effectively a company borrows money. But before we get there, we'll learn how to test the balance sheet for solvency and operational efficiency.

Fundamental No. 4: Current Ratio

With balance sheets, the word "current" means short term, or due and payable within one year. The current ratio is a key fundamental used to measure short-term solvency. It is calculated by dividing current assets by current liabilities, shown mathematically as follows:

Current Ratio = Current Assets ÷ Current Liabilities

In our balance sheet example, the current ratio is 1.0 (10 divided by 10). Consider current ratios below 1.0 a red flag. In such cases, the company's short-term assets cannot cover its short-term debt (liabilities). That's not a positive operating situation.

Fundamental No. 5: Leverage Factor

The current ratio evaluates short-term solvency, but companies can also borrow long-term money (payable in more than one year). In fact, most companies do borrow long-term money, usually to expand operations or invest in other businesses. When it comes to assessing a business, I like to know how much of its assets aren't paid for. To arrive at this number, simply divide what the company owes (total liabilities) by what it owns (total assets). I call this fundamental the leverage factor.

Leverage Factor = Total Liabilities ÷ Total Assets

Leverage is another word for debt, or liabilities. In our example, the leverage factor is 60% ($30 ÷ $50), which, like all other fundamentals, means relatively little by itself. However, if a company is leveraged up to and beyond 95% of its total assets, then it has very little room to borrow additional funds. That's a risky proposition. Too much debt can drive a business into bankruptcy as easily as it can ruin a consumer. The leverage factor is a key fundamental to assessing long-term solvency.

Fundamental No. 6: Unpaid Sales Ratio, or Months Sales Outstanding

The income statement and balance sheet have a few natural relationships that help assess operational proficiency. For instance, accounts receivable (A/R) is the portion of revenues (P&L) not yet paid. To put it another way, A/R represents the amount of sales that are unpaid and due to a company. To be operationally efficient, sales must be collected and converted to cash in a timely manner. This efficiency can be calculated by dividing the amount owed (accounts receivable from the balance sheet) by the amount sold (sales from the income statement), shown mathematically as follows:

Unpaid Sales Factor = Accounts Receivable ÷ Revenues

This answer will usually come in the form a decimal. In our example, the unpaid sales factor is .15, or 15% (3 divided by 20). If the answer to this formula is greater than 1, it means that more than one year of sales is owed to the company by its customers. That's neither good nor efficient cash management.

For a clearer picture, it is helpful to convert the unpaid sales factor into a ratio of months. Since there are twelve months in a year, one month is equal to .083, or 8.3% (1 divided by 12.) The number of months sales are in receivables can be calculated by dividing the unpaid sales factor by .083, shown mathematically below.

Months Sales Outstanding = Unpaid Sales Factor ÷ .083

Continuing with our example, months sales are outstanding is 1.8 months (.15/.083). Again, "good" or "normal" depends on the industry and market segment of that particular stock. Generally speaking, however, companies that produce months sales outstanding of 2.5 or less are best. The best way to assess collection proficiency is to compare the investment you're evaluating against their direct competitors. As you'll see, fundamental comparisons are extremely insightful—once you have the total picture. We're not there yet, but we're getting closer. Let's keep moving.

Fundamental No. 7: Unsold Products Factor, or Inventory Months Supply

The same logic used for unpaid sales can be used to assess how efficiently a company moves its inventory; in others words, how efficiently it produces and supplies products to markets. Inventory from the balance sheet is naturally related to the cost-of-goods-sold item on the P&L. The calculation looks like this:

Inventory ÷ Cost of Sales = Unsold Products Factor

To turn this factor into months, simply divide it by .083, shown below.

Months Supply of Inventory = Unsold Products Factor ÷ .083

Continuing with our demonstration, the calculation for inventory months supply is calculated in the following way.

2 (Inventory) ÷ 10 (Cost of Sales) = .20
.20 ÷ .083 = 2.41 Months Supply of Inventory

Once again, the best way to assess efficiency is to compare the stock you're interested in against a few other companies operating in similar market segments. As a general rule, however, companies with a three-month supply of inventory or less can be considered efficient.

Fundamentals 6 and 7 determine the velocity at which products are sold and converted to cash. Without knowing that, it's easy to get fooled into believing that a high current ratio is good when it truly is not.

For instance, consider a company that experiences a high rate of uncollectible receivables and excessive amounts of inventory that cannot be sold. Its current ratio (current assets ÷ current liabilities) will appear strong; that is, 4.0 or 6.0, even though the company has little cash and is struggling to survive (because it can't collect its sales or sell its inventory). A review of these fundamentals provides you with the insight needed to sniff out that kind of rat.

Fundamental Nos. 8, 9, and 10: Balance Sheet Returns

Besides efficiency, the balance sheet can also be tested for profitability. The two most quoted ratios are return on assets (ROA) and return on equity (ROE). Anytime the word "return" is used, earnings (from the P&L) is the numerator and the other factor is the denominator. These ratios are defined mathematically below.

No. 8: Earnings ÷ Total Assets = Return on Assets (ROA)

No. 9: Earnings ÷ Total Equity = Return on Equity (ROE)

Continuing with our demonstration, the ROA is 6% (3 ÷ 50) and ROE is 15% (3 ÷ 20). Applying standard balance sheet formulas, we can deduce:

No. 10: Return on Assets (ROA) – Return on Equity (ROE) = Return on Liabilities (ROL)

Using the numbers from our example:

ROA – ROE = ROL
6% – 15% = –9%

Since the return on liabilities is a negative number, it is not a "return" at all but in fact a cost. It represents the company's cost of debt. This is good to know, because, as we've learned with subprime mortgage rates, higher interest rates (cost of debt) follow higher risk propositions. Again, certain market segments may experience higher borrowing costs than others. That's why it's important to conduct an apple-to-apple comparison with peers in the industry.

Okay, that's enough for balance sheet fundamentals. There's only one more financial statement to cover and then we can get into the fun stuff of applying these principals to shed new light on our stock selections.

Financial Statement No. 3: The Cash Flow Statement

Large publicly traded companies must be on what's called the accrual method of accounting, meaning that both income and expenses are recorded when they occur, not necessarily when cash is exchanged. As a result, corporations must produce a statement to show how operations affect cash. To put it another way, the cash flow statement shows how cash is created and used in business activity. It does this by breaking down cash activity into three sections:

1. Cash flow from operations (CFO)
2. Cash flow from investing (CFI)
3. Cash flow from financing (CFF)

On the cash flow statement, positive numbers signify sources of cash and negative numbers represent uses of cash. Fig. 5.7 shows a typical cash flow statement.

Cash Flow Statement
Fig. 5.7

Net Income from P&L	**$3.0**	**Notes**
Operating Activities (Cash adjustments to Net Income):		
Depreciation	$3.0	Add Back Noncash P&L Item
Change in Accounts Receivable	$0.8	Got Smaller, Cash Provided
Change in Inventory	($1.0)	Got Larger, Cash Used
Change in Current Liabilities	($0.5)	Got Smaller, Cash Used
Cash Provided or (Used) from Operations (CFO)	**$5.3**	**Net Income + Adjustments**
Investing Activities:		
Capital Expenditures	($10.0)	Purchased equipment: Used
Other Investments	$0.0	
Cash Provided or (Used) from Investing (CFI)	**($10.0)**	**Subtotal Investing**
Financing Activities:		
Dividends Paid	($2.5)	Paid shareholders: Used
Sale or (Purchase) of Stock	$3.0	Issued more stock: Source
Net Borrowings	$5.0	Borrowed more money: Source
Cash Provided or (Used) from Financing (CFF)	**$5.5**	**Subtotal Financing**
Change in Cash	**$0.8**	**Change in Cash vs. Prior Year**

Starting from the bottom, cash from financing (CFF) shows how the company raises or uses cash outside of its operations. A sale or (purchase) of stock refers to the company's own stock. When a company sells its own stock, it raises cash, which, quite obviously, is a source of cash. Purchasing its own stock requires cash: a use. Borrowing more cash is shown as a positive (source of cash), and repaying debt is shown as a negative (a use of cash), just like your checkbook.

The middle item on the statement is cash from investment (CFI), which represents the cash used by a company to invest in itself, like capital expenditures. For this reason, CFI is usually a negative number: a use of cash. If a company invested in a stock portfolio, those investments would also appear here.

Cash flow from operations (CFO) reconciles earnings to cash. It is the top section of the cash flow statement—and the most important number on the page. Consider it a major sign of weakness if the CFO is negative. Operations that do not create cash are inherently more risky than operations that do. If they are not making cash, they are burning it. Never a good sign.

Fundamental No. 11: Cash Conversion Ratio

Earnings are no good unless they convert to cash. This can be assessed by a ratio I call the cash conversion ratio (CCR), shown mathematically below.

Cash Conversion Ratio = Cash From Operations ÷ Earnings

Like the current ratio, the cash conversion ratio (CCR) should always be greater than 1.0. This is to say that cash from operations should always be greater than net income (earnings). Alarms should ring when it's not, because earnings that cannot be transformed into cash aren't real. A CCR below 1.0 also means that many fundamentals, from the P/E ratio to return on equity, can be significantly overstated. The cash conversion ratio is a mechanism to test the quality of earnings, and the fundamentals that rely on earnings for their calculation.

So that's the 1-2-3 of financial statements and my top priority fundamentals. You can't learn everything from fundamentals but you can certainly learn a lot. Remember, the objective with a fundamental review is to corroborate your market experiences. We're looking for consistency in the marketplace and in the fundamentals.

To demonstrate how a fundamental review can be used in building your portfolio, we'll use these fundamentals to assess our stock selections and to assist in ranking them in priority order.

Now the fun begins.

THE FUNDAMENTAL REVIEW

To evaluate the stocks for the 15-51 Indicator, we'll start with our number one industry and work our way down the model. Recall that the top-priority industry is a hybrid allocation consisting of three consumer staple stocks and two consumer service stocks. We'll take them by industry.

Industry 1: Consumer Staples and Services

Consumer Staples

The top three companies on the consumer staple list (see fig. 5.8 on the next page) are included in the 15-51 Indicator portfolio, and I rank them within their respective industries in the order they appear here. Their fundamentals dictated this action.

Fig. 5.8

Company	GM%	NI%	ROA	ROE	ROL (cost of debt)	Current Ratio	Leverage Factor	Inventory Supply	Months Sales Unpaid	Cash Conversion Ratio (CFO/EPS)
Johnson & Johnson	71%	17%	13%	24%	-11%	4.1	46%	3.5	0.2	1.4
Procter & Gamble	51%	14%	8%	17%	-9%	4.7	52%	2.5	0.5	1.3
Church & Dwight	39%	8%	7%	16%	-9%	5.5	57%	1.8	1.4	1.5
Colgate-Palmolive	56%	13%	17%	76%	-59%	3.2	77%	2.3	1.5	1.3
Kimberly-Clark	31%	10%	10%	29%	-19%	3.7	66%	2.3	1.8	1.3

Johnson & Johnson has great gross margins, most probably because it also develops medications, which provide greater gross margins once developed. JnJ also provides solid returns on assets and equity, and has the least leverage of the comparables. I like that flexibility. Its unpaid sales is the lowest, and though its inventory supply is a bit a high, it shows superior strength and efficiency everywhere else.

P&G and Church & Dwight were steady performers but their fundamentals were weaker than Johnson & Johnson's. By using fundamentals to rank them in priority order, these stocks appear (fig. 5.9 on the next page) in the 15-51 Indicator in reverse order from their 13YBM return on investment (ROI).

Fig. 5.9

Company	Fundamental Rank	ROI 13YBM
Johnson & Johnson	1	184%
Procter & Gamble	2	203%
Church & Dwight	3	874%

That's okay. Again, we're not looking for a great portfolio, nor are we looking to stack the deck. We're looking for an above-average market portfolio that indicates strength. Based on fundamentals, this ranking gets us there.

Colgate Palmolive and Kimberly-Clark were thrown in as comparables. Colgate has a much higher return on equity, and much more debt. In fact, its leverage factor and cost of debt are so far out of whack compared to the others that it was enough to scare me off. Kimberly-Clark is weaker than the Indicator's top three stocks on most fronts and doesn't provide a reason to be considered.

Again, there is no right or wrong way to invest. Your stocks will be different from my stocks. No problem. If Colgate finds its way into your portfolio, consider its fundamentals above average in risk (because they are) and then balance that off with a stock with less than average fundamental risk. For instance, Church & Dwight has higher risk fundamentals than JnJ and P&G because it earns profit less efficiently (see GM%, NI%, and the return ratios: ROA and ROE). For that reason Church & Dwight is ranked below them. That is to say, fundamentals are more important than stock price trends for long-term performance.

There can be many successful portfolios with Colgate and Kimberly-Clark included. If you like their products and the way they conduct business in the marketplace, and their fundamentals aren't glaringly bad, then it's okay to invest in them. Remember how durable and flexible the 15-51 model is. Higher-risk stocks can easily be placed lower in priority, which will lessen the impact they will have on your total performance. Keep that in mind when laying out your portfolio.

Okay, let's take a look at the other part of the number one industry, shown in fig. 5.10.

Consumer Services

Fig. 5.10

Company	GM%	NI%	ROA	ROE	ROL (cost of debt)	Current Ratio	Leverage Factor	Inventory Supply	Months Sales Unpaid	Cash Conversion Ratio (CFO/EPS)
Lowe's	35%	6%	9%	17%	-8%	4.0	48%	2.8	0.1	1.5
Home Depot	34%	6%	10%	25%	-15%	3.5	60%	2.7	1.4	1.3
Target	34%	4%	6%	19%	-12%	3.8	66%	1.9	1.7	1.4
Wal-Mart	24%	3%	8%	20%	-12%	0.8	60%	1.5	1.5	1.6

From a fundamental perspective it's a tight race between Lowe's and Home Depot. No doubt about it. But Home Depot has more leverage (debt), which costs more, and it takes them longer to collect their accounts receivable. Lowe's does it better, just as I experienced in the marketplace.

The same goes for the comparison between mass-market retailers Wal-Mart and Target. It's a close one on the fundamental front and despite its slightly higher leverage factor, Target's current ratio is vastly superior to Wal-Mart's (which is below 1.0). That's enough to maintain Target as my choice, for shopping and investment.

Because this industry allocation covers two major markets, components will be rotated by industry. To put the Indicator on a more conservative footing, consumer staples will serve as the dominate allocation in its top industry spot, receiving three stocks. My highest-ranked staple will be followed by the highest-ranked service. Again, fundamentals were used to set the priority rankings in this industry.

Fig. 5.11 shows the layout for Industry 1 in the 15-15 Indicator.

Industry Rank 1
Fig. 5.11

Industry	Consumer Staples/Services
Stock Rank	
1	JnJ
2	Lowe's
3	P&G
4	Target
5	Church & Dwight

Industry 2: Technology

The easiest ways to achieve your objectives is to never forget them and to employ tactics that will ensure success every step of the way. So before we start with this industry, let's revisit the 15-51 Indicator's mission from a different perspective. Its goal is to be an above-average market portfolio, so it will attempt to cover as many market segments and GDP spending classes as possible. We'll do this by staying close to market allocations. We'll also maintain several DJIA components, thus preserving a connection to "the market."

Dow components Boeing and United Technologies serve business and government customers only. Their key fundamentals can be seen in fig. 5.12.

Fig. 5.12

Company	GM%	NI%	ROA	ROE	ROL (cost of debt)	Current Ratio	Leverage Factor	Inventory Supply	Months Sales Unpaid	Cash Conversion Ratio (CFO/EPS)
Boeing	20%	6%	7%	45%	-38%	1.9	85%	2.2	0.4	2.4
UTC	27%	8%	8%	20%	-12%	3.1	61%	2.4	2.2	1.3

Are there better choices serving these market segments? Perhaps. But, again, the 15-51 Indicator is not looking to be the best portfolio ever constructed. It's looking to be an above-average market portfolio and the best way to do that is to own a significant piece of "the market." Dow components Boeing and United Technologies are a means to that end.

The other two technology components will cover the computer market. Apple will top the rankings in this industry because it is one of my favorites, and because it is primarily driven by consumers. This will help diversify this industry by GDP spending class. The final stock allocation will be filled by another Dow component, IBM. Fig. 5.13 shows the fundamental review.

Fig. 5.13

Company	GM%	NI%	ROA	ROE	ROL (cost of debt)	Current Ratio	Leverage Factor	Inventory Supply	Months Sales Unpaid	Cash Conversion Ratio (CFO/EPS)
Apple	34%	15%	12%	23%	-11%	2.8	47%	0.3	2.3	2.0
IBM	42%	11%	9%	37%	-28%	2.7	76%	0.6	3.7	1.5
Microsoft	81%	29%	24%	49%	-24%	2.4	50%	1.0	3.1	1.2
Intel	7%	35%	13%	16%	-4%	6.5	23%	2.2	2.3	1.8
Hewlett-Packard	24%	7%	8%	19%	-11%	1.2	44%	1.2	3.0	1.3

IBM is not the same computing company it used to be, now serving the needs of business more than the consumer. That's why its leverage factor is higher than that of the others. It is a function of how it conducts business.

There is nothing wrong with Apple's fundamentals, which on a profitability level are vastly inferior to Microsoft. But remember, these are two different businesses in two different modes. Microsoft is a mature software company; Apple is innovating hardware and software and also has a retail service. Again, you can't allow fundamentals to be the sole determinant of your investment decisions. They are a piece of the puzzle, beginning with quality products and quality management. On those fronts, and with solid fundamentals, Apple wins the top spot hands down.

Hewlett-Packard and Intel aren't innovating, and it's hard to consider HP anything more than a printer maker. For this reason, they miss the cut. Consequently, Industry 2 in the 15-51 Indicator is ranked as follows (fig. 5.14).

Industry Rank 2
Fig. 5.14

Industry	Technology
Stock Rank	
1	Apple
2	IBM
3	Boeing
4	UTC

Industry 3: Basic and Industrial

Our next industry allocation is another hybrid, consisting of basic and industrial stock components. Because Honda is one of my favorites, we'll evaluate automakers first.

This is one of those market segments where net income percentages rarely get above 10%. It's an industry norm. And though GM operates in the bizarro world, it can provide two valuable lessons. First, a single fundamental viewed in isolation can be extremely misleading. On the surface, GM's return on equity looks great at 104%. However, GM had negative earnings (a loss) and negative equity (a negative net worth), and when divided, the two negatives made a positive. If not for this numerical imperfection, GM's performance would be a disaster from every angle. Second, it's helpful to know that the calculations presented here are based on fiscal years 2007, 2006, and 2005. These fundamentals were therefore the basis for the U.S. government's decision to float GM billions of dollars in 2008, before taking it over in 2009. Let this serve as yet another reason

Fig. 5.15

Company	GM%	NI%	ROA	ROE	ROL (cost of debt)	Current Ratio	Leverage Factor	Inventory Supply	Months Sales Unpaid	Cash Conversion Ratio (CFO/EPS)
Honda	29%	5%	5%	13%	-8%	2.7	64%	1.7	2.5	1.9
Toyota	18%	7%	5%	14%	-9%	2.7	63%	1.0	3.4	1.0
General Motors	7%	-21%	-26%	104%	-130%	2.1	125%	1.4	0.6	(0.2)

to keep government out of enterprise: they make investment decisions based on politics rather than sound investment principals. GM has no role to fill in an above-average portfolio.

Honda and Toyota exhibit solid fundamentals. As discussed in the last chapter, Toyota is simply an automaker and doesn't provide enough diversification for a "market portfolio."

This brings me to another point about portfolio construction. Just as you have reasons for selecting a stock, you must have reasons for positioning them in your portfolio. Stocks should be placed strategically throughout the model to achieve your objectives. Recall that one of the 15-51 Indicator's goals is to create an above-average "market" portfolio, based on the way the market is constructed and the pattern of its activity (GDP). By its inclusion in the 15-51 Indicator, Honda will serve as the first "foreign" stock included in a major U.S. market index, and it makes total sense.

We live in a global marketplace, and Honda is a big part of the American market, measured in both products sold and number of employees. Many Honda products are made in America by

Americans. In this third-ranked industry, Honda tops the list in order to represent all "foreign" enterprises operating here in America, and also because Honda is one of my favorite companies.

After Honda, we need to decide if we're going to stick with Dow component Caterpillar. In fig. 5.16 its fundamentals are compared to John Deere's.

Fig. 5.16

Company	GM%	NI%	ROA	ROE	ROL (cost of debt)	Current Ratio	Leverage Factor	Inventory Supply	Months Sales Unpaid	Cash Conversion Ratio (CFO/EPS)
Caterpillar	19%	8%	6%	40%	-34%	2.5	84%	2.4	4.4	2.2
John Deere	31%	7%	5%	31%	-26%	2.6	83%	1.9	1.7	0.9

I like Deere's fundamentals better than Caterpillar's, but even so, the 15-51 Indicator is staying with Caterpillar. Why?

To stay true to its objectives.

The objective of the 15-51 Indicator is to indicate above-average market returns. Caterpillar is really the portfolio's last chance to add strongly to the business and government spending classes. John Deere has a huge consumer products division; in fact, I own a Deere lawn tractor that I love (corroborated by its strong fundamentals). But again, the Indicator's mission dictates the Caterpillar selection, as the portfolio doesn't need any more exposure to consumer spending patterns.

This same basis is used to maintain the third stock in this industry allocation. 3M is also a Dow component, and the only representative for the industrial/conglomerate industry. By remaining in the 15-51 Indicator, it provides further connection to "the market," and it also presents solid fundamentals. Here they are (fig. 5.17, below).

Fig. 5.17

Company	GM%	NI%	ROA	ROE	ROL (cost of debt)	Current Ratio	Leverage Factor	Inventory Supply	Months Sales Unpaid	Cash Conversion Ratio (CFO/EPS)
3M	48%	17%	17%	35%	-18%	4.6	52%	2.7	2.0	1.0

The purpose of this demonstration, building and ranking stocks for the 15-51 Indicator, is to show you how the process works so you can build a portfolio that will achieve your investment objectives. The way you build your portfolio dictates its patterns of movement.

For example, Industry 1 (Consumer Staples and Services) is heavily weighted to consumer spending, as you would expect. That's why the 15-51 Indicator maintained allocations for IBM, Boeing, and United Technologies in the second-ranked industry, which primarily supplies the business and government GDP spending classes. This hedges the portfolio's exposure to consumer spending, helping minimize the effects of changes in consumer spending patterns.

That's also why Honda's reliability leads the way in Industry 3. Honda sells to multiple GDP spending classes and it consistently produces quality products to multiple market segments. Toyota is too one dimensional for a portfolio constructed for such a purpose. The 15-51 Indicator needs Honda's diversification in order to stay true to its market mission, and my consumer experience.

This too explains why Honda is followed by Caterpillar, which specifically supplies to business and government GDP spending classes. Caterpillar is then followed by 3M, which taps into every GDP spending class (including a large consumer products division). This is diversification by GDP spending class, a tactic used to minimize exposure to any one particular class. All three companies have solid fundamentals, true to the Indicator's mission.

Fig. 5.18 shows how the 15-51 Indicator's third-ranked industry looks.

Industry Rank 3
Fig. 5.18

Industry	Basic/Industrial
Stock Rank	
1	Honda
2	Caterpillar
3	3M

Again, you don't have to maintain a connection to the DJIA by investing in some of its components. That's a tactic used by the 15-51 Indicator to achieve its objectives. When building your portfolio, stay true to who you are and your own objectives. That's most important.

Industry 4: Financial

Let's have some fun with this industry; you know, with the "financial crisis" and all. As we've learned, some industries and market segments have their own unique features and circumstances. And also as we've seen, some rely more heavily on debt than others. The same is true with banks.

Banks do not make products; they borrow money from the government (Federal Reserve) and relend it to consumers and businesses. They also borrow money from consumers (your deposits), pay you a fractional interest rate, and then lend those deposits to other customers at higher rates. As such, bank balance sheets will always appear extremely leveraged. It's the nature of their business.

Before we evaluate this industry, let's refresh our memory about the crash of 2008. News of the "subprime mortgage crisis" broke in February of 2007; despite this, "the market" went on to an all-time high in October 2007. Recall that the housing boom was in full force through most of 2005, until gas prices started to escalate later in that year. Also at this time, interest rates were rising rapidly. Fig. 5.19 shows that chart again.

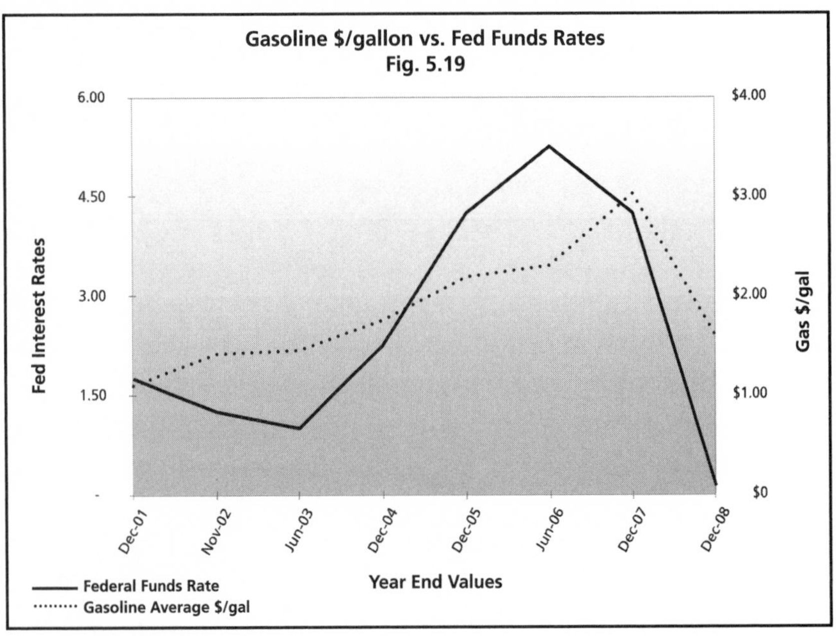

We know that markets do not crash on a whim. It didn't just happen in the fall of 2008. In fact, it had started in earnest in 2006, signaled by the Fed dramatically lowering interest rates. That's why stress should have been evident in bank fundamentals by then. We'll see about that in a moment. For now, we seek to answer these questions: Was weakness apparent in bank fundamentals before the market crashed? If so, when did that weakness first appear?

To determine this, we'll evaluate Dow components Citigroup and JPMorgan Chase against the 15-51 Indicator's selection, Wells Fargo. We'll take them one by one. Here in fig. 5.20 are a select few fundamentals for Citigroup, trended by year.

CITIGROUP
Fig. 5.20

Fiscal Year	2005	2006	2007
Net Income (B)*	$24.589	$21.538	$3.617
Cash From Operations (B)	$31.799	$0.013	-$71.430
Cash Conversion (CFO/E)	1.3	0.0	-19.7
Stock Price	$48.53	$54.55	$28.24

* (B) = Billions

In 2006 Citigroup earned $21 billion but generated just a few pennies in cash. How does that happen? Then, in 2007, earnings dropped to $3 billion (-83%) and operational cash flow was negative by $71 billion. That's a huge red flag.

As a side note, corporate income tax returns are due on March 15; and now with the power of the Internet, those numbers are available soon after. One month after this date, on April 14, 2008, the Dow Jones Industrial Average was at 12,849 and Citigroup's stock price was $25.11. This was a good five months before the Market crashed and long before the stock ended the year at $7.

This is where the Wall Street establishment falls down on the job. Impending doom was apparent in the fundamentals long before disaster struck. But where was your broker, sounding the alarm? And how did the pros do managing your mutual funds?

It's plain to see that it's time to Lose Your Broker.

Here's JPMorgan Chase in fig. 5.21.

JPMORGAN CHASE
Fig. 5.21

Fiscal Year	2005	2006	2007	2008
Net Income (B)*	$8.438	$14.444	$15.365	
Cash From Operations (B)	-$30.236	-$49.579	-$110.560	
Cash Conversion (CFO/E)	-3.6	-3.4	-7.2	
Stock Price	$39.69	$48.30	$40.93	$31.35

* (B) = Billions

I cannot begin to explain how a company can earn $15 billion in profit and lose $110 billion in cash in the same year, but JPMorgan Chase did it in 2007. In fact, JPMorgan Chase had been bleeding cash for years. That's a major red flag, yet its stock price held strong. I don't know why or how it did, nor do I care. Those fundamentals are enough to scare me away from investing in it.

Remember, cash is king. Earnings that do not consistently transform into cash are fake. Investing in companies that consistently burn cash is inherently more risky than investing in companies that create it, especially when news of a "financial crisis" breaks in February 2007. Fig. 5.22 shows Wells Fargo.

WELLS FARGO
Fig. 5.22

Fiscal Year	2005	2006	2007	2008
Net Income (B)*	$7.671	$8.482	$8.057	
Cash From Operations (B)	-$9.333	$32.094	$9.078	
Cash Conversion (CFO/E)	-1.2	3.8	1.1	
Stock Price	$31.42	$35.56	$30.19	$29.48

* (B) = Billions

In 2005 Wells Fargo saw that a financial crisis was coming (we can see this in its cash flow from operations). In 2006 it immediately took action to correct itself, long before the market crashed, probably by liquidating its holdings in asset-backed securities. That's good management. That's a good investment.

Since all banks trade the same product (money), investing in them is all about people. In this light, it's really no surprise that Wells Fargo was a buyer during the fallout of the market crash in 2008. The people who work there love it. Failure was not an option to them. It really is that simple.

Let's move on to the second component of our financial industry allocation. This comparison is between two credit card companies, Amex and Capital One. Fig. 5.23 shows their key fundamentals.

CAPITAL ONE

Fig. 5.23

Company	GM%	NI%	ROA	ROE	ROL (cost of debt)	Current Ratio	Leverage Factor	Inventory Supply	Months Sales Unpaid	Cash Conversion Ratio (CFO/EPS)
Capital One	85%	8%	1%	6%	-5%	1.8	84%	—	3.5	8.3
American Express	100%	13%	3%	36%	-34%	3.7	93%	—	16.0	2.1

This comparison highlights the fact that many companies operating in the same market segment account for things differently. It can be the only reason why Amex reports a 100% gross margin while Capital One produces 85%. They both do the same thing, which makes the difference hard to figure.

I'm a big fan of Amex—I like what they do and how they do it—but I have to say its unpaid sales ratio is high enough to turn me off. That's the reason its current ratio is so high. It's a sign of weakness. And as much as I like Amex, it can't be considered above average. (Remember, it returned a below-average 40% over the course of the 13YBM.)

Capital One is leveraged less, its debt costs less, and it converts its profit to cash at a much stronger pace than Amex. Its net income percentage is smaller but, then again, it's seeking growth more aggressively. It all makes sense. Capital One stays in the 15-51 Indicator.

That said, Wells Fargo gets the number one spot in Industry 4 because of its people; Capital One fills the only other slot. Fig. 5.24 shows us that portion of the 15-51i blueprint.

Industry Rank 4
Fig. 5.24

Industry	Financial
Stock Rank	
1	Wells Fargo
2	Capital One

Perhaps it is fair to question the diversity of this industry. After all, the financial industry is a large one; it includes insurance companies and the notorious business of investment (brokerage). So, yes, this industry might appear a little underdiversified. But my favorite insurance company (Liberty Mutual) isn't publicly traded, and I haven't found my favorite brokerage company yet. Besides, Wells Fargo is a vastly diversified financial institution and has almost every base covered.

You're going to get tired of hearing this, but it's true: investment is more of a discipline than anything else. You must set standards, principals, and core values—and stay true to them. This will provide you with the most confidence, the highest level of comfort, and the best possible investment returns.

Industry 5: Energy

The last industry in the 15-51 Indicator is energy; it receives just one stock selection. Fig. 5.25 shows a comparison between Dow component ExxonMobil and competitor British Petroleum. (These numbers are from 2007, long before the Gulf oil spill in 2010.)

Fig. 5.25

Company	GM%	NI%	ROA	ROE	ROL (cost of debt)	Current Ratio	Leverage Factor	Inventory Supply	Months Sales Unpaid	Cash Conversion Ratio (CFO/EPS)
Exxon Mobil	42%	10%	17%	33%	-17%	4.2	50%	0.6	1.1	1.3
BP	29%	7%	9%	23%	-14%	3.1	60%	1.7	1.6	1.2

In my area, I'm surrounded by Exxon and Mobil gas stations. Since they get most of my money, the best way not to get ticked off about the size of their profits is to own a piece of them. Besides, Exxon is not only a powerhouse energy supplier to the world, but also a very well managed company. Its fundamentals bear that out.

This concludes our fundamental review. Taking everything into account, here's how the finished blueprint for the 15-51 Indicator looks, ranked in priority order in fig. 5.26, on the next page.

Fig. 5.26

Industry Rank	1	2	3	4	5
Industry:	Consumer Staples/ Services	Technology	Basic/ Industrial	Financial	Energy
Stock Rank					
1	JnJ	Apple	Honda	Wells Fargo	Exxon Mobil
2	Lowe's	IBM	Caterpillar	Capital One	
3	P&G	Boeing	3M		
4	Target	UTC			
5	Church & Dwight				

It's not a perfect portfolio by any stretch of the imagination, but it's a good one. Let's see (fig. 5.27) what kind of trend line this portfolio produced over the course of the thirteen-year benchmark period. Hold on to your socks.

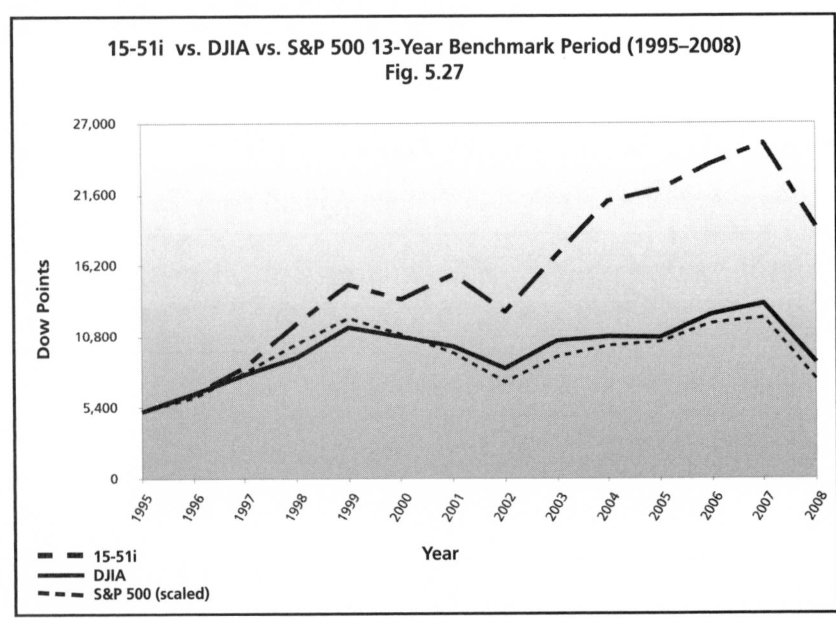

The 15-51i returned a stunning 273% over the course of the 13YBM—after the market crashed. Remember that the DJIA returned 72%, and the lowly S&P 500 gained just 47%. To put it another way, the 15-51 Indicator outperformed the Dow by 379% and the S&P by 581%.

I'd say that's above average.

Let's take a look at the performance comparison in the ten-year benchmarks. Fig. 5.28 shows the 10YBM-05 (1995–2005) and fig. 5.29, on the next page, the 10YBM-08 (1998–2008).

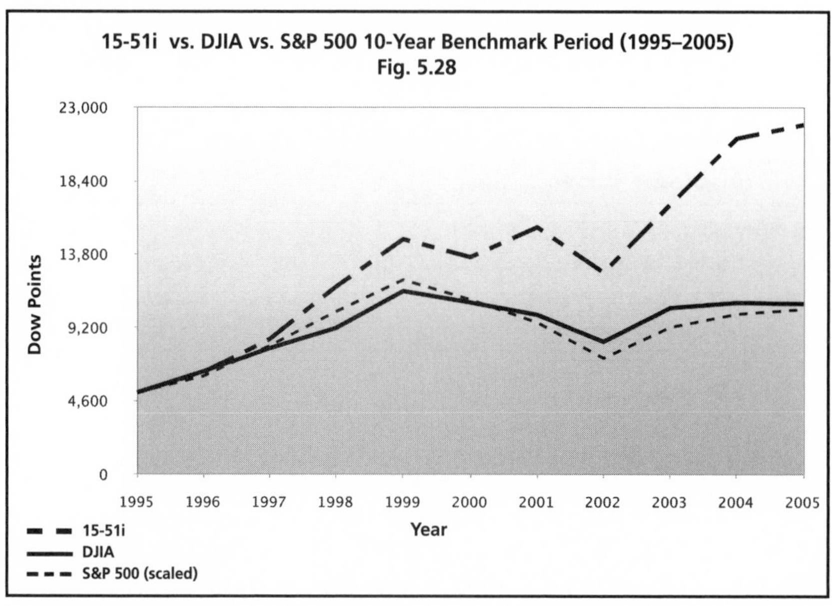

How does that compare to your mutual funds, including those high-risk emerging market follies? Let this serve as proof positive that you don't have to take unnecessary risks to achieve exceptional returns. The table in fig. 5.30, on the next page, compares the 15-51 Indicator, DJIA, and S&P 500.

The 15-51 Indicator is the only portfolio that did not lose ground during the 1998–2008 ten-year period. That's how strength acts in a hostile market. And that's what superior 15-51i construction can do for your portfolio performance!

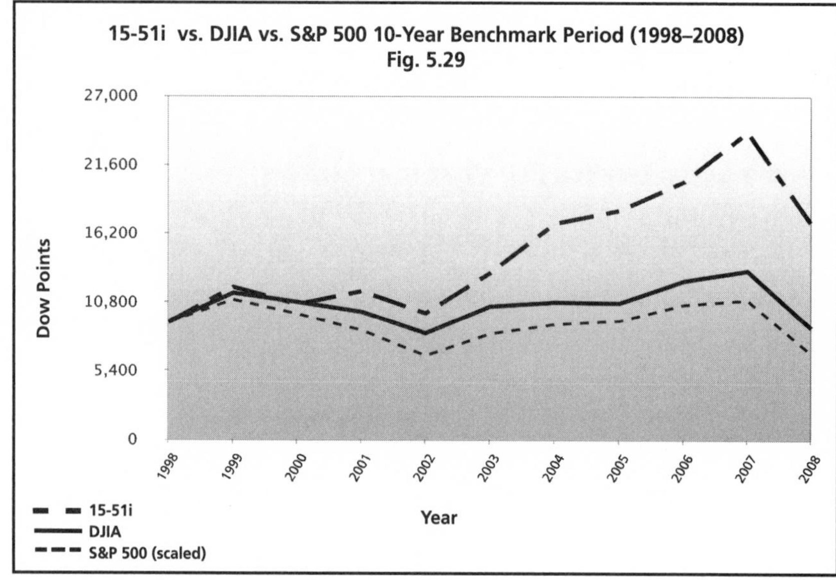

ROI
Fig. 5.30

	13YBM	10YBM-05	10YBM-08
15-51i	273%	329%	85%
DJIA	72%	109%	-4%
S&P 500	47%	103%	-27%

Perhaps the best test of a portfolio is how it behaves under the extreme pressure of a hostile market. Fig. 5.31, on the next page, shows a chart of all three market indicators from "the market" top in October 2007 through the year-end crash of 2008.

Once again, market forces are more powerful than any single investment or collection of investments. So when the market crashes, all stocks, serving all industries, go down. The S&P 500's movements highlight this point, proving that mass diversification cannot limit volatility but actually increases it.

The 15-51i suffers less downside impact, recovers faster, and retains more profit than any other market indicator. This kind of

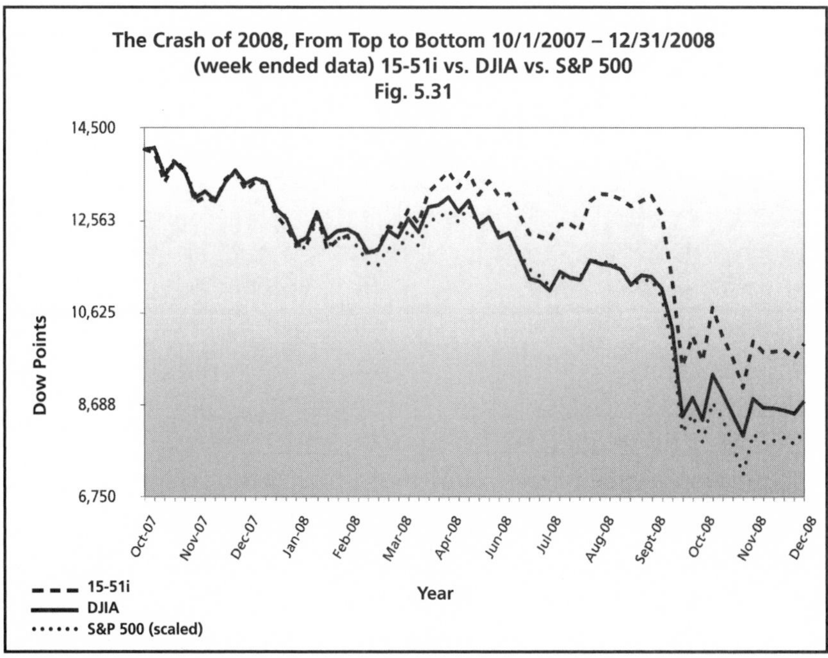

above-average performance makes you extremely comfortable when you invest; and it provides the confidence and steady hand needed in a hostile market. It's so much easier to Buy Low when you're investing in above-average strength at discount prices.

That's the Lose Your Broker difference.

Trust me on this one: the only way to be comfortable with investing is to be comfortable with your investments, with how they're assembled, and with the markets in which you are investing. Period. And though it is true that superior construction and superior components go a long way toward achieving that end, they are not the only tactics you can employ to achieve your desired level of comfort and success.

Expanding your portfolio to other asset classes to mitigate stock market risk, and implementing an effective Buy Low, Sell High strategy to lock in profits can take your performance to a higher level. These are the topics of the next two chapters.

See you there.

CHAPTER 6

Expanding Your Portfolio to Other Asset Classes: Why, and Which Ones?

There are several other investment markets besides the Stock Market (equities); most common are the Bond Market (debt) the Commodity Market (for natural resource products like, gold, oil, and corn), the Money Market (currencies,) and the Foreign Investment Market. In portfolio lingo, these are called asset classes.

Your portfolio does not need allocations in every asset class to be considered "well diversified" or "balanced." A well-diversified portfolio has the proper blend of growth, income, and safety that will make you comfortable and achieve your financial objectives. There is no one right way to do it.

However, portfolios must be comprised of at least two asset classes to be considered efficient. Portfolios with allocations to three asset classes hedge risk more effectively. And then, yes, there are times when access to a fourth asset class might be beneficial. The appropriate number of asset classes for you, and how much of each you need, depends entirely on how aggressively you want to pursue growth and where you want that growth to come from.

For instance, most investors pursue growth in the stock market because it outperforms all other asset classes over the long term. Of all the mutual funds owned, more than 70% are equity funds. Stocks therefore serve as the average investor's core asset class. It is where they place the largest amount of their investment dollars, and where they seek growth.

To remain consistent with reality, stocks will serve as the core asset class in the portfolios we create in this chapter. But it will not be the only asset class. Portfolios consisting entirely of stocks are at the mercy of the stock market for their movement. This is not a very comforting position. To alleviate this burden, we will expand the portfolio to other asset classes.

The reasons for expanding a portfolio beyond stocks are:

1. To mitigate your risk to the stock market
2. To make money when the stock market goes down
3. To implement an effective "buy low, sell high" strategy

A cash allocation is required for efficient investing. Think about it. If the goal of investing is to buy low and sell high—that is, to make money—then common sense tells us that it's difficult to buy low in an up market and just as difficult to sell high in a down market. There's simply not enough opportunity to do both consistently. The only way to be efficient and most successful is to buy stocks in down markets and sell them in up markets, where there is more opportunity to do both consistently.

In order to buy low, the efficient investor must have the capital on hand to buy stocks when the market sells off. Without cash on hand, the unfortunate investor must sell low in order to buy something else low. And that's not cliché. Investors who maximize their investment potential utilize cash reserves to purchase above-average stocks when they go on sale and trade at discounted prices. That's where the real money is to be made.

Besides, cash is king. Nothing can be done without it. And no one has ever gone broke with cash in hand. That in itself is a comforting position, as nothing will calm your nerves more than knowing you haven't gone "all-in" on a sloppy market. Your cash allocation therefore serves a dual purpose. It makes for efficient investing and serves as a hedge to your stock market exposure; as when the stock market slips off the edge, your cash value remains intact.

That is why efficient portfolios must consist of at least two asset classes: a growth element (i.e. stocks) and cash. I know Wall Street brokers hate it when you have money sitting around on the sidelines "not working" and/or "not earning." It's as though your idle cash burns a whole in their pockets. Of course, they make the most money by selling you the most stocks you can afford; the more the merrier. They tell you that you can't achieve your financial objectives unless every dollar is working. That's hogwash. Cash isn't a money maker; it's a mechanism to make money: to Buy Low.

The only risk with cash is inflation: the cost of money. Although that risk can be mitigated by interest income earned in money market accounts, many times that interest does not offset the cost of inflation. If desired, higher-yielding FDIC-insured bank certificate of deposits (CDs) can always be purchased to capture higher interest rates, which will minimize your exposure to inflation. But cash is not where you're looking for growth. It's a stock market hedge and a mechanism for making money.

Okay, so we know that two assets classes (stocks and cash) are required for your portfolio to be most efficient. If you're going to extend your portfolio beyond these two asset classes, then the basic dynamics of the additional asset class should run contrary to your largest investment allocation (usually stocks). In other words, the basic trend of the third asset class should move in a direction opposite to the stock market; this to make money when the stock market declines.

Stocks and bonds have such an inverse relationship, meaning they generally move in opposite directions under the same market conditions. Fig. 6.1 provides a basic illustration.

When Stocks Go Up
Fig. 6.1

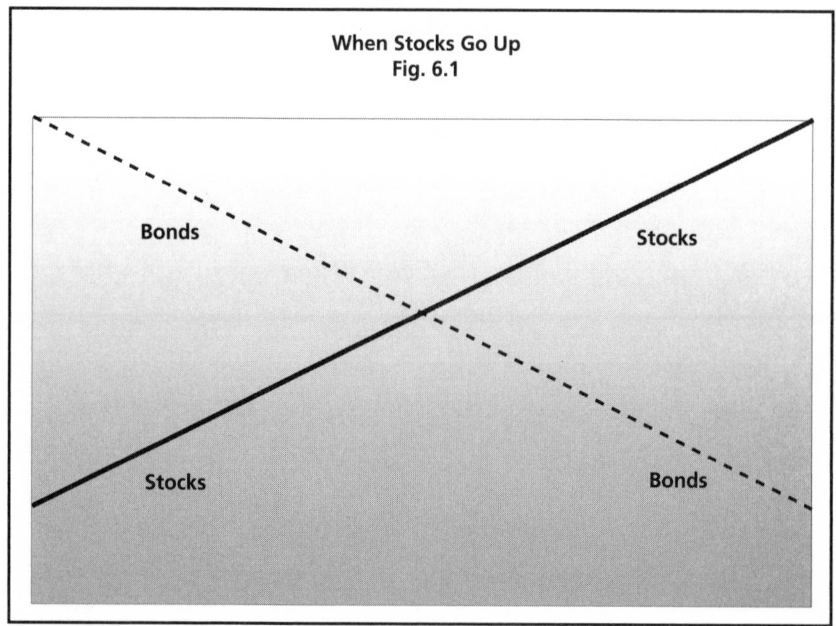

Why is this?

The theory of supply and demand tells us that an appreciating stock market will generate more interest (a.k.a. demand) from investors who are earning lower rates of return in the bond market. Since most investors seek to maximize investment returns, bondholders will sell some portion of their low-earning bonds in favor of higher-returning equities. This increased demand for stocks shortens their supply, forcing their prices to move higher. At this same time, the selling of these bonds increases the supply of bonds, which in turn causes their prices to fall.

Bond values are also driven by interest rates. Let's take a $1,000 bond with a 5% fixed interest rate as an example. If market interest rates rise to 8%, the value of the 5% bond will fall. It's less valuable because borrowers are now offering more interest (8%) for the same $1,000. Put another way, bond values have an inverse relationship with interest rates because as interest rates rise, bond values fall, and vice versa. This can be seen in fig. 6.2, on the next page.

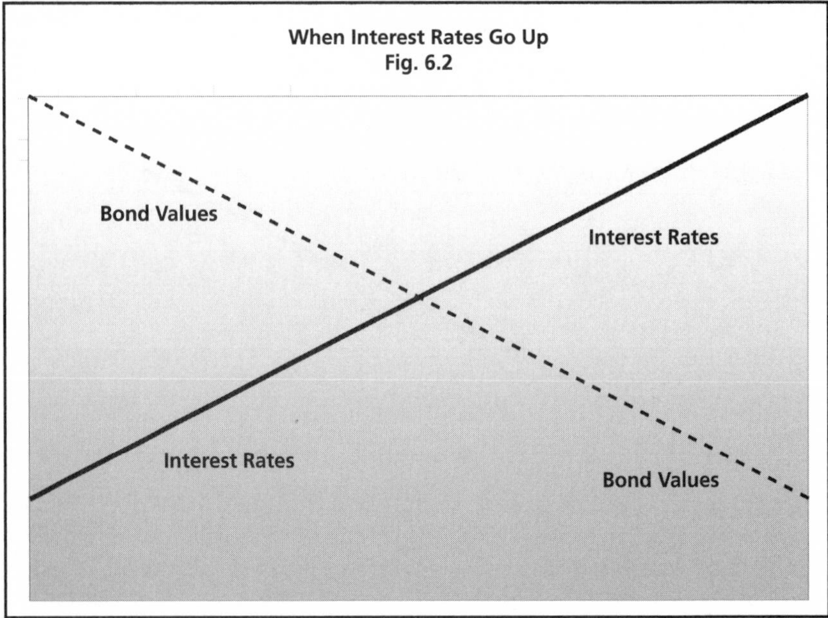

To determine the direction of interest rates, and thus bond values, take your cues from the controlling force of the marketplace. Recall that government establishes key rates of interest through the Federal Reserve and that it raises these rates during times of economic expansion to slow growth and lessen inflationary potential.

Strategically speaking then, the time to buy bonds is when interest rates are up (times of economic expansion), and the time to sell stocks is when stock prices are high (also during economic expansion). This makes the stock and bond relationship a match made in heaven, as the time to sell one generally correlates with the time to buy the other.

Portfolios consisting of these three asset classes—stocks, bonds, and cash—can achieve almost any reasonable portfolio objective. Configured in this manner, the portfolio seeks growth in the stock market and uses an opposite-performing bond allocation to hedge that risk; and it uses a cash allocation to hedge both, provide stability, and promote efficient investing.

If a portfolio is to be extended beyond these three asset classes, then the basic market dynamic of the fourth asset class should run contrary to at least two of the other three assets classes; this in an effort to hedge risk to those markets and to make money when all else fails.

Gold, for instance, normally runs contrary to money (i.e., the U.S. dollar). So when currency depreciates, gold often rises. Gold is considered a "safe haven" because it has always been worth something. For this reason, gold has had persistent value in trade; it has been accepted as payment in even the most disastrous market conditions. Gold is a safety net for money; it's a money hedge. And since debt is only borrowed money, gold is a way to hedge risk to both of those markets (currency and debt).

The only other dedicated asset class we haven't discussed is foreign market investments. I skip over this item because a well-diversified stock portfolio already produces exposure to foreign markets. Consequently, there is no reason for the average investor to dedicate a larger allocation with direct broad-scale investment—a.k.a. international or emerging market mutual fund allocations. Besides, with above-average construction there is no reason to blindly chase the pipe dream of higher returns in these higher-risk asset classes.

These are the asset classes and the purposes they serve in a portfolio. The next step in the process is to determine how much of each class is appropriate. To arrive at these amounts, you need to define your investment posture.

Investment posture is determined by the manner in which you pursue growth. A balanced portfolio by definition pursues growth in a neutral way, without bias to any particular asset class. To put it another way, a balanced portfolio places the same amount of investment dollars in each asset class in the portfolio.

Of course, only you can determine the appropriate level of growth, safety, and income, that's right for you. The purpose of this demonstration is to help you discover what your investment posture is. We'll do so by creating three different portfolios comprised of the same investments, but with three different growth postures—balanced, moderate, and aggressive—so you can see how diversification impacts the performance trend line of your portfolio. Only the allocations between asset classes will change by portfolio; the individual investments will remain the same.

As with every other portfolio in this book, our goal remains the same: to outperform "the market" as defined by the DJIA, over a long period of time. Until now, we have done so with portfolios comprised entirely of stocks. In this chapter, we will achieve the objective with multiple asset-class portfolios and thus defeat the age-old myth that one must take on more risk to reap greater reward.

Our three new portfolios will consist of only three asset classes: stocks, bonds, and cash. This will demonstrate that there is no need to have access to every possible asset class in order to achieve exceptional performance results. Once again, the number of asset classes and their according allocations should be dictated by your overall investment objectives. (It's the only way you can reach them.)

In all three portfolios, the 15-51 Indicator will serve as the stock allocation, which admittedly is not a perfect stock portfolio, nor the best portfolio, but an above-average portfolio. (Why invest in any other kind?) The 15-51i's purpose will be to serve the portfolios' growth objective and will be considered the "aggressive" part of the portfolios.

To balance that risk, the bond allocation will be a conservative one. The U.S. government has never defaulted on an obligation and for that reason is universally considered to be safest investment vehicle. As such, its interest rates are deemed to be "risk-free" rates. And because of this stature, U.S. government debt also offers the lowest interest rates available on the bond market. That is to say:

Safe = Low Interest Rates

And that's okay. We're not looking for growth in the bond market; that's what our stock market allocation is for. The purpose of the bond allocation is to hedge that risk with safety and to do so in an asset class with contrary market dynamics. The 5 Year U.S. Treasury Note (T-note) will be used to fit that bill.

Our cash allocation will increase only by the interest earned on bonds. Inflation, dividends, and interest earned on the cash balance are omitted from calculation, and are therefore assumed to add to zero. In addition, bond movements will be based on the changes in interest rates, not actual free market trading.

Are these few tactics 100% accurate? No, I guess not. But this reminds me of a lesson I learned a long time ago. When I was in business school, many adjunct professors were executives from local industry who taught nights, not for the money but to "give back" to the educational system from which their success derived. Many of them related real experiences that made textbook theories come to life. Others showed videos of leading corporate executives discussing techniques they used to achieve large-scale success. At the time, Jack Welch was transforming General Electric into a powerhouse industrial conglomerate. He was the toast of the town, especially in his own backyard, which is where I found myself. I finished my graduate studies at Sacred Heart University in Fairfield, Connecticut, right around the corner from GE's corporate headquarters.

I remember one particular video in which Jack Welch discussed tactics he used to improve GE's efficiency. He said there were a lot of employees, spending a lot of time, doing a lot of things that didn't add much value. To correct this behavior, he challenged his management team to identify a certain number of these tasks and tag them "IPPANOVAs" (intellectually precise, a pain in the ass to do, and add no value) and then to eliminate them.

The aforementioned items (inflation, dividends, interest earned, etc.) are exactly that: IPPANOVAs. The objectives of this chapter are to provide a conceptual understanding of how expanding a portfolio to multiple classes works and how to effectively build one. That knowledge can be had without the minutia of fractional adjustments.

To prove our results, performance will be tested over the course of the thirteen-year benchmark period (1995–2008) and compared to "the market" (DJIA). In this chapter, each portfolio will start with a nice round $100,000 investment and will be calculated on a strict buy-and-hold methodology; this even knowing that by owning five-year T-notes some action would be required after years five and ten. This limitation will be rectified in the next chapter when the topic of portfolio rebalancing is covered. That said, the portfolios we will test seek growth in three different ways: balanced, moderate, and aggressive, as defined in fig. 6.3.

Three Asset-Class Portfolio Allocation Scenarios
Fig. 6.3

	Balanced	Moderate	Aggressive
Stocks (15-51i)	33%	55%	70%
Bonds (5-Yr. T-note)	33%	25%	20%
Cash	33%	20%	10%
Total	100%	100%	100%

Fig. 6.4, on the next page, shows a chart comparing the returns of these portfolios to the Dow.

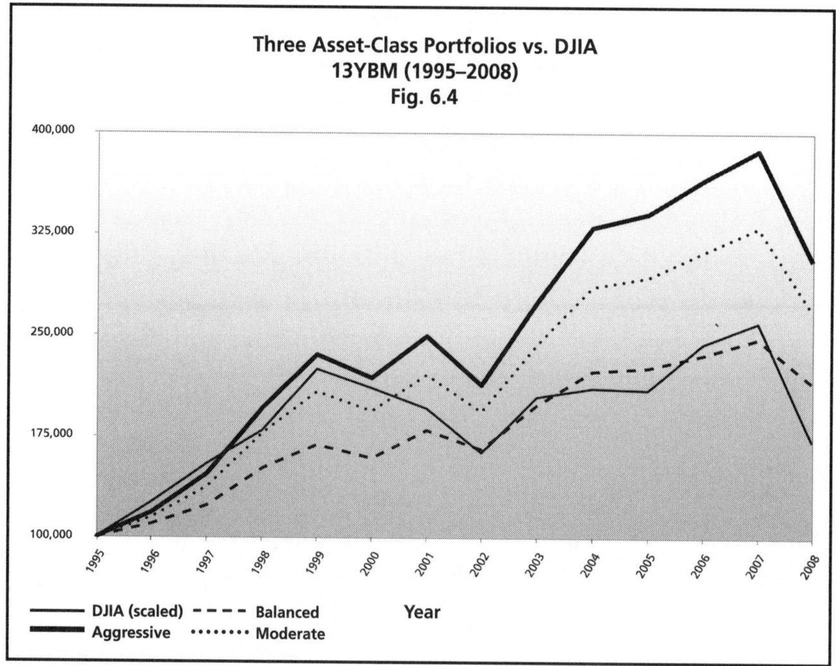

Fig. 6.5 shows the table of returns.

Fig. 6.5

Portfolio	ROI
DJIA	72%
Balanced	115%
Moderate	168%
Aggressive	205%

As one would logically expect, the portfolio that sought growth most aggressively outperformed all other portfolios, and it was also more volatile. Aggressive growth always is. The least aggressive portfolio (Balanced) produced the least volatile trend line, and the least return. Of course.

Remember, all three of these portfolios had cash balances and conservative bond allocations, yet they still beat "the market" over the long term. The Balanced portfolio did so with two-thirds, or 66%, of its assets in cash and U.S. government bonds. It beat the Dow by 43% points, or 60% (43% divided by 72%), with one-third of the capital at risk!

That's less risk and more reward, during an extremely volatile period that ended with the collapse of the financial markets.

How does that compare to your mutual funds?

You see, when you're built for above-average returns, it's easy to achieve them. Superior 15-51 construction allows you to make more money with less risk, even with a set-it-and-forget-it mentality. In these portfolios, no effort was taken to lock in gains or Buy Low and Sell High, for stocks or bonds. Because the 15-51 Indicator returned 273% over the 13YBM, it provides great flexibility when constructing a multiple asset class portfolio. That's why you don't need high-risk emerging market allocations. They're simply not required to succeed.

Fig. 6.6 shows a different-looking chart that compares the performance trends of each asset class.

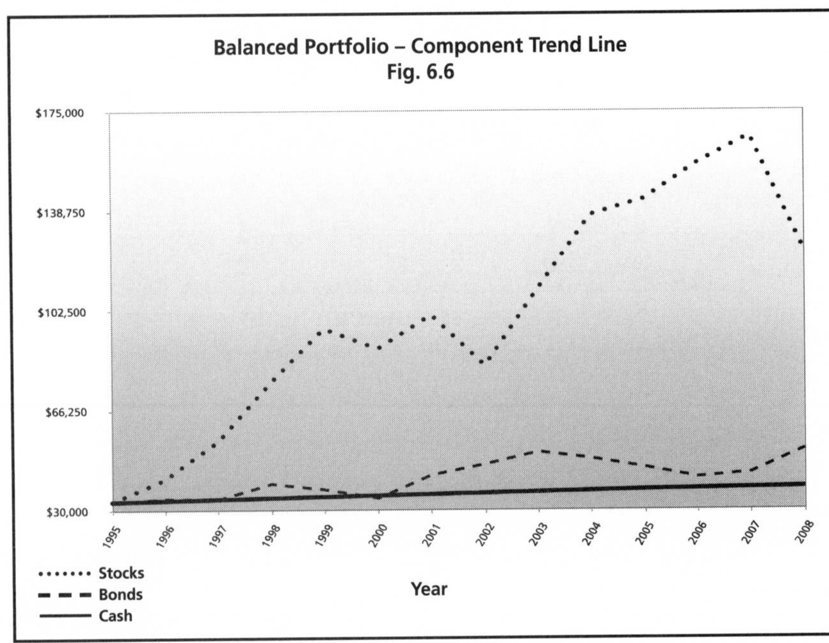

Balanced Portfolio – Component Trend Line
Fig. 6.6

Admittedly, this picture looks a little goofy. The explosive trend line of the 15-51 Indicator is what makes it look so odd. Government bonds can never duplicate that kind of return; in comparison they look like they added very little impact to the portfolio's performance. But that's not the point.

The important concept to grab on to here is the relationship between stocks and bonds, and to see how their values moved in opposite directions. Remember, the bond allocation was a conservative one and thus produced a less volatile trend. Higher-risk bonds with higher interest rates would have produced a much more erratic trend, and perhaps more return. But that wasn't the purpose of our bond allocation.

The purpose of our bond allocation was not growth (a.k.a. high returns); it was to serve as a stock market hedge, to make money when the stock market went down, and to do so with the least amount of risk. This kind of safe hedge to the stock market is nice to have when "the market" melts down.

The cash balance, which is essentially a nonearning asset (as depicted by its relatively flat line in the chart), was there and ready to be employed. Remember, cash is not a money maker, but a mechanism to make money efficiently. You can't buy low without it.

Fig. 6.7 shows a table of returns by asset class for the Balanced portfolio.

Balanced Portfolio
Fig. 6.7

Asset Class	Start (1995)	2008	Gain	ROI
Stocks (15-51i)	$33,333	$124,360	$91,026	273%
Bonds (5-Yr. T-note)	$33,333	$52,038	$18,704	56%
Cash	$33,333	$38,323	$4,990	15%
Total	**$100,000**	**$214,721**	**$114,721**	**115%**

So the market crashed at the end of 2008, and then you look up. There's your portfolio by asset class. Your stocks are up 273%; you have $52,000 in government bonds, and that value is rising; you have $38,000 in cash. That's 90% of your initial investment in cash and government bonds. And you're portfolio is up a total of 115%. Let me ask, Are you uncomfortable with your position?

Or would you rather your nest eggs crash through that basket of mutual funds your broker sold you?

It's time to Lose Your Broker. You, my friend, can do much better.

As I've mentioned, there is no one right or wrong way to invest or allocate your investments by asset class. For some, 80% in stocks might be prudent; for others, 20% might be enough. Select the right blend for you and your objectives. Don't be swayed by talking heads or TV pundits. You know best.

As with every investment decision you make, the first thing to do when establishing your asset allocations is to assess the condition of *the Market* (economy). You want to allocate your portfolio in a manner that will bode well for that condition. If the condition is neutral among asset classes, it's perfectly appropriate to be neutral along with it.

For example, as I sit writing this piece, tax cuts are set to expire. Taxes raise operating costs for business and reduce return on investment. That's bad for business and for investment. On top of this, unemployment remains stubbornly close to 10%. That's bad for consumers. This spells bad news for markets.

Yet national figures place inflation right around 1%, with the Fed funds rate continuing to languish below 1%. The cost of money can only rise from here. And as we know, bonds are simply borrowed money. So when the cost of money rises, so will the cost of debt.

Under these conditions, neither currency nor bonds have much upside. Especially when considering current government action. Massive new legislation and entitlement programs are poised to choke an already struggling and fragile economy. Add to this the fact that the nation's bank, the manufacturer of the U.S. dollar, is printing a ton (billions) of new paper to keep pace with reckless government spending and "deflationary concerns." None of this is good for the dollar, money, or debt.

Consequently, there should be no mystique surrounding the steady rise in gold, now trading at record highs above the $1,300 an ounce mark. The reason for the increased demand for gold is that the money and debt markets are in a state of flux, and the entire world is jittery. Investors are moving to gold to hedge their risks in the bond and currency markets. Considering all of that, the rise in gold is no surprise.

Despite these poor market fundamentals, the DJIA is trading near 10,800 as of October 3, 2010. Once again, the stock market is speculating that things aren't as bad as they are, or that the 2010 elections will greatly impact the market condition. That's pure speculation. Conditions in *the Market* (economy) do not warrant the movement.

So what to do in such sloppy investment environment?

In a market like this, with interest rates and inflation poised to rise, your bond allocations should be short term in duration. During these times, inflation-protected T-bills, called Tips, are a great way to safely generate income. When interest rates move higher, you can extend your durations. Until then, stay short-term and approach growth with a "balanced," or neutral, bias as outlined in fig. 6.8.

Neutral Growth Bias, Four Asset-Class Portfolio
Fig. 6.8

Asset Class	Allocation
Cash	25%
Stocks (15-51)	25%
Bonds (Short-Term Tips)	25%
Gold	25%
Total	100%

When market conditions change, your allocations can and should change along with them. There's no need to overcomplicate matters when building your portfolio. Increase your stock market allocation when GDP is growing steadily and market fundamentals are positive (i.e., unemployment is low) because there are more growth opportunities there, and they're easier to identify, assess, and monitor.

If you're looking for safety, stick to the bond market because it holds the safest investment vehicles (i.e., U.S. bonds). Consider an allocation to a market like gold if the money and credit markets are in a quagmire (as they currently are). And, remember, you can't buy anything without cash. It's a required element for efficient investing.

A multiple asset-class portfolio is the only way to go. Besides hedging risk, increasing efficiency, and providing safety from total loss, a multiple asset-class portfolio can actually make your investment decisions easier. It's an incredibly useful tool for indicating the appropriate times to act.

Answering the previously undeterminable questions of when, why, and how to buy, sell, or hold, is next.

CHAPTER 7

Modifications: Buy, Sell, or Hold—What, When, Why, and How?

Times change. Markets change. And you change. The same should be true for your investment portfolio. Investment is an active sport. Adjustments must be made.

As mentioned, investment is more of a discipline than anything else. The 15-51 construction method is a discipline and so is a multiple asset-class layout. For this reason, they are extremely useful tools for effective portfolio management. Strategies and tactics used to make modifications to your portfolio are the focus of this chapter.

Portfolios are managed on two fronts: from the macro perspective (by asset class) and from the micro perspective (within asset class). We'll examine both views in this chapter. But you should know up front that regardless of perspective the objective is always the same: to buy low and sell high in the most efficient manner possible. Although this is not hard to understand, it is a long conversation. But it also follows basic logic. The first rule of effective portfolio management is to take your cues from what's happening in the marketplace (consumer, business, investment, and GDP), not the stock market as indicated by the Dow Jones Industrial Average. The stock market is full of speculation and often acts with the impulsiveness of an addicted consumer with a billion-dollar bad habit. That's Wall Street. And contrary to its brokers' sales pitches, many of them do in fact try to "time" the market—to sell at the highest and buy at the lowest. That's why Wall Street tends to overreact to everything, good news or bad, in up markets or in down. They're trigger happy.

But you shouldn't be.

Remember, the Dow hit its all-time high one year prior to the collapse of the money and credit markets. Banks were failing in droves in 2007, and that trend continued all the way through 2008. To ignore these market cues is to get caught up in stock market hype and partake in mass market speculation. There's simply no reason to buy into the fluff.

The easiest way to select the right time to act is to consistently monitor your asset allocations and the performance of your investments within those asset classes. Your portfolio allocations are there for a reason; they are your target benchmarks, established to make your portfolio easy to live with. So when actual performance strays beyond these targets and into uncomfortable territory, it's time to act and rebalance your portfolio.

Here's an example. In the previous chapter, the Moderate portfolio was invested in the following manner, and when left alone for the duration of the thirteen-year benchmark period, its performance by asset class produced the following table of returns, as seen in fig. 7.1, on the next page.

Though the moderate portfolio returned 168% versus the DJIA's 72% over the course of the 13YBM, its allocations fell way out of whack by the end of the period. At year ended 2008, stocks represented 77% of the total portfolio (the target was 55%); due to the 15-51 Indicator's above-average performance, the portfolio became underweighted in bonds and cash by double-digit percentages. This is a call for action.

That action is called rebalancing: the process of selling higher-performing investments at high valuations and redirecting those profits to purchase investments trading at lower prices, while shoring up your cash allocation. Capturing profits is

Moderate Portfolio (Three Asset-Class) – Macro Analysis
Fig. 7.1

		Target/Start		13YBM/Finish Year Ended 2008				
Asset Class	Investment	%	$	%	$	Gain	ROI	Allocation +/- Target
Stocks	15-51 Indicator	55%	$55,000	77%	$205,193	$150,193	273%	22%
Bonds	5-Year T-note	25%	$25,000	15%	$39,028	$14,028	56%	-10%
Cash	Money Market	20%	$20,000	9%	$23,743	$3,743	19%	-11%
Total		100%	$100,000	100%	$267,964	$167,964	168%	0%

efficient and effective portfolio management. It's another mechanism to comfortable investing.

We now know what was going on in the market at the end of 2008. The Fed drastically reduced interest rates to encourage borrowing and spending, and to provide banks with a cheap product (money) to profit from. As such, it wasn't the opportune time to purchase bonds, because interest rates were low.

So when was the appropriate time to rebalance this portfolio?

Let us first remember one element of basic market dynamics: the time to buy bonds is when interest rates are up (during market expansion). Fig. 7.2, on the next page, shows the interest rate trend of the five-year T-note over the course of the 13YBM.

Fig. 7.2

	1995	1996	1997	1998	1999	2000	2001	2002	2003	2004	2005	2006	2007	2008
U.S. T-note, 5-Year.	6.4%	6.2%	6.2%	5.2%	5.6%	6.2%	4.6%	3.8%	3.0%	3.4%	4.1%	4.8%	4.4%	2.8%

Fig. 7.3

Asset Class	1995	1996	1997	1998	1999	2000	2001	2002	2003	2004	2005	2006	2007	2008	ROI
Stocks	$55,000	$68,668	$91,088	$126,498	$158,494	$146,421	$166,577	$136,220	$182,106	$226,550	$235,816	$257,040	$273,577	$205,193	273%
Bonds	$25,000	$25,784	$25,627	$29,820	$28,252	$25,862	$32,132	$35,031	$38,362	$36,560	$34,130	$31,387	$32,641	$39,028	56%
Cash	$20,000	$20,319	$20,638	$20,957	$21,276	$21,595	$21,903	$22,211	$22,519	$22,827	$23,135	$23,338	$23,540	$23,743	19%
Total	$100,000	$114,771	$137,353	$177,275	$208,022	$193,878	$220,612	$193,462	$242,987	$285,936	$293,081	$311,765	$329,758	$267,964	168%
Mod. Cum. ROI	start	15%	37%	77%	108%	94%	121%	93%	143%	186%	193%	212%	230%	168%	
DJIA Cum. ROI	start	26%	55%	79%	125%	111%	96%	63%	104%	111%	109%	144%	159%	72%	
Stocks	55%	60%	66%	71%	76%	76%	76%	70%	75%	79%	80%	82%	83%	77%	
Bonds	25%	22%	19%	17%	14%	13%	15%	18%	16%	13%	12%	10%	10%	15%	
Cash	20%	18%	15%	12%	10%	11%	10%	11%	9%	8%	8%	7%	7%	9%	
Total	100%	100%	100%	100%	100%	100%	100%	100%	100%	100%	100%	100%	100%	100%	

Fig. 7.3, on the previous page, shows the yearly performance trend of the Moderate portfolio's asset classes during the same time period. It wasn't rebalanced.

As you can see in the asset allocation percentages shown, there were plenty of opportunities to rebalance this portfolio and sell stocks high and buy bonds with high interest rates. Consequently, we can run wild with hypothetical scenarios. But let's not go crazy with "what if" scenarios. Instead, we'll simply use the expiration dates of the five-year T-notes as the trigger points to rebalance. In other words, the portfolio will be rebalanced twice during the 13YBM, at the end of years 2000 and 2005. (Remember, the tech boom was already busting at the end of 2000, and 2005 was two years before the Dow hit its all-time high. Needless to say, these rebalancing points do not occur at the "perfect" time.)

Once again, the Moderate portfolio began this way at the end of 1995 (fig. 7.4).

Moderate Portfolio
Fig. 7.4

Asset Class	%	$
Stocks	55%	$55,000
Bonds	25%	$25,000
Cash	20%	$20,000
Total	100%	$100,000

The first lot of five-year T-notes expired at the end of 2000. Fig. 7.5, on the next page, shows how the portfolio looked at that time.

First Rebalance Point
Fig. 7.5

Actual						
Asset Class	**FY2000**	**%**	**Target**	**Rebalanced to Target Allocations**	**Adjustment Required**	**Action**
Stocks	$146,421	76%	55%	$106,159	-$40,262	Sell
Bonds	$25,000	13%	25%	$48,254	$23,254	Buy
Cash	$21,595	11%	20%	$38,603	$17,008	Add to Position
Total	$193,016	100%	100%	$193,016	$0	

To rebalance this portfolio at year-end 2000, stocks had to be sold (the DJIA was at 10,788), bonds were bought (at 6.2% interest), and a smooth seventeen grand was reserved to shore up the cash allocation.

Then the next five years went by—September 11, recession, war, recovery, another war. News of the financial crisis hadn't yet hit the street (though, as we know, it reared its ugly head in the fundamentals). The Dow would hit its all-time high almost two years after the second lot of bonds expired in 2005 (when the DJIA was at 10,718). Fig. 7.6, on the next page, shows what the Moderate portfolio looked liked then.

Second Rebalance Point
Fig. 7.6

Actual						
Asset Class	FY2005	%	Target	Rebalanced to Target Allocations	Adjustment Required	Action
Stocks	$200,937	69%	55%	$159,922	-$41,015	Sell
Bonds	$48,254	17%	25%	$72,692	$24,438	Buy
Cash	$41,576	14%	20%	$58,153	$16,578	Add to Position
Total	$290,767	100%	100%	$290,767	$0	

Once again, robust stock market returns threw the asset allocations out of whack by the end of 2005. Stocks had to be sold and another lot of five-year T-notes was purchased, but this time a $73,000 bond purchase was required to bring the portfolio back to its 25% target. This lot of bonds carried a 4.1% interest rate, far below the rates of the prior two lots. Another $16,000 of profit was locked in and added to the cash balance.

Overall, 2006 and 2007 were good years for the stock market, though after hitting its all-time high in October, the Dow began to show weakness late in the fourth quarter of 2007. And then, after a long rocky road in 2008, the market crashed in the fall of that year. The Moderate portfolio, rebalanced twice, ended the year of collapse like this (fig. 7.7 on the next page).

MODERATE PORTFOLIO (rebalanced 2x)
Fig. 7.7

Target %	Start (1995)	Asset Class	Finish (2008)	Actual %	Gain	ROI
55%	$55,000	Stocks	$150,342	49%	$95,342	173%
25%	$25,000	Bonds	$95,127	31%	$70,127	281%
20%	$20,000	Cash	$59,920	20%	$39,920	200%
100%	$100,000	**Total**	$305,389	100%	$205,389	205%

Remember that we reallocated dollars from stocks to bonds and cash twice, making the ROIs look a little kooky. But forget about that. The market crashed at the end of 2008—and then you look up. In a declining stock market, that $55,000 in stocks you began with is now worth $150,000. You have $95,000 in U.S. government bonds and that value is rising (the five-year T-note interest rate was 2.8% in 2008), *and*, because you have sold high and locked in profits, you have $60,000 in cash—that's 60% of your initial investment—ready to invest and buy low.

In all, the Moderate portfolio returned an amazing 205%, more than doubling the DJIA with just a fraction of the risk. That's efficient and effective portfolio management, even with arbitrary rebalancing points. Fig. 7.8, on the next page, shows a chart comparing the Moderate portfolio that was rebalanced against the one that wasn't. Both are compared to the "the market," as defined by the DJIA.

Both Moderate portfolios ran the same trend line in the first five years of the 13YBM, but you can see the effects rebalancing had on the portfolio after that point, especially at the end of 2008. With less capital at risk in the stock market, and more capital in cash and secure government bonds, this portfolio stood

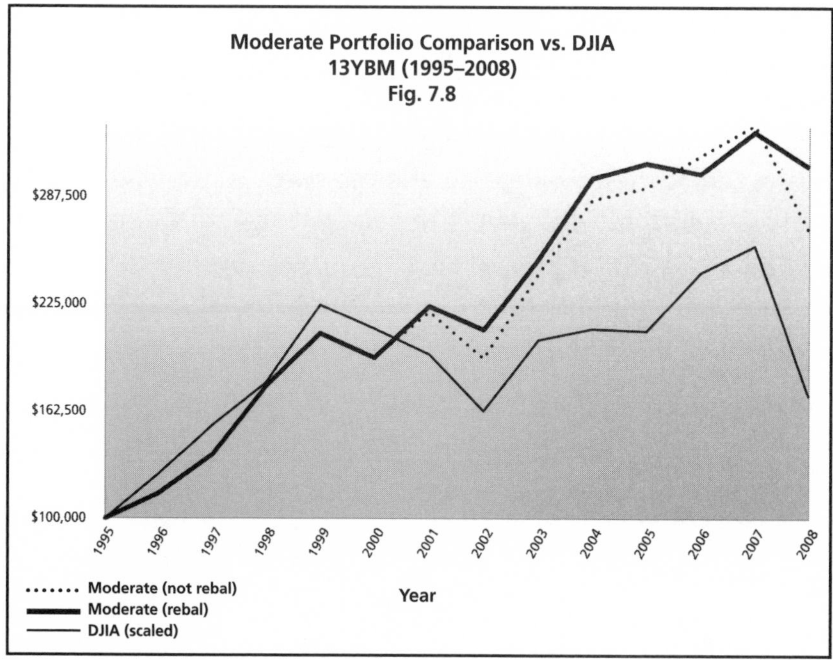

tall in the face of disaster. In fact, if the stock market had gone to zero in 2008, this portfolio still would have returned a 55% gain by way of its cash and bond allocations.

How does that strength stack up to the portfolio your broker threw together?

Multiple asset-class portfolios make investment decisions easy because they indicate action points. Your allocations will change with market activity. When one part of the market is up (say, the stock market), its allocation will increase in value, while a market with contrary dynamics will decrease in value (like bonds). A multiple asset-class portfolio, with its changing allocations, tells you something extremely important: when to sell something high and buy something else low.

That's portfolio management from the asset class, or macro, perspective. Managing a portfolio from the micro perspective is just as easy, and the effects are just as dramatic.

To draw a clear comparison, we will assume a one-asset-class portfolio; just stocks. As such, when the stock portfolio is rebalanced, no dollars will be redirected to bonds or cash. The end result will compare the same amount of capital, invested in the same stocks; the only difference is rebalanced allocations. Once again, the portfolio will be rebalanced twice: at the end of 2000 and 2005. First we'll look at the portfolio by industry and then by individual stocks.

To refresh your memory, fig. 7.9 shows the target allocations for the 15-51 model.

Fig. 7.9

Industry Rank	Industry	15-51 Model Targets
1	Consumer Staples/Services	33%
2	Technology	27%
3	Basic/Industrial	20%
4	Financial	13%
5	Energy	7%
	Total	**100%**

That's how the portfolio was constructed when it commenced on December 31, 1995. Five years later, in 2000, the portfolio strayed from targets as shown in fig. 7.10, on the next page.

Do you see that? Free market stock trading indicated to sell 12% of financial stocks at the end of 2000 because they were running up with cheap and easy money. The housing boom was under way, asset-backed securities were just three years old, Fannie and Freddie were expanding the debt market, and banks were reaping huge benefits. The objective is to buy low and sell high. Because of 15-51 discipline, your portfolio tells you what to do: what to buy and sell.

Fig. 7.10

Industry Rank	Industry	15-51 Model Targets	15-51i Actual in 2000	Adjustment Required	Action
1	Consumer Staples/Services	33%	35%	1.3%	Sell
2	Technology	27%	22%	-5.0%	Buy
3	Basic/Industrial	20%	13%	-7.0%	Buy
4	Financial	13%	25%	12.1%	Sell
5	Energy	7%	5%	-1.3%	Buy
	Total	100%	100%	0.0%	

Let us now assume that these adjustments were made at the end of 2000 and, once again, no dollars were redirected to other asset classes. Instead, the same capital was simply redistributed among the same fifteen above-average stocks. Fig. 7.11 shows what the portfolio looked like five years later, in 2005.

Fig. 7.11

Industry Rank	Industry	15-51 Model Targets	15-51i Actual in 2005	Adjustment Required	Action
1	Consumer Staples/Services	33%	33%	-0.7%	Buy
2	Technology	27%	35%	8.6%	Sell
3	Basic/Industrial	20%	19%	-0.8%	Buy
4	Financial	13%	8%	-5.0%	Buy
5	Energy	7%	5%	-2.1%	Buy
	Total	100%	100%	0.0%	

This time, the allocation indicates to purchase financials, basic/industrials, and energy, while selling lots of technology. News of the "financial crisis" hadn't yet hit the streets (if it had, common sense would have dictated not increasing your investments in that market until the dust settled). But since the epidemic wasn't yet uncovered, these adjustments were made.

That portfolio finished 2008 as shown in fig. 7.12.

Fig. 7.12

Industry Rank	Industry	15-51 Model Targets	15-51i in 2008 (Rebal. 2x)	Change vs. Target
1	Consumer Staples/Services	33%	33%	-0.6%
2	Technology	27%	30%	3.1%
3	Basic/Industrial	20%	16%	-3.5%
4	Financial	13%	11%	-2.6%
5	Energy	7%	10%	3.6%
	Total	100%	100%	0.0%

So that is how the 15-51 Indicator looked after two rebalancings at year-end 2008. If nothing had changed during the course of the 13YBM, meaning nothing had been bought or sold, and thus no rebalancings had taken place, the 15-51 Indicator would have compared to its target allocations as shown in fig. 7.13 on the next page

Fig. 7.13

Industry Rank	Industry	15-51 Model Targets	15-51i Actual (Not Rebal.) in 2008	Change vs. Target
1	Consumer Staples/Services	33%	38%	5.2%
2	Technology	27%	28%	1.1%
3	Basic/Industrial	20%	13%	-7.1%
4	Financial	13%	14%	0.3%
5	Energy	7%	7%	0.5%
	Total	100%	100%	0.0%

Fig. 7.14 shows the comparative chart, followed by a table of returns (fig. 7.15, on the next page).

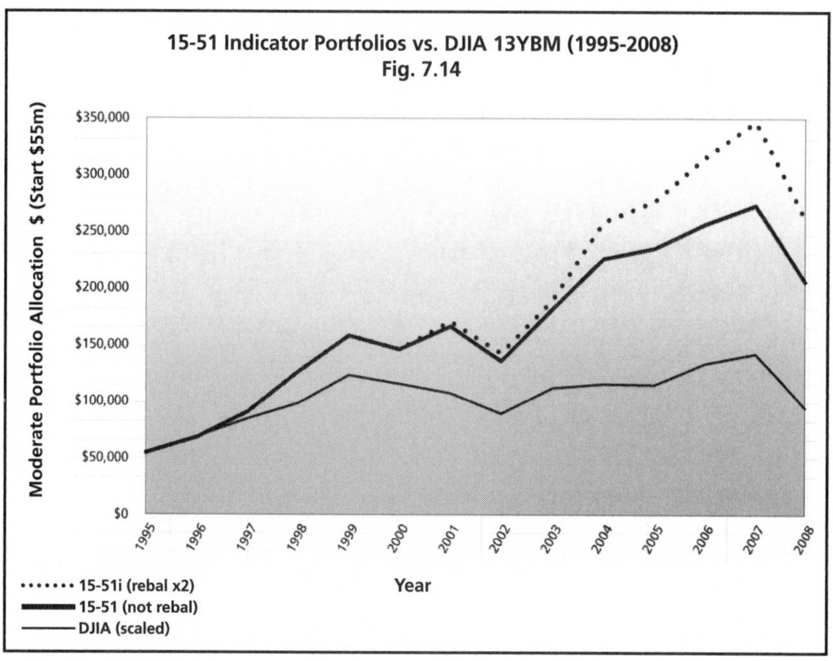

13YBM
Fig. 7.15

Portfolio	ROI	+/- DJIA
15-51i (Rebal. 2x)	374%	302%
15-5i (not Rebal.)	273%	202%
DJIA	72%	0%

Investing is an active sport, and the benefits of that action are clearly shown above. Two rebalancings produced 101% points more of return. Of course, active portfolio management does not rebalance on arbitrary dates at fiscal year-ends, in five-year intervals, as was done in this demonstration. Let conditions of the marketplace, your portfolio allocations, and your objectives drive your actions. Not the stock market.

This is not to say that you should disregard the DJIA. Many times, the Dow will shoot off the initial flare. Remember, the first time most of us heard the words "subprime mortgage" was with HSBC's loan defaults announcement in February 2007. The Dow shook, falling 416 points, or 3.3%, in a single day of trading. That's a signal—a warning to keep your eyes open and reacquaint yourself with your investment plan and objectives to determine your next moves.

As the crisis continued, no one knew whether bank failures were being kept to an isolated few or a major market meltdown. The stock market was volatile and speculation ran roughshod. And even though the DJIA hit its all-time high in October 2007, it was a rocky road. Fig. 7.16, on the next page, shows the 2007 chart again.

The news in 2008 didn't get any better, and banks continued to fold. Industry fundamentals showed weakness, and the Dow was on a declining trend. These were major signals to take

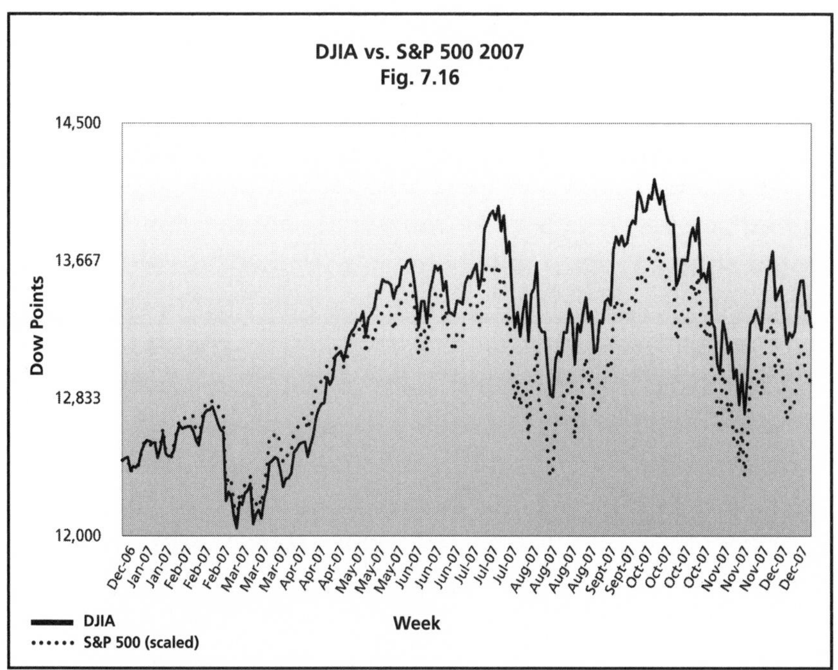
DJIA vs. S&P 500 2007
Fig. 7.16
14,500
13,667
12,833
12,000
Dow Points
Dec-06
Jan-07
Jan-07
Feb-07
Feb-07
Feb-07
Mar-07
Mar-07
Mar-07
Apr-07
Apr-07
Apr-07
May-07
May-07
May-07
Jun-07
Jun-07
Jun-07
Jul-07
Jul-07
Jul-07
Aug-07
Aug-07
Aug-07
Aug-07
Sept-07
Sept-07
Oct-07
Oct-07
Oct-07
Oct-07
Nov-07
Nov-07
Nov-07
Dec-07
Dec-07
Week
DJIA
S&P 500 (scaled)

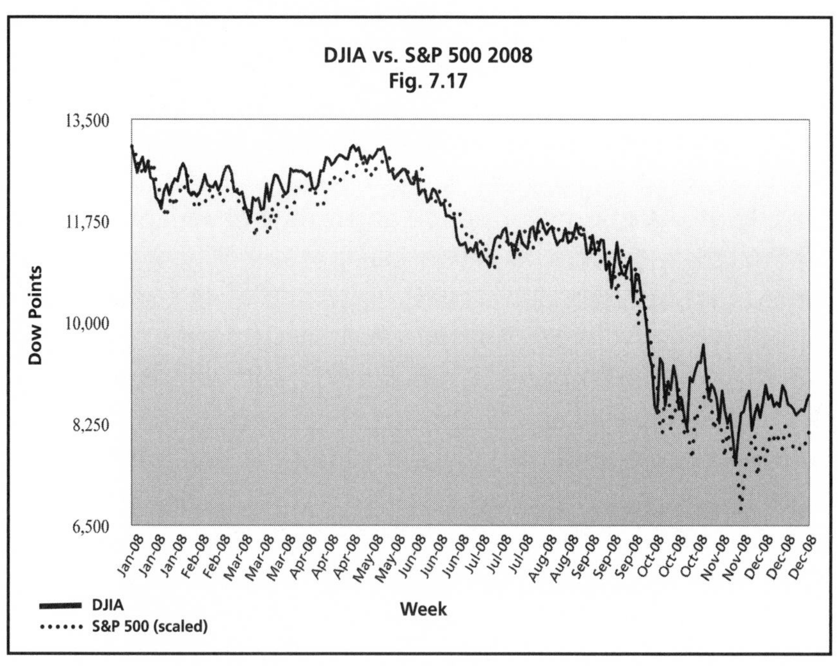
DJIA vs. S&P 500 2008
Fig. 7.17
13,500
11,750
10,000
8,250
6,500
Dow Points
Jan-08
Jan-08
Jan-08
Feb-08
Feb-08
Mar-08
Mar-08
Mar-08
Apr-08
Apr-08
Apr-08
May-08
May-08
Jun-08
Jun-08
Jun-08
Jul-08
Jul-08
Jul-08
Aug-08
Aug-08
Sep-08
Sep-08
Sep-08
Oct-08
Oct-08
Oct-08
Nov-08
Nov-08
Dec-08
Dec-08
Dec-08
Week
DJIA
S&P 500 (scaled)

action. Once again, notice how "the market" provides plenty of opportunity to make portfolio adjustments, thanks to speculation. Fig. 7.17, on the previous page, shows the 2008 chart again.

As we've established, there's no reason to try to sell at the highest point and buy at the lowest. That's not the goal. Your goal should be to buy low and sell high in the most effective and efficient manner you can, while achieving your financial objectives and comfort level. That's success. Perfect timing never factors in.

When you only own two financial stocks, as does the 15-51 Indicator, it's quite easy to mitigate that risk during "crisis" conditions. If, on the other hand, financials was your number one industry, this kind of negative market news should prompt you to reconsider your industry rankings. This can be done quite easily by sliding financial down to a lower industry position, say, four or five, in an effort to minimize your exposure to that market.

Yes, investing is a discipline, but when market conditions change, it's not only appropriate but necessary for your portfolio to also change. Heading into a financial crisis with financials as your number one industry is like heading into a fire with your clothes drenched in gasoline. And when no one—not the Wall Street establishment nor the government—can provide a reasonable assessment of the negative market condition, consider it a dangerous situation and a time to act aggressively.

That's what makes modeling so important. When you understand how your portfolio is constructed and what purpose each part serves, it's very easy to make appropriate adjustments.

Okay, the final aspect of rebalancing is to determine which stocks are to be sold and how much of each one to sell. The next few pages are going to look like a lot of numbers, but the logic is really quite easy to follow. Fig. 7.18 shows the 15-51 Indicator and its stock allocation targets.

Stock rebalancings are done using the same logic as with asset-class or industry (macro) rebalancings. Adjustments will be made at the end of years 2000 and 2005. At these times, stocks will be bought or sold in such a way as to bring them back to their original targets (fig. 7.18).

15-51 Indicator TARGET Allocations
Fig. 7.18

Industry Rank	Equity Rank	Company	Industry	% of Industry	% of Total Stock $
1	1	JnJ	Consumer Staples	33%	11%
1	2	Lowe's	Consumer Services	27%	9%
1	3	P&G	Consumer Staples	20%	7%
1	4	Target	Consumer Services	13%	4%
1	5	Church & Dwight	Consumer Staples	7%	2%
2	1	Apple	Technology	40%	11%
2	2	IBM	Technology	30%	8%
2	3	Boeing	Technology	20%	5%
2	4	UTC	Technology	10%	3%
3	1	Honda	Basic	50%	10%
3	2	Caterpillar	Basic	33%	7%
3	3	3M	Industrial	17%	3%
4	1	Wells Fargo	Financial	67%	9%
4	2	Capital One	Financial	33%	4%
5	1	ExxonMobil	Energy	100%	7%
Total					**100%**

At the first rebalancing point, year ended 2000, the 15-51 Indicator looked as shown in fig. 7.19, with the listed adjustments performed to rebalance the portfolio.

Fig. 7.19

Actual							
Industry Rank	**Equity Rank**	**Company**	**2000**	**% of Total**	**Target % of Total**	**Adjustment Required**	**Action**
1	1	JnJ	$15,019	10%	11%	1%	Buy
1	2	Lowe's	$12,988	9%	9%	0%	Hold
1	3	P&G	$6,930	5%	7%	2%	Buy
1	4	Target	$12,613	9%	4%	-4%	Sell
1	5	Church & Dwight	$3,147	2%	2%	0%	Hold
2	1	Apple	$5,477	4%	11%	7%	Buy
2	2	IBM	$16,372	11%	8%	-3%	Sell
2	3	Boeing	$4,940	3%	5%	2%	Buy
2	4	UTC	$4,862	3%	3%	-1%	Sell
3	1	Honda	$9,732	7%	10%	3%	Buy
3	2	Caterpillar	$5,906	4%	7%	3%	Buy
3	3	3M	$3,328	2%	3%	1%	Buy
4	1	Wells Fargo	$16,501	11%	9%	-2%	Sell
4	2	Capital One	$20,746	14%	4%	-10%	Sell
5	1	Exxon Mobil	$7,859	5%	7%	1%	Buy
Totals			**$146,421**	**100%**	**100%**	**0%**	

At the end of 2005, the allocations changed again and adjustments were once again warranted, as seen in fig. 7.20.

Fig. 7.20

Industry Rank	Equity Rank	Company	2005	% of Total	Target % of Total	Adjustment Required	Action
1	1	JnJ	$18,613	7%	11%	4%	Buy
1	2	Lowe's	$38,993	14%	9%	-5%	Sell
1	3	P&G	$14,406	5%	7%	1%	Buy
1	4	Target	$11,092	4%	4%	0%	Hold
1	5	Church & Dwight	$7,245	3%	2%	0%	Hold
2	1	Apple	$75,457	27%	11%	-17%	Sell
2	2	IBM	$11,328	4%	8%	4%	Buy
2	3	Boeing	$8,311	3%	5%	2%	Buy
2	4	UTC	$2,777	1%	3%	2%	Buy
3	1	Honda	$22,967	8%	10%	2%	Buy
3	2	Caterpillar	$23,838	9%	7%	-2%	Sell
3	3	3M	$6,278	2%	3%	1%	Buy
4	1	Wells Fargo	$14,684	5%	9%	4%	Buy
4	2	Capital One	$8,543	3%	4%	1%	Buy
5	1	Exxon Mobil	$12,614	5%	7%	2%	Buy
Totals			**$277,145**	**100%**	**100%**	**0%**	

And at the end of 2008, after these two rebalancings, the allocation comparison for the 15-51 Indicator can be seen in fig. 7.21.

Fig. 7.21

Industry Rank	Equity Rank	Company	2008	% of Total	Target % of Total	Change v. Target
1	1	JnJ	$31,076	12%	11%	1%
1	2	Lowe's	$15,906	6%	9%	-3%
1	3	P&G	$20,047	8%	7%	1%
1	4	Target	$7,737	3%	4%	-1%
1	5	Church & Dwight	$10,464	4%	2%	2%
2	1	Apple	$37,318	14%	11%	4%
2	2	IBM	$23,566	9%	8%	1%
2	3	Boeing	$9,522	4%	5%	-2%
2	4	UTC	$7,264	3%	3%	0%
3	1	Honda	$20,865	8%	10%	-2%
3	2	Caterpillar	$15,003	6%	7%	-1%
3	3	3M	$7,056	3%	3%	-1%
4	1	Wells Fargo	$23,118	9%	9%	0%
4	2	Capital One	$4,749	2%	4%	-3%
5	1	Exxon Mobil	$26,854	10%	7%	4%
Totals			**$260,544**	**100%**	**100%**	**0%**

Does making these rebalancings require effort?

Yes.

But the return is well worth the price of admission. Remember, the rebalanced portfolio outperformed the 15-51 Indicator by 101% points (a 374% return versus 273%, over the 13YBM). When you sell stocks high, you lock in gains and redirect proceeds to above-average stocks that are selling at discount prices. By selling high you reduce your exposure to overvalued stocks, while increasing your exposure to undervalued ones. Therefore, when the stock market corrects swiftly, like it did in 2008, the portfolio experiences less downside pressure because you have reduced your holdings in stocks with the most inflated prices.

It makes perfect sense.

These rebalancing points were arbitrary, based strictly on the expiration of the five-year T-notes. And since there are no hard and fast rules to rebalancing and there is no right or wrong time to do it, the key is to do it. There's no reason to constantly tinker with your portfolio. You must let your investments work. Take comfort in the strength of your foundation (15-51 construction) and the quality of your investments and allow them to do the work for you. That's the purpose of investment.

Figs. 7.22 and 7.23, on the next page, show two additional views of rebalancing in action. This time we'll view the impact of rebalancing the 15-51 Indicator within ten-year benchmark periods, giving us just one rebalancing for each set of years: 1995–2005 and 1998–2008. In each case, the positive effects of rebalancing can be seen just after the midpoint of the period.

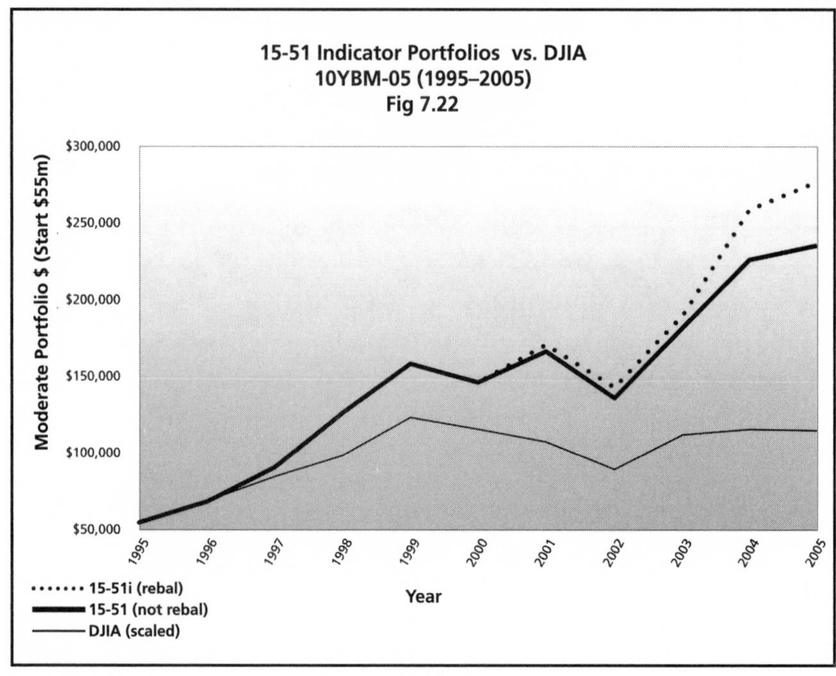
15-51 Indicator Portfolios vs. DJIA
10YBM-05 (1995–2005)
Fig 7.22
Moderate Portfolio $ (Start $55m)
$300,000
$250,000
$200,000
$150,000
$100,000
$50,000
1995
1996
1997
1998
1999
2000
2001
2002
2003
2004
2005
Year
15-51i (rebal)
15-51 (not rebal)
DJIA (scaled)

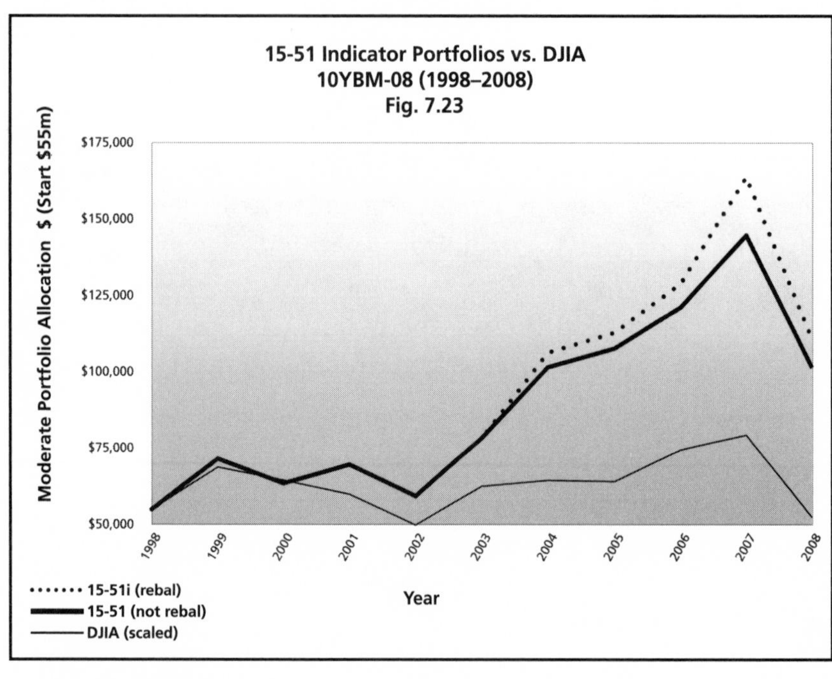
15-51 Indicator Portfolios vs. DJIA
10YBM-08 (1998–2008)
Fig. 7.23
Moderate Portfolio Allocation $ (Start $55m)
$175,000
$150,000
$125,000
$100,000
$75,000
$50,000
1998
1999
2000
2001
2002
2003
2004
2005
2006
2007
2008
Year
15-51i (rebal)
15-51 (not rebal)
DJIA (scaled)

During the ten-year period (10YBM-05), the rebalanced 15-51i portfolio returned 404% versus 329% for the portfolio that wasn't rebalanced. The Dow of course finished up a respectable 109%. Yes, that's impressive. But the next ten-year block (10YBM-08)—you know, the one that replaces the tech boom with the market crash of 2008—is even more striking. Take a look at fig. 7.23 on the previous page. During this period, which ended with the collapse of the financial market, the DJIA lost 4% while the 15-51 Indicator produced an 85% gain. That's pretty good. But the rebalanced portfolio produced an amazing 101% return, just eight points off the Dow's return during the tech boom. Fig. 7.24 shows a table of comparative results.

Return on Investment
Fig. 7.24

Portfolio	13YBM	10YBM-05	10YBM-08
15-51i (rebal)	374%	404%	101%
15-51i (not rebal)	273%	329%	85%
DJIA	72%	109%	-4%

That's what superior construction and active management can do for you.

And that's the who, what, where, and when of effective portfolio management. It's not hard to do or understand. But it does require some effort. And, indeed, it is well worth that effort.

CHAPTER 8

The Lose Your Broker Guarantee, and Some Things to Remember

Perhaps the most important thing to remember about investing is this. You are not the reason for your investment woes—you are the solution. No one cares more about your financial future than you do, and no one will do a better job managing it than you will. You always had the ability, and you always had the experience. Now you have the tools.

Early on in this book I promised you that you could create a portfolio that would outperform the one your broker sold you, and that you could be comfortable doing it. I said that because I knew how easy it is to do. Now you know too.

Keep this book close by. Put it in the bathroom or on the nightstand and read it over and over again, a few pages here and there. You'll find it hard to believe how many different things will pop out, ring a bell, or shed new light each time you go through it.

Lose Your Broker can also help calm your nerves during a hostile market. If you can't make sense of "the market's" movements, return to the Market basics (chapter 2), and then take it step by step through each subsequent chapter until you find the comfort you seek. If after your review you still struggle with the method, or the portfolio you constructed still doesn't perform as you planned, then bring your issues to me.

Beyond the publication of this book, I will also finance, build, and deliver a place on the Web where like-minded investors can go to discuss "the market" and investment. The website, located at www.LoseYourBroker.com, will be totally free of charge and 100% secure. It will provide an unparalleled support network dedicated to you, the average investor.

I will be on the site hosting interactive workshops, chat forums, and webcasts on topics that you will have the opportunity to direct through survey. The site will also feature a public access situation room, where live interactive commentary will take place during hostile markets. And much like a talk radio show, time will be allocated to address your instant messages, questions, and comments.

Regular market commentaries, written in the same straightforward manner as this book, will be posted regularly on LoseYourBroker.com. They will include analyses of all major market indicators as well as the above-average 15-51 Indicator, which should serve as your new benchmark for investment success. (The DJIA, as I have shown, is simply too easy to beat.) The site will also provide easy access to tools designed to facilitate your portfolio construction, fundamental analysis, and rebalancing efforts. These tools will also be available in Microsoft Excel format.

But perhaps the most important feature of the Lose Your Broker website will be the community, the place you can go to connect to investors just like you. These investors will have the same investment aptitude as you, speak the same language, and share the same investment philosophy. This connection will extend the reach of your market research experiences, which in turn will enhance your investment decisions, performance, and comfort level. The more you know about the Market condition, the easier investing is.

LoseYourBroker.com will operate 24/7 until July 4, 2014, and beyond that for as long as I can generate revenue from this book. So tell a friend. The services I've mentioned will be free of charge, included with the price you paid for this book. My goal is to make those dollars the best investment you ever made, because then *Lose Your Broker* will be the best investment I ever made. That's the way investment works.

THINGS TO REMEMBER

Don't Overcomplicate Matters

Clearly define your objectives and keep your tactics simple. Use superior 15-51 construction, quality components, a multiple asset-class portfolio and implement an effective buy low, sell high discipline.

Set Realistic Ambitions

Establish goals like your entire portfolio should outperform the Dow Jones Industrial Average and your stock allocation should outperform the 15-51 Indicator. You have all the tools to do so. If you're still not sure how to allocate your investments by asset class, then approach growth in a neutral way and evenly split your investment dollars across three or four asset classes. Whatever makes you most comfortable. And don't forget, there is no one right way to invest successfully.

Remember to Rebalance

Besides paying huge dividends, rebalancing makes investing easier to handle during volatile markets. Monitor your allocations and compare them to their targets. The best rebalancing point is the one that makes the most sense for *you*, your portfolio, and your objectives. Don't be swayed by anyone "smarter" than you. Recall the effectiveness of arbitrary five-year rebalancing points. Use that demonstration as proof that there is always plenty of time to take successful action. Also remember that investing isn't about buying at the lowest and selling at the highest. It's about buying low and selling high—at the most appropriate times for you.

Consumers Are Market

When making your investment decisions, never forget that it's all about you. You put the fuel into the economic engine. If conditions are good for you, they're good for markets and good for investment. Never sell yourself short. If you're just a grain of sand on a beach, then you're surrounded by many more just like you. Together, you and those around you determine the course of investment. So keep your eyes and ears open. View your daily experiences as those of an investor conducting market research because that is indeed the case.

Don't Try to Time the Stock Market

Know that it's impossible to "time the market." But, in the same vein, it isn't hard to know what the market will do. Take your cues from what's actually happening in the marketplace and its controlling force—government—which can either make a hell of a difference or a different kind of hell. You the investor, with or without a broker, with or without a mutual fund, must know what your government is doing. It's the only way not to get blindsided by your investments.

Don't Count on Uncle Sam

For those of you hoping that government can and will settle the score, it's time to think again. Let me ask you this: was it the government's intention to take over the banking and insurance markets when it created Fannie Mae in 1938, Freddie Mac in 1970, and the CRA in 1977? That which began as a small public option and good intention has nearly turned into a complete government takeover of the financial industry. If this wasn't government's intention, then it really screwed up. It's famous for that.

And now, even with the debacles that are Social Security and Medicare, and with the incredibly weak dollar and ballooning national debt, government has the audacity to insert politics into health care. Have government officials lost their collective mind?

America is in a gigantic mess right now. We rely too heavily on a government that spends too much, borrows too much, and regulates too much—to help too little. These are not positive signs for the market, money, or investment. To reverse course, America must change its posture to pro-growth free market policies. The government needs to get out of the way and let the free market bail itself out. Otherwise, the stock market will continue to trend sideways-to-down (from a Dow midpoint of 10,500).

How can I be sure? That brings me to my final piece of advice.

Monitor Your Market Experiences

Market experiences are investment experiences. Your daily market experiences provide an excellent indication of future stock market movements. So as a final demonstration for this book, let me provide you with my basis for the Dow Jones estimate presented above.

I'm a consumer and also the small-business owner that presidents Bush and Obama always speak about: the "backbone" of American enterprise, the heart and soul of economic vitality. I'm an American entrepreneur, operating at the grassroots of American business and investment. When you sum up the troubles facing America, my situation epitomizes every aspect of it.

For instance, there is a false perception of easy credit in the marketplace today. With low inflation and low interest rates, it appears that money is cheap and easy. But the money isn't moving. High-quality borrowers with sufficient incomes and high credit scores are getting stalled, or entirely cut out, from historic low interest rates.

During the housing boom, it was too easy to get a mortgage. In a notorious practice called "no document" loans, mortgages were provided without employment verification, with no income validation, and without credit scores being factored in. The only thing that mattered was a house's value; that, defined by the government via Fannie and Freddie, determined how much credit a consumer could get. Back then loans up to 125% of inflated market values were common.

The same is true now, but in reverse condition.

Now it is impossible to borrow 81% of a much depressed value, which is still determined by defunct credit facilities Fannie and Freddie. Like the housing boom, it's still about artificial asset values and the government's agenda for the extension of credit. Back then the government was intentionally expanding the debt market. Now it is intentionally contracting it. In both conditions, the government is dictating market activity and causing it to do things against its basic instinct. That's not good for business, investment, or the market, especially if you're an entrepreneur like me, looking to start a new business and put the unemployed back to work.

Many small business owners finance their operations with home loans and equity lines of credit. In preparation for the launch of this publication and its supporting business unit, I looked to refinance my mortgage lines at these historic rates. And though my income and credit scores were above average, I was unable to refinance my loans unless I cut my home equity line by 65% and then doubled the interest rate.

What did I do wrong?

I wasn't looking to get bailed out as were many Wall Street firms in the aftermath of the 2008 crash; I was just looking for market interest rates and a level playing field. But I couldn't get either. That's the government picking winners (those who can get low market rates) and losers (those who can't). How do I know? Because my income, my ability to repay, and the reliability of such repayment never factored into the loan equation. The situation I faced was purely political.

Unfortunately, the only way for me to capture low market rates would be to max out my credit line and then miss several consecutive payments. Then, the bankers told me, they'd have "more flexibility to negotiate." In other words, I had to be in "trouble" in order to get lower rates. Otherwise, I could afford to pay the higher tax on debt.

That's the government incentivizing failure and penalizing success. Not only is that stupid, it's bad for the market and investment. Not to mention the fact that Fannie and Freddie value my home much lower than my local town government does. But then again, the town uses appraised values to charge me property taxes (they want a higher value to assess), while the federal government uses appraised values to determine the amount of credit they will extend to me (it wants to cut debt). That's politics once again. Politicians pollute markets and corrupt business practices. They have no choice. They're driven by politics, not return on investment.

The bottom line is this: if we're going to get America out of this mess, then **We the People** must do it. The more we profit from our investments, the less we need from Social Security and every other hapless government program. We must minimize their effect on us by taking control of our money and our profits. That is the Lose Your Broker mission. Besides, neither the government nor Wall Street has proven to be a worthwhile manager of our hard-earned money. It's time for something different.

It's time to travel the road of financial independence. You have what it takes, the tools, and the know-how. Now it's time to do it.

It's time to Lose Your Broker, Not Your Money.

I'll see you on the Web . . .

APPENDIX

A. 1.1
Sample Portfolio
The 15-51 Format (detail layout)

Industry Rank	1	2	3	4	5	15	Total
No of Stocks	5	4	3	2	1	15	
% of Portfolio	33.3%	26.7%	20.0%	13.3%	6.7%	100%	
Dollar Weight	$3,333	$2,667	$2,000	$1,333	$667	$10,000	**$10,000**

Industry 1

Stock Rank	Weighting	% of Cat.	$	% of Total
1	5	33%	$1,111	11.1%
2	4	27%	$889	8.9%
3	3	20%	$667	6.7%
4	2	13%	$444	4.4%
5	**1**	**7%**	$222	2.2%
5	15	100%	$3,333	**33.3%**

Industry 2

Stock Rank	Weighting	% of Cat.	$	% of Total
1	4	40%	$1,067	10.7%
2	3	30%	$800	8.0%
3	2	20%	$533	5.3%
4	**1**	**10%**	$267	2.7%
4	10	100%	$2,667	26.7%

Industry 3

Stock Rank	Weighting	% of Cat.	$	% of Total
1	3	50%	$1,000	10.0%
2	2	33%	$667	6.7%
3	1	17%	$333	3.3%
3	6	100%	$2,000	20.0%

Industry 4

Stock Rank	Weighting	% of Cat.	$	% of Total
1	2	67%	$889	8.9%
2	1	33%	$444	4.4%
2	3	100%	$1,333	13.3%

Industry 5

Stock Rank	Weighting	% of Cat.	$	% of Total
1	1	100%	$667	6.7%
1	2	100%	$667	6.7%

A. 1.2
Gross Equity Investment $10,000
15-51 Allocation Model (alternate view)

Ranks					
Industry	**Stock**	**Category Weighting**	**% of Category**	**% of Total**	**Investment**
1	1	5	33%	11.1%	$1,111
1	2	4	27%	8.9%	$889
1	3	3	20%	6.7%	$667
1	4	2	13%	4.4%	$444
1	5	1	7%	2.2%	$222
2	1	4	40%	10.7%	$1,067
2	2	3	30%	8.0%	$800
2	3	2	20%	5.3%	$533
2	4	1	10%	2.7%	$267
3	1	3	50%	10.0%	$1,000
3	2	2	33%	6.7%	$667
3	3	1	17%	3.3%	$333
4	1	2	67%	8.9%	$889
4	2	1	33%	4.4%	$444
5	1	1	100%	6.7%	$667
	15		Total	100%	$10,000

A. 1.3
Sample Portfolio
The 16-61 Format (detail layout)

Industry Rank	1	2	3	4	5	6	21	
No of Stocks	6	5	4	3	2	1	21	
% of Portfolio	28.6%	23.8%	19.0%	14.3%	9.5%	4.8%	100%	
Dollar Weight	$2,857	$2,381	$1,905	$1,429	$952	$476	$10,000	$10,000

Industry 1

Stock Rank	Weighting	% of Cat.	$	% of Total
1	6	29%	$816	8.2%
2	5	24%	$680	6.8%
3	4	19%	$544	5.4%
4	3	14%	$408	4.1%
5	2	10%	$272	2.7%
6	**1**	**5%**	$136	1.4%
6	21	100%	$2,857	28.6%

Industry 2

Stock Rank	Weighting	% of Cat.	$	% of Total
1	5	33%	$794	7.9%
2	4	27%	$635	6.3%
3	3	20%	$476	4.8%
4	2	13%	$317	3.2%
5	**1**	**7%**	$159	1.6%
5	15	100%	$2,381	23.8%

A. 1.3, continued
Sample Portfolio
The 16-61 Format (detail layout)

Industry 3

Stock Rank	Weighting	% of Cat.	$	% of Total
1	4	40%	$762	7.6%
2	3	30%	$571	5.7%
3	2	20%	$381	3.8%
4	1	10%	$190	1.9%
4	10	100%	$1,905	19.0%

Industry 4

Stock Rank	Weighting	% of Cat.	$	% of Total
1	3	50%	$714	7.1%
2	2	33%	$476	4.8%
3	1	17%	$238	2.4%
3	6	100%	$1,429	14.3%

Industry 5

Stock Rank	Weighting	% of Cat.	$	% of Total
1	2	67%	$635	6.3%
2	1	33%	$317	3.2%
2	3	100%	$952	9.5%

Industry 6

Stock Rank	Weighting	% of Cat.	$	% of Total
1	1	100%	$476	4.8%
1	1	100%	$476	4.8%

A. 1.4
Gross Equity Investment$10,000
16-61 Allocation Model (alternate view)

Ranks					
Industry	Stock	Category Weighting	% of Category	% of Total	Investment
1	1	6	29%	8.16%	$816
1	2	5	24%	6.80%	$680
1	3	4	19%	5.44%	$544
1	4	3	14%	4.08%	$408
1	5	2	10%	2.72%	$272
1	6	1	5%	1.36%	$136
2	1	5	33%	7.94%	$794
2	2	4	27%	6.35%	$635
2	3	3	20%	4.76%	$476
2	4	2	13%	3.17%	$317
2	5	1	7%	1.59%	$159
3	1	4	40%	7.62%	$762
3	2	3	30%	5.71%	$571
3	3	2	20%	3.81%	$381
3	4	1	10%	1.90%	$190
4	1	3	50%	7.14%	$714
4	2	2	33%	4.76%	$476
4	3	1	17%	2.38%	$238
5	1	2	67%	6.35%	$635
5	2	1	33%	3.17%	$317
6	1	1	100%	4.76%	$476
	21		**Total**	**100%**	**$10,000**

A. 1.5
Sample Portfolio
The 17-71 Format (detail layout)

Industry Rank	1	2	3	4	5	6	7	28	
No of Stocks	7	6	5	4	3	2	1	28	
% of Portfolio	25.0%	21.4%	17.9%	14.3%	10.7%	7.1%	3.6%	100%	
Dollar Weight	$2,500	$2,143	$1,786	$1,429	$1,071	$714	$357	$10,000	$10,000

Industry 1

Stock Rank	Weighting	% of Cat.	$	% of Total
1	7	25%	$625	6.3%
2	6	21%	$536	5.4%
3	5	18%	$446	4.5%
4	4	14%	$357	3.6%
5	3	11%	$268	2.7%
6	2	7%	$179	1.8%
7	1	4%	$89	0.9%
7	28	100%	$2,500	25.0%

Industry 2

Stock Rank	Weighting	% of Cat.	$	% of Total
1	6	29%	$612	6.1%
2	5	24%	$510	5.1%
3	4	19%	$408	4.1%
4	3	14%	$306	3.1%
5	2	10%	$204	2.0%
6	1	5%	$102	1.0%
6	21	100%	$2,143	21.4%

Industry 3

Stock Rank	Weighting	% of Cat.	$	% of Total
1	5	33%	$595	6.0%
2	4	27%	$476	4.8%
3	3	20%	$357	3.6%
4	2	13%	$238	2.4%
5	1	7%	$119	1.2%
5	15	100%	$1,786	17.9%

Industry 4

Stock Rank	Weighting	% of Cat.	$	% of Total
1	4	40%	$571	5.7%
2	3	30%	$429	4.3%
3	2	20%	$286	2.9%
4	1	10%	$143	1.4%
4	10	100%	$1,429	14.3%

Industry 5

Stock Rank	Weighting	% of Cat.	$	% of Total
1	3	50%	$536	5.4%
2	2	33%	$357	3.6%
3	1	17%	$179	1.8%
3	6	100%	$1,071	10.7%

A. 1.5, continued
Sample Portfolio
The 17-71 Format (detail layout)

Industry 6

Stock Rank	Weighting	% of Cat.	$	% of Total
1	2	67%	$476	4.8%
2	1	33%	$238	2.4%
2	3	67%	$714	7.1%

Industry 7

Stock Rank	Weighting	% of Cat.	$	% of Total
1	1	100%	$357	3.6%
1	1	100%	$357	3.6%

A. 1.6
Gross Equity Investment $10,000
17-71 Allocation Model (alternate view)

Ranks					
Industry	Stock	Category Weighting	% of Category	% of Total	Investment
1	1	7	25%	6.3%	$625
1	2	6	21%	5.4%	$536
1	3	5	18%	4.5%	$446
1	4	4	14%	3.6%	$357
1	5	3	11%	2.7%	$268
1	6	2	7%	1.8%	$179
1	7	1	4%	0.9%	$89
2	1	6	29%	6.1%	$612
2	2	5	24%	5.1%	$510
2	3	4	19%	4.1%	$408
2	4	3	14%	3.1%	$306
2	5	2	10%	2.0%	$204
2	6	1	5%	1.0%	$102
3	1	5	33%	6.0%	$595
3	2	4	27%	4.8%	$476
3	3	3	20%	3.6%	$357
3	4	2	13%	2.4%	$238
3	5	1	7%	1.2%	$119
4	1	4	40%	5.7%	$571
4	2	3	30%	4.3%	$429
4	3	2	20%	2.9%	$286
4	4	1	10%	1.4%	$143
5	1	3	50%	5.4%	$536
5	2	2	33%	3.6%	$357
5	3	1	17%	1.8%	$179
6	1	2	67%	4.8%	$476
6	2	1	33%	2.4%	$238
7	1	1	100%	3.6%	$357
	28		Total	100.0%	$10,000

DATE			
OCT 15 '81			
NOV 2 '81			
DEC 15 1986			
JAN 13 1987			
FEB 19 '91			

UNDERSTANDING INFLATION

UNDERSTANDING INFLATION

by

John Case

WILLIAM MORROW AND COMPANY, INC.
New York *1981*

Library of Congress Cataloging in Publication Data

Case, John, 1944-
Understanding inflation.

Includes bibliographical references and index.
1. Inflation (Finance) 2. Inflation (Finance)—
United States. I. Title.
HG229.C35 332.4'1 80-29139
ISBN 0-688-00399-0

Printed in the United States of America

3 4 5 6 7 8 9 10

BOOK DESIGN BY MICHAEL MAUCERI

For Quaker

Foreword

This book is for people who want to know why prices keep going up.

It is not–rest assured–an economics textbook. It contains no equations, one graph, and only a few statistics. Nor is it a book for specialists. Economists interested in the fine points of business-cycle theory or monetary policy will have to look elsewhere. So don't worry if you never (or haven't yet) made it through Economics 101. You don't need to know a thing about supply and demand curves or the theories of John Maynard Keynes in order to read what follows. You may not know much about these matters when you're through. But you should understand inflation.

That of course is no idle ambition. Every morning the papers report some new development on the "inflation front," as if the economy had been transformed into a battle-field. Nearly every day a public official offers a pronouncement or a promise about the high cost of living. Inflation regularly tops opinion-poll lists of Americans' major concerns. If you can understand the subject, you will find the nightly news a good deal less puzzling than it used to be, even if the day's top story is about floating exchange rates or changes in the money supply. You will also find that a considerable amount of what is said about inflation in the press or at the lunch table is confused, misleading, or untrue. Everyone *can* understand inflation, even without a background in economics. But not everyone does.

Inflation is also a useful point of entry into the puzzling behavior of the modern economy. A rapid, continuing rise in prices with no end in sight—the kind of inflation we have experienced since the late 1960s—has never occurred before in American history. For decades, even centuries, prices rose and fell with predictable if not perfect regularity. Since World War II they have moved in only one direction: up. Since about 1967 the rate at which they move up has increased dramatically.

What happened? We like to blame inflation on greedy unions, businesses, or oil sheikhs, on spendthrift governments or chickenhearted politicians. Greed, profligacy, and chickenheartedness are all no doubt widespread. But inflation creates these attributes as much as it is created by them. Moreover, there's no reason to think that these traits were invented ten, fifteen, or even thirty-five years ago. The important chapters in the story of inflation reflect not human vices but human inventiveness. Our own resourcefulness has led us, as through a maze, to a world of apparently permanent inflation. The pages that follow will explain how this came to be.

Three cautions. First, don't expect a simple answer to the problem of inflation. There isn't one. The ways of controlling inflation discussed in the last chapter are messy and imperfect. By the same token, though, the problem is not beyond solution. As with most economic issues, it's a question of what—or who—should be sacrificed.

Second, remember that the American economy is enormously varied. Most of the generalizations in this book allow of exceptions. But don't let the exceptions blind you to the way things work most of the time. Similarly, do not be distracted by what happened to inflation the month before you read this book. Inflation may be getting worse or it may be easing up. But even a temporary improvement is not a sign that the problem is disappearing. Inflation has been with us for some time now. Unless something changes dramatically, it will be with us for a long time to come.

Finally, keep in mind that this is a book about inflation as a social phenomenon and political issue. It is not about inflation as a personal financial problem. There are many books available that treat the latter subject. Some may even contain good advice. But this one discusses what we as a nation ought to do about inflation, not what a few individuals can do to beat it. Only so many people, after all, were able to fit into the *Titanic*'s lifeboats. Better that someone should have told the captain to watch out for icebergs.

Acknowledgments

Thanks to James Campen, Christopher Jencks, Nancy Lyons, and Robert Zevin, all of whom read portions of this book in manuscript form. Most of their suggestions were gratefully accepted. Thanks also to John Brockman, who helped me get started.

Special thanks to my parents, Everett Case and Josephine Young Case, who offered advice and support of many kinds.

Contents

1. The Mixed Curse: Inflation in Perspective

The cost of living has gone up another dollar a quart.
—W. C. FIELDS

Back in 1965, prices did not seem inordinately low.

A dime would no longer buy a cup of coffee in most restaurants, and three dollars wouldn't pay for a copy of the hit new album by a young singer named Bob Dylan. Volkswagens could be driven out of the showroom for less than $2,000, but a fully equipped Pontiac Bonneville station wagon might run as high as $4,700. Ten gallons of Texaco premium cost $3.20, up from $3.10 a few years earlier. A typical new home sold for about $20,000, and mortgage rates had climbed to almost 6 percent.*

People complained about the high cost of living, and the complaints seemed justified. Prices had jumped nearly 75 percent since the end of World War II. And though high annual inflation rates hadn't been seen since the late forties

* Sources for these and other statistics, quotations, and so on, will be found in the Source Notes section at the back of the book.

and early fifties, prices nevertheless kept inching upward a percent or two every year.*

The complainers, of course, didn't know what they were getting in for. But then neither did anybody else.

In 1966 inflation began to heat up a little. Both that year and the next, prices rose more than 3 percent. In 1968 the rate neared 5 percent and in 1969 it topped 6 percent. By the end of the decade a typical item that cost $10 in 1965 was going for $12.05—a 20 percent jump in just five years.

Maybe, people thought, inflation was only temporarily bad—a result of the war in Vietnam. Every other war in America's history had brought hefty price increases. Americans over forty could remember the period right after World War II, when wartime controls were lifted and prices shot up. Even more could remember the inflation brought on by the Korean conflict in 1950 and 1951. But the hope that things were so simple soon vanished. U.S. troop levels in Southeast Asia peaked in 1969. Inflation stayed bad. By 1973 the war was essentially over. Inflation got worse.

Between January 1970 and late October 1979, prices exactly doubled. Inflation during the seventies averaged a little over 7 percent annually—more than triple what it had averaged in the previous two decades.† Nearly every year prices went up faster than they had gone up in *any* year during the fifties and sixties. As the 1970s ended, inflation was well into double digits. In the 1980s the outlook is for more of the same. In all probability prices will double again before another ten years pass.

Most of this book is about where inflation came from, why it has been with us so long, and why it got so much worse

---

* See the Appendix for an explanation and discussion of the various measures of inflation. Throughout this book, "prices" will refer to the Labor Department's Consumer Price Index and "inflation" or the "inflation rate" to percentage changes in the index (unless otherwise specified).

† An average rise of 7 percent a year leads to a cumulative 100 percent rise over ten years because of compounding.

during the seventies. The book will also discuss what can be done about inflation. Before these mysteries are unraveled, though, it helps to consider the nature of the beast. Like all objects of fear and loathing, inflation has grown larger than life, and in the process has engendered a set of cautionary tales. Inflation, it is said, is making us poorer by the day. It saps our economic strength, discourages hard work, undermines thrift, eats away at earnings. There is enough truth in these charges to make them credible.

The whole story, however, is not so simple. Like the Lord, inflation giveth and inflation taketh away. Also like the Lord, inflation gets blamed for the negative side of the ledger, while the positive side is chalked up to our own intelligence and hard work. The analogy ends here: inflation is beyond doubt a curse. But its effects, which this chapter will scrutinize, are mixed.

Inflation is not making us poorer

During the 1970s, prices doubled. Yet most Americans were making more than twice as much at the end of the decade as they were making at the beginning. Most families' purchasing power rose. The purchasing power of some of our society's most vulnerable groups—the elderly, for example—rose even faster than the average. Some people are better off than they were, some worse off. But in general the poor are no poorer, the rich no richer. Some goods and services are relatively cheaper than they used to be, some relatively more expensive.

Economists calculate these changes in what they call real terms—real wages, real prices, and so forth.* To figure real changes, all you need is a standard of comparison, like last year or 1970; then you adjust your figures for the effects of inflation. If you made $100 a week in 1970 and $200 a week

* Another phrase that means the same thing is "constant dollars." If two prices are calculated in constant dollars—1970 dollars, for example—then the later price is discounted by the amount of inflation that occurred in the interim.

in 1980, for example, your real wages (or your purchasing power) hardly changed at all. If you got a 12 percent raise in 1979, when inflation was running at 13 percent, you wound up making 1 percent less in real terms than before.

Between 1970 and 1979, average after-tax income rose about 25 percent per person in real terms. Except for the economic downturn of 1974–75 and the beginnings of recession in 1979, it rose steadily throughout the decade. Average income rose almost as fast in the 1970s as it had in the boom years of the 1960s.

In real terms, a lot of things are easier to afford now than they were in 1970 (see box, p. 19). Nearly everything is cheaper in this sense than it was in the Depression, despite what those who lived through it tell their children and grandchildren. Eggs, for example, went for about 38¢ a dozen in 1935. To earn that much, a typical worker (if he or she had a job) had to work nearly three quarters of an hour. In 1980 eggs cost about 88¢ a dozen. That took the typical wage earner about seven-and-a-half minutes to earn. By the same measurement, a color television set "cost" perhaps eighty-six hours of work in 1970. In 1980 a similar set cost only forty-two hours.

Sometimes, of course, real prices rise. If the world really is running out of oil, for instance, the price will eventually go up with or without the Organization of Petroleum Exporting Countries. And a hospital with a lot of modern sophisticated equipment in it will cost more per day in real terms than a hospital of the 1950s. As long as the economy is growing, though, most of the things we buy will be easier to afford every year. Inflation drives up prices, but in a growing economy people's income rises even faster.

Where the money went

A moment's reflection will convince you that it would be hard for inflation to be making *everyone* poorer. You and I and everybody else are spending a lot more money than we used to. But the stores, landlords, and banks that get the

TEN ITEMS THAT WERE EASIER TO AFFORD IN 1980 THAN IN 1970 . . .

Item	*Price Increase*
Potatoes	69%
Rent (residential)	79%
Clothing (men's & boys')	40%
TV sets	3%
Whiskey	29%
New cars	67%
Public transportation	81%
Refrigerators & freezers	57%
Telephone services	31%
Property taxes (residential)	56%

Consumer Price Index, same period up 110.7%

After-tax income, per person up 136%

& A FEW OF THE ITEMS THAT WENT UP THE FASTEST . . .

Fish & seafood	174%
Gasoline	257%
Hospital room	180%
Soft drinks	234%
Home maintenance services	141%

NOTE: Price increases for each item reflect changes in individual components of the Consumer Price Index. They compare the index figure for May 1980 with the 1970 annual-average index figure for the item in question. "After-tax income" compares the per capita disposable income figure for 1970 ($3,348) with the Census Bureau's figure for May 1980 ($7,894).

money don't just sit on it. They spend it—on wages, supplies, dividends, investments, and so forth. So do the governments that are collecting more and more of your money in taxes. Every dollar that comes in goes out—to pay a teacher or a tax collector, to provide benefits like social security, to build roads or cruise missiles. You may not like what businesses and governments do with your money, but you can't accuse them of not spending it. And one person's expenditure is another person's income.*

Money, of course, may be ending up in other people's pockets instead of yours. If stock dividends skyrocket while real wages fall—and you don't own any stock—then all the averages in the world won't convince you that you're better off than you used to be. The issue of who's getting the income may therefore be just as important as whether average income has kept up with inflation. And indeed, some specific groups have gained economic ground during the last ten years while other groups have fallen behind.

Welfare recipients—despite all the rhetoric about America's overgenerous welfare programs—have done badly. Average benefits under the Aid to Families with Dependent Children (AFDC) system dropped about 20 percent in real terms between 1970 and 1978. Single-parent families in general didn't do so well. Families headed by a single woman—about a sixth of all families, at last count—just about maintained their purchasing power in the last decade while other families' real incomes were increasing. Workers dependent on the minimum wage almost kept up but not quite: the federal minimum for most workers rose from $1.60 an hour in 1970 to $3.10 in 1980 while prices were a little more than doubling.

People employed in retail trade, finance, insurance, and real estate, on the average, lost ground. Librarians and college professors did too—full professors' real incomes dropped

* If a lot of money were flowing abroad, of course, Americans could be getting poorer while others were getting richer. And it's true that the United States' balance of payments has been getting worse, thanks in part to the rising price of imported oil. Still, the numbers are not huge. In 1977 through 1979, we imported about $30 billion a year worth of goods more than we exported, or roughly 1.5 percent of the Gross National Product. And the "current account" balance, which measures things like income from investments abroad as well as from exports, has actually been in surplus for much of the last decade.

nearly 10 percent between 1967 and 1978. Vacuum-cleaner salesmen, Avon ladies, household workers, and free-lance writers have all, by some reports, done poorly. So have cowboys. "Five, six years ago," one range rider in Arizona told a reporter, "the average cowboy in these parts made about three hundred dollars a month, along with room and board. Today he's still making about three hundred."

On the other side of the ledger, steelworkers have done well. Their average earnings rose from about $7,500 in 1967 to more than $19,500 in 1978—a gain, after inflation, of 35 percent. Most other blue-collar workers who belong to strong unions have more than kept up with rising prices. So have most federal employees, accountants, schoolteachers, police, and keypunch operators.

Among those who have more than kept pace—surprisingly, given the traditional belief that inflation hurts retired people most of all—are the elderly. The median income of those over sixty-five rose more than the average between 1970 and 1978. The proportion of old people under the government's poverty line fell from 25 percent in 1970 (about twice the national average) to 14 percent in 1977 (only a little more than the national average). One key to this unexpected development is social security, which accounts for roughly half of all the income going to the elderly. Benefits rose in real terms during the early years of the decade, and since 1975 have been increased yearly to keep up with the Consumer Price Index. Another key is private pensions. Since many private pension plans began after World War II, they cover a larger fraction of the elderly today than they did ten years ago. None of this, of course, means that the elderly have been handed the keys to Fort Knox. Their incomes, on the average, are lower than other people's, and many live perilously close to the poverty line. Those who counted on savings accounts or fixed-income pension plans to see them through have lost a good deal to inflation. On the whole, though, the situation of the elderly as a group has been getting better rather than worse.

Overall, the distribution of income has changed scarcely at all during the last decade. Neither the roiling inflation of the 1970s nor any other factor has made the poor significantly poorer or the rich significantly richer. Economists measure income distribution by dividing the population up into fifths (commonly called quintiles) according to how much money people are receiving. In 1978 you were in the highest quintile if your family's income was more than $28,632. Income under $8,720 put you in the bottom quintile. If your family brought in $17,640 you were right in the middle.

In 1970, the poorest quintile of families got 5.4 percent of the income, or a little more than one twentieth of the total. The richest quintile garnered 41 percent, or more than two fifths of the total. Thus the average family in the top group was bringing in nearly eight times what the average family in the bottom group was getting. In 1978 the bottom quintile's share was 5.2 percent and the top's was 41.5 percent. Everything else had stayed roughly the same too. Individuals may have moved up or down, but the economic ladder stayed put.

For the most part, different groups' winnings and losings cannot be blamed on inflation. Wage and other income variations depend more on politics and on changes in the marketplace than on changes in the price level. The elderly, for instance, have grown more numerous, and Congress has discovered that it is good politics to make sure that social security at least keeps up with inflation. Raising welfare benefits is not as popular, so those who depend on programs like Aid to Families with Dependent Children don't do as well. Oil-rig employees in Texas are likely to have done better in the last ten years than shoe-industry workers in Maine. People with skills that are in short supply and high demand—good corporate lawyers, for example, or electronic data-processing engineers—will do better than those who can more easily be replaced. Unionized workers will win wage gains more easily than unorganized workers, and so on.

Inflation's effects, moreover, frequently cut both ways. For

FALLING BEHIND INFLATION

• *Chief executive officers* of major American corporations saw their compensation increase only 9.7 percent in 1979 while inflation hit 13.3 percent, according to a study by Arthur Young & Company. The executives' salaries ranged from a low of $193,300 (CEO's in utility companies) to a high of $454,200 (CEO's in the petroleum and chemical industries).

• *Loan sharks* have maintained constant interest rates during the 1970s despite spiraling inflation, says an FBI special agent who supervises the Boston office's organized crime squad. The typical rate, the agent said, is about 5 percent a week, though it varies with the size of the loan and how well you know your neighborhood loan shark. The loan shark's business seems to increase with inflation: "investigators believe more persons may seek loan-shark money as inflation rises and credit becomes tighter," said one report.

SOURCES: "Executive Raises Trail Inflation Rate," *The New York Times,* August 26, 1980; Richard J. Connolly, "Loansharks Holding the Line on Inflation," *The Boston Globe,* May 19, 1980.

example, inflation is supposed to hurt those who work in industries like automobiles or electronics that must compete with imports. If the other country's prices are standing still, it does; U.S. goods get priced out of the market. But for most of the 1970s prices were going up faster in every other large industrial nation except West Germany than they were in the United States. So inflation "helped" those industries rather than hurt them. Similarly, inflation is supposed to hurt those who live on fixed incomes. It does. But most Americans do not live on fixed incomes. Those who do are as likely to be rich bondholders clipping their coupons as poor pensioners with no social security.

INFLATION IN THE NECESSITIES

One interesting notion making the rounds in the late 1970s was that inflation made the poor worse off because of what they spent their money on. The argument, first developed by economists associated with a group called the Exploratory Project for Economic Alternatives (later the National Center for Economic Alternatives) in Washington, was called the "four necessities" theory.

According to the theory, four basic necessities of life —food, fuel, housing, and health care—were going up in price faster than other goods and services. Since the poor presumably spend a larger fraction of their income than the rich on necessities, their purchasing power was going down faster than the purchasing power of those who were better off to begin with. The rapid rise in food and oil prices during the 1970s lent credibility to the argument.

Other studies, however, disagreed with its premises and its conclusions. Both the Cambridge (Massachusetts) economics magazine *Dollars and Sense* and Brookings researcher Joseph J. Minarik pointed out that the theory (as *Dollars and Sense* put it) "does not correctly identify the dividing line between luxuries and necessities." Clothing, for instance, is not counted in the necessities column—and clothing prices rose more slowly than most in the 1970s. And the "food" component of the Consumer Price Index, as Minarik noted, "includes not only basic food items but also sirloin steaks and restaurant dinners—hardly essential fare."

Moreover, calculations by *Dollars and Sense* and by sociologist Christopher Jencks showed that the actual market basket of goods that poor people spent their money on rose in price at about the same rate as everyone else's market baskets. The magazine reported its findings this way: "Dividing consumer spending into thirty different items, and calculating price indexes for each tenth of the population from the poorest to the richest, D&S found that from 1967 to 1978 the price indexes for each tenth increased between 93.4% and 95.0%. That is, the degree of inflation experienced by different groups varied only slightly." What about food and oil? The theory, *Dollars and Sense* said, "overlooks the fact that these prices move in spurts, whereas other prices rose steadily though less dramatically. From 1975 through 1978, food and gasoline prices rose more slowly than consumer prices as a whole."

In a sense of course this debate is beside the point. Some poor people have probably not lost ground to inflation during the last decade—thanks in part, as Minarik points out, to the "implicit indexing of medicare, medicaid, and various forms of rent subsidies, and [to] the explicit indexing of food stamps." Other poor people undoubtedly have lost ground. But the poor are in many ways more vulnerable to any economic reversal than are those with more to lose. A lost job or a rising fuel bill is hard to cope with if you have nothing besides welfare to fall back on. And the uncertainty of inflation will weigh more heavily on those who are barely getting by than on those with more of an economic cushion.

NOTE: The original study was published as "Understanding the New Inflation: The Importance of the Basic Necessities" (Washington: Exploratory Project for Economic Alternatives, 1977). The study's principal author, Leslie Ellen Nulty, developed a similar argument in "How Inflation Hits the Majority," *Challenge: The Magazine of Economic Affairs*, January/February 1979, pp. 32–38. The response by Jencks appeared in *Working Papers for a New Society*, September/October 1978, pp. 8–11 ff.; the *Dollars and Sense* critique is in the magazine's October 1979 issue, pp. 14–15; and the Minarik critique can be found in the *Brookings Bulletin*, vol. XVI, number 4 (1980), pp. 8–10.

Nest eggs and homes: inflation's effects on assets

"The only thing wealth does for some people," wrote the Comte de Rivarol in the late eighteenth century, "is make them worry about losing it." Inflationary times inevitably increase the number of worriers, for rising prices do have indisputable effects on assets. As with the income-expenditure balance sheet, though, the effects are mixed. And the question of who's really poorer because of inflation remains as obscure as before.

At the end of 1978, stock prices on the New York Stock Exchange were more than 30 percent lower (in real terms) than in 1970—and 1970 itself was an unusually poor year for stocks, with prices already nearly 25 percent below their 1965 level. The value of long-term corporate triple-A-rated bonds fell by almost half over the same period. In 1980 it looked for a while as if the bottom would drop out of the long-term bond market altogether. Though values subsequently recovered, it was no longer a place where the jittery investor could find a haven.

The reason for the decline in stock prices is the subject of considerable debate among economists, brokers, and the investors who lost at least the buttons off their shirts. Inflation is only one among several villains that commonly get blamed. With bonds, inflation's role is harder to deny. Rising prices in fact may have done in the long-term bond market all by themselves.

One undeniable effect of inflation is that it drives up interest rates—not the interest you get on your bank account, necessarily, since that's regulated by law, but the interest rates on bonds and other devices by which businesses and governments borrow money. Interest rates rise partly because nobody wants to lend money unless they can make a little profit over and above the expected rate of inflation.

Now suppose you own a $10,000 bond paying 5 percent, purchased, say, in 1966, and coming to maturity (that's when the bond issuer gives you your money back) in 1996. In stable times, your bond is worth essentially $10,000 because you can sell it for something approximating that figure on the open market. In inflationary times, though, you're in trouble. New bonds issued by corporations are paying 8, 10, or even 15 percent. No one wants your bond unless they can get it for substantially less than its face value. The bond's market price—its value to you right now—has dropped. The only way you'll get your $10,000 back is to hold the bond to maturity, and by that time your ten grand may buy you no more than a ten-speed bicycle.

So financial assets haven't done very well, thanks in part to inflation. Who's poorer? Banks, insurance companies, pension funds, and other institutional investors are. So are the very rich. At last count, about four fifths of the American people owned no stocks or bonds. About half of all the stock and three fifths of all the bonds owned by individuals were owned by people in the richest 1 percent of the population. Doubtless people in this category believe that hard times are upon us; doubtless too, some worthy individuals who are not rich have been hard hit by the drop in stocks and bonds. But their cries of anguish should not be allowed to obscure the silence with which most Americans greet the changes that shake Wall Street.

The main asset that a lot of people do own is a home. Here the trend has been exactly opposite. Between 1970 and 1978 the price of existing homes (as distinct from newly built homes) rose almost two thirds more than average prices. This rapid increase is usually reported in terms of the hardships it places on young families and others looking to buy a house. It can also be viewed as a dramatic rise in the value of the primary asset owned by the average American. According to economist Alan Greenspan, homes increased in value a total of more than a trillion dollars between 1974 and 1980. "Inflation is not all bad," California Senator Alan Cranston is reported to have said. "After all, it has allowed every

American to live in a more expensive neighborhood without moving."

Homeowners' equity undoubtedly rose even faster than home values. If you buy a house for $50,000, with $10,000 down and a $40,000 mortgage, you are said to have $10,000 worth of equity in the house. Suppose now that you can sell the house for $55,000. Your equity has risen from $10,000 to $15,000, an increase of 50 percent.

The cost of a house would have gone up in the 1970s with or without inflation, primarily because the baby-boom generation (born in the years after World War II) was getting to home-buying age and was bidding the prices up. But inflation played a part too. Investors and speculators saw early on that real estate values were consistently beating inflation, and so began to buy more property. As they did so, prices rose. More investors and speculators were then attracted to real estate, and more middle-income families stretched their budgets to buy a home because it looked like a good investment.

Also, for most of the 1970s, mortgage interest rates were low compared to the rate of inflation. If you borrowed money at 8 percent to buy a house while inflation was nearing double digits, your loan essentially cost you nothing. At the same time, inflation-induced wage and salary hikes were driving everyone into higher tax brackets. The tax breaks the government gives homeowners–you can deduct both mortgage interest payments and property taxes from your taxable income, which is a little like allowing tenants to deduct half or even three quarters of their rent–thus became ever more important. Both of these effects increased the number of potential buyers and made it possible for people to afford more expensive homes than they otherwise could.

The rise in the value of homes as opposed to stocks and bonds does not mean that the poor have been surreptitiously getting rich or the rich poor. Many of the poor don't own homes and many of the rich own a lot of them. Stockholders have lost some portfolio value, but the after-tax profits that pay their dividends have remained generally healthy for most of the decade. Those who sell houses are richer, but those who buy them are poorer; sometimes the same person does both, and winds up back where he or she started. On the whole, probably the very richest people (with the most financial assets) have lost some of their wealth and probably a lot of middle-income people have gained some wealth. How much these gains and losses might come to, no one knows.

The money illusion

Despite all these numbers, a lot of us feel that we're worse off than we used to be. If we didn't feel that way we wouldn't worry about inflation. And inflation is consistently near the top of the list when polltakers ask people what they think is America's number-one problem.

Why should this be? The very rich and the very poor, as we have seen, have good reason to be aggrieved with inflation. At the top, rising prices have undermined more than a few bond portfolios. At the bottom, welfare benefits have not kept up with the cost of living and thus have fallen in real terms. Yet if prices had remained stable, benefits probably would have too. Legislators are never overjoyed with the prospect of raising welfare levels, but they don't particularly like to cut them either.

Other losers, though, are in some ways deceived by rising prices. If prices remained stable, those who lost economic ground would have seen their incomes fall. Workers in declining industries or regions would have lost their jobs, or would have been forced to take wage cuts. Owners of failing businesses and partly vacant buildings would have seen profits drop off and rents dry up. In inflationary times, most of those who are losing ground see their money incomes rising—just not as fast as prices. The true villain is whatever has caused their real income to drop—new competition, business reversals, bad management, shifts in technology or in taste. But the only villain that shows its face is inflation.

Everybody else is subject to a similar kind of money illusion, even when their real incomes are going up. Most of us feel entitled to a raise in pay as we grow older, gain seniority, advance in career or profession. These raises are supposed to enable us to take winter vacations in the Caribbean one year or buy a new motorboat the next. Most of us get the raises. But inflation makes us uncertain as to what the raises will be worth, and seems to eat up every additional dollar. MIT economist Lester C. Thurow, noting that real incomes rose 16 percent between 1972 and 1978 while money incomes went up 74 percent, describes the effect this way: "If the milkman were a moneyman, and you expected him to deliver $74 to your door in the morning but instead he delivered only $16, you would feel cheated. You are $16 better off than you were, but you can imagine what life would be like with the $74. You may even be able to convince yourself that your real standard of living has fallen." Thus does a rising price level camouflage what is really taking place.

In keeping with this role as smokescreen and scapegoat, inflation has concealed one real change in the economy that is helping us all feel poorer. This is the relatively sluggish growth in many people's real wages. In 1960 the typical worker in private industry was making $2.09 an hour. By 1965 this wage had risen to $2.46 and by 1970 to $3.23. Allowing for inflation, the increase worked out to an average gain of about 1.8 percent a year.

By 1975 the wage had gone up to $4.53 an hour, and by 1979 it was $6.16. This time, though, real gains amounted to only about 2 percent over the whole decade. The major reason was that in the 1973–75 recession—and again in 1979—real wages for this group of workers fell, and the drops in those years brought down the decade's average. In 1979, the typical private-sector worker was making little more, in real terms, than he or she was making in 1970.*

To be sure, average incomes were rising: remember the

* Note that this comparison refers to hourly wages. Much has been made of the fact that average *weekly* earnings have stagnated or even fallen, depending on what year you start from. Weekly wage statistics,

average after-tax income figures mentioned above. Average incomes went up partly because many sources of income rose faster than the wages of rank-and-file private-sector workers. Social security benefits, government employees' wages, and many higher-level salaries all did better than inflation. Incomes also went up because a larger fraction of the population was working. If, for example, your spouse went to work for the first time during the 1970s, your family's real income undoubtedly rose regardless of how well you yourself were keeping up with inflation. But the improvement in your standard of living may not have given you much satisfaction for long. Spending the money proved easy—in fact you may have known what the money would go for (college educations, old medical bills) before your spouse went to work. And now you have to worry about whether both of you can keep up with inflation, because there's no one left to go to work. When both members of a couple are working, a family is as likely to feel strapped as it is to feel well-provided for. In that sense the relative prosperity of the 1970s was small comfort, and worries about keeping up with inflation persisted.

The trouble with inflation

This chapter's objective, so far, has been to relieve inflation of some of its extraneous burdens—to put it in perspective. Not all the economic hardships we feel are due to inflation. Not all are even as real as they seem. If the story ended here, the moral would be simply to

---

however, lump together full-time and part-time workers. Since part-timers are more numerous today than they used to be, the average can look low even when hourly wages are rising.

The hourly figures too are subject to interpretation. According to *The Wall Street Journal*, for instance, Labor Department economist Paul Ryscavage believes that the larger number of young people in the work force these days—because they typically earn less than older workers—may be pulling down the average wage, "even though all workers may individually be as well off as workers of their ages have ever been."

learn to live with the beast. Unfortunately it doesn't.

For one thing, America is not alone in the world. Americans are generally well protected against the proverbial ravages of inflation. So are the citizens of most other industrialized countries (even Israel, where the inflation rate hit 111.4 percent in 1979). Citizens of poor countries are not. In Ghana during the 1970s, the price of food rose almost half again as fast as average prices, to the point where a couple of pounds of fish or poultry cost the typical worker a full day's wages. In Peru, workers' purchasing power dropped by half between 1976 and 1980, and the price of bread rose tenfold. The noncommunist world's economy is highly interconnected, and America is in many ways at the center. When the United States sneezes, it used to be said, the rest of the world catches cold. Now the United States has a cold and the rest of the world is lucky if it gets off with double pneumonia.

Inflation's effects at home can't easily be ignored either. It may not be making us poorer, but it does make us uncertain. And uncertainty has effects of its own.

Suppose you knew that prices were going to go up 10 percent a year, inexorably and invariably. If you knew that your income was going to rise at least that much every year—plus whatever you could add through working harder, moving up the hierarchy, or bargaining for a share of your company's profits—you wouldn't be nervous at all. The 10 percent annual price hike would quickly be reflected both in interest rates on mortgages and other loans and in what you could earn on your money in a savings bank or other investment. You would mentally adjust to prices doubling about every seven years, knowing that the price increases weren't "real."

If you knew prices were going up 10 percent but didn't know how much your income would go up, you'd be considerably more nervous. The chances are you would do whatever you could—take two jobs, press for militant union activity, lobby for special treatment for your business, and so on—to ensure that your income would keep pace. It might not take too long before most workers got cost-of-living adjustments written into their contracts. (Slightly less than half of the unionized workers covered by major collective bargaining agreements now have these adjustments.)

The situation at present is even worse than this. You think prices will rise, but you don't know how much, and there's always the chance of inflation rates up around 20 percent or more. Unless you have an unusually good job (or happen to own a few oil wells, in which case you may not care), you have no way of knowing whether your income will keep pace. Most investments are uncertain. Even borrowing is risky, because the economy might take a sharp downturn. That, you think, might cure inflation, but you might be out of a job. Uncertainty is a fact of life. But inflation intensifies it, and before long the economy begins to look like a giant lottery, with winners and losers chosen at random.

Businesses face the same kind of uncertainty. Why build a new plant or modernize the old one if you aren't sure what's happening to the economy, or how much things will cost next year? On the other hand, maybe you should build or modernize right now, before prices go up again. Is it prudent to borrow money, even though interest rates seem unbelievably high? Maybe it's foolish *not* to borrow money. Interest rates may go still higher tomorrow, and if inflation gets worse you'll be repaying your loan in ever-cheaper dollars.

The results of this kind of uncertainty and the widely remarked "loss of confidence" it has apparently led to are by no means clear. At worst, as some economists believe, uncertainty makes businesses unwilling to invest, consumers unwilling to save, and everyone unwilling to work hard, innovate, and be productive. Economic growth thus slows to a crawl. At best, uncertainty makes for a highly volatile economic environment, in which every organized group is desperately trying to push its own interests to the exclusion of everybody else's. This may be the economic reality behind the "me decade" recently ended. It may also be the reason for the apparent stalemate of governmental initiative. When all are screaming loudly, the safest course for a politician is to do nothing that offends anyone. Ordinarily that means doing nothing at all.

Worst of all, inflation has a dismaying tendency to feed on itself. As long as it's mild, as in the 1950s and early 1960s, it can be tolerated and held in check. When it begins to get worse, as it did in the late 1960s and 1970s, presidents of the United States and chairmen of the Federal Reserve Board feel they have to do something before it gets out of control. Their attempts usually entail engineering a recession, as in 1974–75 and again in 1980. Recessions by definition lower our standard of living. Production falls and real incomes drop. If inflation weren't so bad, the measures employed against it might not have to be so drastic.

Before we examine how inflation got this far, it is worth remembering that what we're looking at is an unprecedented phenomenon. The American economy has always had periods of rising prices. Today's prices, however, have been rising consistently for more than forty years, and have doubled in the last ten. Inflation of this sort is new to history.

For most of the nineteenth century—except during wartime—prices edged downward. A basket of goods that cost $50 in 1800 was selling for $42 in 1820, $30 in 1840, $27 in 1860, $29 in 1880, and $25 in 1900. The first four decades of this century seemed little different. World War I brought inflation, but prices fell 10 percent in the recession of 1921 and 6 percent more in 1922. When the Great Depression hit, prices dropped an average of 6 percent a year for four years. They fell again in 1938 and 1939 after rising a little in the middle thirties. The pattern was clear: war and boom times brought inflation, and a slump then ended it. Prices returned to normal.

After World War II, prices stopped falling. Now they rose a little every year. If the economy was in recession they might stop rising momentarily, but when the recession ended they resumed their upward course. In the 1970s prices rose faster than ever and were harder to check. The recession of 1974–75, for example, was by all accounts the worst of the postwar era. It did what observers hoped it would: ended the threat of runaway inflation. Prices had been rising 12 percent in 1974; they rose only 5 to 7 percent in the following three years. But note the difference. In the old days, a recession made *prices* fall. Inflation disappeared altogether. Now only the *rate of inflation* fell. Prices kept on rising and, despite the recession, were still going up faster than they had in almost any previous year.

The way our economy works, in short, had changed. The next several chapters will trace these changes. Some go back to the late nineteenth century, before their inflationary effects were noticed. Some appeared in the Depression, and some in the years during and immediately after World War II. All these changes help account for the apparently irreversible inflation we have experienced since the war. Finally, some changes turned up only in the 1970s, and explain the virulence of inflation during the last ten years.

Many readers doubtless have a theory as to which change will turn out to be the villain. Some will blame the minimum wage, the disappearance of the gold standard, federal budget deficits. Others will look at the swollen Pentagon budget, corporate profiteering, the abuses of Big Labor, or the ineptitude of the Federal Reserve. For the moment, all such theories should be set aside. The story of inflation is not a potboiler, where the culprit will be revealed at the end. It is more like a jigsaw puzzle, with each piece fitting together in a particular way and at the end revealing a picture you didn't know was there.

The various pieces have historical roots, but understanding them involves looking at the present as much as at the past—and eventually at that enigmatic golden age between 1945 and 1965, which ended with people grousing about the high cost of living. The starting point, inevitably, is prices, for without rising prices there is no inflation.

2. The Inflationary System: Big Business

Prices, we generally assume, are set by supply and demand.

"Demand" means how much consumers are willing to spend for something—how badly they want it, and how much they can afford to pay for it. "Supply" means how much is available for sale at various possible prices. If consumers want more of something than is immediately available, the price rises. If they want less, the price falls. The moving price, in turn, attracts more buyers or sellers as the case may be.

This introductory lesson in economics is not entirely useless. It explains why sporting goods stores that bought too many skis in October put them on sale in March (demand has fallen relative to supply). It also explains why the price of oranges rises after a cold winter in Florida (supply has fallen relative to demand). Supply and demand can even explain the way a whole market behaves: the stock market, for instance. Suppose Mobil Oil discovers a new offshore strike. More people now want to buy Mobil shares than wanted to yesterday, and fewer people want to sell them. So the price of a share rises. Now suppose that the Justice Department hauls Mobil into court on serious price-fixing charges. The stock suddenly doesn't look so good, and the price falls.

The market as a whole responds to supply and demand just the way an individual stock does. Favorable economic news persuades a few more investors to buy stocks, and the Dow-Jones goes up. Unfavorable economic news—the election of a Democrat to the presidency, traditionally—causes the market to fall. Supply and demand vary as investors' perceptions, expectations, and strategies change.* Stock prices respond to these changes with astonishing sensitivity and quickness. They do so, of course, because of competition. A dim-witted broker trying to peddle a stock for more than the going price wouldn't find any takers. Buyers would simply take their business to the next broker in line.

Elsewhere in the economy, however, things aren't so simple. To be sure, economists frequently use the same word: a "market" is simply all the ways by which buyers and sellers of anything get in touch with one another and conduct their business. But the market for toothpaste, for psychoanalysis, or for the services of a computer programmer doesn't look much like the New York Stock Exchange. In these markets, supply and demand are but dim shadows of their former selves. They are limited, interfered with, regulated, propped up, constrained, or controlled. Competition is muted, restricted, or banished entirely. Prices, as a result, do not glide effortlessly up and down the way they do on the stock market. They move jerkily, and they depend more on what the seller decides than on what the marketplace determines.

Most markets, to put it succinctly, are rigged. Since they are rigged to favor the seller rather than the buyer, prices will go up more easily than they go down. That is the First —maybe the Only—Law of Inflation. The next few chapters will explain how it works. In the meantime, note only that rigging a market is neither as difficult nor as reprehensible as it might seem. The mechanisms by which various companies, industries, professions, and workers accomplish it

* The long-run supply of stock—that is, the total number of shares issued by companies listed on a stock exchange—is huge, and changes only by small increments. "Supply" in this context means existing shares that are offered for sale on the market.

will not, once they are pointed out, sound either strange or evil.

Managing the marketplace

In 1882, an oatmeal producer named Henry P. Crowell built a fancy new mill—"the first in the world," as one historian describes it, that could "grade, clean, hull, cut, package, and ship oatmeal to interstate markets in a continuous process." The only trouble with the mill was that there weren't enough buyers for all the oatmeal it could turn out.

Then Crowell hit upon an idea. He packaged his brand—it was called Quaker Oats—and called it a breakfast cereal, a commodity that was virtually unknown in America at the time. He advertised it heavily, employing box-top premiums, prizes, testimonials, scientific endorsements, and other gimmicks. He set up sales offices to market the product and hired field agents to buy oats directly from midwestern farmers. In 1888 Crowell joined with two other big producers of oatmeal to form the American Cereal Company, and thirteen years later the firm became the Quaker Oats Company. It shortly added new products—wheat cereals, farina, hominy, cornmeal, specialized baby foods, and animal feeds—and by 1917 was the fifteenth largest food products concern in the country.

Today Quaker Oats is, so to speak, a medium-sized giant corporation. It does about two billion dollars' worth of business a year, and ranks twenty-fourth in size among food-processing companies. In breakfast cereals Quaker is now fourth, behind Kellogg's, General Mills, and General Foods. Together these four firms sell nearly all of the breakfast cereal sold in America. Among their brand names are Puffed Rice, Puffed Wheat, Life, Corn Bran, Cap'n Crunch, Crunch Berries, Quips, Total, Body Buddies, Count Chocula, Boo Berry, Cocoa Puffs, Kix, and Trix, as well as the familiar Wheaties, Cheerios, Corn Flakes, and the like.

With appropriate variations, the story of Quaker Oats and its colleagues in the cereal business is the story of the several hundred other giant industrial firms that dominate the $2.5 trillion American economy. In the late nineteenth century, the rapid spread of railroad lines opened up huge markets, and made it possible for manufacturers to obtain large supplies of raw materials relatively cheaply. The abundance of coal for steam engines meant that factories no longer had to rely on water power to run their machinery; it also made possible the development of new industrial processes requiring intense heat, such as the Bessemer process of steel production. Other technological development, on the order of Henry Crowell's continuous-process mill, vastly increased the speed at which plants could turn out finished products. Companies that first took advantage of the new techniques and new markets grew very large very quickly. Typically a few of the biggest then combined into one even larger behemoth, just as Crowell joined with his erstwhile competitors to form American Cereal.

At present, the 500 largest industrial firms—Quaker Oats ranks 176th on *Fortune* magazine's famous list—do an average of nearly $3 billion worth of business a year. Together they account for more than three quarters of everything manufactured in America. They employ approximately one worker out of every six—an average of 32,400 per firm. They own more than a trillion dollars' worth of assets, and in 1979 made more than $78 billion in profits.

Typically, a few of these giant firms dominate an industry, often with several other good-sized companies doing most of the remaining business. All manufacture and market a variety of individual products. Most of these are sold on a brand-name basis: they are differentiated from others in the industry and advertised for their special advantages. These advantages may be real, as with an unusually dependable television set. Or they may be imaginary, as with the gusto that characterizes the life of Schlitz drinkers.

The companies are for the most part highly integrated. They own outright some of the farms, mines, and manufacturers that supply them with materials, parts, and equip-

OTHER BIG COMPANIES

Large size is not limited to industrial concerns.

• In *retailing*, Sears, Roebuck & Company did some $17 billion worth of business in 1979, about 2 percent of total retail sales in that year. Safeway and K mart, two other giant retailers, each did more than $12 billion worth.

• In the *food and lodging* industry, McDonald's, Marriott, and Holiday Inns are all billion-dollar corporations. In *communications*, the giants are Time, Inc. ($2.5 billion in sales for 1979), the Times-Mirror Company ($1.6 billion), the Gannett chain ($1 billion), and of course the broadcasting networks.

• The largest *banks* in America are BankAmerica (based in California) and Citicorp (based in New York). The biggest insurance company is Aetna Life & Casualty. And the biggest company of all, measured by profits and by number of employees, is the American Telephone & Telegraph Company.

SOURCE: "*Business Week*'s Corporate Scoreboard: How 1,200 Companies Performed in 1979," *Business Week,* March 17, 1980, pp. 81–116.

ment. U.S. Steel, for instance, gets two thirds of the coal it uses from its own mines. In other cases they establish long-term contracts with their suppliers, often on terms they themselves dictate. They assure markets for their products not only through sophisticated selling techniques (of which conventional advertising is only a part) but through an extensive sales force, network of distributors, or both. The reason for their long reach is not obscure. No billion-dollar corporation can afford to depend on uncontrolled sources of supply. Nor can it produce a million boxes of oatmeal or a hundred thousand steel ingots and hope that somebody somewhere will buy them at a reasonable price. Supply and demand are thus managed, not by the invisible hand of the marketplace but by the visible hand (in historian Alfred D. Chandler's phrase) of corporate management.

No industry is exactly typical. One, though, can be seen as prototypical: it illustrates in virtually pure form how the big companies conduct their business. Art students learn technique by studying the masters. Students of the economy can learn much from those who have cultivated the art of managing the marketplace.

In 1880, a man named James Bonsack filed for a patent on a machine capable of manufacturing cigarettes. As William Bennett describes it, the machine "poured a uniform flow of tobacco through a device resembling the wool feeder of a carding machine into a thin strip of paper. The paper was rolled into a single continuous tube. As it emerged from the machine, the tobacco-filled tube was cut into equal lengths." At the time, the most highly skilled worker could turn out several thousand handmade cigarettes a day. Bonsack's machine produced over 70,000 a day while still in its experimental stages; by the late 1880s it could make over 120,000 a day. "Fifteen such machines," writes Alfred D. Chandler, "could fill the total demand for cigarettes in the United States in 1880, and thirty could have saturated the 1885 market."

James B. Duke, a North Carolina tobacco entrepreneur, signed a contract with Bonsack in 1885. In 1890 Duke and four other firms joined to form the American Tobacco Company. By 1900, after pioneering in some of the advertising and marketing techniques that Quaker Oats's Crowell and others would later imitate, Duke controlled more than three fifths of the smoking and chewing tobacco industry. In 1911 the American Tobacco Company was broken up by the Supreme Court in an antitrust decision. The three new companies that were created after the decision–R.J. Reynolds, Liggett & Myers, and P. Lorillard–accounted, along with American Tobacco, for over 90 percent of the cigarette market by 1925.

Today, some of the companies have new names. American Brands has replaced American Tobacco (no more "tobacco is our middle name" ads), and the Liggett Group has replaced Liggett & Myers. Lorillard is a division of Loew's Corporation. R.J. Reynolds ranks thirty-ninth on *Fortune*'s list of the 500 largest industrial companies; Philip Morris ranks forty-ninth. These five companies, along with the Brown & Williamson Tobacco Corp. (a subsidiary of a British concern), produce virtually all of the roughly 700 billion cigarettes manufactured in America. Reynolds and Philip Morris alone account for over 60 percent of the market.

Production is even more highly mechanized than it used to be. At Philip Morris's modern Richmond, Virginia, plant, reports *The Boston Globe,* machines do virtually all the work: "From the time workers peel the wooden sides from the 1000-pound hogsheads of tobacco there is not another hand operation until workers stack cases of packaged cigarettes in the packing room." The cigarettes themselves have undergone refinement as well. "Much of the tobacco in modern cigarettes," says the *Globe,* "has been pulverized to a paste, homogenized, sterilized, reconstituted, freeze-dried, chemically altered . . . and then sprayed with flavors that sound more like the recipe for chicken curry or candy than cigarettes." These flavors include "cardamom, pepper, clove, nutmeg, cascarilla, vanilla, rum, honey, raisin, prune, dates, and the old standbys cocoa and licorice. And these are just the natural flavors."

Nowhere, however, have the improvements been as dramatic as in marketing. The companies have a lot at stake in this area. According to industry analysts, 1 percent of the cigarette market amounts to about $100 million worth of sales, or about $20 million in pre-tax profits. To increase their market share, the companies have hit upon an unusual but effective strategy: "dividing the smoking population into relatively tiny sociological groups," as *The Wall Street Journal* describes it, "and then aiming one or more brands at each group." Once most smokers "chose from among three brands: Camel, Chesterfield, and Lucky Strike. Today, more than 160 brands adorn the retail shelves."

Brands are differentiated from each other, and directed at the target population, partly by the content and style of their advertising: "Vantage and Merit, for example, are aimed at young women, and Camel and Winston are aimed mostly at rural smokers." They are also differentiated by paper color, package color, location and style of filter, length, and package design. Long cigarettes and recessed filters appeal to women. The brown paper of More cigarettes "is supposed to convey a 'riverboat gambler look.' " Red packs suggest flavor, green packs coolness, white packs safety. Philip Morris "heightened the appeal to the stylish of its Benson & Hedges brand by printing the company's Park Avenue address on the front and back of each pack." The same company's Merit brand—in a package with big yellow, brown, and orange racing stripes—"is intended to connote a 'flamboyant, young-in-spirit image.' " One company market-tested thirty-three different packages before deciding on a blue, gold, and red design (Viceroy Rich Lights).

All this costs money. The industry spent nearly half a billion dollars on newspaper and magazine advertising alone in 1978, and the investment necessary to bring out a new cigarette has recently been estimated as high as $50 million. But it has paid off. Despite a ban on television advertising and despite increasingly stringent health warnings printed at the government's behest on all advertisements and cigarette packages, per capita consumption of cigarettes has stayed roughly constant at about 4,000 per year, or an average of half a pack a day for smokers and nonsmokers alike. Industry profits, meanwhile, went up 32 percent in 1979 over 1978, a gain in real terms of nearly one fifth.

Managing prices

Even if you don't smoke, one fact about cigarettes is unlikely to have escaped you. You do not see signs on the window of the grocery store down the street saying "Camels—special this week. Only 50¢ the pack." Nor do you see magazine ads contending that Winstons cost less than Marlboros. As every smoker knows, cigarettes all cost the same. If this were the stock market, we would be forced to conclude that the ratio of supply to demand was the same for every brand. Moreover, since cigarette prices all go up at the same time, the ratio would always have to be changing at the same rate. Since it is the cigarette market, we may entertain more plausible hypotheses as to why cigarettes all cost the same. These hypotheses, however, will have to apply to a lot of different industries, for cigarettes are more nearly typical of the way things are priced than are stocks. Ordinarily, big companies sell their wares at prices very similar to those of their competitors. Ordinarily, too, these prices change by similar amounts at roughly the same time. To understand why prices behave this way is to understand one important element of inflation.

Sometimes prices are similar because companies have conspired to fix them. In a single week in 1980, for example, *The Wall Street Journal* reported that four big gypsum firms had settled a fifteen-year-old price-fixing suit brought by the Justice Department; that five companies had been indicted on charges of fixing the prices for glassine and greaseproof paper; and that two school-supply companies were close to settling a Federal Trade Commission and grand-jury investigation charging them with fixing the price of wax crayons. Indictments and settlements, of course, do not constitute guilt. But the number of cases suggests that price-fixing is not yet a thing of the past.

More often, price-fixing is unnecessary. One firm simply

acts as "price leader," with the others following suit. For many years U.S. Steel played this role in its industry. "About 20 years ago," writes economist Robert R. Nathan, "when Estes Kefauver was chairman of the Senate Subcommittee on Monopoly, he had some steel executives testifying before him. He said to one steel executive, 'When U.S. Steel raised its price 5.738 percent, why did you raise your price 5.738 percent?' The fellow answered, 'To be competitive.' " The usage has grown common. The phrase "competitive prices," in the lexicon of the business world, usually means prices that are the same as everybody else's, not prices designed to undercut the competition.

Recently, U.S. Steel has come on hard times. This has not changed the practice of price leadership, only the roles. "U.S. Steel Corp.," reported *The Wall Street Journal* in March of 1980, "joined several other major steelmakers in a 5% average price increase on sheet and strip products." Around the same time, the Aluminum Company of America (Alcoa) raised that metal's price from 66¢ to 72¢ a pound. "Other major producers," commented the *Journal* drily, "are expected to follow." A day later, the *Journal* reported that General Motors was raising new-car prices 2.2 percent. Within seven days Ford, American Motors, Chrysler, and Volkswagen announced increases in the same range. Ford's and Chrysler's were exactly 2.2 percent.

At times the prices charged by big companies for their consumer goods seem unnecessarily high. Bristol-Myers' Bufferin, for example, was retailing for $2.35 per 100-tablet bottle as this book went to press. The price was roughly comparable to that of other nationally advertised pain relievers: Anacin ($2.66), and Excedrin ($2.39). It did not compare so well with a bottle of generic buffered aspirin manufactured by the Republic Drug Corporation of Buffalo, New York, and located on the pharmacist's shelf right next to the Bufferin. That product—essentially identical to Bufferin—was going for $1.85, or about 80 percent of what Bufferin cost.

Other times the prices of manufactured goods seem reason-

CIGARETTES AND STOCKS

How Two Sets of Prices Rose and Fell in the 1970s

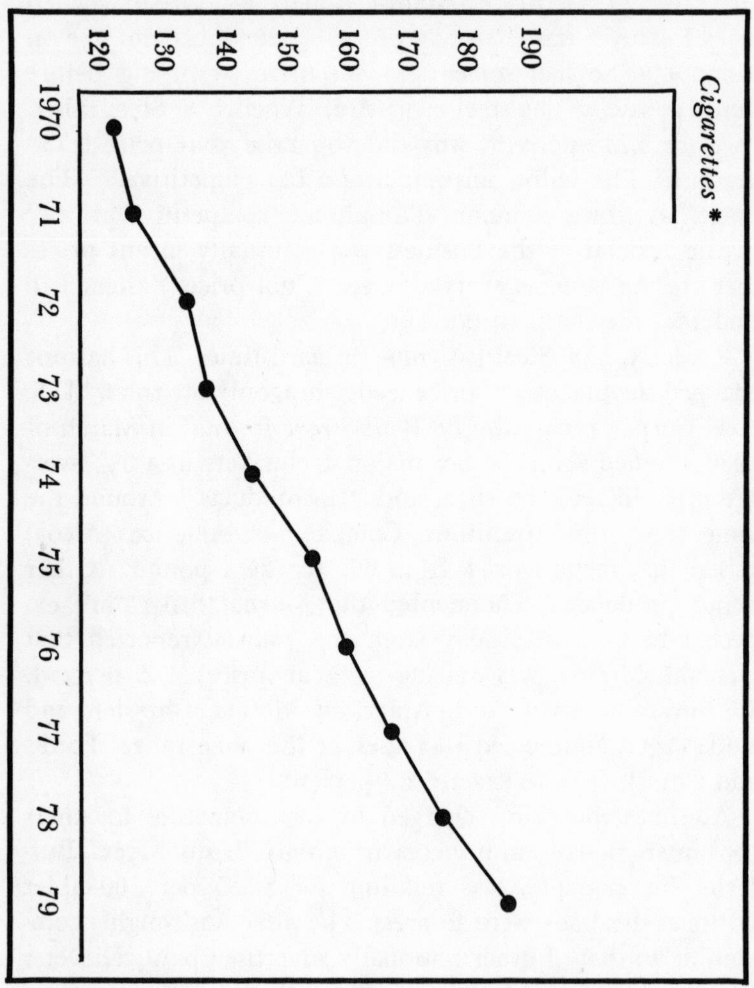

* "Tobacco Products" price index, Bureau of Labor Statistics

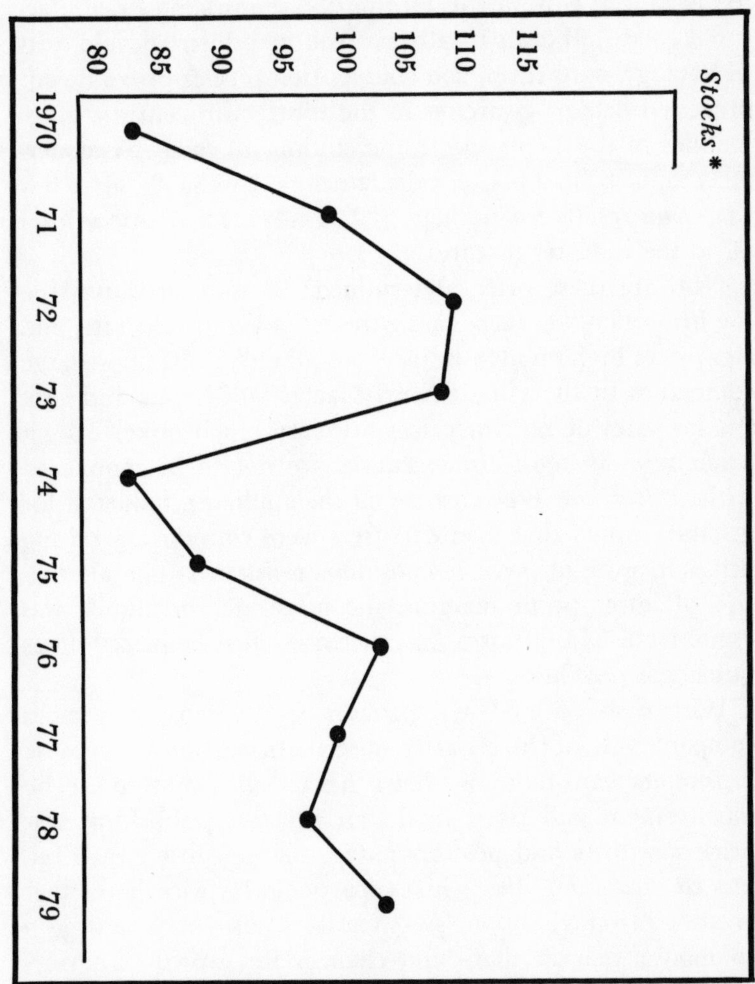

* Standard & Poor's common index (500 stocks)

SOURCES: The "tobacco products" price index is found in the *Handbook of Labor Statistics,* and is updated in the *Monthly Labor Review.* Standard & Poor's common index appears in the *Statistical Abstract,* p. 543, and is updated in the Commerce Department's monthly magazine *Survey of Current Business.*

able; certainly they are low in comparison with what they would be if the goods were manufactured by hand or with less advanced equipment. Ordinarily, the prices of manufactured goods fall dramatically as a young industry develops its technology, costs drop, and competition pushes prices down: processed oats or cigarettes in the nineteenth century, automobiles in the 1920s, electronic equipment today. A moderately sophisticated pocket calculator that cost $150 only a few years ago retails for perhaps $22.95 now. Then prices level off as the industry matures.

How are these prices determined? By most accounts, the big firm calculates its costs, figures a "target" profit rate, and sets prices high enough to meet that target. Since most large companies in the same industry face similar costs and seek similar rates of return, prices are very much alike. Target profit rates in most circumstances are not to be monkeyed with. A *Business Week* article on the appliance industry, for instance, noted that manufacturers were considering raising prices in spite of possible consumer resistance. The alternative of lower profit margins, the magazine concluded, was "untenable." In all cases, cost increases must be passed on as quickly as possible.

With costs covered and profit rates assured, however, a company will not necessarily raise its prices simply because consumers want more of what it has to sell. Doing so can be inconvenient and risky, in that it involves publishing new price schedules and possibly antagonizing a firm's distributors or customers. Price hikes, particularly price hikes that are not matched by one's competitors, also may damage a company's market share and chances for growth. Management teams that pursue such courses may find themselves unpopular with shareholders and boards of directors.

In principle, almost any big company could cut its prices dramatically for a while and spend a lot of money advertising the fact. It might thereby attract a lot of new customers, grow bigger, and maybe even drive its competitors out of business.

In practice, cutthroat competition of this sort is rare. One reason is that the antitrust laws frown on successful attempts to put one's competitors out of business; R. J. Reynolds needs Philip Morris and Liggett just as General Motors needs Ford and Chrysler. A second reason is that the logic of mass marketing may not allow for significant variation in price. Procter & Gamble presumably makes a lot of money on Tide because it sells so much of the stuff (it considers the exact amount a trade secret), not because it turns a large profit on each box that is sold. Yet Tide would have to be substantially cheaper than, say, Fab to induce the habitual user of the latter to switch over. A price cut of a dime, which may be a large fraction of P&G's profit on a box of Tide, won't do the trick; consumers looking for bargains in detergents can already find discount brands going for 70 or 80 percent of the nationally advertised brands (and not doing as well). Unless P&G could put Colgate-Palmolive and the others out of business quickly—an event hard to imagine—it would find itself in the proverbial unhappy position of trying to sell at a loss and make it up in volume.*

A third reason is that price cutting by one firm would doubtless engender immediate retribution. Businesses learned about the possibilities for mutual destruction by this means in the nineteenth century. The railroads, which were the first giant enterprises to operate on a national scale, competed so strenuously by slashing their prices that, in Alfred D. Chandler's words, "the logic of such competition appeared to be bankruptcy for all." Railroad men therefore devoted enormous energies to setting up associa-

* "Cents off" coupons—a form of temporary discounting that is about as close as most companies get to lowering their prices—has more in common with box-top premiums and other advertising gimmicks than with true price competition. Consider the difference between a coupon entitling the bearer to 22¢ off his or her next box of Tide, and an announcement by Procter & Gamble that henceforth it would sell Tide for 10 percent less than the detergents made by any competitor. The latter is unimaginable—and not because P&G couldn't afford to do it.

tions, pools, and cartels to set rates for all.* Other businesses followed suit. In the 1870s, writes Chandler, virtually every industry in America had established trade associations "for the purpose of controlling price and production"; by the 1880s these federations "had become part of the normal way of doing business" and frequently "allocated specific markets to different firms." The associations were fragile creatures, however, for they had no legal authority over their members. Much more effective, from the businessman's point of view, was to combine with your competitors into one big company (American Tobacco, U.S. Steel); to set up an overarching trust that owned many hitherto competing firms (Standard Oil); or simply to buy out the competition.† "Most businessmen believed in competition—theoretically," says the writer Frederick Lewis Allen about turn-of-the-century capitalism. "But in practice there was a ceaseless search for ways in which to prevent it." Thanks to that search—and despite the Sherman Antitrust Act, passed in 1890—the industrial economy by the time of World War I looked very much as it does today: a few big firms dominating most industries, and little if any price competition.

To be sure, price cutting has not disappeared. But it crops up mainly in unusual circumstances, and it may run counter to the laws of supply and demand as often as it

* The passage of the Interstate Commerce Act in 1887 in effect accomplished for the railroads what they had been unable to accomplish for themselves. The act called for "just and reasonable rates" and "prohibited temporary short-lived rate changes."

† Until 1888 it was in most cases illegal for one corporation to own stock in another. "Buying out" another company therefore meant that the owners of Company A had to buy up Company B's stock: a costly and risky procedure for the individuals involved. In its 1888–89 session, however, the New Jersey legislature passed a law permitting corporations registered in that state to buy stock in other corporations. To no one's surprise, this move touched off a rush of companies wanting to register (for a small fee) in New Jersey. The state's revenues rose considerably, and "New Jersey holding companies" became a familiar feature of the economic landscape.

obeys them. In 1980, for instance, several major airlines were waging a price war on their profitable East Coast and transcontinental flights. Phased deregulation of the air had begun, ending decades of rate setting by the Civil Aeronautics Board, and the airlines were experimenting with ways to increase their market. Not one, however, was happy with the situation; industry earnings dropped substantially in the first year of deregulation, thanks largely to the rising cost of jet fuel and the new competitive pressures.

It wasn't long before the airlines were inventing new ways to compete without slashing fares. United, American, and TWA began to offer lottery tickets by which passengers (and others who requested them) could win extra trips and other prizes. The hope, explained *New York Times* writer Winston Williams, was that games of chance would "provide the competitive outlet that is needed to minimize costly fare wars such as those now being waged. . . ." At the same time the airlines were quietly raising fares, despite the fact that passenger traffic was down 3 percent in the first three months of 1980.

Automobile companies too were engaged in a little price competition, and they weren't any happier than the airlines. Chrysler's unprecedented program of rebates in 1979 and 1980, which included, at one point, a $50 bonus paid to anyone who so much as test-drove a Chrysler car and then went on to buy it or any other car, was a response to a drastic drop in sales following the company's announcement of possible bankruptcy. Ford was offering rebates too, though for a while its logic was the opposite of Chrysler's. Ford was "rebating its popular Fairmonts and Thunderbirds," one report noted, "but offering no rebates on the sluggish LTD." The logic? " 'We fish where the fish are biting,' says Ford VP and division manager Phillip E. Benton Jr. Ford figures it can get 'more bang for the buck' rebating the better sellers." All these rebates, of course, were coming at a time when sticker prices were rising that 2.2 percent mentioned above (2.2 percent of a $7,000 list price is $154). And the sticker price hikes, which were still there when the rebating programs were over, occurred in spite of the fact that sales of American cars were plummeting.

Sticky prices and inflation

This sketch of the industrial system and the way it sets its prices has dramatic implications for the economy as a whole and for inflation in particular. MIT economist Robert M. Solow, in a memorably curious turn of phrase, has termed this effect "the upward bias of sticky down."

Some price, somewhere, is rising in real terms all the time. A bad harvest raises the price of grain by restricting supply. Speculation in the silver futures market raises the price of the metal and thereby the cost of manufacturing photographic film. Strong demand for small, fuel-efficient cars persuades General Motors to hike the price of its compact X-body line. A new wage settlement raises the cost of doing business in the aluminum industry, and aluminum firms raise the price of ingots.

These price increases reverberate through the economy. More expensive grain means more expensive flour, not only for the consumer buying five pounds of Gold Medal, but also for ITT Continental Baking Company and for Dunkin' Donuts. The price of wheat-based breakfast cereals may go up a little, and the price of cereals based on other grains (oats, rice) may rise too "to stay competitive." Higher aluminum prices lead not only to higher costs for aluminum products like soft drink cans, they may also persuade the steel industry that it can get away with hiking its prices a little. Or, to turn the example around, a generous wage settlement for aluminum workers may encourage the steelworkers to demand a higher wage settlement than otherwise, in turn leading to higher steel prices.

Economists call this process "leapfrogging," Companies and unions come to expect a certain pattern of relative prices, not only within an industry but among different industries. Price hikes in an industry facing higher costs encourage discretionary price hikes by other industries seeking to redress the balance or simply to enlarge profit margins a little.

Theoretically, prices should be dropping here and there too, thanks to abundant harvests, cheap silver, slackening demand for cars, or lower wages (more likely, wage settlements that are more than compensated for by gains in output per worker). Some prices actually do fall. Agricultural prices drop when harvests are good, though not too far, as we shall see in the next chapter. Raw materials prices sometimes go down too, as do the prices of industrial bulk materials (processed metals, chemicals, and the like). These price changes should also reverberate throughout the economy.

They don't. Cost savings—unless they are dramatic, as with changes in technology—are rarely passed on to consumers. When business falls off (when demand declines, in the economist's terminology) prices don't: as the British economist Joan Robinson puts it, "It is considered very bad form to start cutting prices, and sometimes they are even raised 'in order to cover costs.'" During the recessionary period from May 1974 to March 1975, the late Brookings economist Arthur Okun pointed out, the prices of industrial raw materials fell an average of 15 percent. "During that same 10-month interval," wrote Okun, "producers' prices of finished goods other than food and fuel rose by 10 percent." At around the same time, the world price of sugar jumped to a record 66¢ a pound, and the prices of processed foods requiring a lot of sugar soared. Later sugar dropped to 6¢ a pound. "Soft drinks and other products containing sugar or corn sweeteners declined somewhat," an analysis in *The New York Times* observed, "but not in proportion to the drop in price of the commodity."

No conspiracy is necessary to effect this result. Cost savings from lower raw materials prices may not amount to much for most companies, and wages and overhead expenses probably aren't decreasing. "Don't expect these lower input prices to be reflected in consumer prices," a Labor Department official cautioned a reporter in 1980 when a few raw materials had begun to drop. "There are energy and labor costs which easily take up the slack of these lower input prices." Most important, the same factors that militate against price competition militate against price cuts in general. Companies may not have much leeway to cut prices, and they certainly do not want to get involved in a price war with their competitors if it can be avoided. A responsible management will not look askance at an unusually good profit now and then, particularly if it thinks raw materials costs are likely to go up again before too long. And the competitive pressure that would drive prices down is virtually nonexistent.

Kodak offers a textbook example of sticky prices. The Rochester, New York, giant–30th on the *Fortune* 500, with more than $8 billion in sales–accounts for about 90 percent of the photographic film sold in the United States. In late 1979 and early 1980, the Hunt brothers from Dallas were speculating heavily in the silver futures market, driving prices up to nearly $50 a troy ounce. Silver is a prime component of photographic film, and Kodak raised its prices accordingly–nearly 100 percent on X-ray film, according to *Business Week*, and an average of 27 percent on other products.

By April 1980 the price of silver had dropped to around $14 an ounce, not far from where it had been the previous fall. Kodak, faced with modest competitive pressures in specialty-film areas, reduced the price of X-ray film about 20 percent in two months and trimmed the price of professional 35-millimeter motion-picture film. It also cut some other prices–though not, the *Times* noted, the "10 to 20 percent increases in instant, 110 and 35-millimeter film" announced earlier. "Even when prices decline," said the *Times*, "they seldom make it all the way back to their previous levels." The movie film on which Kodak cut its prices went from

$70.20 a roll to $61.70 after the cuts. The same film "sold for $42.50 a roll until last October 26."

In general, *Business Week* noted, the company was "likely to maintain most of the other price increases announced in December." As a result it "stood to improve margins and earnings substantially." On May 1, 1980, Kodak announced first-quarter earnings 10 percent higher than the previous year's.

Companies faced with declining sales—the time when economic theory says they should cut prices—usually have a variety of options to choose from. If investors decide they want fewer shares of Coca-Cola stock, the price falls. If consumers decide they want to drink less Coke, the price stays the same but the company mounts a new advertising campaign ("Have a Coke and a Smile"). If things really get desperate—as they have in recent years for the likes of Lockheed, U.S. Steel, and Chrysler—the government can be called in to bail the company out (or at least protect it from imports).

Most typically, however, a firm's response to declining sales is simply to cut back production rather than adjust its prices. When Firestone realized in 1980 that its bias-ply tires were not selling well, it didn't cut the price; it closed six plants, throwing more than 7,000 people out of work. The economist Gardiner C. Means, in a famous 1934 memorandum to the Secretary of Agriculture, found that the idle plants of the Depression were in large measure attributable to production cutbacks of this sort. In markets that were largely competitive, such as agriculture, producers kept on producing but prices fell. In large industrial markets, production dropped and prices stayed largely where they were.

To return to the stock market for a moment, the price of a stock varies because "supply" and "demand" are moving autonomously, in response to the decisions of many different investors. In product markets, however, a big company can control how much of something it supplies (Firestone tires,

Winstons, Quaker Oats). It can also influence consumers' decisions about how much to buy, through advertising and other marketing techniques. Supply and demand are still there, but they are subject to manipulation. And the price at which goods are sold need not move at all.

This is one example—probably the most important one—of a system of markets that is rigged to favor the seller rather than the buyer. The market for most of the brand-name industrial products we buy is rigged in the sense that each manufacturer is big enough to exercise considerable control over the supply of its products, the demand for its products, and thereby its products' prices. Prices rise easily; they fall with difficulty.

All this does not mean that big corporations face no competition. General Motors must compete not only with Ford and Chrysler but with Volkswagen and Toyota—even, in a sense, with trains and buses. But the competition seldom turns primarily on price. Nor does it mean that the big corporations somehow "cause" inflation. They are by no means inconsequential; their price and wage patterns, for example, frequently serve as guidelines for smaller companies and even for government agencies. But they have as much incentive to keep prices low, thereby expanding their market shares and enhancing their prospects for growth, as they have to keep them high.

What is important about the big companies is not that they systematically jack their prices up higher than they should, by whatever standard, but that they have a significant amount of discretion over what their prices will be. If costs go up, prices will too—quickly. If costs drop, prices might go down a little—slowly—or they may not move at all. If business is good, companies won't necessarily raise their prices. But if it's bad, they are highly unlikely to cut them, and may even raise them to maintain profit margins. The "upward bias of sticky down" means only that prices tend to adjust upwards. In that sense the industrial system builds a predisposition to inflation into our economy.

The industrial system, in any event, has been around since the early decades of this century. Yet the years from 1890 to 1940 witnessed some of the more pronounced deflations the industrial world had ever seen Evidently we need more pieces to the puzzle. One of the more important ones, the subject of the next chapter, is the fact that the secret has gotten out. Big companies can protect themselves from falling prices by manipulating supply, demand, and often the price itself. So, as it turns out, can a large fraction of the other firms and individuals who make up the American economy.

3. The Inflationary System: Not-So-Big Business

The giant corporations that dominate America's industrial economy are hard to ignore. So is the fact that these companies exercise considerable influence over the various markets in which they operate. They determine, in large measure, how much of their products they will sell and at what price. When business turns down or competition intensifies, they develop new product mixes or new marketing strategies rather than accept lower prices and consequently lower earnings. Nor is this behavior thought peculiar. There are few who believe that large corporations can, should, or are likely to act otherwise.

Once in a while, of course, even a ranking member of the *Fortune* 500 discovers that the marketplace is out of control. Thus General Motors, Ford, and Chrysler awoke one morning in 1980 to find that no amount of advertising was persuading consumers to buy their gas guzzlers, and all three firms began to report record losses. Companies as big and as diverse as U.S. Steel and A&P have come upon hard times in recent years. And the competition, as with the airline rate war described earlier, can sometimes get cutthroat. Throughout the business world, profits fluctuate and corporate managers worry.

It is tempting, when the news of a giant in trouble hits the headlines, to assume that big corporations aren't so powerful after all. The occasional price war or business setback is taken as evidence that the marketplace works: that the consumer is sovereign and competition effective. This belief is comforting, for it fits the image of a free-enterprise, free-market economy that most of us carry around in our heads—it's the way capitalism ought to work. If big companies really could dominate the marketplace, why would business executives get ulcers?

What happens occasionally, however, should not blind us to what happens regularly. The Lockheed 1011 Tri-Star widebody jet is sometimes grounded by storms, just like a Piper Cub. But if you believe that the Tri-Star is as dependent upon low winds and good visibility as a smaller plane, you'll be left with a serious misconception about its ability to fly a regular schedule. Similarly, the worries of corporate managers usually focus on matters like whether this year's profits will outpace last year's. This can be a topic of some concern to the manager: if profits don't pick up, his or her career may not go far either. But only in unusual circumstances do such fluctuations affect the fundamental economic health of the large corporation. The market rules only in extreme situations.

A more persuasive view of America as a predominantly market-dominated free-enterprise system focuses on the parts of the economy not populated by giant firms. A walk through the streets of a big city reveals dozens of grocery stores, pharmacies, restaurants, and apparel shops. A glance through the *Yellow Pages* turns up hundreds of small manufacturers, tradespeople, dentists, and construction firms. The countryside nearly everywhere in America is dotted with farms. None of these enterprises wields anything like the economic clout of a Quaker Oats or a Kodak. For them, it seems, the market must reign supreme, and capitalism must work the way it is supposed to.

Where prices are concerned, though, the distinction between the giants and everybody else is not always clear. Like the big firms, small companies frequently find ways to compete without cutting prices. Some trades manage to keep prices up by limiting the number of people licensed to do business. Others are the beneficiaries of extensive government intervention in the marketplace. In all these instances supply and demand are manipulated, and prices are influenced either directly or indirectly by the seller. These rigged markets lead to sticky prices, hence inflation, as surely as the control exercised by the *Fortune* 500.

Small businesses

In any sizable metropolitan area in the northern part of this country, a family with an oil-burning furnace can find dozens of companies willing and eager to supply it with oil. All will deliver anywhere in the metropolitan area with reasonable reliability. All offer essentially the same product: Exxon's home heating oil No. 2 is no different from Texaco's. And all provide the same convenience of doing business. A phone call does the trick.*

No supplier of oil, therefore, can afford to charge his customers more than a fraction of a cent more per gallon than his competitors do. If he tried to do so, he would soon find himself out of business. If the price of oil at wholesale should drop (which it still does once in a very great while), the savings would probably be passed on quickly to consumers. Kellogg's may know that its two or three main competitors are not going to get involved in cutting prices, but the Ajax Oil Company knows no such thing about its thirty-seven competitors.

A consumer looking for a hair stylist is entering a marketplace quite different from that faced by the oil-burning homeowner. The chances are that there are only a few hair stylists within easy walking distance of home or job, and why look any farther? Experimentation will reveal that some are more

* "Discount" oil dealers, which can be found in some cities, fall into a separate category. They do charge less for their oil, but they typically offer no free maintenance and repair service. Nor do they send out bills: the rule is cash on delivery. Thus their "product" is different from that sold by most dealers.

competent, friendly, and efficient than others; that some play loud rock music while others are as quiet as the public library; and that some are more expensive than others. All of these considerations will enter a customer's decision about which establishment to patronize. Price may be decidedly secondary. Its effect may even be opposite from the expected. A more expensive establishment may confer a sense of prestige and self-worth on the customer that cut-rate stylists can't match.

The oil dealer facing a loss of business cannot usually do much about it. Advertising won't help: it just costs money, and he doesn't have much to advertise that is different from any other dealer. Very likely the drop in business reflects declining demand for the whole industry. Consumers may be keeping their homes cooler or switching to natural gas. If the situation keeps up, companies that can afford to do so will cut prices a little to compete more effectively. Those that cannot afford to do so will be forced out of business.

The hair stylist faced with declining business has other choices short of shutting up shop. She can advertise, maybe just by passing out flyers in the neighborhood. She can install a new carpet or get rid of a surly employee. She can lower her prices, or raise them. (The latter, in the euphemistic terminology of business, is called repositioning oneself in the market.) No such choice is open to the oil dealer.

Oil dealers and hair stylists, in short, face two different kinds of markets. One kind, the oil dealer's, is very much like the stock market. There are many sellers, and what they offer for sale is essentially identical. Since everyone has to charge the going rate, the price automatically falls to its "market" level—the level determined by supply and demand. The other kind, the hair stylist's, is more like the world of the large corporation. The goods and services being offered are particular combinations of quality, convenience, service, aesthetic appeal, advertised virtues, and so forth. Price is of course a part of the package. But the seller has a good deal of discretion over what it will be, and frequently can choose to compete on other turf entirely.

Most smaller companies operate in a marketplace somewhere between these two extremes. The supermarket business in most cities, for instance, exhibits a considerable amount of price competition. The printing business, though also highly competitive, exhibits a good deal less; press capacities, quality controls, and ancillary services are usually as important as price in determining who gets the customers. In many businesses each company sells to a small geographic market. In others each company sells a highly differentiated or unique product—Cantonese meals, for example, prepared by a well-known chef. In both cases firms can end up as relatively big fish in relatively small ponds. Prices then behave the way they do in the world of giant corporations. If companies don't have too much competition in their particular market niche, and if they can offer customers the right combination of quality, variety, and service, they automatically have some discretion over the prices they charge. When this is the case, prices won't fall as easily as they do in markets that resemble the stock market.

Licensing

Frequently there is no way by which an entrepreneur or company can grow large or easily distinguish itself from the competition. Except in the smallest of cities, general-practice lawyers will find several other attorneys happy to take their business away. So will plumbers and liquor-store owners. In this circumstance, it is advantageous to be able to limit by law the number of people in your line of work.

A surprising number of industries and trades have been successful in obtaining such a limitation. You can't set up a radio or television station without approval from the Federal Communications Commission. You can't run an airline without an OK from the Civil Aeronautics Board. A proposal for a new bank requires approval by the state banking commission or some other governmental agency. If you want to do business in interstate trucking, you need a go-ahead from the Interstate Commerce Commission. Doctors, lawyers, architects, accountants, pharmacists, stockbrokers, dentists, plumbers, and electricians are some of the more common tradespeople who ordinarily require a license to operate. Some of the less common occupations in this category were listed not long ago by a writer named Peter Meyer. "A study being conducted by the Labor Department," Meyer wrote, "finds that some 350 different occupations are now licensed by state authorities and another 500 occupations require state certification or registration. A cross section of jobs that now need licenses includes falconry, hairdressing, well-pump sales, weather modifying, social work (fifteen different categories), hunting and trapping guide, shampooing (hair), television-antenna installation, phrenology, prophylactic sales, tattooing, lightning-rod installation, and cesspool cleaning."

Obviously there are good reasons for licensing many of these professions, notably those related to medicine. But the rationale (or lack of it) in any given case should not obscure the economic effects of licensing. Most licenses are contingent upon successful completion of extensive, often costly, educational or apprenticeship programs. The time and expense required by such programs work wonders in keeping down the number of applications for licenses. The difficulties of obtaining a license may help create a sense of fellowship and common interest among those who succeed. Frequently the licensing board itself is run by members of the profession in question, thus ensuring that the licensees' interests will be looked after.

Sometimes a license to operate carries a fee schedule along with it. Thus interstate trucking rates are set by the ICC; and taxi fares (though not tips) are usually set by the city agency that dispenses taxi licenses. These fee schedules are seldom painful. Trucking companies, according to *Business Week,* have been making profits as high as 20 percent; the recent deregulation bill may or may not cut these profits.*

* The bill, passed in mid-1980, does not remove the ICC's jurisdiction over truck routes and freight rates, as deregulation proponents had originally hoped. It does make entry into the business easier by shift-

There are about 12,000 taxicabs licensed to operate in New York City. The licenses, called medallions, can be bought and sold on the open market, and in 1980 were going for as much as $68,000. This fact led some observers to conclude that things couldn't be as bad as the industry had claimed when it asked for a rate hike that year. If the situation really was so dismal, *The New York Times* asked editorially, "why then are prospective taxi owners willing to pay between $53,000 and $68,000 for the right to run a cab in the city?" Fares were evidently higher than they would have been if anyone was free to operate a cab.

In most regulated industries, rates are not set by public agencies. Restrictions on who can sell something become all the more important. Keeping down the number of competitors not only reduces the chance of direct price competition—remember Kellogg's versus the Ajax Oil Company—it also facilitates informal measures aimed at rigging markets or manipulating prices. It is hard to imagine, for example, that a plumber could charge $25 (sometimes twice that in big cities) just for walking in a customer's front door if plumbing were a profession open to all comers. It is also hard to imagine that other trades could have gotten away with price-fixing as long as they did. Lawyers, until recently, were provided with "minimum fee schedules" by state bar associations, which, though not legally binding, helped establish a price floor for legal services. The American Society of Anesthesiology, until recently, required hospitals to hire its members on a fee-for-service basis rather than at a salary, a device that turned out to raise the cost of anesthesiology and the incomes of anesthesiologists. Only recently have opticians in many states been allowed to advertise the price of eyeglasses or pharmacists the price of drugs. For a long time, professional associa-

---

ing the burden of proof from those who propose new service to those who oppose it. It requires truckers, beginning in 1984, to apply individually to the ICC for certain rate changes, rather than agreeing on rates beforehand and applying jointly. And it allows firms to raise or lower rates 10 percent without an OK from the ICC.

tions and regulatory boards were able to shield many such trades from the rigors of the marketplace.

Laws, court cases, and Federal Trade Commission decisions during the last few years have limited the variety and scope of practices like these, and of similar anticompetitive measures in unregulated industries. Congress, in the Consumer Goods Pricing Act of 1975, outlawed state "fair trade" laws and its own Miller-Tydings Act, both of which were designed to protect small retailers from "unfair" price competition. The Supreme Court in 1977 ruled that lawyers have a constitutional right to advertise—a decision, according to reports, that has led to lower legal fees in some areas. Both the Federal Trade Commission and the Justice Department began in 1980 to investigate "industry practices" aimed at fixing prices; among such practices, said one report, "are the specific assignment of dealerships by territory; the policy of an industry or area leader to set prices and smaller companies to base theirs on those levels; producers selling only to wholesalers or retailers gearing their prices to those suggested, and use of credit . . . [to] keep prices at set levels." So the tide may be turning. How far it will flow out remains to be seen.

"No business," writes management consultant Rolf H. Wild, "particularly welcomes competition, because real competition is expensive and detrimental to the competitors." Measures designed to increase competition will therefore provoke howls of pain—much like the howls that the 1980 trucking deregulation bill elicited from the American Trucking Associations. Without competition, however, there is little downward pressure on prices. Regulated rates and rules about who can supply a particular good or service both lead to prices that are sticky. From the affected business's point of view, that's a pleasant situation.

Housing and health care

Not all industries lend themselves to supply restrictions. Rather than let themselves be buffeted by the ill winds of the marketplace, though, some have found ways to prop up consumer demand for what they sell. This too has a salutary effect on price from the seller's point of view. The usual means by which demand is kept high is government subsidy. The usual rationale, often unexceptionable, is that the items being sold are critical to the nation's well-being. The best examples are housing and health care. Together they account for about a quarter of the average household's expenses.

Median prices of existing homes rose about 65 percent more than the Consumer Price Index during the 1970s. New-home prices went up about twice as much as the index. The average price of a new house in 1980 was $72,000. The increase, as noted earlier, is due to many factors, the baby boom and inflation among them. Without the government, however, housing would not be where it is today.

Consider the homeowner's tax break all by itself. The Johnsons—a hypothetical family of four with an income of $20,000—would have paid $2,271 to Washington in 1979 if they took the standard deduction on Form 1040. But suppose the Johnsons own a $60,000 house, with a 5-year-old mortgage of $40,000 at 9 percent. Interest on the mortgage loan comes to perhaps $3,000 a year. Property taxes are probably another $1,200. Both are tax-deductible. So they fill out Schedule A and find that housing expenses alone reduce their tax liability by about $250. And now that they're filling out Schedule A anyway, they can take deductions for medical expenses, charitable contributions, credit-card and other interest costs, and so on. All might be worth another $100 or so off the tax bill. As long as the Johnsons own their own home (and keep it well mortgaged) the government might as well send them a check for $350 every year. If the Johnsons get richer, even if they get richer only in nominal terms because of inflation, the size of the check increases. If they buy a more expensive house or get a more expensive mortgage, the check gets bigger too. Overall, these tax breaks cost the government an estimated $14 billion in uncollected revenue in fiscal 1979.

That isn't all the government does. Since 1968 it has subsidized construction of housing for low- and moderate-income families on a substantial scale. For much longer than that, the Veterans Administration and the Federal Housing Administration (FHA) have been guaranteeing mortgage loans. Families taking advantage of these programs can borrow at low interest rates with smaller down payments than banks would otherwise require. And the programs are frequently expanded. In 1977, for instance, Congress lowered the down payment required on FHA-insured mortgages. Other measures reduced the taxes most homeowners must pay when they sell their house and buy a new one, and changed mortgage-repayment rules to permit lower payments in the first years of a mortgage.

As interest rates rose during 1980, buyers were forced out of the market and home prices fell a small amount. Realtors tried to postpone the fall as long as they could; in lieu of reducing prices, *The Wall Street Journal* reported, some were pursuing gimmicks like giving away a compact car with the purchase of a sufficiently expensive home.* Meanwhile, the *Journal* also noted, the declining housing market "was provoking anguished cries from builders and unions for a multi-billion-dollar infusion of federal mortgage subsidies." Insofar as the government rescues the industry—and it is always under considerable pressure to do so from prospective buyers and sellers as well as from trade groups—prices do not easily go down.

In health care, which has risen in cost about 10 percent more than the Consumer Price Index as a whole during the 1970s, inflation is built into the financing system. As Harvard

---

* A $5,000 car is better than a $5,000 price cut from the broker's point of view because he or she can't collect a commission on the price cut. Also, many brokers are themselves real estate owners or developers and have an interest in keeping nominal prices up.

Brokers' commissions, which represent the price of brokers' services, seem to stay constant regardless of trends in home prices. One midwestern broker who attempted to reduce his commission when faced with a sagging market was immediately accused by his colleagues of "unethical" behavior.

sociologists Paul Starr and Gosta Esping-Andersen explain it, three factors affect the price of health care. First is the fact that "payment for most medical care today is made by a 'third party' "—Blue Cross, Medicare, or a conventional insurance company. So neither the patient nor the hospital nor the doctor providing the care has to pay out of pocket for what is "sold." Second, doctors and hospitals get paid on a fee-for-service basis: the more treatment that is prescribed, the more money the provider makes. Third, "reimbursements to hospitals and other institutions under Medicare and Blue Cross are determined on the basis of costs." The result is that "the hospital that spends wantonly today will reap its rewards in higher rates of reimbursement tomorrow." Medicare, which was passed in 1965, was particularly profligate. Hospitals could compute their costs in two different ways and use whichever method proved most favorable; and they got an extra 2 percent on top to cover "whatever costs might have been omitted."

The direct effect of Medicare and Medicaid was to make fully paid hospital coverage available to a poor and elderly population that hitherto had been unable to afford it. Their indirect effect was to increase hospital spending dramatically. "In the year before Medicare," write Starr and Esping-Andersen, "hospital costs were rising at about 6 percent annually; in the year afterward, they rose 16 percent. Between 1965 and 1977, hospital expenditures quintupled from $13.1 billion to $65.6 billion—an average increase of 14 percent a year, more than double the rise in the consumer price index and higher than medical costs overall." Spending on Medicare, meanwhile, has been doubling every four years. In 1980, according to *The New York Times*, it was expected to reach $34 billion.

The world of health care—particularly hospital care, which now accounts for over 40 percent of all medical expenditures —is not one of price competition: quite the opposite. It is a world of approved fee schedules and reimbursements. Nor is it sensitive (as the housing industry is) to declining demand due to bad business conditions. People who are sick do not put off getting treated. Some have already paid the bill anyway, through payroll deductions for Blue Cross or another insurance plan. For others the government will pick up the tab. As a result the health care system exhibits, in the Harvard experts' words, "a continuously high rate of inflation that is apparently impervious to changes in the economy."

Farming

The scope of free, unrestricted, competitive markets, as the reader will notice, is getting smaller. Most manufacturing is excluded. So are the regulated utilities, the big retailers like Sears and service companies like Marriott, many smaller retailing and service concerns, a lot of the trades and professions, now housing and health care. In most cases competition has not vanished. Companies still have to take into account what their customers want and can afford, and how much their competitors are charging. But most have found ways to tame the competitive jungle—to keep down the number of competitors, for instance, or to make sure that there are plenty of customers for all.

Once that's done, prices are no longer as flexible as they once were. They still can move up. But they don't fall so easily. If the housing market is bad, you rarely find builders and lumber companies slashing their prices, or homeowners selling out at a loss. Instead you find most people waiting until things get better, and in the meantime asking for government help.

The one part of the economy where free markets really do seem to work is agriculture. You can see the evidence in the supermarket every week. The prices of unprocessed foods—meat, dairy products, eggs, coffee, and so on—really do go up and down, just as they are supposed to. The newspapers correctly remind us that these fluctuations reflect changes in supply or demand, usually supply, since consumer demand for food items remains essentially constant. Between 1976 and 1977, as coffee drinkers will remember, bad harvests in

Brazil led to an 85 percent increase in the price of coffee, $1.87 a pound to $3.47 a pound on the average. By mid-1979, however, the price had dropped nearly 25 percent, back down to $2.67. Yet the average price level was rising 20 percent in the same period.

From the farmer's point of view, the market is pretty effective too: he sells his produce for whatever it will bring (although large midwestern grain farmers sometimes stockpile it in hopes of getting a better price). Considered as businesses, most farmers are small. Yet the market for farm produce is regional or national in scope. Even the producer of a highly perishable commodity, the Vermont dairy farmer, say, rarely sells his wares to his neighbors. Instead, his milk is marketed by big dairy enterprises and cooperatives throughout New England.

For nearly fifty years, however, the government has propped up or manipulated the market for farm produce in a variety of ways. The Agricultural Adjustment Act of 1933, signed by Roosevelt on May 12 of that year, provided for benefit payments to farmers who agreed to limit production; it also allowed for "marketing agreements" to fix prices for agricultural commodities. Later the government established support prices at which it would, if necessary, buy farm output. And in 1973 it instituted the so-called target price system, which allowed market prices to fluctuate more than before (and thus keep U.S. grain competitive on the world market) while still maintaining farmers' incomes. If the market price for wheat, say, falls 25¢ a bushel below the target, the government mails the farmer a check for 25¢ times every bushel he sells. Target prices are supposed to reflect a combination of farm costs, expected demand, and world market prices. They are issued annually, and can be increased (but not decreased) at any time by the Secretary of Agriculture. The temptation to increase them in an election year can prove irresistible: Jimmy Carter, for example, announced higher targets for some crops not long before the 1980 election.

The system varies from crop to crop. Dairy farmers, for

example, sell their milk to bottlers and processors at prices that are not allowed to fall below government-established minimums. If more milk is produced than processors can eventually sell, the processors take it anyway and turn it into butter, cheese, and powdered milk. An agency called the Commodity Credit Corporation then buys the surplus products and stores them in government warehouses. They can be sold only at prices at least 5 percent higher than the support level. Meanwhile, the government limits imports of dairy products to protect domestic farmers and processors from foreign competition.

Under a 1979 law, minimum dairy prices must be adjusted twice (rather than once) a year to keep up with inflation. Because of the way the Department of Agriculture calculates these adjustments, support prices have been rising faster than milk producers' costs. The semiannual adjustment in April 1980, according to *The New York Times,* would mean an extra $7,500 in gross income over a six-month period for a dairy farm with fifty cows. It would raise the price of milk to the consumer an estimated 8¢ per gallon, and the price of butter and cheese about 9¢ a pound. The whole program was expected to cost the government nearly a billion dollars in 1980.

Tobacco farmers grow their crop on "allotments" determined by the federal government; it is the only crop whose production is still strictly limited. In the 1930s, when the price of tobacco had dropped to 6¢ a pound, the government began assigning tobacco-growing rights to farmers on the basis of how much they had traditionally raised. These allotments, which have changed little over the years, limit both the number of tobacco farmers and the amount of tobacco that can be grown. "A farmer who doesn't have an allotment," as one writer explains it, "can't grow tobacco today unless he finds someone willing to lease him growing rights or else sell him land with an allotment." Land with an allotment, not surprisingly, is considerably more expensive than comparable land without one.

The Department of Agriculture also supports tobacco prices; any tobacco not sold at the government-determined minimum price is purchased by a company operating with federal money. The company stores it in warehouses until prices go up, then sells it for a profit, and pays back the loan. The plan makes tobacco more expensive than it otherwise would be and helps those who grow it considerably. "A 'bacca farmer just can't operate and not make money," one North Carolina grower told a reporter.

More fruit and vegetable farmers live in California than in any other state; California is the leading producer of artichokes, asparagus, lima beans, broccoli, Brussels sprouts, cantaloupes, carrots, cauliflower, celery, garlic, honeydew, lettuce, onions, spinach, strawberries, peaches, pears, grapes, plums, lemons, and tomatoes. Fruits and vegetables are not covered by federal price support programs. Often, however, producers will band together and issue "marketing orders" that set standards for the produce, thus insuring themselves against unanticipated excess supply. And a few of the vegetables—tomatoes, for example—are grown in ways that resemble industrial production. California grows 85 percent of U.S. tomatoes. The 600 or so big farm operations that raise them plant an average of over 350 acres apiece. The fruit they plant is genetically selected for a variety of characteristics: "thick-walledness, less acidity, more uniform ripening, oblongness, leafiness, and high yield," as the writer Mark Kramer describes them. It is harvested by huge machines a week or two after airplanes have sprayed the entire crop with ethylene, an agent that hastens ripening. Six of the machines can harvest a 766-acre field bearing 100 million tomatoes in about a month.

Seven out of every eight tomatoes are bought for processing rather than fresh consumption. Four canners—Del Monte, Heinz, Campbell, and Libby, McNeill, & Libby—sell 72 percent of the nation's tomato sauce and a substantial fraction of most other tomato products. In recent years, large growers and canning companies have set up a system called "joint contracting" for producing tomatoes. Under this system, both parties share the expense (and responsibility) of "investing" in the crop: seeds, herbicides and pesticides, machinery, water, labor, and management. The tomatoes are "sold" by farmer to canner at a price agreed upon in an advance contract.

"Under this sort of business condition," observes Kramer, "the marketplace is fully occupied by giants. It is no place for the little guy with a truckload or two of tomatoes—even if his price is right. Farmers who once planted twenty or thirty acres of cannery tomatoes as a speculative complement to other farming endeavors are for the most part out of the picture, with no place to market their crops and no place to finance their operating expenses."

In all these cases, the normal fluctuations of the market are softened, and prices are prevented from falling too far. It is worth remembering too that most of the food we eat does not exactly go straight from the farm to the supermarket. Instead, like tomatoes, it is canned, frozen, processed, packaged, and marketed like an industrial product. Pringles, Sugar Smacks, even Dannon Yogurt are produced and sold by some of the biggest companies in America. (Dannon's parent is the giant Beatrice conglomerate, which also owns Canada Dry, Schweppes, RC Cola, Sunbeam Bread, and dozens of other companies.) They are extensively processed, heavily advertised, and sold at a premium. Their price responds to farm-price fluctuations the way Kodak film prices respond to silver fluctuations: easy up, sticky down.

Back to the marketplace?

Since by now the devout inflation-fighter will be appropriately indignant about corporate and governmental meddling with the market, it is worth a moment to consider the alternative. Again, agriculture is a useful example. Before the Agricultural Adjustment Act of 1933, farmers really did operate in what was essentially a free market. As we should expect in such a market, food prices rose and fell with ease, reflecting supply and demand with considerable accuracy.

The best years for the farmer under this system came during and right after World War I: as the historian Lester V. Chandler describes it, "cotton rose from about 12 cents to 35 cents a pound, wheat from about 90 cents to $2.16 a bushel, and corn from about 65 cents to $1.52 a bushel." The parity ratio—a measure of farm-product prices in relation to farm costs—rose from 100 in the base period of 1910–1914 to a high of 120 in 1917. Farmers bought more land and brought new land under cultivation. They bought new equipment. To finance it all they went deeper in debt.

Between May 1920 and the end of 1921, farm prices dropped more than 40 percent. Net farm income, thanks to the larger debt load, decreased nearly 60 percent. For most of the 1920s, parity hovered around 90. In retrospect, the cause of this decline is clear: farm output had increased substantially and demand, thanks to a rapidly shrinking export market, had not kept pace. During the Depression things got worse. The prices paid farmers for their produce dropped by more than half between 1929 and 1932; parity bottomed out at 58. Net farm income decreased almost 70 percent in the same period.

By the time of the Agricultural Adjustment Act in 1933, roughly half of all the farms mortgaged in the United States were reported delinquent.* Farm output, however, did not drop; in fact it was slightly higher in 1932 than in 1929. The reason was that no individual farmer had much to gain by restricting his own output, and there was no effective way by which farmers could work together to restrain output.

* By no means were all of these mortgages foreclosed. In many cases creditors were tolerant of farmers' difficulties; in others they simply despaired of being able to do anything with a foreclosed farm. In some places, farmers joined together to prevent foreclosure, occasionally throwing the foreclosers off the place bodily, occasionally through more subtle means. In Shelby, Nebraska, says Lester Chandler, "A farm mortgaged to a bank for $4,100 was bid in by friendly neighbors for $49.50 and turned back to the owner." The practice was not unknown elsewhere too.

Farming might be a bad business, but there were no jobs available anywhere else anyway.

Until 1933, in other words, farmers were at the mercy of supply and demand conditions over which they had no control. Their incomes boomed in good times, plummeted in bad times. Though agriculture is in some ways a special case, much the same will be true of any unregulated, uncontrolled free market. New England fishermen, for example, are in much the same situation now that farmers were in before 1933. Unlike Canada, which regulates the size of its fishing fleet, the United States leaves its fishermen largely unregulated. When prices are good more boats go out and bring back more fish. The resulting oversupply depresses prices and hurts everyone's incomes. Some fishing boats go bankrupt, and supply eventually decreases. Ironically, the low prices received by the fishermen in times of oversupply do not show up in the retail price of fish. Drops in fresh fish prices, say economists at the University of Rhode Island, "fail to show up at the retail level because the retail market for fish is relatively uncompetitive." "We don't like to fluctuate our prices too much," one fish store owner told a reporter.

In a competitive marketplace like fishing, those who sell a particular good or service are under the thumb of impersonal forces. In the world of Adam Smith, that works out to everybody's benefit. In the real world, it means that a business's income may change dramatically: riches one minute, poverty the next, and you never know what's around the corner. Few sane people can be happy with such a situation indefinitely.

Some businesses control the marketplace by growing large enough to manipulate their own supply, demand, and prices. Those who cannot grow so big must rely on governmental action for the same end. Over the years, a large number of groups have convinced legislators in Washington and elsewhere that what they do is important enough to merit governmental protection or support. As a result, a substantial fraction of our economy is protected against the drop in incomes that would result from free competition and freely falling prices. Prices are sticky down. So, as the next chapter will explain, are wages.

There is much to be said for an economy in which those who provide goods and services are protected in these ways. Life is more secure. Planning is easier. Maybe more gets produced. Such an economy, however, cannot easily avoid inflation. Unless prices can fall as easily as they rise, the long-term trend can only be upward.

4. The Inflationary System: Labor

Unfettered competition is a little like corporal punishment in the schools. It is esteemed by the traditionally minded, except those old enough to remember its use. It has fallen into disrepute in the modern age. Some would bring it back, though usually for their neighbors rather than for themselves. Others are glad to see it gone.

Even people in the latter category, however, should not blind themselves to the effects of its disappearance. School children arguably have a right not to be rapped on the knuckles with a rattan cane. But a major incentive to good behavior has been lost. Similarly, businesses may fare better in a world where government bailouts, subsidies, and other forms of protection have replaced competition and the threat of bankruptcy. But a major incentive to flexible pricing policies has vanished as well.

To be sure, vestiges of the marketplace remain. And if *costs* were dropping, prices might too. More competition and less protection would doubtless hasten the process. But even monopolistic Kodak cut its prices a little when silver fell. If other costs fell too, it would probably have cut them even more. "Other costs," of course, are the rub. Most of them are labor costs, the wages and salaries paid those who do the work. For reasons this chapter will explain, these costs seldom fall. Because wages are "sticky down," prices are too.

Like prices, wages were once flexible: they went down as

well as up. A mason working on the Erie Canal in New York State made an average of $2.50 a day in 1876 and only $2.00 a day two years later; the "common labor" wage on the canal dropped from $1.50 to $1.00 over the same period. Blacksmiths earning $2.66 a day in 1871 were getting only $2.31 by the end of the decade. A worker in a textile plant saw her wages drop more than 10 percent between 1893 and 1898. Average hourly wages for all manufacturing workers went down in 1894, 1898, 1908, and again in the early 1920s. The long-run trend, of course, was up, as the economy grew and production increased. But whenever business dropped off both prices and wages were likely to decline.

The labor market that brought about this flexibility in wages, however, was not particularly pleasant to behold. One writer observed the Chicago factories around 1900:

> On cold, rainy mornings, at the dusk of dawn, I have been awakened, two hours before my rising time, by the monotonous clatter of hobnailed boots on the plank sidewalks, as the procession to the factory passed under my window. Heavy, brooding men; tired, anxious women; thinly dressed, unkempt little girls and frail, joyless lads passed along, half awake, not one uttering a word, as they hurried to the great factory. . . . Hundreds of others, obviously a hungrier, poorer lot . . . waited in front of a closed gate until finally a great red-bearded man came out and selected twenty-three of the strongest, best-looking men. For these the gates were opened, and the others, with downcast eyes, marched off to seek employment elsewhere or to sit at home, or in a saloon, or in a lodging house. . . .

Nor is this description overdrawn, despite the lugubrious prose. With unions representing only about 3 percent of the labor force and enjoying no governmental protection, employers could essentially hire and fire at will. The hours of work were long (typically 60 a week in 1900), accidents frequent, and safety precautions few. Minimum-wage laws and workers' compensation were unknown. Even child labor was not yet illegal: the first law regulating the employment of people between the ages of fourteen and eighteen wasn't passed until 1916, and it was declared unconstitutional shortly thereafter.* In 1900, about a quarter of the boys and a tenth of the girls between age ten and age fifteen were working. In a sense, wages were the least of a worker's problems. When wages went down prices usually did too, so real wages didn't change much. Still, knowing that the employer can and will cut your pay if things look bad does not increase one's peace of mind, especially if the wages aren't much above the poverty level to begin with.

The Depression of the 1930s underscored the effects of this kind of labor market. Nearly a quarter of the labor force was out of work. Production workers' hourly wages fell more than 20 percent between 1929 and 1933. Unions were still small and weak in the early thirties, and government had not yet begun to regulate conditions of work. Workers were still on their own, and doing worse than ever.

A decade of Depression and five years of war, however, essentially transformed the relationship between employer and employee. The changes were rooted in the new politics of the thirties, and in the new economics of postwar America. Today we take most of them for granted, and even complain now and then that unions and government interfere too

---

* That law banned the employment of children under fourteen in factories and those under sixteen in mines. It was declared unconstitutional in 1918. A milder law passed in 1919 was held unconstitutional in 1920. An attempt by the American Federation of Labor to amend the Constitution so that Congress could pass a child-labor law was never successful. "When ratification came before the voters of Massachusetts," writes one historian, "Daniel Cardinal O'Connell and other high-ranking prelates of the Roman Catholic Church attacked the proposal and urged its defeat." One may suppose that the interests of employers coincided with the interests of at least some Catholic workers, whose incomes depended on everyone in the family working.

Child labor was not finally regulated on a national scale until the Fair Labor Standards Act of 1938.

much with companies' ability to run their own affairs. Those who manage companies (or would like to) also complain about the fact that wages, like prices, are sticky down. Probably the grousing is inevitable. But it's a measure, in a sense, of how far we have come from the "free" labor markets of the past. A review of how we got where we are today shows not only how but why the labor market contributes to inflation.

Unions before the Depression

At the Carnegie Company's Homestead Steel Works near Pittsburgh, the contract between management and its 3,800 employees was due to expire in July 1892. In those days a union called the Amalgamated Association of Iron, Steel, and Tin Workers represented about a quarter of the nation's steelworkers. Its strongest local was at Homestead. In fact the local essentially controlled the way the plant operated. The skilled workers who dominated the union worked much like independent contractors. They produced steel with company equipment but largely according to union rules, and they hired and paid their own unskilled help. By agreement, the company's payments to the skilled workers rose and fell with the market price of steel.

Homestead at the time was run by an accomplished union-buster named Henry Clay Frick, who was second in command only to Andrew Carnegie himself. Frick didn't like the way the plant was working. The burgeoning market for steel in the 1880s had brought intense competition to the industry, and the union-dominated production system made it virtually impossible for management to cut costs by figuring out ways for the workers to produce more. Shortly before the contract ended Frick built a fence topped with barbed wire around the plant. He also, writes Katherine Stone, "had platforms for sentinels constructed and holes for rifles put in along the fence; and he had barracks built inside it to house strikebreakers." On June 25 the corporation secretary announced that henceforth the company would make its own decision about wage scales and about the terms of the new contract. The issue, said Frick, was "whether the Carnegie Company or the Amalgamated Association shall have absolute control of our plant and business at Homestead."

Four days later the plant's employees voted to go out on strike. Frick had already requested Robert Pinkerton to assemble, in secret, 300 of his guards to help break the strike. On the night of July 4 the Pinkertons were put on barges at a point below Pittsburgh and towed up the Ohio River and then the Monongahela by a tugboat named *Little Bill.* A union lookout in Pittsburgh noticed the barges and wired the strikers. When the Pinkertons arrived, a crowd of thousands, some armed, was waiting on the riverbank to meet them.

"The Pinkertons," writes the historian Philip Taft, "pushed a gangplank ashore, and one of the crowd threw himself before them to prevent their passage. During the argument a shot was fired, followed by a volley from the crowd and general firing from the barges. Two strikers and two Pinkertons were killed.

"Two hours later, another attempt at landing was made, and it was met by a fusillade from the strikers who were now partially protected by embankments of steel and iron. The Pinkertons again retreated to their boats and answered the strikers' fire through the windows and port holes. The tugboat *Little Bill,* which had carried the barges to their destination, now sought to bring them back. It was met by a volley of shot and finally escaped up the river to Pittsburgh, leaving the barges exposed. Oil was spread on the river in the hope of burning the barges, and dynamite was thrown at them, but these maneuvers failed. Finally, the Pinkertons raised a white flag as a token of surrender, but for a time it was ignored. By five o'clock in the evening, Hugh O'Donnell, the chairman of the strikers' advisory committee, agreed to the surrender of the Pinkertons and assured them safe passage. The crowd was of another mind; it swept over the barges and carried off the movable goods, and the Pinkertons fared badly as they ran through a gauntlet of men, women, and children who had seen some of their friends and relatives felled or killed."

The Amalgamated's victory was short-lived. The following week Governor Robert E. Pattison of Pennsylvania ordered 7,000 troops to Homestead, where they forced the strikers out of the plant. By July 15 the furnaces were lit again, and on July 22 a new work force of nonunion men entered the plant. On November 14 the strikers voted to return to work, their demands wholly unmet. Within two years the Amalgamated, its morale broken, had lost almost half of its membership.

Thus was inaugurated—in steel, at least—the Golden Age of Union-Busting. In 1901 the Amalgamated greeted the new century by losing a series of strikes against several of the companies that made up the new United States Steel Corporation. In 1909 the American Sheet and Tin Plate Company (part of U.S. Steel) announced that henceforth its plants would all be operated as nonunion shops and that wages would be cut. The Amalgamated walked out, requesting help from the rest of the labor movement. Thirty-six unions responded by launching an organizing drive, but to no avail. After fourteen months the Amalgamated gave up the strike. By 1911 its membership numbered just over 4,000.

In 1918 the American Federation of Labor launched another organizing drive, this one under the aegis of the National Committee for Organizing the Iron and Steel Workers. In September of 1919, shortly after the end of World War I, some 367,000 steelworkers went out on strike. By modern standards they weren't asking much: an eight-hour day with one day off in every seven; abolition of the twenty-four-hour shift; and a guarantee of collective bargaining rights. Nevertheless they met fierce opposition. The governor of Indiana sent first the National Guard and then federal troops to Gary to maintain order. The companies began reopening their plants with nonunion workers. On January 5, 1920, after eighteen strikers and two others had been killed, the executive board of the Amalgamated requested an end to the strike. The other unions quickly complied, and the strike was over, a failure.

In 1936 the weak Amalgamated, under strong pressure from the new Committee for Industrial Organization led by United Mine Workers president John L. Lewis, agreed to go along with yet another organizing campaign. This one was to be engineered and funded (to the tune of half a million dollars) by the CIO. The Steel Workers Organizing Committee (SWOC) was set up to launch the drive. As its first move, the historian William E. Leuchtenburg observes, it "brazenly rented offices in downtown Pittsburgh on the thirty-sixth floor of the Grant Building, an edifice which housed more steel barons than any other in the nation." More than 200 organizers spread out over the steel regions, and again workers signed up in droves.

This time the opposition came from what was quaintly known as Little Steel—the giant corporations of Republic Steel, Youngstown Sheet and Tube, Inland, and Bethlehem Steel, "little" only by comparison with U.S. Steel. A strike began on May 25, 1937. Again there was bloodshed. On Memorial Day in Chicago, a protest meeting called by the union ended with ten strikers dead at the hands of police. A Republic Steel plant in Monroe, Michigan, was opened by 200 special police. In Johnstown, Pennsylvania, a "citizens committee" formed to fight the strike encouraged violence against picketing workers, and the Bethlehem Steel plant there supplied itself with tear gas and munitions. Governor George H. Earle declared martial law and sent in troops. Later that month Ohio governor Martin L. Davey sent troops to Youngstown after a picket was killed at the Sheet and Tube plant. Slowly the mills reopened. Eighteen had been killed and 168 injured.

In the meantime, however, the Golden Age had ended. Within a few years all the Little Steel companies had been compelled to recognize and to sign contracts with the Steel

Workers Organizing Committee. U.S. Steel, meanwhile, had "folded without a fight" and signed a contract with the union granting a wage boost and a forty-hour week. Jones & Laughlin, Wheeling Steel, and Caterpillar Tractor signed contracts too. The SWOC, which already boasted 325,000 members by early 1937, continued to grow. In 1942 the Committee, together with the aging remains of the old Amalgamated Association, formed the United Steel Workers of America. The steel industry, after half a century of union-busting, had been organized in about five years.

The turning point

What made the difference, of course, was the New Deal. Not so much Franklin D. Roosevelt himself: FDR, says Leuchtenburg, was "somewhat perturbed at being cast in the role of midwife of industrial unionism." But the Democratic landslide of 1932 and the new political climate it reflected were making possible initiatives that would have sunk in a well of apoplexy and disbelief only a few years before.

In December 1932, for example, Alabama Senator Hugo Black introduced a bill aimed at creating more employment by cutting the work week to an unheard-of 30 hours; AFL president William Green "startled the country, and perhaps himself" by threatening a general strike in support. The Senate passed the bill shortly after Roosevelt's inauguration. FDR in turn set in motion the hearings and studies that would soon lead to the National Industrial Recovery Act. The NIRA set up procedures allowing businesses to establish industrial practices and to fix prices without fear of the antitrust laws; its Blue Eagle and the slogan "We Do Our Part" quickly became familiar features on store windows, factory walls, and newspaper mastheads. At Senator Robert Wagner's insistence it contained a famous provision—Section 7A—stipulating that the new industrial codes set minimum wages and maximum hours for labor and guaranteeing the right to collective bargaining.

The effect was dramatic. "In the grimy alleys of Birmingham, in the drab bars of Akron, on Seattle's wharves, workers were saying what for so long they had not dared to say: 'Organize!' " John L. Lewis's United Mine Workers added 350,000 new members in 1933 and 1934. The American Federation of Labor took on 800,000 new members in 1933 alone. The NIRA was declared unconstitutional by the Supreme Court in 1935, in the so-called sick chicken decision.* But shortly thereafter Roosevelt signed an even more far-reaching piece of legislation. The Wagner Act, as it was known, created the National Labor Relations Board and established the procedure for unionizing a plant that is still in effect today. Under the act, workers in a plant can petition the board for a "certification" election establishing a particular union as their bargaining agent. If a majority of workers votes yes in the election, the employer must recognize the union as bargaining agent for all the employees in a unit.

The law's provisions have never stopped employers from appealing election results and finding other ways to stall. The thirties were no exception to this rule, particularly since most employers were in doubt as to the law's constitutionality. U.S. Steel capitulated, but it was several years bebefore government pressure forced the Little Steel companies to accept unionization. The auto companies recognized the United Auto Workers only after a wave of sit-down strikes, beginning in 1936 at General Motors Fisher Body No. 1 plant in Flint, Michigan. But the tide nevertheless was flowing. "As steel and auto went," writes Leuchtenburg, "so went much of the nation."

After an eight-week strike in March and April, 1937, Firestone Tire & Rubber capitulated to the United

* So called because the plaintiff was a Brooklyn poultry firm convicted of violating the National Recovery Administration's codes on several counts, including selling diseased chickens. With the law behind the codes declared unconstitutional, the firm's conviction had to be reversed.

> Rubber Workers. By the end of 1937, General Electric, RCA-Victor, and Philco had recognized the United Electrical and Radio Workers. The Textile Workers Organizing Committee, run by Sidney Hillman, brought into line industry titans like American Woolen in Lawrence; by early October, it boasted 450,000 members.

Meanwhile, starting in 1934, John L. Lewis and his allies had begun pressuring the American Federation of Labor to begin organizing "industrial unions"—unions that included everyone working in an industry rather than, as with most of the AFL unions, the members of a specific trade or craft. The AFL wasn't buying the idea. At its 1935 convention Lewis punched Big Bill Hutcheson of the Carpenters Union in the face, and the AFL voted down a report favoring industrial unionism by a three-to-two margin. Shortly thereafter Lewis and eight other union leaders established the Committee for Industrial Organization, and in October 1938 the Congress of Industrial Organizations was born. The CIO was responsible for most of the large-scale organizing drives that swelled the ranks of American labor.

Swell them they did. In 1930 about 3.4 million workers, not quite 7 percent of the total labor force, belonged to a union. By 1940, the figures were 8.7 million and 15 percent; by 1950, 14.3 million and 22 percent. They haven't varied much since. In 1976 about 20 million workers—one out of every five, and one of every four nonfarm workers—belonged to a union. The Teamsters alone have nearly 2 million members. Five other unions include an average of more than a million members each.

The gross statistics of union representation and the widely touted fact that union membership has been dropping off as a percentage of the total labor force don't do justice to unions' impact on the economy. For one thing, unions are concentrated in key economic sectors. More than half the workers in most manufacturing industries belong to a union.

THE TEN BIGGEST UNIONS IN AMERICA

Union	*Membership (1978)*
Intl'l Brotherhood of Teamsters	1,973,272
United Auto Workers	1,544,859
National Education Association *	1,470,212
United Steel Workers of America	1,300,000
Int'l Brotherhood of Electrical Workers	991,228
Int'l Association of Machinists	943,280
United Brotherhood of Carpenters	820,000
Retail Clerks International Union	650,876
Laborers' International Union	650,000
American Federation of State, County, and Municipal Employees	648,160

* The NEA, though not a traditional union, has in recent years begun to function much like a union, partly because of competition with the American Federation of Teachers, AFL-CIO.

Except for the Teamsters, Auto Workers, and NEA, all unions listed belong to the AFL-CIO.

SOURCE: *The World Almanac and Book of Facts,* 1980 (New York: Newspaper Enterprise Association, 1979), p. 111.

In transportation and construction the figure is over 75 percent. Some unions regulate the supply of labor: the building trades, for example, where union membership is often a precondition to getting a job. All engage in collective bargaining and thereby help determine wage rates and working conditions for their members.

Unions' indirect influence extends even farther. Many nonunion employers peg their wages to the scale established by some union. Some do this by custom, others because they are afraid their own plants will be organized if they don't. The same fear of unionization effectively precludes wage cutting in many industries. Under the Davis-Bacon Act (another product of the Depression) and subsequent legislation, firms working on government contracts or on federally assisted projects must usually pay union-scale wages. And union wage gains often drive up the salaries of white-collar and managerial employees who are thought entitled to earn more than blue-collar workers.

Unions, in short, are an enormous monkey wrench in the works of a flexible labor market. Once in a while you read of a union that has agreed to accept a wage cut—"Union Accord on Pay Cuts Averts Closing," read one headline about a 1980 agreement between Uniroyal and the United Rubber Workers. This is a news story on the order of man bites dog. For the most part, unions effectively prevent wages from falling. Unless union leaders can win wage gains, they don't get reelected. Unless a contract contains an increase, the membership will reject it. Employers who would like to cut wages nearly always cannot.

Instead, of course, they raise prices. If wages cannot fall, prices seldom can either. And one more piece of the inflationary puzzle is in place.

Income security

Unions aren't the only interference with the labor market. The government meddles too. Once again the roots of this meddling lie in the Great Depression.

If the labor market is to work the way it used to, people who are not working should not eat. If they have some other means of support, they may choose not to work at all, or they may choose to work only when wages are high enough and other conditions of employment are fair. Nor will they be disposed to accept wage cuts. Faced with one, they're likely to quit instead.

Before the 1930s, people who were out of work had little to fall back on. It didn't make much difference whether they had been fired or laid off, had quit, had taken sick or grown old, or were needed at home to care for children. If they had some savings (or a pension plan, in the case of the elderly, which only a few had), they might get by for a while. If not, they were dependent upon relatives, friends, and whatever provisions their state, county, municipality, or church made for relief. "Welfare" of this sort was not ordinarily generous. Nor did it need to be as long as most of the population lived and worked on farms. With the growth of cities and industry, though, living off the land was not so easy. When times were hard people were in trouble. And never were times harder than in the thirties. In 1932, total spending for relief by states, counties, and municipalities (there was no federal relief at the time) came to about $366 million. That averaged out to about $30 a year for each of the 12 million unemployed.

Shortly after Roosevelt's election, an agency called the Federal Emergency Relief Administration began dishing out money. In 1934 relief spending came to about a billion dollars, with more than half the total coming from Washington. The government also began putting the unemployed to work. The Civil Works Administration set up by Harry Hopkins in 1933 was employing more than four million people by mid-January of the following year. The Public Works Administration directed by Harold Ickes moved more slowly, but it was soon building everything from rural post offices to New York's Triborough Bridge. The Civilian Conservation Corps sent unemployed men off to work camps in the country, and the National Youth Administration in seven years "gave part-time employment to more than six hundred thousand college students and to over one and a half million high school students." The Works Progress Administration created in 1935 employed some three million jobless workers.

In 1935, Roosevelt signed into law the Social Security Act. The act created not only the familiar system of payments to the retired but a host of other programs as well: the first national unemployment insurance system, federal aid to families with dependent children (precursor of the best-known "welfare" program today), aid to the blind and the elderly poor. The funding was not large, and a lot of workers were excluded from coverage. But the principle the act embodied helped transform the labor market almost as much as unions did.

Today, Old Age, Survivors, Disability and Health Insurance (OASDHI)—the full name of the social security program—covers most of the working population. In 1980 more than 35 million people were receiving benefits. Those not covered and those without other sources of income are eligible for the Supplemental Security Income program, begun in 1974 and now covering more than four million people. Mothers with young children and no other means of support are eligible for Aid to Families with Dependent Children (AFDC). Most workers who are laid off can get unemployment benefits of roughly half their previous wages for between six and nine months (sometimes up to a year). Some workers get supplemental benefits paid for by their employer or union, often adding up to 90 percent of their average wage. People who lose their jobs because of competition from imports are eligible for additional government aid under the Trade Adjustment Assistance Program.

Medicare pays doctors' fees and hospital bills for the elderly (it's the "health" part of OASDHI). Medicaid, though variable from state to state, does essentially the same for the poor. Everybody with incomes under a certain figure (the cutoff in 1980 was between $800 and $1,000 a month, depending on individual circumstances) can get food stamps from the U.S. Department of Agriculture. All told, "transfer payments" like these add up to more than one eighth of all personal income in the United States. They account for roughly two fifths of the federal government's spending and nearly a third of all government spending (state and local as well as federal).

Theoretically, most of the programs are fully available only to those who are not working. Even social security recipients lose a dollar of benefits for every two dollars they earn (over a certain minimum) up to age 72. "Not working," however, is partly a matter of what else is available. In 1890, nearly seven out of every ten men over sixty-five were either working or looking for work. The proportion now is about two out of ten. If social security did not exist, the figure still might not be as high now as it was in 1890, since Americans are richer now on the average than they used to be. But it would surely be higher than it is.

A similar point can be made about welfare, unemployment insurance, and the like. Those who oppose such programs claim they encourage sloth and degeneracy by making it possible for people to avoid working. The claim is usually overstated: very few people deliberately rely on welfare or unemployment for extended periods of time. But there is a grain of truth in it. Welfare, unemployment insurance, and other transfer payments do make it possible for people to get along for a while without jobs. They also make it possible for employers to lay off workers without consigning them to living out of garbage cans. In the old days this option wasn't available. Hard-pressed employers more frequently cut their workers' wages, and hard-pressed workers more frequently accepted those cuts.

One other modern development keeps wages from falling, at least at the bottom end of the scale: the minimum wage. Again we take it for granted; and again it was a long time coming. The codes of the National Recovery Administration were the first attempt to establish national minimums, but they weren't very effective. Not until the Fair Labor Standards Act of 1938 was a minimum wage enacted. Even that didn't have easy sailing. Southerners in Congress feared, with some justification, that the bill was a conspiracy dreamed up by northern businessmen to undermine the South's cheap-labor factories. The American Federation of Labor, which at first gave the bill a lukewarm endorsement, shortly came out against it. The minimum wage, AFL president William Green noted sagely, "tends to become the maximum."

On May 3, 1938, though, Florida senator Claude Pepper won handily in a well-publicized primary; he owed his victory, by all accounts, to his support for the bill. Within two months the act was law. There were many exemptions. Representative Martin Dies at one point filed a satirical amendment calling for the administration to determine "whether anyone is subject to this bill." Nevertheless, the act covered about 11 million workers, and immediately raised the wages or lowered the hours of more than a million. The initial minimum wage was 25¢ an hour and the maximum work week 44 hours. A year later the minimum rose to 30¢ and the week decreased to 42; an additional 3 million workers benefited.

On January 1, 1981, the minimum wage rose to $3.35 an hour. About 75 million workers are covered by its provisions, including half a million agricultural workers and more than a million household employees; both groups had no coverage at all prior to 1966. The minimum is not inordinately high, at least by historical standards. In 1950, for example, it was more than half of the average hourly earnings of production workers in manufacturing. By 1979 it had dropped to 45 percent of that average.

How the labor market works

If wages were set by supply and demand interacting in something approaching a free labor market, we might expect workers to be paid less in bad times, when unemployment was high and a lot of people were looking for work, and more in good times. In the past that's pretty much how things worked. Now, wages still tend to rise when the economy is booming. But they very rarely fall. Part of the reason, as we have seen, is unions and the fear of unions. Another part is the many government programs that put a "floor" under wages and that make unemployment or retirement more tolerable alternatives than they used to be. A third factor is the peculiar nature of the labor market itself. Some economists, in fact, believe that the labor market's characteristics are as important as unions and government transfers in persuading employers not to cut wages. These economists point out that, though wages used to fall, they usually didn't fall far enough to get rid of unemployment. In this view wages have always been "sticky down," and are just more so today. Three peculiarities of the labor market help keep them so.

1. *There is no single labor market.* Employers looking for workers do not automatically take the first warm body that walks in the front door. Some want particular skills, experience, or credentials. Others want a particular skin color, sex, or personal manner. Most workers, by the same token, are not looking for the first job that comes along. If they were, our current unemployment rate would ensure that no want ad in the newspaper ran for more than a day. Rather, workers are looking for jobs that match their skills or interests, that are in areas where they have experience, that are easy to get to, that have good fringe benefits or a good future. Some want temporary or part-time work; others are seeking full-time, year-round employment. Some are looking in San Diego, others in Hoboken. If you are unemployed and there are a thousand jobs available in your city, you might consider applying for ten.

2. *The wage goes with the job.* Jim Rice may be considerably more valuable to the Boston Red Sox than a lesser outfielder and hence commands more money than most. But the difference between one welder, typist, or salesclerk and another is harder to measure; nor are their skills as scarce as Jim Rice's. So employers typically offer the same wage to all applicants: "The job pays $285 a week." What the actual wage is depends more on the region and industry than on an individual's skills or qualifications. The same unskilled

laborer who makes the minimum wage packing shrimp in Louisiana will make maybe twice as much working in a northern manufacturing plant. A truck driver's wage may vary by nearly 100 percent depending on the size of the company he works for and what he is hauling. Yet there is no evidence a driver's skills have anything to do with these variables.

3. Labor is the only commodity that has an opinion about what it is worth. It has to be "purchased" over and over again: the employee makes an implicit decision every day about whether to show up for work or quit. Workers who feel they aren't being paid fairly will quit sooner, and in the meantime will be less cooperative and productive. Employers thus have an interest in paying a wage their workers consider fair, not so much for reasons of altruism as for reasons of practicality. A stable, contented work force is worth money. Some employers, in fact, raise their workers' wages whenever they can for precisely this reason. Nearly all refuse to cut wages for the same reason.

All these features of the labor market mean that conventional rules of supply and demand don't necessarily apply in determining labor's "price." Unemployment among West Virginia coal miners—an excess supply of labor, in economic terms—does not lead to lower wages among California aerospace workers. An abundance of competent truck drivers working for small, low-wage firms does not induce big firms to cut the wages of their truckers. A company just starting up will normally pay prevailing wages for its industry or region regardless of the number of applicants for work; anything less would be unfair.

The fairness of a given wage, by and large, seems to be determined not by any absolute standard but by what other people are making. City police compare their wages to those of fire fighters. Auto workers compare theirs to the wages earned by unionized steelworkers. College professors in

Philadelphia look at what college professors in Arizona are making. Government accountants look at what accountants working for banks are getting. Everyone compares their wages to those of their friends, relatives, and neighbors who are similarly situated.

The result is what the labor economist John T. Dunlop long ago christened "wage contours"—patterns of wages that prevail throughout an industry, a profession, a region, or an occupational group. These contours may rise together but usually bear a constant relationship to each other. They may change slowly over time, reflecting shifts in the supply of, and demand for, different kinds of workers. In the short run, though, the contours are a much stronger influence on wages than fluctuations in supply and demand. In 1980, for example, there was a nationwide shortage of nurses, to the point where some hospitals tried offering a "bounty" of $500 to any employee who brought in a registered nurse for employment. Despite the shortage, average nurses' wages were only $6.78 an hour, about the same as a secretary's in many parts of the country.

Raising nurses' pay to, say, $12 an hour (about $25,000 a year, still less than a graduate of the Harvard Business School can expect to make in his or her first job) would undoubtedly work wonders to alleviate this shortage. Older nurses would return to work. Nurses staying home with the children would discover the benefits of day care. Eager students would flock to nursing schools. Hospitals wouldn't necessarily be any worse off in the short run, since they are usually reimbursed for whatever they spend anyway. But the wage contour of the medical profession would be turned inside out. Doctors, medical technicians, lab workers, and orderlies would demand immediate pay hikes. So would dental hygienists, licensed practical nurses, physical therapists, school health officers, and members of a dozen other professions. Employers who responded to these demands with a lesson in the economics of supply and demand would not find themselves winning many arguments. Knowing this, they are unlikely to monkey with nurses' wages in the first place.

Wages, in sum, are determined by employers, but without much leeway. Companies with unionized shops (or shops that are in danger of being unionized) must worry about what the union wants. Companies with low-wage workers have to comply with the minimum-wage laws. All are more likely to lay off workers when business is bad than they are to cut wages. Most employers have to take into account what their employees think of as fair, and what their employees could be making elsewhere or receiving from the government. Most, obviously, do not want to pay more for labor than they have to. But they often have to pay more (and sometimes get to pay less, as with nurses) than simple rules of supply and demand say they "should."

Wages go up, over time, partly because workers expect to get raises, which seems fair, and partly because unions have the power to force them up. They also go up because of the comparison effect of wage contours. All these factors work in only one direction, like a ratchet. Because wages tend to move only one way, prices do too. Both are easy up, sticky down.

The story, however, is not yet complete. In particular, "sticky" does not mean "stuck." It is easier for prices and wages to rise than it is for them to fall. That does not mean that no prices and wages ever fall; nor does it mean they will be equally sticky in all situations. A truly impressive depression, for example, might make both prices and wages come unstuck. In the 1930s, prices of even the goods offered by giant companies dropped some, and wages even in unionized firms fell. Maybe, despite all that has changed since then, another depression of that magnitude would have the same effect. Yet no depression that bad has occurred for forty years, and none is likely to occur in the foreseeable future. To understand why this is so is to understand the last piece of the inflationary puzzle.

5. The Inflationary System: Government

Inflation, people once thought, was an ailment of the business cycle. When times were good and business was booming, prices rose. When the economy turned down, prices fell.

The logic behind this view is simple enough. In good times, everyone is working. Businesses are investing and consumers are buying. When workers demand higher wages they are likely to get them; employers are feeling optimistic, maybe even generous, and don't want to risk a dissatisfied work force. Prices that are responsive to supply and demand go up because demand is high. Prices that are determined on a cost-plus basis go up too, as wage hikes and other cost increases are passed on to the consumer.

In bad times, the opposite occurs. Demand drops and inventories pile up. Business executives get nervous and don't invest. Workers, fearful for their jobs, don't demand higher wages. Many get laid off anyway as their employers cut back production. Unemployment rises, and consumer spending falls off even more. Business gets worse. With demand down, prices fall.

For a good part of our country's history, the economy boomed and crashed in just this way. Its movements were at times dramatic and painful, but they were largely without long-term effects since in a year or two the tide would turn the other way. Prices rose and fell with the economy as a whole.

Back then, inflation was a boon. It signaled good times: booming production, high wages, cheaper dollars with which to pay off debts. Deflation—falling prices—was the enemy. As prices fell wages were likely to fall too. And debt, figured in real terms, mounted. Paying off a large mortgage with a dollar that takes more time to earn than it used to take is not a happy prospect. Bankers and other lenders, of course, saw things from the opposite perspective, so there were always plenty of loud voices warning against the dangers of inflation. For most, though, a period of rising prices meant prosperity. Economic life may have resembled a roller coaster, but at least it had its ups as well as its downs.

In the 1930s, the roller-coaster ride ended. The economy coasted down the track and just stayed there, instead of going up the next loop. No one, least of all the economists and politicians of the time, had foreseen such a breakdown, and few indeed were more than dimly aware that it had occurred. Most just kept studying the tracks they had already traveled over and predicting that pretty soon the car would get moving again. Happily, one economist saw a little more clearly than most. His name was John Maynard Keynes (rhymes with rains), and he both analyzed the difficulty and prescribed a cure. Over time, most of his prescriptions were adopted, though not always deliberately and not always as Keynes would have wanted.

In the process, the economic roller coaster has been banked, leveled, graded, straightened, and smoothed out to the point where it is almost unrecognizable. The modern Keynesian economy still has its business cycles. If the old cycles were Demolition Derbies, though, the modern ones are amusement-park-style Kiddie Bumper Cars: tame, and not capable of doing too much damage. Almost incidentally, they have lost their capacity to control rising prices.

The story of this change is the story of the growth of government. It begins in the 1930s.

Out of the Depression

Not everyone remembers the Great Depression. Most Americans—about 70 percent, at last count—were born after 1935, when it was half over. Still, it has been widely written up, and nearly everyone knows an anecdote or two from their parents or grandparents. So a few reminders can substitute for a complete description.

Production—gross national product—began to fall even before the famous stock market crash of October 1929. Total GNP dropped 30 percent in the four years after the crash. Investment levels fell nearly 90 percent. In 1932 the steel industry was operating at about 12 percent of capacity. Automobile production was off 65 percent, residential construction 95 percent. Eighty-five thousand businesses failed, notes the economist Robert L. Heilbroner, and by 1933 "the average standard of living was back where it had been twenty years before."

Unemployment was highest in the industrial cities and regions. About two fifths of Chicago's workers were out of a job by October 1931. In Detroit roughly a third were jobless, in Cincinnati about a quarter. There was no unemployment insurance and little welfare. Needy families in Cincinnati got $7 or $8 a week, the equivalent of maybe $35 or $40 today. In rural Pennsylvania families got $8 to $12 a month. In Chicago, writes the historian Lester V. Chandler, the unemployed "had lost $2 million of wages a day, but only $100,000 a day was available for relief. Help was being given only to the totally destitute."

Somewhere between one million and two million people, mostly men, took to the road. Many "threw together makeshift shacks of boxes and scrap metal" that were known as Hoovervilles. The largest was in St. Louis. Others could be found below Riverside Drive in New York City, under the Pulaski Skyway in New Jersey, "along the banks of the Tennessee in Knoxville," and "in the huge dumps off Blue Island Avenue in Chicago." There was "scarcely a city that did not harbor at least one" such settlement.

Wage cuts began in earnest in 1931 and continued in 1932. A National Industrial Conference Board study of a number of businesses found that 90 percent had lowered wages and salaries by about a fifth. Farm workers' wages fell by half. Counting both the employed and the unemployed, American workers as a group were earning only 60 percent (80 percent in real terms) of what they had earned before the Depression.

Two questions about the Depression plague those who have grown up after World War II. One is how people survived. Some of course didn't; they died from starvation or lack of medical care. Some others, writes Lester V. Chandler, "would have met the same end if they had been too proud to paw through garbage for scraps of food." But most managed to get by one way or another. The twenties had been relatively prosperous, and many people had some savings or assets (a house, for instance) to borrow against. For those without resources, grocers sometimes extended credit, at least until they too went broke. Landlords often refused to evict tenants who couldn't pay the rent; some were kind, others simply realized they couldn't rent the apartments to anyone else anyway. People pulled together. The "invisible relief" of help from family, neighbors, and friends probably kept a lot of people from starving.

The other question is why people put up with it for so long—why, in short, the government didn't do something. The answer is apparent from the history sketched above, but it is still surprising to the modern ear. Depressions were a part of life. Government wasn't expected to do anything about them, and wouldn't have known what to do in any case.

Just ten years before the crash of 1929, for example, America experienced a sharp postwar slowdown. Output fell over 15 percent between 1918 and 1921. Unemployment rose to nearly 12 percent in 1921. Yet by 1922 the economy was on the mend: in that year GNP rose 16 percent. Nor were the early twenties unique. The nation had experienced panics, crashes, and crises throughout the nineteenth century (including a five-year slump in the 1870s) and again in 1907. "We have been passing," said Herbert Hoover in May 1930, "through one of those great economic storms which periodically bring hardship and suffering upon our people.

A RECESSION BY ANY OTHER NAME

During the last century and until 1907, the United States had panics, and that, unabashedly, was what they were called. But, by 1907, language was becoming, like so much else, the servant of economic interest. To minimize the shock to confidence, businessmen and bankers had started to explain that any current economic setback was not really a panic, only a crisis. They were undeterred by the use of this term in a much more ominous context—that of the ultimate capitalist crisis—by Marx. By the 1920s, however, the word crisis had also acquired the fearsome connotation of the event it described. Accordingly, men offered reassurance by explaining that it was not a crisis, only a depression. A very soft word. Then the Great Depression associated the most frightful of economic misfortunes with that term, and economic semanticists now explained that no depression was in prospect, at most only a recession. In the 1950s, when there was a modest setback, economists and public officials were united in denying that it was a recession—only a sidewise movement or a rolling readjustment. Mr. Herbert Stein, the amiable man whose difficult honor it was to serve as the economic voice of Richard Nixon, would have referred to the panic of 1893 as a growth correction.

—John Kenneth Galbraith,
Money, p. 103.

While the crash only took place six months ago, I am convinced that we have now passed the worst and with continued unity of effort we shall rapidly recover." In the light of history, Hoover's statement is both less Panglossian and less disingenuous than it sounds today. Like most other Americans, he had little reason to believe that this was the storm that would very nearly capsize the ship.

By the economic theory of the day, depressions were self-correcting. As production fell, wages and prices would too. So would the rate of interest, since with nobody doing much borrowing the supply of money would be greater than the demand for it. Eventually labor, money, and everything else would get so cheap that businesses would find it profitable to invest. A few would do so, putting some people back to work and putting more money in circulation. Then a few more would do so, and the economy would gradually get moving.

In the thirties, however, the theory didn't work. Economists and historians disagree about the reasons, but at least three factors seem important. For one thing, the economy was no longer a collection of farms and small businesses. Investing in a steel mill or an automobile plant is a little different from plowing an extra field or putting a new wing on your shoemaking shop; it requires both more money and more optimism about the prospects. So investment lagged and kept on lagging.

Second, wages and prices fell, but not as far or as fast as they once had. Only agriculture behaved the way economists expected it to. There, wages and prices both fell by half. In industry, however, wage cuts were not so dramatic, and the real wages of those who kept their jobs fell scarcely at all. Industrial prices dropped, but not as much as other prices.

Third, interest rates were not allowed to move freely, and wouldn't have made much difference anyway. Since its inception in 1914, the Federal Reserve Board had lent money to banks belonging to the Federal Reserve System at what is termed the discount rate. When the board thought the economy should be slowed, it would raise the discount rate. Banks would then find it more expensive to borrow money and would raise their own loan rates. When the Fed thought the economy should be stimulated, it would lower the discount rate, with the opposite effect. The Fed's thinking, however, was not always clear. In 1921, with the economy in recession, it raised the discount rate to an unprecedented level of 6 percent, thus making the recession worse. In 1929 and 1930 it let the interest rate fall, but slowly.

Nevertheless, the rate reached 1.5 percent in 1931. If cheap money were enough to make business pick up, business should have picked up. It didn't. The reason—this was one of Keynes's main insights—was that business executives may not think they can make a profit on investment no matter how little it costs to borrow money. If things look bleak enough—and they did, with so many people out of work and factories lying idle—only a fool would think about building a new plant.

The only thing that would get the economy going again, Keynes saw, was for someone to spend money. Consumers couldn't; most of them were just barely getting by as it was. Businesses wouldn't, since the prospects for making money looked so gloomy. The only part of the economy that could be made to spend money was the government. So the government, Keynes argued, should borrow and spend as much as it possibly could. All that spending would create jobs, put money in people's pockets, lead to higher consumer spending and better business conditions. It would "prime the pump," and pretty soon the water would begin to flow of its own accord.

Roosevelt's administration, for the most part, never understood this theory. The federal government's spending did go up, from $4.6 billion in 1933 to $8.8 billion in 1939. But the increase was due more to pragmatic problem-solving than to conscious economic policy. If the administration had known what it was doing, it wouldn't have made so many mistakes. In 1937, for example, another downturn was threatening the still-shaky recovery from the depths of 1933. Yet Roosevelt reduced government spending. Partly as a result, says William Leuchtenburg, the economy in 1938 "plunged downhill" and Roosevelt "did not know how to stop it."

What pulled the country out of the Depression was precisely what Keynes had advocated: massive government spending. The reason for all the spending, though, was not the New Deal's war against poverty and unemployment, such as it was; it was the Allies' war against the Germans and the Japanese. By 1942 the federal government's outlays had risen to almost four times their 1939 level and over seven times what they had been in 1932. Unemployment virtually disappeared and production skyrocketed. America was back at work, the Depression over.

Stabilizing the economy

Depression never came back. Despite fears of a postwar slump, the economy rapidly converted to peacetime operation. Production kept rising, and unemployment stayed low. To be sure, we still get recessions, seven since the end of World War II, counting the most recent (which started in 1980). But by historical standards these are pretty puny affairs. The longest and worst postwar slump to date took place in 1974 and 1975. Real output fell an average of 1.3 percent a year for two years, and unemployment among nonfarm workers peaked at just under 10 percent. The recession of 1919–21 by contrast, never mind the Great Depression itself, saw output fall an average of more than 5 percent a year for three years and nonfarm unemployment rise to almost 20 percent.

Not coincidentally prices fell by a fair measure in 1920 and 1921. In 1974 and 1975 the rate of inflation eventually slowed, but prices kept going up. Whipping inflation, evidently, requires a good old-fashioned slump, not one of the delicate modern variety. Unhappily for inflation-whippers the modern economy does not easily lend itself to old-fashioned slumps. The reason can be summed up in a word: government. Five major developments since 1932—some attributable to Keynes's ideas, others to the exigencies of modern life and politics—have reshaped government's economic role. As a result we now have an economy that is largely protected against depressions of the 1930s variety. We also have one that is inordinately vulnerable to inflation.

The five changes are of course interrelated. All, in different ways, mark a tremendous increase in the importance of what transpires in Washington.

1. Government employment

In 1929, the federal government employed 579,559 civilians. Just over half worked for the Post Office. Not quite 20 percent were attached to the War and Navy departments. Only about 30 percent of the total—180,000 people—worked for every other branch of the federal government. Counting both these civilian employees and the military (roughly 255,000 soldiers, sailors, and marines), the federal government in 1929 employed slightly less than 2 percent of the labor force. State and local governments employed another 2.5 million, or about 5 percent of the labor force. All told, one American worker in fifteen worked for government at some level.

Today the Defense Department alone employs more civilians (almost a million) than the whole federal government did back then. The federal government as a whole employs nearly 3 million civilians and more than 2 million military personnel on active duty. State and local employment has burgeoned to almost 13 million. Counting the armed forces, government at some level now employs about 17 percent of the labor force. Indirect government employment—people working for firms with government contracts, for example—has been estimated to include another 11 percent of the labor force. So more than a quarter of U.S. workers depend directly or indirectly on government expenditure.

From the employee's point of view, working for the government is pleasant because you seldom get laid off. The well-publicized cutbacks of city workers during the past few years don't contradict this statement, they're just the exception that proves the rule. When twenty police officers lose their jobs it's a scandal; when two thousand rubber workers lose theirs it's a fact of life. Unemployment rates for people who have worked in government are lower than for any other major occupational group: they're usually less than half the national average. The reason, of course, is that businesses lay off some workers any time sales drop, or whenever the future looks bleak. Governments don't face the same constraints. Only when a particular jurisdiction finds it hard to raise taxes—New York City, for instance, or Cleveland—will it even begin to think about layoffs. And even then the federal government (which always has plenty of money, for reasons we'll get to shortly) can often be called in to help.

From the economist's point of view, all these government workers are an immense stabilizing force on the economy. When business is slow, industries begin laying off workers. Production falls; so does purchasing power. Immediately things look worse than they did before. So more businesses lay off workers, and the downturn gets more severe. Not so with the government. Business may be bad, but children still have to be taught, the roads maintained, and criminals put in jail. Moreover, Congress may decide to fund a new missile system or build a new dam—thereby increasing government employment—precisely *because* business looks bad. Thus the business cycle is stabilized or even counteracted by a large government sector.

2. *Transfer payments*

State and local employment has grown considerably in recent years. It doubled, for example, between 1960 and 1978. Civilian and military federal employment, however, has increased only a little since the late forties and has actually fallen off in the last ten years. What has accounted for the recent growth in federal spending is transfer payments.

As the last chapter observed, transfer payments are essentially an invention of the last fifty years. In 1929 about the only money the federal government paid out to individuals other than its employees went to veterans and bondholders. In 1979 transfer payments (*excluding* interest on bonds) came to more than $200 billion, or roughly 40 percent of total federal outlays. In the 1970s alone transfer payments increased 76 percent in real terms.

When numbers like these appear in the newspaper, irate citizens frequently conclude that welfare recipients are gobbling up more and more of their tax dollars. In fact most of the transfer payments represent programs that we don't usually think of as "welfare." A hypothetical tax dollar going to transfer payments—hypothetical only because the taxes that actually pay for these programs come from many different sources—would be divided up this way: About 75¢ goes to cash benefits—45¢ to social security, 10¢ to retired federal employees, 5¢ apiece to veterans, welfare recipients, the unemployed, and miscellaneous other beneficiaries. The other 25¢ goes to in-kind benefits: food stamps, public housing, and (the largest) Medicare.

From the recipient's point of view, these transfers make retirement or lack of work a lot more tolerable than they otherwise might be. They also provide something of an alternative to jobs that pay too little, or jobs where the employer tries to cut wages. From the point of view of the whole economy, transfers are a tremendously important way of stabilizing purchasing power. The poor and the elderly have considerably more income to spend than they otherwise might. Workers who lose their jobs get unemployment benefits, giving them some money to spend too. In the past, even the threat of a slump led people to cut their spending; the slump itself might reduce their incomes to zero. Today recessions can be painful, but our incomes fall nowhere near as far or as fast as they once did. So the downturn is apt to be less severe, and recovery that much quicker.*

3. Fiscal policy

Government spending of all kinds adds up to about a third of gross national product. Washington's disbursements alone account for more than a fifth of GNP. (Though state and local governments employ more people, the federal government's enormous transfer payments give it a much bigger budget.) All this spending helps anchor the economy through the business cycle, maintaining people's purchasing power during bad times and good. The federal budget plays another role too: it can counteract the business cycle by running in deficit when the economy is slow and running in surplus when the economy is booming. This "countercyclical" effect, as economists term it, reflects the government's "fiscal" or tax-and-spending policies.

A budget surplus is simple enough to understand. Washington, in effect, is taking more money out of the economy than it is putting back in. So purchasing power is less than it otherwise would be. Less gets bought, less is produced, and the economy slows down. Insofar as that eases pressure on prices and wages, inflation should slow down too.

---

* Readers with a logical turn of mind or a little training in economics will realize that where the money for transfer payments comes from is just as important as where it goes. Other things being equal, after all, a transfer payment that gives Mr. Jones $100 to spend may reduce Mr. Smith's income by the same amount, and purchasing power won't change a bit.

In general, people with lower incomes spend a higher proportion of their money than people with higher incomes. (The latter are more apt to save some instead of spending it.) So if you take $100 from a rich man and give it to a poor one, chances are that more of it will be spent. By and large, transfer payments like social security, unemployment, and welfare take money from those who are working and give it to those who would otherwise have little or no money. So more money is spent and total purchasing power rises.

Deficits are a little harder to comprehend but not much. The key to understanding federal deficits is to remember that the government is simply borrowing the extra money that it's spending. The factory worker who buys saving bonds on a payroll deduction plan and the New York bank that buys a million dollars' worth of Treasury bills are both lending the government money to cover its deficit. As the government borrows, the national debt increases. But this is not, in most cases, a cause for alarm. Just as a company can borrow more and more every year as long as business is good and the firm is growing, the government can borrow more and more as long as the economy is growing. The national debt has increased in dollar terms every year since 1950. But debt as a proportion of GNP has grown smaller almost every year. The debt "burden" on the taxpayers is thus decreasing, despite the fact that government deficits in the 1970s hit record levels.*

More worrisome than the national debt is what might happen if the government does *not* run a deficit. Without a defi-

---

* "Burden" is the wrong word in any case. To understand why, imagine what would happen if the debt were suddenly paid off. A company that is in debt owes money to "outsiders"—banks, bondholders, and so forth. A government that is in debt owes money for the most part to its own taxpaying citizens. Suppose Congress votes tomorrow to pay off the national debt this year. The move requires a stiff new tax—nearly $800 billion worth—but Congress passes it, the taxpayers pay it, and everyone holding a U.S. government security is paid off.

The immediate effect is an enormous redistribution of income. Those who own no government bonds are a lot poorer, those who own many are a lot richer, in cash terms. But the bondholders no longer have the assets they once had. No savings bonds for their old age; no Treasury bonds to pass on to their grandchildren. Doubtless they will be looking for something to do with all their newfound cash. Doubtless too the federal government will want to borrow some money to finance all the food stamps, unemployment benefits, and the like made necessary by the tax-induced impoverishment of everybody else. Maybe the people who have just been paid off would like to lend their money again—U.S. government bonds, after all, are probably the safest investment in the world. So the debt, in a short time, is re-created.

cit there's a good chance that purchasing power (economists call it aggregate demand) won't be sufficient to keep the economy going at full speed. Why this should be so is no mystery. Suppose, for example, that you make $20,000 a year. According to the way these things are figured, you have produced $20,000 worth of goods or services that somebody now has to buy. But you may not want to spend your whole $20,000. You may want to put a little in the bank, or maybe buy some stocks or bonds. In good times, businesses are looking for ways to expand: building a new plant, say, or replacing old machinery with the latest model. To do so they need to borrow money. So they sell you a bond, or they go to the same bank you put your savings in, borrow your savings, and spend it. In that case every dollar that has been earned gets spent, and the economy keeps humming.

But suppose business looks bad, and companies aren't doing much investing. Your savings, and everybody else's, start to pile up in the banks. Now you have "produced" more dollars than you're spending. Everybody else who's doing any saving has done the same thing. Unsold goods begin to pile up on the shelves. Companies notice this and begin to cut back production. A recession threatens.

Here's where the government steps in. If it borrows your money (either directly or from the bank) and spends it, the money you saved will stay in circulation. Everything that is produced will be bought. No unsold goods on the shelves, no cutbacks. In fact business will look good: companies too will want to borrow so they can expand, and the economy will grow. But note that the government must run a deficit in order to assure this happy result. It must spend all it takes in in taxes, borrow some more, and spend that too. It has to spend your savings as well as its "own" money. It can run a surplus only when it's willing to risk recession (to fight inflation, say), or when it believes that business will invest enough on its own to keep the economy hopping.

The government budget's countercyclical effect varies automatically with what the rest of the economy is doing. When unemployment rises, spending for jobless benefits and other relief programs goes up too. Yet tax revenues fall, since people who aren't working don't pay taxes. So the federal balance sheet tilts toward a deficit. When the economy is booming, on the other hand, tax revenues rise and spending falls, thereby tending to create a surplus.

In principle, whatever administration is in power sets its fiscal policy by adjusting tax and spending levels to achieve the desired effect. If recession threatens, the government should cut taxes or increase spending, thereby boosting purchasing power. If inflation is thought to be the greater danger, the supposed cure is to increase taxes or reduce spending. In real life, of course, the choice is seldom so simple. The trade-off between inflation and recession (as we shall see in Chapter Eight) is not always clear. And political considerations always impart a certain asymmetry to fiscal policy changes. Any politician will find it easier to cut taxes than to raise them. Politicians will also find it easier to increase spending, thereby keeping various interest groups and federal agencies happy, than to cut it.

Fiscal policy therefore more often focuses on stimulating the economy than on slowing it down. In the past twenty years the budget has been in significant surplus exactly twice. The result is higher levels of employment and fewer (or milder) recessions than we otherwise might have had. Another result, probably, is more inflation.

4. Monetary policy

Like an engine that runs on gasoline, the economy runs on money. If there isn't enough, the economy won't run very fast, and will be prone to fits and starts. Plenty of money will not, all by itself, ensure a fast-growing, smoothly working economy; you still need people, businesses, and governments willing and able to spend that money. But if you don't have the money you can't have the spending.

The word "money" in ordinary parlance usually refers to currency: bills and coins. Those who accuse the government of cheapening the dollar frequently accuse it of "printing too much money," as if the presses that turn out $5 bills were working overtime. In reality, of course, most of what we use as money isn't currency at all; it's the "money" that is in our checking accounts.

This money is neither more nor less than a bookkeeping account on the bank's ledgers. It is created, in part, by the banking system itself.

Suppose, for example, you take $1,000 in cash to a bank and open an account. You now have a brand-new checkbook, and you know you can write checks up to a total of $1,000. Suppose at the same time your neighbor applies to the same bank for a loan of $1,000. When she gets the loan, the bank doesn't necessarily give her your $1,000 in cash; more likely it gives her a checkbook too and credits her account with $1,000. Now you and she have a total of $2,000 to draw on, but the bank, let us assume, only has your original $1,000 in currency. As long as neither of you wants $1,000 in cash at the same time, the bank is sitting pretty. By this process the supply of money—that is, the total deposits the banking system carries on its books—grows well beyond the volume of cash that is in circulation at any given time.

Obviously, however, there has to be some limit on the amount of money so created. If banks lend mony to all comers, they'll soon find themselves in trouble. And if the banking system creates too much money in relation to what there is to buy, the excess purchasing power will drive prices up. The dollar will be worth less, then, simply because there are too many dollars in circulation.

The growth of the money supply can be limited in two ways. One is the way of "hard" money, fiscal responsibility, reliance on the market. The other is the way of "soft" money and political interference with the market. By all the standards of good conservatism, the first sounds preferable. When it was tried, however, it had two rather severe drawbanks. Coping with these drawbacks led to the inflationary monetary system we have today.

Under the traditional system of managing the money supply (in effect in this country throughout much of the nineteenth century and changed only gradually in the twentieth) every paper dollar is theoretically redeemable in gold. The government can issue only as much currency as it can safely cover with the gold in its vaults. Banks have to have access to enough currency or gold to satisfy any of their depositors who want it. The gold standard thus imposes rather severe limits on how fast the money supply can grow.

A country's gold supply depends on how much of the metal is being mined, and on how much is coming in from abroad to purchase goods and services. Its need for money, however, depends on how much real economic activity there is—how much people want to borrow and spend. If people want to borrow and spend more money than is easily available with the existing gold supply, interest rates shoot up. Banks make fewer loans, and businesses don't invest. The supply of money can thus limit economic growth. It may even provoke a recession. That's why the Populists—William Jennings Bryan and his followers, for instance—fought so hard against the gold standard. If more money were available (if, for example, all the currency could be backed by silver as well as gold), then booms would be longer, panics fewer. The price to be paid—inflation—was one the Populists were willing to pay.

In a series of steps beginning with Roosevelt's 1933 ban on gold transactions and ending with Nixon's renunciation of the international gold standard in 1971, the United States went "off gold." The particular reasons for each step were different. Ultimately, however, gold is too inflexible a standard for a rapidly growing economy. If we were still on the gold standard, we would either be limiting ourselves to a very slow rate of growth (essentially the rate at which gold could be obtained) or else we would constantly be making the dollar worth less in terms of the amount of gold it would buy. The former choice would be disastrous for the economy. The latter, though theoretically possible, would appear to undermine ("devalue") the currency repeatedly by deliberate government action. A rapidly expanding economy can't work with a money supply that is fixed either by fiat or by custom, any more than a growing number of automobiles can easily run on the oil produced by a fixed number of wells.

So the dollar today has no "gold backing" at all. If you take a $1 bill to the Treasury and ask for metal you will probably be given a Susan B. Anthony copper-and-nickel coin, worth less than 3¢ melted down. Instead, limits on the money supply are set, through a variety of devices, by the Federal Reserve System. The Fed tells banks how much money they can lend in proportion to their "reserves" (currency and money the banks keep on deposit at the Fed). It sets the discount rate at which it will loan money to banks, thus influencing other interest rates. And it buys and sells government securities on the open market, thus pumping money into the system (when it buys) or taking money out of the system (when it sells).

The details of these procedures are intricate. The only people who really care about them are those who get paid to do so. For the rest of us, the important point is simple enough. The rate at which the money supply is allowed to grow is now determined not by gold or any other impersonal force, but by the Federal Reserve. The Fed officials who determine how fast the money supply will grow are not elected, but they are appointed by the president and are not wholly insensitive either to his wishes or to Congress. If they keep too tight a lid on the money supply, recession is likely to threaten. Recessions are not popular with elected officials, particularly with presidents seeking reelection. In ordinary times, therefore, the Fed has a strong incentive to let the money supply grow. As it does, prices tend to rise.

Fiscal and monetary policy—tax-and-spending policies on the one hand, regulating the money supply on the other—fit together in an important way. In real life, there is no such thing as running a deficit exactly big enough to make sure that "everything that is produced will be bought," as in the simplified explanation above. Instead the government tries to run whatever deficit it thinks is necessary to stimulate the economy. An expanding economy, however, typically requires *new* money, which is exactly what the Fed provides when it buys a bond from the Treasury.* The deficit is thus "monetized," in the language of economics, and both total spending and the money supply expand.

On the other side of the ledger, an expansionary fiscal policy ensures that expansionary monetary policy will work. In the 1930s, remember, the money supply didn't grow despite the rock-bottom interest rates: nobody was doing any borrowing. A big government deficit, though, means that new money will automatically be spent. Again, total spending and the money supply increase together.

5. *The end of "panics"*

The old monetary system's second drawback was that it relied largely on prudence (and the marketplace) to enforce its constraints. A prudent banker, in theory, would lend only as much as he could safely "cover" with gold or currency. Despite their carefully cultivated image, however, bankers are seldom more prudent or less greedy than other human beings. So in practice the operating principle was let the depositor beware. If you put your money in a bank that wasn't run carefully, so much the worse for you.

What happened was this. If a panic was in the air, or if some depositors began to get nervous about a bank's financial soundness, a lot of them might show up at the teller's window all at once, demanding cash. If the depositors wanted more cash than the bank had or could get, it had to close for a while. Now it was really in trouble. When it reopened, virtually every depositor would be waiting in line to take out

* The Fed typically pays for its bonds by crediting the Treasury's account on its books. The effect is the same as if it paid for the bonds with newly printed Federal Reserve Notes (currency).

his or her money. In most cases there was no way the bank could get enough cash to satisfy all its depositors. So it simply shut up shop. In the language of the time, a "run" on the bank led to its "failure."

Banks often failed in groups, not only because similar economic circumstances affected them all, but also because a bank failure in the next neighborhood might make depositors in your neighborhood worry about their own bank. Between 1870 and 1900 at least ten banks in the United States failed every single year. In each of four years, more than a hundred banks failed, and in one year (1893), nearly five hundred went under. In the twentieth century things got worse. Between 1900 and 1920 dozens of banks failed every year. From 1920 through 1929 at least 500 banks closed their doors almost every year. When the Depression hit, the number soared to more than 1,000 a year. In 1933, more than 4,000 banks shut down.

When banks failed, their deposits vanished into the depths of bankruptcy proceedings; with luck, depositors might get a little money back when the assets and liabilities of the bank were toted up. But frequently the deposits vanished into thin air. The 4,000 banks that closed in 1933, for example, took with them some $3.6 billion in deposits. The money supply could thus contract violently at any point, causing untold hardship to people's lives and livelihoods and significantly worsening any incipient slump. People whose checking accounts have just disappeared are not likely to win prizes for big spending. And banks that have just gone under aren't likely to be making many loans.

In 1933, Congress passed and Roosevelt signed the Glass-Steagall Act, a law reforming the banking system. A major provision of the act provided for the separation of investment banks from commercial banks. A minor provision, not much noticed at the time, established the Federal Deposit Insurance Corporation. The new FDIC insured bank deposits up to $5,000 per depositor. Over the years that limit has been raised: it now insures bank deposits up to $100,000 per depositor.

In one little-noticed swoop the fear that had led to runs on banks was legislated out of existence. If deposits were insured by the government, there was no need to make sure they were there. Over a period of years, bank failures grew rare. In the 1970s, exactly eleven banks failed. Thanks to the FDIC, little money was lost by depositors. In most cases, the failed banks were simply taken over by healthy ones in the banker's equivalent of a shotgun marriage.

The government has set up other mechanisms as well to prevent the kind of panic that in the past usually preceded a slump. The Federal Reserve sets limits ("margin requirements") on how much stock you can buy with money borrowed from your broker, thus preventing the wild stock speculation that preceded the Crash of 1929. The Securities and Exchange Commission and the Commodity Futures Trading Commission regulate offerings and procedures in the financial markets. The FDIC, however, is probably the most important, because bank failures affect not only public confidence but the actual supply of money. In recent years some have argued that the FDIC is in trouble, because its reserve funds have been steadily shrinking in proportion to the amount of insured deposits. So far it has passed all its tests, including helping to rescue the mammoth First Pennsylvania Corporation in 1980, an endeavor that involved nearly $500 million in assistance to the financially troubled bank. If the FDIC does get in trouble in the future, so will the monetary system that has so far kept economic slumps from worsening as rapidly as they once did.

The inflationary system

With this chapter, most of the pieces that make up the jigsaw puzzle of inflation are now in place.

If prices responded directly to supply and demand—the way they do on the stock market, say—they would rise and fall with equal facility. They don't. Supply, demand, and prices themselves are manipulated in most parts of the economy in a variety of ways. Giant industrial firms control their own markets and strenuously avoid price cutting whenever possible. Smaller firms are sometimes big enough in their own markets to get away with the same behavior. Plumbers, lawyers, and a host of other tradespeople make sure they don't have too many competitors by setting up stringent rules about who is allowed to practice. Some try to work on fixed fee schedules as well. Farmers, doctors, home builders, and electric utility companies sell their goods or services at prices that are determined or propped up by the government. The marketplace, in short, is rigged. People have found ways to protect themselves from the market's invisible hand. Prices can still go up, but they go down only with difficulty.

The same is true of wages. Unions, or an employer's fear of unions, can usually protect workers against wage cuts. Minimum wage laws and income-transfer payments help protect workers at the low end of the scale from wage cuts. Moreover, workers have opinions about what constitutes a fair day's pay. An employer who cuts wages below the standard does so at his peril.

A real depression might shake this whole applecart. It might break the conventions that keep wages from falling. It might make companies desperate enough for sales that they would begin to slash prices. It might make the government so poor that it could no longer afford health care for all, tax breaks for homeowners, price supports for farmers, and bailouts for endangered companies. A depression of this magnitude, however, is unlikely. The government itself employs so many people that the economy isn't as vulnerable to the business cycle as it once was. Government transfer payments help maintain purchasing power when people can't find work. Budget deficits ensure that total spending keeps up with production. A regulated banking system under the Fed's control allows the money supply to expand as required and protect it from violent contractions. Booms are thus fed, busts cushioned. The slumps that we do get seem no longer capable of wringing inflation out of the economy.

All these developments, in short, have created a system where inflation is hard to avoid. If prices are to fall as well as rise, then the economy must contract sharply as well as expand. Workers must be willing to accept wage cuts, and prices must be driven down by competition. As a nation we have learned to protect ourselves from these grim possibilities. But that very protection leads to inflation. Wage hikes and price increases ripple through the economy, driving other prices up. There is no comparable force driving prices down.

There is, however, one more piece of the puzzle still to be laid in place. Most of the institutions, policies, and practices described so far were in operation by the end of World War II. Yet for twenty years from 1945 to 1965 inflation was almost always gentle, with prices going up a percent or two a year. In the mid-1960s someone apparently kicked the throttle up a couple of notches, and in recent years the engines seem to have been running on All Ahead Full. To understand *this* inflation—the double-digit variety, the kind that makes headlines in the newspapers and seems to eat holes in our wallets—we need to look not just at a system but at the peculiar history of the last fifteen years.

6. Why Things Got Worse in the 1970s

Nazi Germany surrendered to the Allies on May 7, 1945. Three months later, on August 6 and 9, the United States dropped atomic bombs on the Japanese cities of Hiroshima and Nagasaki. Japan surrendered on August 14, 1945, and World War II was over.

In 1946 the troops came home. Factories shut down their wartime production lines, and America's gross national product fell nearly 12 percent. Inflation, held in check by price controls during the war, hit 8 percent soon after the controls were lifted. The next year things got worse. Output continued to fall for a while, and prices jumped even more. War, true to form, had been hell. Now peace was starting to look like some kind of economic purgatory, haunted on the one side by the ghost of the Depression and on the other by the specter of runaway inflation.

During the next twenty years, that purgatory would be transformed into Hog Heaven. Homes in the suburbs, Buicks in the garages, chickens in every pot.

Not that the apparitions vanished immediately. But it seemed, just as it had before the war, that the one scared away the other. In 1948 inflation looked bad but production was booming. In 1949 and 1950 the economy slid downhill but inflation disappeared altogether. (Prices actually fell a little between December 1948 and December 1949.) During the 1950s periods of good times and modest inflation alternated with periods of mild recession. But the economy grew more than 3 percent a year in real terms: Americans were getting progressively richer.

In the early 1960s the pace picked up and the specters disappeared. John F. Kennedy, campaigning against Eisenhower's vice president during the last of Eisenhower's recessions, promised to "get this country moving again." A few more people (about 119,000 out of a total vote for both candidates of over 68 million) thought he would do a better job of it than Richard M. Nixon. They may have been right. Production rose 6.6 percent between 1961 and 1962, about double the average annual growth rate of the previous decade. From then on it went up 4, 5, or 6 percent every year: no more recessions. Prices kept inching upward, but even more slowly than they had in the fifties. Up to 1966, inflation under Presidents Kennedy and Johnson was never more than 1.9 percent a year.

A growing economy with plenty for all, low unemployment, steady prices: such was the vision of what Henry Luce had first christened the American Century. There was more to it, of course. America was also to lead the Free World, to fight communism, to instruct the unwashed in the virtues of democracy and free enterprise. And it would have to do something about the poverty and discrimination that were slowly entering the national consciousness at home. But none of this was possible without a strong, growing economy. And it looked as if the Democrats in the early 1960s had somehow found the secret. As GNP rose, America's promise seemed boundless.

Now, fifteen years have passed and the vision has collapsed. What seemed like the Promised Land feels today like a fool's paradise.

The changes came almost unnoticeably. During those fifteen years, American armed forces lost a minor war but no major one. The nation's physical security was no more threatened than it had been in the era of Kennedy, Khrushchev, and the Cuban missile crisis. No depression destroyed the American economy; despite a couple of recessions it continued to grow nearly as fast as it had in the good years. But in the end events teamed up to overwhelm some of the power and most of the promise of the American empire. Vietnam, and the protest it engendered; Watergate; the energy crisis; and finally the Iranian hostages all combined to create and reinforce an image of America as a helpless giant, corrupt and corrupting, an idea whose time was past.

Behind the general disillusion was a real decline in the United States's capacity to control international events. Also behind it were some new economic realities. Productivity, or output per hour, rose less than half as fast in the 1970s as in the two previous decades. Factory workers' real wages rose by half between 1950 and 1969; since then they have increased scarcely at all. Unemployment in the seventies averaged more than a full percentage point higher than unemployment in the fifties and sixties.

Nowhere was the difference so marked or so widely felt as in the rate of inflation. Some of the gloomy contrasts have been mentioned in earlier chapters. For the two decades beginning in 1950, the Consumer Price Index rose an average of just over 2 percent a year. In the 1970s it went up an average of about 7 percent a year. The long-term inflation rate, in other words, more than tripled. Between the Korean War and 1965, the *most* prices rose in any one year was 3 percent in 1957. Since 1970 the *least* they have risen is 3.4 percent (in 1971 and 1972). The average annual price rise for the last decade is more than double the highest annual increase between 1951 and 1968. In 1974 and again in 1979, inflation hit double digits.

As the inflation rate got worse, pundits and politicians began to single out villains. The Vietnam War was a logical candidate until the war ended and prices kept going up. Nixon's inept and contradictory economic policies came in for their share of the blame too, though Nixon's defenders correctly observed that he was not the first president in recent memory to pursue inept and contradictory policies. In the early 1970s a variety of random occurrences—a failure of the anchovy crop off the coast of Peru, a bad harvest in the Soviet Union—seemed to be contributing to rising prices. The Organization of Petroleum Exporting Countries (OPEC) too was a favorite culprit, though those who traced all our difficulties to "the Arabs" weren't always sure why inflation had been so bad before the 1973 oil embargo.

All these villains did play a part in the drama, of course, and the rest of this chapter will explain each one's role. Spotlighting the actors, however, should not blind us to the sets, stages, and theaters where they're performing: without the economic structures described in the preceding chapters, what happened during the seventies might have turned out quite differently. Then too, the important actors weren't always the ones that got star billing. Those who manipulate the murky world of international finance, for example, turned up frequently on center stage, though the audience's attention as often as not was elsewhere. Inflation in the seventies was a curious morality play in which most of us, most of the time, weren't quite sure what was happening. The only certainty was that prices kept on going up.

Wartime deficits, recession, and controls

Beginning in 1966 or so, successive administrations pursued policies that were remarkably effective in stimulating inflation. Policies that might have curbed it were postponed, curtailed, or never even considered.

• On June 29, 1966, American pilots began bombing Hanoi, the capital city of North Vietnam. The signal was unmistakable: henceforth it would be the United States's war, not just the South Vietnamese government's, to win or lose. By the end of 1966, U.S. troop levels in South Vietnam had risen to 385,000—more than double the number of a year earlier—with another 100,000 stationed offshore or in Thailand. In the next two years an additional 160,000 arrived, bringing the total to over half a million before withdrawals began in 1969.

The fighting required hefty increases in the Pentagon's budget. Military spending rose from not quite $50 billion in 1965 to $55 billion in 1966 and almost $70 billion in 1967, finally peaking at nearly $80 billion in 1969. After stalling as long as he could, Johnson asked Congress for a surtax to pay for the war's costs in 1967. As the president expected, Congress was not pleased with the prospect of raising taxes to pay for an unpopular conflict and took months to accede to the request. By the time the new tax was enacted in June 1968, the federal budget deficit had climbed to $25 billion.

By today's standards that deficit looks small, at least until you correct for inflation. At the time it was twice as big as the largest previous deficit for any year since the end of World War II, and it was five times the average budget deficit of the previous seven years. With unemployment at a near-record low of 3.6 percent, meaning that the economy was operating at very nearly full capacity, a deficit that big would bring inflation unless the Fed kept a very tight lid on the money supply. It didn't. In 1968 prices jumped more than 4 percent and in 1969 more than 6 percent.

• In 1968, Robert F. Kennedy and Martin Luther King, Jr., died at the hands of assassins. The Soviet Union invaded Czechoslovakia. A nation of freaks invaded Woodstock, New York, for the granddaddy of all rock festivals. And Richard M. Nixon was elected president of the United States for the first time.

Nixon proceeded, very slowly, to disengage from Vietnam. Peace talks had begun shortly before his election, and some troops were withdrawn beginning in July 1969. The policy of Vietnamization, meaning it was no longer "our" war but "theirs," was announced on November 3. Defense spending leveled off, and thanks to Johnson's surtax the federal budget began to show a small surplus. Worried about inflation,

Federal Reserve chairman William McChesney Martin tightened the screws on the money supply a little. Output fell, and by 1970 the economy was in recession for the first time in a decade.

The recession did not last long. Having lost the 1960 election because of Eisenhower's recession, Nixon was determined that 1972 should be a year of economic expansion. For three years the government proceeded to run big budget deficits, and the money supply expanded. (Martin's term at the Fed had expired in January 1970, and when Arthur Burns was sworn in as its new chairman Nixon is reported to have said, "Dr. Burns, please give us some money.") In 1971 the economy grew 3 percent. In 1972 the growth rate was back up near 6 percent.

Unlike every previous postwar recession, the 1969–70 slump put scarcely a dent in inflation. Prices rose more than 5 percent during 1970 and were going up at about the same rate in early 1971. In retrospect, it seems likely that Nixon administered the wrong medicine. Recessions typically lead to price drops in highly competitive industries like textiles and farming. Prices in industries dominated by a few big firms may not fall at all: managers may instead decide to raise prices to maintain profit margins. In the event, that's just what happened. The wholesale price of farm products fell, and prices in competitive industries rose only slightly. But prices went up 6 or 8 percent in concentrated industries like transportation equipment, machinery, and metal products. For most of the 1960s, the government's chief weapon against price hikes by big firms that dominated their markets was "jawboning"—using a combination of threats and persuasion to dissuade companies from raising their prices. Nixon and his advisers believed that jawboning was an ill-advised form of intervention in the market system. His reward for this belief was an unusual (at the time) combination of recession and inflation.

• In July 1971, Dr. Paul W. McCracken, then chairman

of Nixon's Council of Economic Advisers, wrote an article in *The Washington Post* against wage and price controls. "General wage and price control," he intoned, "would be a serious threat to individual freedom." A few weeks later, Nixon invited McCracken and other top aides to an urgent meeting at Camp David. Right after the meeting–Sunday night, August 15–he announced a ninety-day wage and price freeze.

The freeze was Phase I of what was dubbed the New Economic Policy. Phase II, a system of wage and price controls administered in good bureaucratic fashion by a Price Commission and a Pay Board overseen by a Cost of Living Council, began in November. In 1972 Nixon was reelected by a startling margin: only Massachusetts and Washington D.C. gave their electoral votes to his opponent. It wasn't long before he had terminated Phase II and announced the beginning of Phase III. This phase both reduced the scope of controls and left their "administration" more up to companies and unions themselves. Prices started to take off again. Nixon again froze wages and prices (June 1973), and imposed a new system of controls known as Phase IV.

Phase IV soon petered out. By then Nixon had other things on his mind anyway. In early 1973 the Watergate break-in defendants were found guilty, and in June former Nixon counsel John Dean began singing to the Senate about the cancer growing on the presidency. A year later, after a series of Watergate revelations, resignations, and impeachment hearings, Nixon resigned.

While they were in effect, Nixon's Phase II wage and price controls didn't work so badly. To be sure, a lot of items weren't covered: food prices, for example, rose nearly 5 percent from the end of 1971 to the end of 1972. And there were irrationalities. Chickens for broiling came under price controls: plucked and ready for use they were no longer considered a "raw agricultural product" and hence were not exempt. Since they were a popular consumer item, the Price Commission was not enthusiastic about letting their price go up. Feed grain for chickens, however, was outside the commission's jurisdiction, and its price rose rapidly. In short order poultry farmers found their costs of production outpacing the price they were allowed to get for their broilers.

For all the problems, inflation was held at least partly in check. Prices rose only 3.4 percent overall in 1972, and consumer prices other than food went up only about 2.5 percent. The vaguer guidelines of 1973's Phase III were predictably less effective. "Major corporations," wrote the economist Robert Lekachman, "interpreted Phase III as full of sound and fury, signifying nothing."

The departure from Phase II's strict controls, as John Kenneth Galbraith put it, reflected the novel notion "that if a policy is working, it should be abandoned." Politically, of course, the controls had already worked: they had gotten Nixon reelected in 1972. For more than a year before the election he had managed to stimulate the economy into recovery while avoiding the drastic price hikes everyone feared. He had also placated the growing number of voices in Congress and elsewhere who were demanding measures to control inflation. In political terms it was a well-conceived and well-executed policy. Economically its effects were temporary. When controls were lifted, inflation revived.

International finance: the shrinking dollar

Wage and price controls, though dominating the headlines, made up only half of Nixon's New Economic Policy. In fact, as then–Treasury Secretary George P. Shultz and others have suggested, they may have been designed partly to distract attention from the policy's international side.

Ordinarily, nobody's attention has to be distracted from international economic matters: attention is seldom on them in the first place. Ordinarily too, pronouncements on the subject have as much political effect as pronouncements on National Library Week. This time Nixon had reason to feel that the impact might be greater than usual. In 1971 there were funny things going on with the world's money. As the decade progressed the situation got worse. Eventually the international monetary system of the postwar period essentially collapsed, and a new, makeshift system emerged to take its place. In that change lay the roots of more inflation.

For twenty-five years after World War II, the dollar had been the linchpin of international finance. It was the one currency everyone was willing to accept, and it was the yardstick against which everybody else's money was measured. The reasons for its emergence in the postwar years weren't hard to find. It was issued, as the writer Nicholas von Hoffman put it, "by the government of the one society in the world that had a lot to sell." It also seemed safe. America's military might and political stability encouraged people to believe that the dollar would be worth just as much tomorrow as it was today. So did the Treasury's promise to redeem dollars for gold at $35 to the ounce.* It wasn't long before international trade came to be conducted almost exclusively in dollars. And just as a growing economy needs an expanding money supply, so the growing volume of international trade required an ever-expanding supply of dollars.

This need meshed nicely with the dominant economic and political role the United States was playing in the postwar world. With the vast European market temporarily devastated, American companies built plants abroad, and American investors bought the stocks and bonds issued by European firms. The United States government sought to win friends and influence people by maintaining a huge military establishment overseas. American citizens took cheap European vacations and bought cheap Japanese goods. To be sure, the United States was exporting considerably more goods than it imported, meaning that on trade alone we were making money in the international marketplace. But American investments, military spending, tourism, and other expenditures abroad tipped the international ledger

---

* Though Americans had been unable to trade their dollars in for gold since 1933, foreign banks could still do so.

the other way. Our "balance of payments," as economists put it, was recurrently "in deficit."

In the past, accounts between nations were customarily settled in gold. A payments deficit thus usually led to an outflow of gold and was a sign of trouble. Too many deficits and your gold supply would run out, at which point nobody would want your money. For the United States the situation was a little different. Foreign banks and companies wanted dollars to finance international trade, and so were willing to accept them in lieu of gold. It was a little like, in economist Paul M. Sweezy's words, "owning a free gold mine"—or like being the banker in a game of Monopoly, with the right to use the bank's money as your own.

The only trouble was that it probably couldn't last. Once the European and Japanese economies were fully rebuilt, American exports would face stiffer competition on the world market. That would reduce the surplus we were earning on trade and thus enlarge the payments deficit. Yet the dollar, to maintain its value, had to remain both sufficiently stable and sufficiently scarce in the eyes of other nations' businesses and banks. If there were a surplus of dollars—or if people lost confidence in the dollar and wanted to exchange it for gold—the jig was up.

As the 1960s progressed, in fact, the dollar was looking a little shaky. The Vietnam War (and America's war-generated inflation) cast doubts on the dollar's stability. Yet the expenditures required to pay for the war contributed to payments deficits that were bigger than ever. Already by 1965 there were more dollars in the hands of foreign banks than the gold in Fort Knox was worth. By 1970 foreign bankers and others held upwards of $40 billion while America's gold supply (at $35 an ounce) was worth only $10 billion. Now if anyone began to worry about the dollar's stability and ask for gold instead, the resultant run on the bank we were operating would empty Fort Knox quicker than a burglar in a jewelry drawer—except that the United States would lock the gates and call out the cavalry long before any raiders could reach the fort. Seeing this, no big foreign bank pressed its luck.

Presidents had tried various measures to stem the balance of payments deficit and thus bolster confidence in the dollar; President Kennedy, for example, imposed an "interest equalization tax" aimed at discouraging Americans from buying foreign securities. All such measures were like fingers in a crumbling dike. The only answer from one point of view was to devalue the dollar—to make it worth less in terms of gold and in terms of foreign currencies than it had been before. Such a move would make imports more expensive and exports cheaper; a big enough devaluation would automatically reverse the payments deficit as consumers adjusted

THE INCREASE IN THE INFLATION RATE

(Percent change in the Consumer Price Index, December to December)

The 1950s		*The 1960s*		*The 1970s*	
1950	5.8%	1960	1.5%	1970	5.5%
1951	5.9	1961	.7	1971	3.4
1952	.9	1962	1.2	1972	3.4
1953	.6	1963	1.6	1973	8.8
1954	—.5	1964	1.2	1974	12.2
1955	.4	1965	1.9	1975	7.0
1956	2.9	1966	3.4	1976	4.8
1957	3.0	1967	3.0	1977	6.8
1958	1.8	1968	4.7	1978	9.0
1959	1.5	1969	6.1	1979	13.3
Ten-year average: 2.2%		Ten-year average: 2.5%		Ten-year average: 7.4%	

SOURCE: *Economic Report of the President*, p. 263.

to these new prices and began buying more U.S. goods. It would also make our gold supply worth more in dollars than it had been.

From another point of view, though, devaluation would be a robbery big enough to make the Brink's job look like shoplifting a Hershey bar. No devaluation is ever popular with other countries—what helps Nation A's exports, after all, hurts the exports of Nations B through Z—and competitive devaluations in the early 1930s helped make the Depression as bad as it was. When the currency being devalued is the dollar, other countries pay a double price. For many years they had been accumulating dollars in lieu of gold, secure in the belief they were as good as gold. Now the Monopoly banker, who has been shoveling out money to all who would take it, announces that everybody's money is suddenly worth less than it used to be. The output of the free gold mine turns out to be fool's gold, and those who have been holding it look like suckers. For this reason the United States postponed devaluation again and again.

In the end it could be postponed no longer. By the spring of 1971, Americans were importing more goods than they exported; the dollar surplus on trade, which for so long had made manageable the deficits racked up by the Pentagon, investors, and tourists, had disappeared, and the outflow of dollars grew to a flood. In May, speculators and everybody else began to trade in their dollars for other currencies; the Germans quit buying them on May 5 when they were asked to sell a billion dollars' worth of marks in the first hour of business. In early August, the Bank of England asked the Fed in effect to guarantee the value of $750 million it had purchased during July. That meant the Fed would take the loss if the dollar were devalued, and it meant other countries would soon be asking for the same guarantee. At that point Nixon called his advisers to Camp David—quickly.

On August 15, at the same time he announced the price freeze, Nixon proclaimed that the United States would no longer redeem dollars for gold ("closing the gold window," the move was delicately termed). He also announced a 10 percent surcharge on all U.S. imports—a kind of backhanded, one-way devaluation of the dollar—knowing that other countries would now have to come to the table to negotiate new exchange rates. By the end of the year, an international conference at the Smithsonian in Washington had ratified new rates. Despite Nixon's description of it as "the most significant monetary agreement in the history of the world," it wasn't enough. In early 1973 the dollar was devalued again, and new rates negotiated.

But before long the central banks found it impossible to keep up any semblance of fixed exchange rates, mainly because countries were experiencing different rates of inflation. Most major currencies, including the dollar, began to "float" against each other, rising and falling on the marketplace as banks, governments, businesses, and individuals bought and sold each one. The dollar floated downwards in relation to the currencies of its main industrial competitors. In 1970 it was worth 357 Japanese yen, 3.6 West German marks, and 5.5 French francs. By 1980 the figures were 210 yen, 1.8 marks, and a little over 4 francs. It was quite a fall, and it came about mostly because the United States tried to get away with playing Monopoly a little too long.

The aftermath—plus OPEC

When Phase II's strict controls were removed in early 1973, prices began to take off like a Saturn rocket. Part of the reason was the delayed effects of devaluation. Other changes in the world's finances and politics played a role too.

• In 1972, the world was awash with money. Early in the year—it was an election year, remember—the Fed began to pump money into the U.S. banking system, cutting the discount rate and letting other interest rates fall. The German central bank followed suit, partly to prevent American investors from worsening the U.S. balance of payments situation (and thus the whole shaky system) by buying up higher-interest German bonds. The British, French, and Japanese were pursuing expansionary policies too. Between 1970 and 1972 the world's supply of "international money" (mainly the gold and major currencies held by central banks) grew 70 percent. In 1973 it rose another 18 percent.

Meanwhile, the years 1971 and 1972 brought a series of agricultural disasters. Much of Africa was riddled with drought. Asian rice crops failed. The anchovy crop—anchovies are used in livestock feed—mysteriously failed to turn up off the coast of Peru. With a lot of money chasing scarce goods, world commodity prices went up 65 percent from the end of 1971 to the spring of 1973. "There was pressure from all directions," writes Martin Mayer in his book *The Fate of the Dollar,* "on the world's productive capacities."

Into this tight market stepped Russian grain buyers. The Soviets had bought a considerable amount of grain in 1970 and 1971 though they had bumper crops of their own. In 1972 their harvest failed, and with the dollar devalued U.S. grain looked like a bargain. On July 10 the U.S. government announced that the Soviet Union would be buying $750 million worth of grain over a three-year period. "Suddenly," says *Washington Post* journalist Dan Morgan in his book *Merchants of Grain,* "the United States was hemorrhaging grain. Monumental tie-ups and traffic jams occurred as thousands of freight trains full of grain converged on the Gulf Coast ports of New Orleans and Houston." The massive exports, which reduced U.S. wheat stocks from 23.5 million tons to under 7 million tons in about a year, were "only partially the doing of the Russians." Other countries too were looking for cheap U.S. produce, and "when grain prices began to rise, customers panicked, and many nations bid up the price."

The next year—1973—high prices rippled through the Farm Belt. High corn prices, as Morgan explains it, led to a beef shortage; feedlot operators couldn't afford to buy cattle at the going rate, so ranchers sold young animals to the slaughterhouses instead. Pig farmers decided to sell their grain rather than feed it to their hogs; pork prices came down as the pigs were slaughtered, but soon went back up as "fewer sows produced fewer new litters." By the end of the year consumer food prices were up 20 percent; the Consumer Price Index had jumped 8.8 percent. And oil had scarcely risen at all.

• The Organization of Petroleum Exporting Countries had been around for a while. It was modeled, the financial writer Adam Smith has pointed out, on the Texas Railroad Commission. "Back when the problem was too much oil," writes Smith, "producers worried about how to keep the price up. The Texas Railroad Commission, which was in charge of oil in that state, would restrict production. If the price started to sag, the commission would reduce the number of days per month that producers could pump.

"In the fifties, a Venezuelan petroleum lawyer called Juan Pablo Pérez Alfonso was in political exile in the United States. He believed that the major oil companies were keeping Venezuela's oil prices down by increasing the production in the Persian Gulf, where it was cheaper, and he studied the activities of the Texans. In 1959, Pérez Alfonso was not only back in Venezuela under a new government, he was Minister of Mines, and he set about creating an international Texas Railroad Commission—without Texans, in fact—to oppose the major oil companies. In 1960, Saudi Arabia, Iran, Iraq, and Kuwait joined Venezuela as charter members of OPEC."

During the 1960s OPEC didn't accomplish much. Back then, the United States was importing only a fifth of the oil Americans used. And it had plenty of spare production capacity: in fact, when the Suez crisis created a temporary shortage in Europe in 1956 we had stepped up production to help meet European needs. As late as 1970 imports amounted to less than a quarter of total U.S. oil use. The world price of oil hit its postwar peak in 1957 at just over $2 a barrel and had been declining ever since.

In the early 1970s the picture began to change. U.S. production was slowly falling, yet demand was on the rise. By 1973 imports had jumped to nearly two fifths of total oil consumption, and a substantial fraction of the imported oil was coming from the Middle East. Then hostilities broke out between the Arabs and the Israelis. Middle Eastern oil producers announced a 70 percent hike in the price of their petroleum, and the Arab nations announced an embargo on oil shipments to the United States. Though the war soon ended, OPEC had gotten the boost it needed. Another price hike, announced in December, brought the wellhead price of Middle Eastern oil to $7.11 a barrel, an increase of nearly fourfold over the October 1 level. That increase showed up almost immediately in the prices Americans paid for gasoline, heating oil, and electric power. The "energy" component of the Consumer Price Index rose nearly 30 percent between 1973 and 1974.

• Oil is not like sardines. If the price of imported sardines rose fourfold, consumers would suddenly discover a taste for the domestic variety, or for herring, or for anchovies, or for salmon. Even if consumer demand did for some reason hold constant, the sardine part of the Consumer Price Index isn't inordinately large. Nor are sardines used for much besides hors d'oeuvres and sandwiches. Oil, by contrast, is hard to replace. Cars may someday run on alcohol or methane, but they don't yet. Home furnaces and electric power plants once burned coal, but most don't anymore. And oil is necessary for a variety of manufactured products, from fertilizer to Baggies.

It is, in short, a particularly powerful example of a general phenomenon. When the price of something goes up, consumer demand is supposed to go down. In the long run, that's probably what will happen, provided the price increases stick. In the short run, though, if the product in question is OPEC oil, South African chromium, or even high-quality Japanese television sets, buyers may decide to keep on buying despite higher prices. When that happens the result is inflation. OPEC had raised the price of oil, and devaluation had raised the price of every other import.

The reverse applies to exports. Shortages and devaluation led to skyrocketing demand for U.S. agricultural products. In the long run, supply might catch up with that demand. In the short run, prices went through the roof. Again, consumers had to pay them. You can get by without steak, but not without foodstuffs made from grain. When you pay those high prices, that too is inflation.

The lessons of inflation

With all these factors at work, the United States and everybody else in the capitalist world lived through a period of hell-for-leather inflation that was entirely new to Americans. Prices rose 9 percent in 1973, 12 percent in 1974, and 7 percent in 1975. At the same time the U.S. economy was plunging like a broken-legged horse into a ravine of recession. The chaos of those years—coped with only lamely by President Gerald Ford, who at one point was passing out buttons marked WIN (for Whip Inflation Now)—set the stage for the chronic inflation of the last five years. For like any good morality play this Western drama taught a number of lessons.

Jimmy Carter's administration learned a lesson it took four years to forget: If Recession Doesn't Stop Inflation, Then Why Have a Recession? To be sure, economists could and did point to the fact that the inflation rate slowed up measurably in the years right after the 1973–75 slump. But that argument came up short when set against the claims of political strategists that the recession had cost Ford the 1976 election. (As with Kennedy against Nixon in 1960, the popular vote was close.) Thanks to the recession, Ford had left a big budget deficit; with the recession over, Carter made it bigger. From 1975 through 1979 the government's deficit never dropped below $27 billion. Usually it was almost double that figure.

Businesses learned a variety of lessons. One was to anticipate inflation in their pricing policies. A survey by *Business Week* turned up a variety of strategies for keeping up with rising prices: more frequent price reviews, surcharges reflecting increased costs, escalators reflecting cost-of-living increases. "Where we can, we're trying to get complete escalators included in the contract," a midwestern heavy-goods producer told the magazine. "Where we have to bid a fixed price, we just add 12% a year to offset inflation." Unions learned a similar lesson. They bargained hard, as ever, for wage increases. And they tried more than ever to get cost-of-living adjustments (COLAs) included in the contract.

Businesses and consumers also learned a maxim that would have caused conservative corporate treasurers and family men of the past to throw up their hands in despair. The maxim was simple: Live on Borrowed Money. Real interest rates—interest rates discounted by the inflation rate—were frequently low, sometimes even negative. Business debt escalated, hitting a record level of 53.9 percent of GNP in 1979. For consumers it was the Decade of the Credit Card. Master Charge (now MasterCard) made its appearance in 1966. BankAmericard became VISA in the mid-1970s. Outstanding "revolving" credit, the kind you get with those two cards as well as with Sears and other charge accounts, rose from $5 billion in 1970 to $52 billion at the end of 1979, a real increase of about fivefold. Total consumer credit went up by about a third (in real terms) in the same interval. Mortgage debt, meanwhile, was jumping from $474 billion in 1970 to $1.3 trillion by the end of 1979, a real increase of nearly 40 percent.

There were other lessons too. The Federal Reserve learned it had better provide plenty of money for all this borrowing and spending; the money supply rose an average of 12 percent a year between 1975 and 1979. Banks learned several ways to get around whatever restrictions the Fed did try to implement. Thus the largely unregulated "Eurodollar" market (composed of dollar deposits held by banks not located in the United States) mushroomed. So did hitherto obscure financial instruments like certificates of deposit and repurchase agreements, both aimed at circumventing various monetary regulations. On the international front, Carter and others decided not to worry too much about the value of the dollar. It plunged in 1978 but recovered somewhat in 1979.

In the end, though, it all boiled down to one big lesson: inflation is here to stay. For most of the postwar period, people had expected prices to rise, but so slowly as to be almost imperceptible, a percent or two each year. Now they expected prices to rise 5 or 10 percent a year, and that changed their behavior. "It is no longer taken for granted," wrote the economist Robert L. Heilbroner, "that what goes up must come down; on the contrary, what goes up will probably continue to go up indefinitely. With such attitudes, corporations do not feel a need to furl sails rapidly the instant a recession blows up, nor do households feel a need to practice thrift, even if their incomes fall. Unions are emboldened to ask for aggressive wage settlements, because they know their members have the backstop of unemployment compensation behind them. The unemployed do not feel the necessity of taking any kind of work, because the welfare system permits individuals to refuse work they do not like." Wages and prices, always sticky, stopped falling altogether for most of the 1970s. And steep increases one year fed steep increases the next. When people expect rapid inflation, they act accordingly. Those very actions—the borrowing and spending, the cost-of-living allowances, the anticipatory pricing—ensure that inflation will be worse than ever.

Things got worse in the early 1970s because of a series of discrete circumstances. The recession of 1969–70 was brief, and didn't begin to dent price hikes in industries dominated by a few big firms. Price controls served to get Nixon reelected (though it's doubtful they were really necessary, given his large margin over McGovern), but they only postponed inflation. Devaluation made all imports a little more expensive and OPEC made imported oil a lot more expensive. Food prices skyrocketed as the Russians and others began buying up newly cheap U.S. grain. The inflation grew so virulent that the worst recession since World War II seemed at the time only to make it worse.

By the mid-1970s, inflation had been bad for ten years and the end wasn't in sight. People had already begun to adjust: now they learned to adjust more quickly and in more ways. Unions and corporations anticipated price hikes; businesses and consumers borrowed and spent. Fearful of a recession, the Fed let the money supply grow. Congress and the administration kept government deficits high. The recession at the end of the 1970s was a strong dose of old-fashioned medicine, but whether it would be administered in sufficient quantity, and indeed whether it was still potent at all, was open to question. The prospect, as the 1980s began, was for more of the same—despite the changing of the guard in Washington.

Chapter Eight will take up the question of whether anything can be done about this inflation. First it may help to summarize the overall picture—to reexamine the puzzle from a few different angles, figuring out how much of what people say about inflation is true, and how the history can best be understood. Once that is done, we will be in a position to consider whether there are any effective solutions or whether, like actors in a long-running play, we are compelled to confront the same problems and go through the same motions over and over again.

7. The Causes of Inflation: A Summing-Up

At one time or another during the last ten years, the following individuals, groups, numbers, policies, institutions, and social or natural phenomena have been blamed for inflation:

—Irresponsible labor leaders, corporation executives, farmers, and consumers;

—Federal budget deficits, resulting from taxes that are too low to cover governmental expenditures; on the other hand, taxes alleged to be so high they discourage work, savings, and investments;

—Interest rates so high that they add noticeably to the cost of homes, cars, and other goods that are bought with borrowed money; also, interest rates not high enough to discourage such borrowing;

—Social-welfare spending (including social security), which accounts for about half of federal outlays; also the Pentagon, which accounts for about a quarter;

—OPEC, also known as "the Arabs," a usage that must surprise the Venezuelans, Nigerians, and Iranians, who together provided the United States with about 30 percent of its imported oil during the 1970s; also the seven major oil companies;

—The Board of Governors of the Federal Reserve System, in particular Arthur Burns and Paul Volcker, the last two chairmen; the banks they regulate; the banks they don't regulate (such as overseas banks and branches); and the money supply itself;

—Jimmy Carter, Gerald Ford, Richard Nixon, and anybody else who had something to say about the way the economy is run; also Lyndon Johnson and his war;

—The Russians, who until recently bought a lot of grain from the United States; the grain dealers who sold it to them; and the U.S. Department of Agriculture, which made it all possible;

—And a potpourri of other factors, including government regulation, the Consumer Price Index (which is thought to overstate inflation—see the Appendix), minimum wage laws, speculation, war, peace, international exchange rates, bad weather, falling productivity, declining moral fiber, and that missing anchovy crop off the coast of Peru.

Once in a while—the last item, for example—an alleged cause of inflation will be reported mainly for the air of knowledge it imparts to the speaker. (Not everyone understands the importance of anchovies in the world economy.) More often, discussions as to who or what is responsible for inflation are simply a way of laying one's preferences and prejudices on the table. When an editorialist or your luncheon companion observes that something is inflationary, it's a safe bet you're going to hear about something he or she doesn't like.

Many of the purported villains listed above have turned up in the preceding chapters. The purpose of this chapter is not to go over old ground, nor is it to scrutinize the case against all the culprits that haven't yet made their appearance. The objectives here are simpler but in the end more useful. One is to illustrate the futility of blaming inflation on some of the more frequently accused miscreants. Another is to look at the whole inflationary system in historical perspective. Both endeavors will reveal much about how inflation should—and should not—be controlled.

Government regulation

In the 1960s and 1970s, the federal government passed a lot of laws that business people weren't particularly fond of: regulations about waste disposal and air pollution, about health and safety at the workplace, even about the racial and sexual makeup of the labor force. In the white businessman's view of the situation, profits were going up in smoke: they were burned up in a furnace stoked by a sixty-eight-year-old Spanish-surnamed gay woman in a wheelchair, who was wearing $1,500 worth of safety equipment. The ashes went up a 50-foot-high stack topped with a scrubbing apparatus costing $2 million. Everyone else working in the plant was back at the office filling out government forms.

Not surprisingly, business executives wanted to fight these regulations. The trouble is, it doesn't sound good to defend your right to pollute the air and water, to let your employees be killed or maimed, or to continue hiring on the basis of sex and skin color. The lobbyists and public relations firms hired to put forth business's point of view had to come up with a better angle. Happily, one was at hand: inflation. Since most regulations add to the cost of doing business, most must therefore add to product prices. When prices go up, as Calvin Coolidge might have said, inflation results. Since nobody likes inflation, it follows that nobody should like the regulations.

There is little doubt that many regulations do add to the cost of doing business. How much they add is less than certain. The conservative economist Murray Weidenbaum, who has studied the subject in detail, estimates that the total cost of government regulation is more than $100 billion: about 4 percent of GNP. Mark Green and Norman Waitzman, associates of Ralph Nader who have also studied the subject, contend that Weidenbaum's estimate is overblown, and cite a Government Accounting Office estimate of regulatory costs only one third as great. Green and Waitzman also note that only 30 percent of Weidenbaum's estimate is attributable to "social" regulation of the sort mentioned above; the rest is due to "cartel" agencies like the Interstate Commerce Commission that regulate competition and rate setting, and to paperwork. Cartel regulation, of course, does not come in for the same kind of opprobrium from business as do the regulations of agencies like the Occupational Safety and Health Administration (OSHA) and the Equal Employment Opportunity Commission.

In any event, adding to the cost of doing business is not the same thing as causing inflation. For one thing, any given regulation increases costs only once. It may make a product more expensive–once. It does not lead to continuing price increases. For another, effective regulations lead to products that are qualitatively different from what was being produced before. If Sony brings out a cassette recorder that works and sounds better than last year's model but costs more, few would describe that price hike as inflationary. If General Motors produces a car that pollutes less air and that injured fewer workers while it was in production, that car too may cost more. Like the Sony recorder, it's worth more.*

---

* The benefits of regulation, though hard to measure, are also usually overlooked in the debate about regulation's costs. Nicholas A. Ashford of MIT's Center for Policy Alternatives has listed some examples of such benefits:

> Water pollution control, in a breakdown, produces a reduction in water-borne disease valued at $100 million to $1 billion a year, provides recreational potential valued at up to $9.4 billion a year and substantially increases property values. And these evaluations do not take into account programs directed at such long-term or large-scale problems as carcinogens in water supplies, stratospheric ozone depletion, atmospheric sulfate transport or acid rain.
>
> Inspections by the Occupational Safety and Health Administration are estimated to have prevented between 40,000 and 60,000 accidents in which workdays would have been lost and up to 350 deaths in both 1974 and 1975. . . .
>
> As a result of consumer product safety regulations, child-resistant drug packaging has prevented an estimated 34,000 injuries from accidental drug ingestion between 1973 and 1976. Crib safety standards

Minimum wage laws

Those who believe that people should have the right to work for less than $3.35 an hour—not quite $7,000 a year, assuming full-time year-round employment—are quick to criticize minimum-wage laws as inflationary. Minimum wages do undoubtedly make a few things more expensive than they otherwise would be: laundry service, McDonald's hamburgers, and car washes come to mind. But they are seldom inflationary. Between 1970 and 1980 the minimum wage rose 94 percent. Average manufacturing wages and the Consumer Price Index both rose more. Thus people working for the minimum wage have not even kept up with inflation, let alone caused it. Moreover, only a small fraction of the U.S. work force earns no more than the minimum wage. Blaming inflation in general on a rising minimum wage is like saying that New York Yankee ticket prices are so high because the bat boy makes so much money.

There are two specific situations in which a small amount of inflation can plausibly be attributed to the minimum wage. First, in a year when the minimum goes up faster than other wages or prices it tends to lift the average rate of inflation. Thus in 1978 it rose 15 percent, and, according to economists Robert Gough and Robin Siegel, it thereby added a tenth of a percentage point to the inflation rate. Second, when increases in the minimum wage are mandated in advance (as was the January 1981 increase to $3.35 an hour), other low-wage workers may demand similar increases to maintain traditional wage differentials. How significant

---

have reduced crib-related injuries to infants by 44 percent since 1974. . . .

There are other kinds of benefits too. Without government fuel economy standards, for example, Detroit would probably have made fewer small cars in the last few years, and would have taken an even worse beating than it did in 1979 and 1980 when consumers began buying more small automobiles.

this effect may be, particularly with other wages and prices rising rapidly anyway, is hard to judge.*

OPEC

Blaming OPEC for inflation–in fact, hating OPEC in general–is for an American about as hard as denouncing the Russians for invading Afghanistan. Xenophobes dislike the ominous Arab character of many OPEC nations. Conservative free-marketeers oppose OPEC because it is a cartel. Liberals and radicals object to the traditional, almost feudal nature of some of the more important OPEC states, and note that a lot of the new oil wealth does not get widely distributed. Everybody dislikes paying more for gas and heating oil. About the only Americans who may, in their most private moments, thank the Lord for OPEC are those who own large shares in the oil companies. Between 1972 and 1978 the petroleum industry's net income increased (in real terms) 47 percent.

Between 1973 and mid-1980, the energy component of the Consumer Price Index essentially tripled. Everything else rose only 80 percent. So oil price hikes really do account for a good part of our inflation. Energy costs by most estimates account for about a tenth of our economy's output. A 20 percent hike in energy costs, therefore, generates two points of inflation all by itself. The worst price boosts came

* There are two other arguments against the minimum wage. One is that it discourages employers from hiring low-wage workers and thus hurts the very people it is trying to help. This effect may be counterbalanced by the fact that low-wage workers *with* jobs earn more under a minimum-wage law than they otherwise would; the evidence is mixed. The second argument is that the minimum wage actually has a perverse effect on the distribution of income. Since many of the workers in minimum-wage jobs are teenagers, and since teenagers from more affluent families are more likely to get jobs than poor teenagers, the minimum wage seems to help the middle class more than the poor. On both points see Christopher Jencks, "The Minimum Wage Controversy," *Working Papers for a New Society*, March/April 1978, pp. 12–14.

in 1973–74 and in 1979. The rest of the time, oil went up no faster than other items.

OPEC, however, did not act alone. The oil companies, though opposing the increases, were able to pass them on to consumers; company profits thus increased substantially, as did the value of the reserves they hold in non-OPEC countries like the United States and Canada. Consumers, for their part, kept on buying oil and gasoline for a long time regardless of the price: while the wellhead cost was rising from less than $2 to nearly $30 a barrel, U.S. imports were rising from 2.2 million to 6.2 million barrels a day. Most important, the West's central banks and international monetary institutions made sure there was plenty of money around to buy the oil.

To understand the importance of this last phenomenon, imagine, as Robert L. Heilbroner has suggested, that all the coal producers in the nineteenth century got together and formed a domestic version of OPEC aimed at regulating the price of coal. Imagine too that they, like OPEC, started off by jacking the price up to four times what it had been. No one, says Heilbroner, would come to the conclusion that such a move would be inflationary:

> Instead, a coal OPEC would have resulted in the wholesale shutting down of coal mines unable to sell their product; in the drastic curtailment of steel output as plant managers cut back their unprofitable operations; in a decline of purchasing from the businesses and households affected by this turn of events; and thereafter in a fall in "carloadings," the index of general economic activity we used before GNP was invented.

Some such decline actually resulted from the modern OPEC's moves. The initial price jump of late 1973 and early 1974 worsened, if it did not actually cause, the recession that extended to 1975. The price hikes of 1979 probably contributed to the recession of 1980.

OPEC's measures did not touch off worldwide depression,

however, because the money supply was large enough to accommodate the new prices. Remember all those dollars that were floating around? When OPEC nations were paid, they deposited the dollars in American or European banks. The banks in turn "recycled" the "petrodollars," as the new language had it, by lending out the money to poorer nations so they could pay their oil bills. It's exactly as if Americans, faced with the hypothetical coal OPEC of the nineteenth century, had simply borrowed all the money they needed to pay their coal bills and kept right on buying as much as before. Back then, this couldn't have happened—gold and prudence, as explained above, combined to limit the supply of money available for borrowing. In 1973 the limits were off: gold was irrelevant, and the United States kept churning out dollars. Inflation, not depression, was the result.

Government spending (liberal version)

Among the charges leveled against the Defense Department by liberals and other foreign-policy doves is the assertion that fat Pentagon budgets cause inflation. Since the accusation comes from people who oppose much arms spending anyway, it is somewhat suspect, like business charges that government regulation is inflationary. Still, the argument is not entirely specious. Even a conservative writer like Alfred L. Malabre, Jr., of *The Wall Street Journal* has asserted that "military spending tends to exert a particularly inflationary impact."

How can this be? At the simplest level, the belief that defense spending is inflationary hinges on the notion that people are being paid to produce something they can't buy. Thus the income in people's pockets adds up to more than the supply of consumer goods available for purchase, and prices rise accordingly. The flaw in this argument is that it could be applied to nearly everything the government buys for us—parks, dams, state universities, and so forth. From the viewpoint of the economy as a whole, military preparedness is just as much a "purchase" as the nine million cars Americans bought last year, and the Pentagon in this respect is no more responsible for inflation than the automobile industry. Only to the extent that military forces are a total waste of money, and maintaining them therefore akin to digging holes and filling them up again, does the argument make sense. But then the issue should be wasted resources, not higher prices.

Fat Pentagon budgets probably do feed inflation indirectly. They help keep government spending high, stabilizing the economy and preventing a depression. And the Defense Department, despite recent efforts to control costs, is not known for parsimony. As a result most contracts work on a cost-plus basis. A Columbia University engineering professor, Lloyd J. Dumas, describes the effects this way:

> No firm that knows its customers will cover all of its costs—including guaranteed profits—will hold back on spending. The inevitable freewheeling attitude bids up the prices of the various productive resources the various firms buy—resources also needed by civilian firms. In this way the defense budget fuels "cost push" inflation.

Then too, U.S. military spending abroad—the costs of empire, as some commentators have put it—is a prime component of the American payments deficit. As Dumas notes, the United States gained $49 billion on trade alone between the mid-1950s and the mid-1970s. During the same period we spent more than $54 billion abroad for military purposes. "Military spending," Dumas concludes, "thus turned a positive trade situation into a negative overall flow, and caused dollars to pile up overseas." Eventually all those dollars made devaluation necessary, with inflationary effects as described in the last chapter.

Finally, the defense budget represents an enormous diversion of skilled manpower—scientists, mathematicians, engineers—to military endeavors. In principle, these same professionals might otherwise have been working on technological improvements in the civilian economy, which in turn would have led to faster growth rates, higher productivity, and, conceivably, less inflation. The professionals might also have been unemployed. It depends, as with so much else in political debate, on what you assume the government would have done if it hadn't spent so much money on defense. Is defense spending inflationary? Like the old woman who was asked "How's your husband?" a reasonable answer is, Compared to what?

Government spending (conservative version)

Where liberals like to blame the generals for inflation, conservatives like to blame welfare mothers and other less influential recipients of governmental largesse. Government, say the conservatives, dishes out too much money to people who aren't working, and pays too many bureaucrats to provide unwanted or unneeded social services to the poor. Cutbacks in this area would reduce the size of the federal budget, lower the chance of a deficit, and in general encourage more people to work more than they do now. The result would be greater output and less inflation.

Circumstantially, the conservatives have a better case than the liberals. In the late 1960s, rising defense expenditures contributed to Vietnam-era inflation. Since then, however—and during the years when inflation has been at its worst—defense spending has been falling, both as a proportion of GNP and as a share of the federal budget. Governmental transfer payments, in contrast, have been rising steeply. "Income security" passed "national defense" on the budget ledger in fiscal 1974 and has been going up ever since. Logically too the conservatives have a prima facie case. A sharp reduction in social security, welfare benefits, and other transfer programs might lead more people to seek work, might make low-wage workers more willing to accept wage cuts, and almost certainly would make total purchasing power decline, thus precipitating a recession. The recession in turn might be sharp and steep enough to dampen inflation considerably.

In the long run the effects of such moves are harder to predict. Most West European countries spend considerably more on social welfare than the United States, yet inflation rates in Europe vary widely. Then too, the desirability, morality, and political feasibility of the conservative prescription are open to some question. At last count, approximately fifty-five million Americans were receiving a sizable fraction of their income in the form of a government check, with the largest chunk coming from social security payments. A small amount of extra inflation may be a reasonable price to pay for the modest degree of income security enjoyed by Americans who are retired or unemployed.

In general, using inflation as a political club does not make for particularly persuasive arguments. Business executives would be better off pointing out the waste engendered by foolish government regulations than they are in charging that all regulation is inflationary. Liberals are better off attacking the fat in the Pentagon's budget, or even the whole concept of a spiraling arms race in a thermonuclear world, than in laying inflation at its doorstep. After all, those who believe that what OSHA or the Navy does is important are probably willing to put up with whatever inflation they may cause. The same is true of transfer payments.

Deficit spending

Liberals and conservatives alike often agree that federal budget deficits are inflationary. In early 1980, for example—before the recession was recognized for what it was—Democrats and Republicans in Congress competed to see who could come up with a balanced-budget proposal first. There is no doubt that big budget deficits can, at times, generate inflation, as long as the Fed is willing to expand the money supply accordingly. Lyndon Johnson's Vietnam deficits are a prime example. But the matter is not as simple as it sometimes seems.

In principle, you want to run a deficit whenever the economy is running well below capacity and there is widespread unemployment. The only question is how big the deficit should be. Economists try to estimate it by figuring what the budget would look like if everyone were working and paying taxes; that high-employment budget, as it is known, should be roughly in balance. For most of the 1970s, the high-employment budget was in deficit, though not by large amounts. Ironically, one year in which the high-employment budget was in surplus was 1974—the year, until 1979, of the worst inflation ever. So the connection between deficits and price increases is not always clear.

Other comparisons also undermine the apparent link between deficits and inflation. "We had inflation in 1920," notes the historian Arthur Schlesinger Jr. in an article in *The Wall Street Journal*, "when the federal budget ran a surplus. We had appalling deflation in 1930–33—when the federal budget was running unprecedented peacetime deficits. In 1975–76 inflation declined from 12% to 4.8%—while the budget ran deficits of $112 billion. . . . Or take a look abroad. West Germany today has a budget deficit at least two and a half times as large as ours in relation to gross national product—and an inflation rate one fourth of ours."

Finally, looking at Washington's role in the whole government sector of the economy may put the matter in the perspective it needs. In 1979, the federal government ran a $10.5 billion deficit. State and local governments, meanwhile, were running a surplus of over $24 billion. Yet Washington was transferring about $80 billion to states and localities through various aid programs. If that figure had been cut by $10 billion the federal budget would have been in balance; state and local governments would have had less of a surplus; and the inflation rate would not have budged.

Too much money

One source of inflation that nearly everyone agrees on is that you can't have inflation without a lot of money. The

WHAT HAPPENS WHEN THE FEDERAL GOVERNMENT TRIES TO BALANCE THE BUDGET

In March of 1980, shortly before the recession stuck its nose under the tent, President Carter announced some new anti-inflation measures, including a balanced budget. As budget cuts were being discussed in Congress, Democratic Senator Thomas B. Eagleton traveled to his home state of Missouri. There, according to a report in *The Wall Street Journal,* he encountered any number of good reasons to oppose a balanced budget:

- A black minister pleaded with him, "Please don't let them cut the youth program for this summer."
- A building-industry group applauded him for bringing hundreds of millions of dollars in federal construction projects to Missouri; the group's president also told the *Journal* it would "do its best to see that the budgetary axe falls somewhere else."
- In St. Louis, a Job Corps director urged him to defend federal employment programs.
- At a pig farmers' convention, a top official urged him not to let Washington cut the pork research budget.
- An International Association of Machinists official wanted to make sure Labor Department programs didn't get cut.

usual way of explaining this fact is to liken the economy to an auction. Imagine an auction where food, clothing, and other necessities of life are being sold. If there are 100 people with $100 apiece in their pockets, it's a safe bet that $10,000 will be spent. Suppose now that someone comes along and gives everybody an extra $100. People's desires for what's being sold have not changed, nor has the total supply of goods being offered. Yet now, in all likelihood, $20,000

• A leader of the Missouri State Nurses Association said she would refuse to support the senator if he "persists in cutting the nursing-aid budget."

• A man rushed up to him at an airport and announced he was counting on Eagleton to help "increase federal support for diabetes research," and at another airport the board of directors of a Kansas City antipoverty program waylaid Eagleton to demand more money for their projects.

• In Hannibal, a Laborers Union official announced bluntly that Senator Eagleton was "going to have to reconsider his thoughts" about budget cutting.

Back at the White House, meanwhile, officials counting the mail reported that nearly everyone supported Carter's goal of a balanced budget. Letters about specific budget cuts, however, were running 96 percent against the reductions. Maybe President Reagan will have better luck.

SOURCES: David Ignatius, "Democrats' Distress: In This Election Year, Balancing of the Budget is a Real Juggling Act," *The Wall Street Journal*, March 14, 1980. Also, Judith Miller, "Congress Under Siege by Lobbyists Pleading Against Budget Slash," *The New York Times*, March 20, 1980.

will be spent: the buyers will bid prices up to double their previous level. Take away half the money, similarly, and you cut prices in half.

Historically, as Milton Friedman and others have demonstrated, changes in the stock of money correlate pretty well with changes in the price level. During the 1970s, for example, the money supply rose considerably faster than it had in the 1950s and 1960s. Moreover, it rose a lot faster than real output. If the two had gone up at the same rate, the average price level might have stayed constant—a little more money would have been chasing a few more goods. As it was, a lot more money was chasing a few more goods. The result was inflation.

Though there is little disagreement that inflation requires more money in circulation, there is much disagreement about whether it makes sense to say that too much money is the cause of inflation. Money, remember, is all the devices people use to store their purchasing power—currency, checking accounts, savings accounts, and (depending on which measure you're using) any of half a dozen other social inventions. Every time you use your VISA card or a corporation borrows on its line of credit at the bank, the "money supply" expands.

Now suppose we're back at the auction—only this time, instead of $100 in cash in our pockets, we have our checkbooks, complete with a reserve-credit provision that allows us to borrow another $500 each from the bank. Suppose too that the auctioneer, being no fool, has suddenly realized that his commissions will go up if he can double the price he gets for his wares. So he takes what he hoped to get for each item, doubles it, and announces that the bids will start there. People need the goods: they grumble, but they write checks for whatever it takes. They then leave the auction, go to work, and demand a raise from the boss. He has heard that prices in the region are doubling—doubling!—and he doesn't want to jeopardize his business by risking a strike. So he gives his workers a 75 percent raise and hikes his prices 90 percent. And he borrows from the bank to finance the higher wage bill until he can begin selling his products at the new prices.

The community, without a doubt, is experiencing inflation. The money supply is expanding too. But did the increase in money cause the inflation? Only in a limited sense. Other causes of the inflation were the auctioneer's raising prices, the workers' demands on the boss, the boss's decision to raise his prices, and so on. Blaming inflation on too much money is like saying the bathtub overflowed because there was too much water. You also need to know why the spigot was left on, what's wrong with the drainpipe, and who was trying to take a bath.

In the real world, of course, the Federal Reserve System is supposed to control both the spigot and the drain. It buys and sells government bonds, thus pumping money into the economy or taking money out. It tells banks how much they can lend out, and it manipulates interest rates, thus encouraging or discouraging borrowing.* None of these tools, it should be pointed out, is exactly like working a bathtub faucet and stopper. It is more like directing a huge crowd through a museum exhibit: you can set up all the signs and ropes you want to, but you can't always be sure people will do what they're supposed to. Rising interest rates, for example, may dissuade some people from borrowing. They may persuade others that interest rates are shooting up and they had better borrow now before things get any worse. Similarly, falling demand due to tight money may persuade some businesses to lower prices. It may persuade others just to cut production.

Monetary policy is thus a clumsy tool. It is also a tool whose use can be hazardous. These are subjects we shall consider in more detail in the next chapter, when we examine possible cures for inflation. For the moment a simple trade-off should be kept in mind. Rising prices—remember the coal OPEC—can lead consumers to purchase less, businesses to cut back, and economic activity to drop.

* For most of the recent past, the Fed "watched" interest rates, and intervened in the economy whenever it thought interest rates were too high or too low. Most recently, under Paul Volcker, it has taken to "watching" the money supply and intervening only when the supply seems to be growing too fast or too slow. As a result, interest rates seem to fluctuate more widely and rapidly in the short term than they used to; whether the new policy will be different in other ways is yet to be seen.

But buyers are also likely to look around for more money by demanding higher wages, raising their own prices, asking for government help, maybe borrowing a little in the meantime. If the central bank provides the money that lets all this take place, it is causing inflation in the limited sense noted above. If it doesn't, prices might come down, as companies and unions find they can't make them stick. But production too will drop. And the administration that is in office when all this occurs may not stay in office long.

The causes of inflation

Examining the money supply brings us back to seeing the economy for what it is: a system. Most of the culprits accused of causing inflation are not wholly innocent—even government regulations and minimum wage laws have something to do with rising prices—but most get blamed way out of proportion to the damage they actually do. Alone, none could cause more than a little inflation. Put together, and inserted into a system where the potential for inflation is built in, they can cause a lot. Social scientists, when examining the causes of a complex phenomenon, frequently speak of predisposing and precipitating factors. That's probably the best way to look at the causes of inflation. A predisposition to inflation is built into the fundamental structures of our economy. With those structures in place, many different factors can touch off or worsen an inflationary spiral. The last five chapters have spelled out both the basic structures and the precipitating events of the last decade, shaping the whole picture one piece at a time. Now it's time to look at what we've got and consider the implications.

The first essential element is this. *Most of the important participants in our economy—companies, industries, professions, workers, interest groups—are able to exercise some influence over how the economic pie gets divvied up.* We have seen lots of examples.

• Big firms have the economic muscle to persuade consumers to buy (and suppliers to sell) at prices determined, within broad limits, by the firms themselves. Small firms in particular markets can often get away with the same behavior. All seek to "maintain profit margins," meaning to make sure they get their share.

• Farmers, doctors, home builders, defense-industry workers, the elderly, welfare mothers, and dozens of other groups draw part or all of their incomes from a variety of government programs. So too, of course, do teachers, tax collectors, and everyone else on government payrolls. All can lobby, bargain, support candidates, and otherwise seek to increase the share of the pot going to them.

• Funeral directors, plumbers, doctors, lawyers, social workers, beauticians, electricians, architects, and many other professionals and tradespeople exercise considerable influence, usually through state licensing authorities, over who may set up shop in their field. They are also sometimes able to establish formal or informal fee schedules, preventing too much price competition.

• Workers who belong to a union can vote for leaders who win (or promise to win) big wage gains. Workers who don't belong to a union can threaten to form or join one. Other workers can quit, threaten to leave, slow down, smoke dope, perform acts of sabotage, and generally not cooperate if the conditions of employment (including wage levels) are unacceptable.

Seen as a competition for real resources, some of this jostling for a piece of the pie cancels itself out. Food stamp recipients and aerospace workers have to compete for a share of the federal budget; General Motors and the United Auto Workers must compete for whatever consumers wind up spending on automobiles. In terms of prices and wages, though, all the jostling has the same effect. Anyone faced with an apparent drop in income—lower wages, higher production costs, less government support, whatever—screams bloody murder. Everyone, given half a chance, asks for more. As a result both prices and wages tend to ratchet upward. It is often easier for employers, particularly if they are big enough, to grant higher wages and then raise prices rather than risk a strike. It is easier for Congress to approve a new program or increase subsidy levels, thus making at least one group of constituents very happy, than to take the opposite measures. To be sure, every price increase, wage hike, or new federal program is likely to provoke cries of irresponsibility from editorial writers and other sidewalk superintendents of the economy. What the hand-wringers forget is that the capitalist system is built on the notion that everybody will—indeed, should—try to make as much money as they can, and that our political system is built on the notion that legislators should try to get reelected. "Responsible" union leaders, corporation executives, and politicians, like nice guys, finish last. In that fact lies one prime source of our economy's predisposition to inflation.

The other essential element is the *enormous importance of government spending in the economy.* Thanks to its huge size, the government can stimulate economic activity and expand the money supply almost at will, thereby smoothing out the business cycle and preventing depressions.

This, more than anything else, is what separates the modern era from the past: it is the fundamental reason why prices have never fallen more than a trivial amount since 1940. People have always tried to control the prices they received for their wares or the wages they were paid for their labor: guilds, industry associations, and other conspiracies in restraint of trade crop up regularly in economic history. People have also tried to increase their incomes by currying favor with the authorities, getting special concessions or tariff protections. But in the past most such attempts at monkeying with the marketplace soon failed. Until the twentieth century few companies were big enough. Until the 1930s few unions were strong enough. Before World War II, governments were too small to make much difference.

Most important, the various structures weren't able to survive hard times. Panic and depression led businesses to forget about their agreements not to cut prices. Workers facing layoff (with no unemployment benefits) readily deserted the union and accepted a wage cut. With tax revenues down statesmen suddenly became penurious. Bank failures and the resultant shrinkage of the money supply forced reductions all around anyway. Prices had nowhere to go but down.

Today—so far anyway—we have no more depressions of the old-fashioned variety. There are recessions, sometimes touched off by factors beyond the government's control, other times deliberately encouraged in hopes of bringing prices down. But when the economy turns down, a number of stabilizers come into action. Tax revenues fall, government spending rises, and the federal deficit swells. The Fed is likely to ease its restraints on the money supply, letting interest rates drop and pumping money into the economy by buying the bonds that the government issues to finance its deficits. Politicians soon begin talking about tax cuts, and, when a cut finally passes, consumers have more spending money. With all these factors working together the economy soon picks up.

In principle, the government could devote as much attention to preventing inflation as it does to preventing depression. It could raise taxes and tighten up the money supply at the first hint of a jump in the Consumer Price Index. It could lay off its employees, cut transfer payments, allow banks to fail and workers to be laid off without compensation. No political genius is required to see why such measures might be unpopular. Policies aimed at fighting recession have the enormous virtue, from a politician's viewpoint, of putting more money into voters' pockets. Policies aimed at fighting inflation necessarily take money out of voters' pockets.* Thus the asymmetry. The system is predisposed

* The West Germans and Swiss have been more successful than some in controlling inflation partly because a large part of the cost has been borne by southern European "guest workers," who mostly do not vote. Lester C. Thurow argues that the number of workers expelled by the Germans and Swiss in one year is roughly equivalent to an unemploy-

toward inflation on what economists call the macro level as well as on the "micro" level of firms, professions, and industries.

Precipitating factors

Despite this structure, inflation can for a while be held in check. But peculiar conditions are required. You need frequent recessions, and probably the memory of a Great Depression too, just so people don't get too confident in the future. You need a populace that's too disorganized or too powerless to win too many benefits from the government. You need to dominate the international economy, just to make sure that nothing from abroad upsets the applecart. And you need to have productivity rising quickly so that workers' wages and corporate profits can both rise without price increases. This was the recipe for the relative price stability of the 1950s and early 1960s.

With the structure in place, though, any one of four factors can touch off inflation or make it worse. And once it gets going, one big factor—expectations—will be enough to keep it going.

1. Demand-pull inflation. This is the Vietnam-era variety. Government runs a big budget deficit on top of an economy operating near capacity, the Fed accommodates, and too much money winds up chasing too few goods. In principle, booming private investment can create the same situation.

2. Administrative inflation.* This kind can take a variety

---

ment rate approaching 30 percent in this country. He adds that both the West Germans and the Swiss enjoyed the benefits of an appreciating currency in the mid-1970s because their currencies had been undervalued in the old system.

* The term was coined by the economist Gardiner C. Means. It includes some of what economists usually call cost-push inflation (caused by union wage increases) and some of what Means calls profit-push inflation (caused by companies trying to maintain profit margins). "Administrative," in his view, was an appropriately neutral term.

of forms. Unions can negotiate catch-up wage increases even when productivity hasn't improved. Companies, if they're big enough, can raise prices even when the demand for their product has dropped off. A government policy—price supports, for example—can fix prices at steadily increasing levels.

3. "Price shock" inflation. Bad harvests, shortages, wars, external cartels like OPEC, and temporary imbalances in the economy can lead to sharply rising prices for particular goods. These price hikes can reverberate through the economy, lifting the prices both of derivative goods (like petrochemicals and fertilizer) and competitive goods (like coal and natural gas).

4. International inflation. This is brought on by a drop in the value of a nation's currency. When the dollar was devalued, the price of imports rose. So did the price of goods like wheat that could be exported, since increased exports meant a smaller supply for the domestic market.

In the 1970s we got it all. Prices rose and rose, with no end in sight. And that generated the worst inflation of all, the inflation of expectations. When people expect prices to go up, they spend money as if it were going out of style, borrowing as much as they can. So overall demand stays high. Unions bargain for generous settlements and companies jack up prices as much as they can. Farmers and other commodity producers sometimes hold their wares off the market, thus creating a temporary shortage, in hopes of getting a better price later. The dollar looks less attractive to international investors and speculators, so its value falls and prices rise.

Everybody who's not keeping up, meanwhile, looks to the government for help. Fearful that the whole overheated structure will collapse, as it started to in 1973–74, the government runs up big deficits and pumps up the money supply, making sure that all the rising prices can be accommodated. Only in late 1979 and early 1980 did Washington begin to apply the brakes, tightening up the money supply and talking about balanced budgets. By then the recession was under way, and in November Jimmy Carter paid the price.

To return for a moment to that list of villains at the beginning of this chapter, each one's place should now be a little clearer. Anything that drives some prices up (OPEC, the Russians, the anchovies) can be a cause of inflation simply because prices of other goods are unlikely to fall. Everyone who manages the economy (presidents, Federal Reserve chairmen, and so on) has a strong incentive to allow inflation because the alternative might be deep depression. When people charge that something they don't like is inflationary—defense spending, say—they usually have unspoken assumptions (often wrong) about what would happen if the object of their dislike were done away with. When people disagree about a cause of inflation (whether taxes and interest rates are too high or too low, for instance), it's usually because they have different ideas about what would happen if the phenomenon in question were changed. There are still, in economics, a lot of things we don't know.

From the viewpoint of history, the cause of inflation on the broadest level can readily be summed up. A free-market, competitive, dog-eat-dog uncontrolled capitalist economy is nobody's paradise. Businesses, facing prices they can't predict and markets they can't control, fear for their economic health. Workers, without control over their wages or their terms of employment, fear for their physical health. Those who can't work fear for their lives. The evidence of this fear is written in the history of the twentieth century. Companies have grown large enough to ensure their survival and profitability in all but the direst straits. Workers, farmers, the elderly, and dozens of other groups have struggled to make the government responsive to their needs and have won huge gains. Economists and political leaders learned that the business cycle can, within broad limits, be controlled; from that time on no administration could afford to risk more than a short recession. In the meantime the government grew large enough not only to meet at least some of the needs of those who were putting forth claims, but also to manage the economy, make sure that there was plenty of money (and to spend it if necessary), and thereby to stabilize the cycle.

The cause of inflation, in a word, has been the long, tortuous, and largely successful escape from the terrible insecurity of the marketplace—from the chilling fingers of the invisible hand.

8. Can Inflation Be Controlled?

There is a simple means of getting rid of the never-ending inflation we have experienced for the last few decades. It works quickly, and it's guaranteed effective.

The first step is to eliminate all the ways the government interferes with the free operation of the marketplace. Abolish social security, welfare, unemployment compensation, minimum-wage and child-labor laws. Declare the National Labor Relations Act null and void. Do away with farm price supports, the Civil Aeronautics Board, the Interstate Commerce Commission, and all the other institutions that restrict competition and help keep prices up. At the state and local levels, get rid of licensing requirements for lawyers, doctors, taxi drivers, plumbers, and other restricted trades.

The second step is to abolish most of the rest of the government. No more housing programs, food stamps, interstate highways, Medicare and Medicaid. No more bloated Pentagon: cut the Defense Department's budget by 95 percent. (That would still give it about $7 billion, enough to maintain what used to be thought of as a peacetime army.) In states and localities, get along with fewer bureaucrats, teachers, road workers, librarians, sanitation workers, and police. Cut taxes accordingly.

The third step is to restrict the growth of the money

supply. The dollar could be backed by a commodity—gold will do—and the stock of money regulated by the supply of that commodity. Banks should sink or swim on their own: no more restrictions on competition among banks, and no more Federal Deposit Insurance Corporation.

So far, all we have done is to go back to about 1914. We have removed the stabilizing influence of a huge government, and we have rendered expansionary fiscal or monetary policies impossible or ineffectual. We have lubricated the mechanisms that set wages and prices with a healthy squirt of competition. Thanks to all these measures, prices will soon begin to fall as well as rise.

To be safe, though, we should set a firm upper limit, not too big, on the size of business enterprises, then break up any company larger than that. (If the limit were $1 million in annual sales, we would have to break up about 300,000 concerns but could leave about 14 million intact.) Big corporations can't cause inflation all by themselves, as the early years of this century showed us. But they can usually keep prices from falling too far in the parts of the economy where they are dominant. Unless they are broken up, the burden of controlling inflation through falling prices would fall mainly on farmers and small businesses. That would be an unstable arrangement at best. So we had better ensure real competition throughout the economy.

This kind of anti-inflation program is only partly fanciful. The economist Milton Friedman, host of the popular television series *Free to Choose* and coauthor with Rose Friedman of the best-selling book of the same name, espouses some of the proposals outlined above. *The Wall Street Journal*'s editorial page (whose editor, Robert L. Bartley, won a Pulitzer Prize for editorial writing in 1980) would also go along with some. So, in his more private moments, might Ronald Reagan. A large number of Americans read and agree with Friedman and the *Journal*. A larger number voted for Reagan in 1980. The mood of the country, it is said, has turned conservative. There are some who suppose the time is ripe for a return to the past.

But political moods come cheap. Campaign rhetoric notwithstanding, neither the current administration nor any other in the foreseeable future will come close to proposing anything like such a program.* Budget and program cuts, if there are any, will be limited to small fractions of what the government does. No one will suggest abolishing welfare or unemployment benefits, let alone social security, and expect to be taken seriously; and no one, least of all the conservatives mentioned above, will propose a big reduction in the size of the Pentagon's activities. Neither presidents nor Congress will risk the anger of farmers, doctors, home builders, or unions by proposing to do away with the special programs or protections each group now enjoys. And none will seriously attempt to break up the big corporations.

Those who lament this state of affairs frequently blame it on political chickenheartedness. It could more accurately be blamed on political good sense. Most government programs came into being because they served real needs. Many still do. Even those that seem to have grown all out of proportion to the need they once served have active, vocal defenders. A radical reform—abolishing price supports, say—hurts at least one group directly and immediately. If it helps anyone, say by lowering food prices, the effect is felt only gradually and in small amounts. The political calculations, therefore, all point toward not fiddling too much with

---

* Sometimes there is less even to the campaign rhetoric than meets the eye. Two months before the 1980 election, for example, Ronald Reagan made headlines by proposing to slash federal spending by $195 billion. This sounded like a radical cut in the budget. In reality, however, his plan called for only a 2 percent budget reduction in 1981, followed by annual cuts gradually increasing to 7 percent in 1985. They added up to a total of $195 billion on the assumption that federal spending would otherwise climb to about $900 billion by 1985. No mention was made of which programs would be cut, except of course for "waste and inefficiency." If such a plan is ever laid before Congress, it will be interesting to see how far it gets.

the system. American politics *is* fundamentally conservative, but it is the kind of conservatism that seeks to maintain the status quo, not the kind, like Friedman's, that yearns for a different social order.

Fierce political struggles, of course, will be fought over all these issues—over taxes, tariffs, price support levels, health insurance plans, new housing programs, weapons systems, and social security benefits. But nearly all will take place, as economists say, at the margin. Reagan's conservatism, like that of most elected Republicans, is tempered by a healthy dose of pragmatism. Congress will debate budget cuts of a percent or two, probably while increasing military spending. It will consider lopping off one or two of the federal bureaucracy's less important arms. It will cut taxes—but not far below where they would have been if inflation hadn't been driving everyone into higher tax brackets. All these battles will make a difference to those who win or lose jobs, influence, or a few extra budget dollars in Washington. To the rest of us they will mean little. They will have virtually no effect on the major political and economic institutions that have been created over the past fifty years. And they will have virtually no effect on inflation.

Controlling inflation with recession

The middle-of-the-road approach to stopping inflation, and hence the most common one, is not to dismantle the political economy but to control it through fiscal and monetary policies. The typical metaphors for this approach involve automobiles and stoves. Inflation is said to occur when the economy is "going too fast," or when it is "overheated." To stop inflation, the government has to "put on the brakes" or "turn down the heat." The assumption behind both metaphors is that an inflationary economy is operating at very nearly full capacity. Demand is pressing on supply, and prices are therefore tending to rise. Congress can slow it down (or cool it off) by raising taxes or cutting spending, thus removing purchasing power from the economy. The Fed can achieve the same result by raising interest rates or otherwise tightening up the money supply.

In the best of all possible worlds, tightening up the budget or the purse strings a little would dampen inflation without causing any ill effects elsewhere in the economy. In the real world, as all are aware, things are seldom so precise. The economy is an enormous, complex system. It has a momentum of its own, which varies with market shifts, technological developments, investment patterns, and so on. The government's tools to affect this system are at best blunt instruments. Budget cuts require months to take effect. Tax hikes and tight-money policies can work faster, but nobody knows at any point how steep the tax increase should be or how high interest rates should go. Nor do they know to what extent the reduction in purchasing power will show up in the form of reduced production rather than lower prices. If the policies aren't stringent enough, inflation continues. If they are too stringent the economy slips into recession. A government trying to avoid both resembles a drunk walking a tightrope in a high wind.*

Those who propose cutting federal spending without reducing taxes and those who propose get-tough monetary policies are thus proposing that we fight inflation by risking and if necessary enduring a recession. All the discussion of slowing down and cooling off the economy should not be

---

* Economists used to write a good deal about the "Phillips Curve," a line on a graph that seemed to show a predictable trade-off between inflation and unemployment. Increase unemployment a small amount, the curve seemed to say, and you will reduce inflation by a corresponding amount.

For most of the 1950s and 1960s, the curve fit the data pretty well: prices rose a little in good times, when most people were working, and rose scarcely at all in times of relatively high unemployment. In the 1970s, though, devotees of the Phillips curve for the most part folded up their pads of graph paper and began to interest themselves in other things. What had been a comparatively smooth curve now was looking like the doodlings of a creative chimpanzee. Hence the difficulty at present of knowing how much recession is needed to curb inflation.

allowed to obscure this fact. If recessions could be avoided, elected governments would almost certainly avoid them. Yet they occur—provoked, encouraged, or worsened by deliberate governmental policy, carried out in the name of fighting inflation. The recession of 1980 is only the most recent example. It was, wrote economists Martin and Kathleen Feldstein, "the result of a deliberate *and desirable* policy designed to slow the rate of inflation" (emphasis added). Reagan, too, is likely to court recession by tightening up the purse strings.

The policy of throwing recessions at inflation is not, of course, foolish on its face. It was the panics and depressions of the past that once wrung inflation out of the economy. Even in modern times there is little doubt that recessions can change the behavior of some businesses, workers, and consumers in ways that might affect inflation. "In a recession," as business-cycle specialist Geoffrey H. Moore explains it, "businesses try to cut costs, and are often successful. They are forced to shave profit margins and give discounts to get rid of heavy inventories. The cost of holding even a normal inventory—in terms of interest charges—is likely to prove excessive. Some businesses fail, and sell out for what they can get. Overtime work is cut back or eliminated, which not only reduces costs but reduces the incomes of workers who have been earning the high overtime rates. Layoffs occur, wage increases are deferred, and the uncertainty about jobs and earnings makes people cautious about spending for frills, postpone big ticket purchases, seek ways to economize, borrow less. Construction projects get postponed, delayed, or stretched out. Banks take a hard look at new loans, and may urge repayment instead of refinancing existing loans.

"All these factors," Moore concludes, "make it more difficult to raise prices and more difficult to get wage increases. More prices remain steady and some fall."

If everything were so clear-cut, we might glumly decide that a little recession was good for us now and then. But recession's record as a cure for inflation is spotty at best. The reasons for that spottiness are built into our political system as surely as the behavior Moore describes. And because its effectiveness is open to doubt, the hardships recession causes can't be so easily glossed over or accepted. Lost jobs and failed businesses, after all, are easy to accept only when they aren't your own.

The record—and the reasons

Since World War II, there have been seven economic downturns, counting the one that began in 1980.* The rate of inflation, measured over six-month intervals, has turned downward nine times in the same period.† The two phenomena are almost certainly connected. But the connections are not simple, and in recent years they have been growing tenuous.

In theory, the inflation rate should peak during a recession: prices may keep going up for a while as higher costs are passed along, but the factors cited by Professor Moore should make prices rise more slowly than before. That's essentially the way things worked in 1954, 1970, and 1973–75. In 1949, however, prices bottomed out during the recession; the inflation rate had been falling already, and it would soon shoot up because of the Korean War. The recessions of 1958 and 1960 also followed rather than preceded drops in the inflation rate—rather as if medicine were administered after the patient's fever had broken—and in 1966–67 inflation eased a bit without a measurable downturn.

Like a drug used against an increasingly resistant infection, recession doesn't cure inflation as well as it once did. For fifteen years after World War II, prices essentially stopped rising before or shortly after an economic down-

---

* A rule-of-thumb definition of a recession is a drop in real GNP over two successive three-month measuring periods. The semiofficial arbiter of recessions is an outfit in Cambridge, Massachusetts, called the National Bureau of Economic Research.

† Note here that what slowed was the inflation *rate*, not prices. When inflation drops from 6 percent a year to 4 percent, prices are still going up.

turn. In the 1970s, though, with prices going up much faster than they used to, recession never came close to doing away with inflation. The long, deep, and painful slowdown of 1973–75, the worst since the Depression, cut the inflation rate from a high of 12 percent in 1974 to a low of 5 percent in 1976. But the new low was higher than any inflation America experienced between 1951 and 1968. Recession still "worked." But its effects were not what they once had been.

The reasons for recession's blemished record do not bode well for its effectiveness as a cure for inflation in the near future. Essentially, tight-money and tight-budget policies face three obstacles.

One is the uncertainties of timing and magnitude already noted. It is hard to determine what the economy was doing three months ago, let alone what it will be doing three months hence. So no one ever knows how much slowing down the economy "needs." Recessionary measures may come too soon or too late, and they may be too severe or too weak. In either case, the policy is apt to appear misguided, and those who implement it to appear foolish or heartless. When inflation is bad, the risks are magnified by the size of recession thought necessary to curb it.

The second obstacle is the political problem suggested in the last chapter. Anti-inflationary policies—high interest rates, balanced budgets—necessarily remove purchasing power from the economy. Taxes go up, government spending goes down, borrowing gets harder. On paper, this sounds simple enough. In practice the difficulties are enormous. Congress has never been fond of raising taxes. It is even less fond of angering constituencies and federal agencies by cutting back their programs. Even the Fed has problems in maintaining a tight monetary policy. Its governors do not have to be elected, and their terms run for fourteen years, which is supposed to insulate them from political pressures. Still, every Fed chairman in recent memory has worried about how to justify tight-money policies to members of Congress who don't like them. Also, stringent policies may conflict with another of the Fed's purposes, which is to serve as guarantor of the banking system's health and, when the occasion calls for it, lender of last resort. In the 1973–75 recession, the Franklin National Bank in New York failed. In early 1980, the Hunt brothers' speculation in the silver futures market almost brought about the collapse not only of the silver market itself but of some major brokerage firms. In both cases the Fed had a hand in arranging the solution: a takeover of Franklin National, a bailout loan for the Hunts.

The tighter the Fed's monetary policies are, the more banks and big companies are apt to find themselves in trouble, requiring some kind of government help if whole systems are not to collapse. The Fed's dilemma, as the economist Robert B. Zevin has described it, is that in inflationary times it ends up trying to squeeze an egg. It wants to apply pressure to the economy, but it doesn't want to have to clean up the mess when things begin to crack. Again, the dangers are hard to avoid. "Since the mid-1960s," writes Washington University economist Hyman P. Minsky, "the Federal Reserve has been able to force a contraction only as it has taken the economy to the brink of financial crisis."

Because of these political difficulties, nobody wants to maintain a recession too long. Yet it may take a very long time, especially now, for recession to have a noticeable effect on prices. That is the third obstacle faced by the policy of fighting inflation with recession.

If prices responded quickly and accurately to a slowdown in demand, like prices in the stock market, then a recession would rapidly slow or even reverse the rate of inflation. Some prices really do respond this way: spot market prices for industrial commodities, for example, usually fall during a recession. Most prices, however, do not. Some prices fall, but only after six months or a year, when contracts can be rewritten or new deals negotiated. Other prices don't move at all. Most just keep rising. Some go up because the part of the economy in question (government, say, or medicine) doesn't change much during a recession. Others rise because costs are continuing to increase, or because manufacturers are desperately trying to cut losses or protect profit margins. The year 1980, for example, was one of the worst years the domestic auto industry has ever faced; at one point sales were off 25 percent from 1979 levels. Yet average new-car selling prices rose between 6 and 9 percent.

Tight-budget and tight-money policies will always, if they are stringent enough, reduce *spending*. But *prices* will fall only where they are responsive to demand. When prices are going up because of three-year union contracts, because of corporate needs to cover costs or decisions to increase margins, because of external factors like OPEC, or because of governmental policies like Medicare or higher wages for government workers, inflation continues in spite of spending cutbacks, and production drops. That is the recipe for "stagflation."

Is recession worth it?

Even if a recession makes a dent in the inflation rate, its costs are not negligible.

In a recession, production drops off. Businesses fail and workers lose their jobs. Consumers, as economist Moore allows, have to tighten their belts and get by on less. The drop in output, of course, is one reason prices don't fall as far or as quickly as they otherwise might. When people are buying fewer cars, General Motors doesn't cut the price, it just makes a smaller number. The same is true of many manufacturing industries. According to the late Arthur Okun, a member of the Council of Economic Advisers under Lyndon Johnson, "90 percent of the effect [of a prolonged recession] is lost output and jobs, and only 10 percent is diminished inflation." President Carter's Council of Economic Advisers, in their 1980 Economic Report, seemed to agree with Okun. "Unfortunately," the report read, "the overall rate of wage and price increases in the American economy, while not immune to the effects of idle capacity and unemployment, is not highly sensitive to moderate changes in economic slack." Translated from the language of economic policy makers, this means that recession might slow inflation a little but is unlikely to dampen it much. What we get instead is a lot of "idle capacity and unemployment."

Whether recession is worth this cost in lost output and unemployment depends in large measure on whom you're talking to. *The Wall Street Journal* wondered in 1980 whether "the nation now is willing to suffer the degree of economic pain that a substantial reduction in inflation would surely entail." But nations don't suffer pain; people do. Managers of banks and large businesses, academic economists with tenure, most policy analysts and government officials are unlikely to feel a recession's effects personally. Some may even benefit. Hard times tend to squeeze out smaller competitors in an industry, thus strengthening the position of big companies. Hard times may also soften workers' wage demands, thus enabling many employers to maintain or increase profit margins.

The burden of recession, by contrast, usually falls on people who weren't doing so well to begin with. Workers in economically marginal industries and companies suffer. So do workers in highly volatile, boom-and-bust industries like construction. So do those who were last hired and are now first fired. The burden, as it turns out, is borne disproportionately by Black and Hispanic workers, by female workers, and by the young.* Those who gain from recession are not all rich,

* "Often," writes Lester C. Thurow, "the argument is made that women and children should be more than proportionally drafted into the war on inflation because there are fewer harsh economic consequences when they suffer unemployment since they have families to fall back upon. I have yet to hear this argument made by women or young workers; it ignores a very large number of women and young workers who are family heads or come from low-income families. It also ignores the long-run consequences of having a generation of young people who have either dropped out of the economy or have not gained

and those who suffer are not all poor. But the effects grow considerably less noticeable as you go up the income scale. Not coincidentally, that's where you find most of the people who prescribe recession as a cure for inflation. "In all recorded history," writes management consultant Peter Drucker, "there has not been one economist who has had to worry about where the next meal would come from."

The case for controls

The main cause of inflation, as we have seen, is that a lot of different groups have the ability to make effective claims on how the economic pie gets divided up. Unions demand wage increases. Companies raise their prices without fear of being undersold. Those whose incomes depend on government lobby their representatives for more money, knowing that representatives have an interest in going along whenever they can. When the Fed accommodates all these demands by letting the money supply expand–and it usually has little choice if it wants to avoid a recession–the result is rising prices.

The solution to inflation, however, is not to do away with people's ability to make claims on the economy, abolishing unions, big corporations, government programs, and so forth. Nor is it simply to put a lid on the money supply. Both cures put us back where we started, and wreak disproportionate havoc on those who can least afford it. *The solution instead is to control the claims themselves.* So far we have tried to do this piecemeal, through jawboning, fiscal restraint, and trying to hold down increases in programs like welfare or farm price supports. That hasn't worked well, mostly because a piecemeal approach puts an unfair burden on those who happen to be first in line, or who are politically weakest. Any company, union, or government beneficiary worth its

---

the work experiences that lead to skills in later life. What do we do when today's unemployed twenty-year-old becomes the next generation's unemployed forty-year-old?"

FIGHTING INFLATION OURSELVES?

"Should We Blame Uncle Sam for All He Spends, or Blame Ourselves for All We Ask?" read the headline on a two-page advertisement that turned up one day in 1980 in *Business Week.* The ad, which was placed by the American Council of Life Insurance, invited readers "to join us in an earnest effort to bring [inflation] under control." All you had to do was fill in the coupon at the bottom of the page; the council would "see that our nation's leaders in Washington hear of your concern."

"I Vote to Self-Control Inflation," the coupon read. "I will not ask for or support government programs that require deficit spending."

Leaving aside the question of which programs are the ones that require deficit spending, the ad called to mind a letter that had appeared shortly before in *The New York Times.* "In this year of high inflation," the letter read, "everyone must sacrifice. The poor will give up food stamps and summer jobs; the rich will give up Federal programs to aid the poor."

Source: This particular ad appeared in *Business Week,* July 7, 1980, pp. 16–17. The letter was written by Paul Rosenbaum and was dated April 18, 1980.

salt will not easily buy the notion that the fight against inflation begins with them, and that others may or may not join later.

The only way to do it is all at once: to control, explicitly, the prices businesses are allowed to set, the wages workers are allowed to earn, and all the other decisions that affect the share of society's resources going to different groups. This does not mean, as we shall see in a moment, that the government has to run the economy. Nor does it mean we have to fight inflation through a wartime-style program of shortages and rationing. It means only that the private sector's freedom to raise prices and wages indefinitely has to be restrained. And it means that the parts of the economy where the government is most involved will have to be restructured so that people's incomes are controlled as well as supported. None of this will be smooth sailing. But the subject at hand is how to curb inflation without causing undue economic distress, not how to make everybody happy. A system of controls, warts and all, is the only anti-inflationary program that seems even roughly fair to all and likely to increase rather than undermine people's sense of security. For just those reasons it seems both potentially feasible and potentially effective.

Political feasibility

Like most proposals designed to curb inflation, wage and price controls provoke a measure of fear and loathing. The economics profession, with only a few exceptions, regards them with about the same affection the Church lavished on the theories of Galileo. Business might accept wage controls and labor might accept price controls, but the standoff between the two ensures that we'll never get one without the other, and neither group is especially happy with that prospect. There is reason for suspicion even on the part of the general public. Controls have traditionally been employed only in wartime, not the happiest of associations. They were last used by a president whose intentions and competence were open to some doubt. And they would be administered by the only institution the public mistrusts as much as Big Business and Big Labor: Big Government.

Nevertheless, opposition to controls is neither as widespread nor as unchangeable as it sometimes appears. Voters generally support a policy of controls whenever inflation gets particularly virulent. A *New York Times*/CBS poll in February 1980, for example, found nearly two thirds of its respondents supporting controls, and other polls have elicited similar reactions. Senator Edward M. Kennedy's espousal of controls during the 1980 primaries did not hurt his campaign noticeably, and indeed may have contributed to his victories in the large industrial states. Even the opposition from business and academic quarters does not seem set in granite. In 1980, before the recession hit and the rate of inflation eased a little, several prominent economists began to debate the case for controls. The magazine *Business Week*, ordinarily a mirror of conventionally conservative views, supported them editorially.

At some point during the next few years it seems highly likely that some form of wage and price controls will be imposed. (Exactly what form is open to question—see box, below.) The reason will not be ideological—Reagan opposes

VARIATIONS

This chapter discusses wage and price controls in their classic form—that is, ceiling prices and wages fixed and enforced by a government agency, as in World War II and in the early 1970s. Other, less thoroughgoing forms of wage and price control have been proposed too. "Real wage insurance" would give workers a tax break if the cost of living rose faster than a government-determined ceiling on wage increases. The "tax-based income plan" (TIP) proposed by economists Sidney Weintraub and Henry C. Wallich would tax companies whose total payrolls (blue- and white-collar) rose beyond a certain amount. Either of these, or yet another variation, may be implemented in lieu of comprehensive controls.

We have little way of knowing how effective any such plan would be. The wage-price guidelines of the last twenty years, an even milder form of controls, proved themselves effective in periods of mild inflation (the 1960s) and ineffective in periods of virulent inflation controls—but that other attempts to curb inflation have failed. Suppose, for example, that the Labor Department one day announces that the latest round of collective bargaining will produce record-setting wage increases. An OPEC meeting a week later announces a 10 percent oil price hike. A bad harvest the previous summer begins to show up in higher prices at the supermarket, and mortgage rates again hit 20 percent.

Before long the government announces a monthly jump in the Consumer Price Index of 2.1 percent, translating into an annual inflation rate of over 25 percent. The president announces on television that inflation is expected to abate next month (it is frequently expected to abate next month, at least by the administration in power), but that he will

(the 1970s). Today, companies that anticipated sharply rising costs might choose to accept tax penalties rather than forgo their own desired price increases.

The discussion in this chapter focuses on classic wage and price controls rather than variations like TIP for two reasons. Number one: we can assume that strict controls really will hold down prices, and focus on the issue of whether they produce deleterious side effects. With loose controls, both questions are up for grabs. Number two: you don't necessarily gain much by substituting incentives or tax penalties for outright wage and price ceilings. As *The New Republic* has pointed out, to the extent that half measures work, they cause the same potential inefficiencies and problems as full-scale controls. To the extent that they don't cause those problems they aren't working. Lester C. Thurow adds that tax-based incomes plans are "just equivalent to a set of wage and price controls with a predetermined set of financial penalties for violators. Catching the violators and enforcing the rules [are] no less difficult or expensive."

ask Congress for the authority to impose wage and price controls in case it does not. The next month, after a startling round of anticipatory wage demands and price hikes, the CPI again jumps 2 percent and controls are imposed. A few economists wring their hands. The public, rightly recognizing there was no other way out, applauds.

Effectiveness

Will controls work? Economists' opposition to wage and price controls is based largely on the belief that they never have and therefore never can. This view has percolated through the business community and helps account for the policy's unpopularity there. But the case against controls is a little like an old battleship: rusty, leaky, and more appropriate to the last war than the current one. The objections, when scrutinized, turn out to be full of holes.

1. *Controls are like putting a lid on a boiling kettle instead of turning down the heat.* This analogy—back to the cookstove again—crops up repeatedly in newspaper editorials, in statements by political officials, and in the "image" advertisements by which large corporations monger their opinions to magazine readers. Its message is that price controls address the symptom rather than the cause of inflation. The reason for rising prices (in this view) is too much government spending, or maybe too rapid a rise in the money supply, and it is these factors rather than prices that ought to be controlled.

If inflation were solely a case of too much money chasing too few goods, as the government-spending and easy-money arguments imply, then the analogy would be valid. Controls really wouldn't work. Something else would be noticeable too. The economy would be operating at very nearly full capacity. Plants would be running two or three shifts, and jobs would be easily available to all. High demand and high prices, after all, should mean good times for business, and business should therefore be working overtime to sell all it can. Since few businesses are in fact working overtime right now and since the past ten years have not been a period of notably rapid economic growth, something may be wrong with the analogy.

The trouble, of course, is that the argument assumes the economy works much like the stock market, with prices rising only in response to high demand. The real world, as we have seen, is considerably more complicated. Only a small number of prices respond quickly and accurately to changes in supply and demand. Others are raised to protect profit margins—the auto industry, for example—whether or not business is good. Most simply go up whenever costs, especially labor costs, rise.

Controls by definition prevent companies from arbitrarily raising their prices. They also put a lid on most costs, including wages. So in most cases the reason for high prices—the cause of inflation, in effect—simply vanishes. In this sense controls really do turn down the heat; they reduce the upward pressure on prices.

2. *Controls won't work because too much of the economy is outside the jurisdiction of the United States government.* We can't control the price of OPEC oil, for instance, or the world price of wheat, copper, and other internationally traded commodities. If we try, and if the U.S. price is lower than the world price, we simply won't get the goods.

This point is indisputably true. The only economic leverage we have over OPEC is to use less oil and hope that will make prices come down. We have virtually no leverage over the world price of commodities we don't produce ourselves, and little enough over the price of those (wheat, for instance) where we are one producer among several. The price of imported goods will therefore have to rise whenever the world price goes up. Businesses that use these goods should be allowed to pass on part of the cost increases—only part, so as to encourage conservation. Consumers will just have to pay the higher prices. The same may hold true for some goods produced here and sold on the world market. Or we may decide to hold the price down and institute export controls, so that the whole supply doesn't get shipped abroad.

Does this mean that price controls won't work? Obviously not. The fact that we cannot control the price of oil or wheat does not mean we can't control the price of housing, health care, processed foods, coal, secretarial service, or high-school teaching. Rising world prices will inevitably lead to some inflation here at home. A 10 percent jump in the price of oil, for example, might cause one percentage point of inflation in the United States. But the purpose of controls is not to abolish all price increases forever: it is to halt the inflationary spiral. Few would object to paying Kellogg's an extra penny a box for cereal because the price of wheat has gone up, or to paying Blue Cross an extra 1 percent in premiums because hospital fuel bills are on the rise. What we don't like is paying 10, 15, or 20 percent more every year on all such items because the cost of everything else has gone up that much too.

3. *Prices are an important economic "signal." If they are not set by the marketplace, we'll get shortages and black markets. Remember World War II.* To understand this argument, return for a moment to the stock market. Suppose Xerox is selling for 58½, and suppose further that a simple-minded president decides to curb inflation by setting ceiling prices for stock. The Securities and Exchange Commission soon announces that the maximum selling price for Xerox will be 60.

Two weeks later, the company announces a technological breakthrough that promises to improve its profit picture, and investors flock to buy its stock. In normal times, the price would rise sharply—up to a point where the number of shares investors wanted to buy equaled the number that other investors wanted to sell. With price controls on, though, buyers can't bid the price up past 60, and only a few people are willing to sell their shares at that price. At this point one of two things happens. Buyers who obey the law go away empty-handed. The others begin making under-the-table deals with Xerox shareholders, raising the effective price of the stock to whatever the traffic will bear. Thus do shortages and black markets appear when prices are held down below the market level.

Note that in reading this explanation, however, you had to suspend disbelief at a critical point, namely that a president would impose price controls on the stock market. Controls on the stock market are entirely unnecessary, and not only because stock is not a commodity in the usual sense. Stock prices move down as well as up. The market itself is an effective control. Where the economy works like the stock market, controls are similarly unnecessary. The price of most agricultural produce, for example, rises and falls (at least down to the support price) as supply and demand change. So do the prices of manufactured goods in highly competitive industries like clothing, and the prices of some industrial commodities like bulk chemicals. In most of these cases, prices can be allowed to rise as the market permits, because the market doesn't permit much. So no shortages will develop here except those occasioned by real factors like bad harvests.

In other cases, however, the market is largely ineffective. The price of automobiles should be controlled because the Big Three have shown themselves ready, willing, and able to raise prices regardless of market conditions. So with most goods manufactured by highly concentrated industries. The price of health care—doctors' fees, hospital charges—should be controlled because the government has (rightly) interfered so much with the marketplace that competition no longer does its job. And the price of labor—wages—should be controlled not only because it is such an important part of other prices but because the labor market is ineffective in pushing wages down.

In none of these cases are long-term shortages likely to develop. The effect of price controls on highly concentrated industries would be to turn them, in effect, into regulated public utilities, producing at fixed prices for an assured return. There is no shortage of capacity in the regulated sectors of the economy. Where health care is concerned, we already have an overabundance of most facilities and personnel: the problem is that they are poorly distributed. And as for the labor market, there are shortages and bottlenecks already, as with nurses. Would they get worse under a system of wage controls? In fact the opposite might happen: the wage controllers could let the wages of occupations where there are shortages go up while holding others in the same "wage contour" steady.

The widespread shortages that people over fifty remember from World War II were due not to price controls per se but to the fact that there was a war on. Occasionally, peacetime controls might lead to a temporary shortage of something too: no chicken in the supermarket, long waiting periods to buy an automatic washer. That will be a sign that the price schedule needs adjustment. Again, we might get a little inflation. But we would not get an inflationary spiral.

4. *Every time price controls are lifted, inflation reappears.* By this reasoning food stamps must be ineffective too: if the program were terminated tomorrow, poor people would again go hungry. If inflation reappears when controls are lifted, then you lifted them too soon. Unless the economy can be changed in ways that make inflation less likely, or unless a regime of controls itself begins to change people's long-term expectations and behavior, controls may have to be permanent.

5. *But permanent—or semipermanent—price controls will require a huge bureaucracy. And they infringe on our freedom by putting the government in the position of telling businesses how much they can charge and workers how much they can make.* Permanent controls will in fact require a fair-sized bureaucracy. So does nearly everything else that operates on a large scale: the telephone company, the United Auto Workers, the social security system, the Pentagon. The

bureaucracy at times will seem inept. It need not, however, be as large as many government agencies. Nor need it be any more incompetent, ineffectual, and corrupt than, say, the Internal Revenue Service. As with most things political, it depends on who's in charge and on what the governing rules and expectations are. The experience under Nixon was not necessarily a fair test.

The extent to which price controls infringe on our economic freedom is hard to measure. Economic freedom is neither indivisible nor inalienable by anyone's standard. We already pay taxes and submit to extensive government regulation; both are infringements on our ability to get and spend as we choose. The press critic A. J. Liebling once pointed out that freedom of the press is guaranteed to the man who owns one. Similarly, the freedom to determine prices or to set wages, let alone the freedom to determine our own income, is not a freedom most people enjoy. Those who have it will of course give it up reluctantly. The rest of us should not concern ourselves unduly.

There is probably less to wage and price controls than meets the eye. Like other major reforms of the political economy—the graduated income tax, the introduction of social security, government protection for union organizing—controls are an expedient way of dealing with what has become a pressing problem. Like those other reforms, controls will provoke some loud shrieks of agony and a lot of low-grade carping. Eventually, people will get used to them.

Controls will never work perfectly. Nor will they solve many of the various problems that plague the U. S. economy. Nevertheless, they seem worth trying. Inflation may not be the monster it is frequently made out to be, but it does cause a lot of uncertainty and worry, and it always threatens to run away with itself. No other policy has proved effective against it. If we can implement a system of wage and price controls equitably, reasonably, and without unrealistic hopes or expectations, we should be able to curb it.

Other measures

Once price and wage controls are in effect, there are many other ways the government can begin restructuring the economy to prevent recurrent price increases.

• Where the government itself sets wages, prices, and benefits, it can hold them largely constant over time. Thus federal wage levels, social security benefits, or farm price supports would be allowed to rise only after a conscious decision to allocate more of the nation's real income to federal employees, the elderly, or farmers.

• Where the government regulates supply and demand, it can pursue policies aimed at lowering prices. Paradoxically, the policies may sometimes involve using the marketplace. Airline deregulation, for example, has evidently lowered many air fares, and trucking deregulation should have the same effect. In other instances prices will need explicit control. A license to operate a television station, a law firm, a plumbing business or a funeral home, just like a taxicab medallion, should carry a maximum fee schedule along with it. Only if there are no applicants for licenses should we conclude that the fee schedule is too low. If there are many it is probably too high.

• Where the government pays a good part of the bill, as in health care, it needs to set rates more thoroughly and explicitly than it does now. The trick here may be to have the government pay all the bills through some sort of national health scheme, as in England or Canada; it then has an almost inescapable incentive to keep costs in line. Though their systems differ, both nations spend considerably less of their GNP on health care than we do. Yet both Canadians and the English are as healthy as Americans.

• Where the government is drawn willy-nilly into an economic sector, as it has been drawn into energy, it has to pay attention to controlling prices. Gasoline and home heating oil, for instance, should have been rationed the minute it became clear that OPEC could make the new prices stick. Nearly all drivers and homeowners, I suspect, would have preferred a guaranteed allotment of both commodities at a lower price to an uncertain allotment at a considerably higher price. Moreover, the reduced consumption enforced by rationing would have given us a substantial bargaining weapon in negotiations with OPEC.

• Fiscal and monetary policies should not be ignored. The high-employment budget should normally be balanced, the money supply allowed to grow at a modest pace. Levels of spending and money supply growth should be determined pragmatically: avoiding recession on the one hand and the shortages occasioned by high-demand price controls on the other. As at present, this balance will never be perfect. But the dangers on the inflation side will be less, and the chance of avoiding recession that much greater.

Without comprehensive wage and price controls, measures aimed at holding down prices in one part of the economy seem unfair, and the government seldom pursues them. Nor can it easily hold down demand through fiscal and monetary policies without provoking recession, and even then prices may still keep rising. With controls in place, all such policies become possible. Demands from individual groups can be refused because everyone is being asked to sacrifice. And fiscal and monetary policies can be eased a little without risking runaway inflation.

Inflation is a problem that can be solved. The solution, it is true, involves the government deeply in all parts of the economy. This may be lamented by many. But the government is already deeply involved in the economy. Its involvement is a prime reason for the inflation we have experienced for the last thirty-five years. There is little chance of reducing that involvement; nor, in most instances, is there good reason to do so. So we need to proceed to the next logical step, and create the means by which inflation, like so many other aspects of the economy, can be subjected to control.

Epilogue:
After Inflation

In a sense, both inflation itself and the attempts to control it are symptoms of a deeper struggle within the American economy. This deeper conflict is likely to intensify if we succeed in curbing price increases. It is of course the struggle over how the economic pie will be divided up. It used to take place on terms quite different from today's.

In the past, the money pie itself was more or less fixed. Rising prices or wages would, over time, be balanced by falling prices or wages. Then as now, average incomes could rise in real terms only as more was produced. But now money incomes can rise even if real incomes don't.

Also, economic power was in the past distributed quite differently. Economic power is the ability to influence how much of the pie you get. For most of history, essentially the only people who wielded any such power were those who owned land or commanded armies. In the industrial age, the corporations that first capitalized on new markets and new technologies grew large enough to gain economic power, as did the banks and investment houses that provided the capital for all this growth. Eventually other groups, working through the medium of a vastly expanded government apparatus, began to catch up. Today farmers, unionized workers, government employees, doctors, the elderly, and dozens of other groups wield some economic power. The federal government supports or provides a substantial fraction of their income, and they have all won a measure of influence over the government's decisions.

Given these two conditions—a *political* economy, and no firm limit on money incomes—inflation is inevitable. The real economic pie, as always, can grow only as more is produced. But the money pie tends to grow whenever companies raise prices, unions raise wages, and government spends more money. The function of inflation is evident in this context. Every individual act—a price hike, a wage boost, more federal spending—makes somebody think they're getting ahead of somebody else. Since so many people have the power to win such gains and since not everybody can win real increases except to the extent the economy is growing, there has to be a way by which people who think they are winning can turn out to be losing. The way is inflation.

Inflation has a peculiar virtue in this role: it camouflages real changes and thus deflects anger. In an earlier era, when people's incomes were more at the mercy of the elements or the marketplace than they are now, there was no one to blame for economic misfortune and nowhere to turn for economic help. In a political economy the opposite is the case. Any economic agent—a company, an industry, a group of workers, even a region—faced with declining economic fortunes or wanting to increase its share of the pie will look to the government for help. Democratic government, by its nature, is both visible and accommodating. Its actions are a matter of public record and concern. Its officials win popularity, stature, and reelection by granting requests, by spending money, by providing employment rather than by doing the opposite.

Inflation is a way by which the government can appear to be giving out more than it has. It is also a way by which the amount everyone gets can be invisibly reduced, without any particular administration, agency, or member of Congress seeming to be responsible. It allows the struggle over the economic pie to proceed, all the while, as Yale economist James Tobin has put it, "blindly, impartially, impersonally, and nonpolitically" scaling down its outcomes. Inflation is not, of course, wholly invisible, a fact that partially explains the popular outcry against it. But its persistence in the face of widespread opposition suggests that it is a useful veil in maintaining the system as it has come to be. For a while, at least, it keeps people happy.

The imposition of wage and price controls would make explicit what so far has been largely implicit. Some people's wages and prices would still rise, in response to the economic needs and pressures mentioned in the last chapter. But one person's increase would no longer be sufficient justification for another's. Theoretically, for example, a Wage and Price Administration might let hospitals raise nurses' pay in order to alleviate the shortage. It would not then be expected to let doctors', technicians', and orderlies' incomes go up.

The visibility of this governmental intervention in the economy raises the ultimate questions behind the struggle over the economic pie. The questions are these. What is a fair distribution of income? And what distribution of income is consistent with a strong, growing economy? Most political debate revolves around these questions even today. But the questions are answered largely on an ad hoc basis—should wheat price supports be raised this year?—and the apparent answers are then adjusted by inflation into a real gain or real loss for those concerned. A system of wage and price controls requires more explicit choices and makes winners and losers more visible. The struggle over the pie is likely to intensify for precisely this reason.

In a sense, then, the test for the American economy isn't inflation at all, but what happens when inflation is controlled. At that point the role of government will be out in the open, and the struggle begun on a new footing. If the economy grows so rapidly that all remain generally satisfied with their relative shares, then the conflict may never come to a head. If we somehow reach agreement on what constitutes a fair distribution of income, then that agreement itself will define the limits of the conflict. At present, both rapid economic growth and a consensus about income distribution remain elusive objectives.

Our difficulty in reaching these goals, however, does not reflect a lack of knowledge. It reflects the fact that there are several possible solutions to both problems, each one representing different beliefs and different economic interests. The particular path that is chosen will be influenced by philosophic and economic argument, and it will in the end be determined by the way interests clash—by politics. The end of inflation, if it comes, will thus mark the beginning of both a new debate and a new political struggle over how —and for whose benefit—the economy should be managed.

Appendix:
How the Inflation Rate Is Calculated

The most common measure of inflation in the United States is the Consumer Price Index (CPI), a number published each month by the government's Bureau of Labor Statistics.* If the CPI in January is 1 percent higher than the CPI for December, inflation (which is usually reported on a yearly basis) is said to have hit 12 or 13 percent.† When news reports announce last month's or last year's inflation rate or "increase in the cost of living," it is usually the change in the CPI they're referring to.

The CPI does not measure "prices" as a whole. Even if that were possible it wouldn't make much sense: you wouldn't know how much weight to give automobiles, say, as opposed to transistor radios or dental services. Instead, Bureau of Labor Statistics re-

---

* Actually two numbers. The traditional CPI measures the prices of goods and services purchased by "urban wage earners and clerical workers." A broader CPI introduced in 1978 measures the prices of goods and services purchased by "all urban consumers"—in other words, a slightly different market basket, reflecting the buying habits of a somewhat larger group of people. The former is now called CPI-W, the latter CPI-U. So far the two indices have not differed significantly.

† 1 percent monthly increase gives a 12 percent yearly increase if it is not compounded. With compounding, the rate works out to 12.7 percent. Different news reports treat this problem in different ways.

searchers attempt to determine what a typical household spends its money on. The bureau then ascertains the prices of these items from month to month, weighting them according to their share of the family budget. If they cost 1 percent more this month than they did last month, the CPI goes up 1 percent.

Every so often, obviously, the bureau must update the "market basket" that it is pricing. An index that reflects the price of washtubs won't mean much if everyone is buying automatic washing machines. The latest survey of what people spend their money on took place in 1972 and 1973, and it is this basket of goods and services that is "priced" by today's CPI. As it happens, the CPI stood at 133.1 in 1973. (It was arbitrarily set at 100 for 1967.) By 1979 it had reached 217.4. So if you were a typical family and set out to buy the exact same mixture of goods and services in 1979 that you bought in 1973, it would have cost you 63 percent more.

The inflation rate as measured by the CPI is not quite the same thing as an increase in the cost of living. For one thing, the CPI doesn't include taxes. For another, the index measures the price of a specific collection of goods and services over time. Real families, however, don't buy the same mixture of goods and services over time. In 1972 and 1973, for instance, gasoline was still cheap. So our typical family probably owned an Oldsmobile V-8 and took it for a spin in the country every Sunday. Today the same family probably owns a Honda Civic and goes jogging on Sunday instead of driving. Its expenditure on gasoline may have risen only a little, despite the steep price increases. The CPI, however, assumes the family is buying just as much gasoline as before, and the "inflation rate" reflects that assumption.

Also, it is hard for the CPI to separate out inflation—price increases for the same item—from changes in the items themselves. Suppose Sears brings out a newly designed Kenmore dishwasher priced $50 higher than last year's model. Only part of that increase, presumably, is inflation. Another part should represent improvements in the product's quality, attractiveness, or features. The Bureau of Labor Statistics uses various methods to "correct" for quality improvements so that it is always comparing a similar market basket from one year to the next. But the calculations are rough and the judgments sometimes subjective, particularly when a service like medical care is the item in question. Over several years, an apparent increase in the cost of living may represent a higher standard of living (more efficient cars, better medical care) as much as it represents inflation.

Finally, the way the CPI calculates the price of owning a home overstates the cost of living for most families. Housing costs are an important component of the CPI, yet home ownership is a unique kind of expenditure. Part of what the homeowner spends on housing is analogous to rent—current consumption of housing, exactly like the money spent on eggs or hi-fi music systems. Another part represents an investment, like buying stocks or bonds. The price people pay for their homes reflects not only how much they would be willing to pay in rent (if rental housing were the only kind available) but how much they want to invest in real estate. Sharply rising home prices are therefore quite different from sharply rising gasoline prices or clothing prices in their impact on the cost of living. If you're paying a lot for a home, it may be because you have deliberately chosen to do so in hopes your investment will pay off when you sell.

There's a technical problem involved here too. At present, the CPI calculates the cost of buying a home at current home prices and mortgage interest rates. This does not mean, as is sometimes alleged, that the Bureau of Labor Statistics assumes every homeowner is repurchasing and refinancing a home every month. Rather, it assumes that the same number of people who bought homes in 1972 and 1973 are buying them today. And it counts the total of their expenditures—purchase price, financing costs, and so on—as the total home-purchase component of the CPI. All the people who are assumed not to be buying a home are assumed to have no home-purchase expenditures at all. So when current home prices and interest rates are shooting up, the CPI rises rapidly too. Yet most homeowners' mortgage payments—an important part of their cost of living—may not have changed at all.

Other methods of calculating the price of owning a home can easily be imagined, and the bureau has considered adopting one or another of them. It could, for example, try to figure out homeowners' actual outlays in a given month—mortgage payments, taxes, and so forth. That would lump together recent buyers (who are paying today's interest rates) with buyers who are paying interest rates of years past. Alternatively, it could try to figure out what a typical owner-occupied home might rent for, and use that figure as an index of a homeowner's costs. In both cases, rising home prices and interest rates wouldn't push the CPI up so quickly.

Changing the way the CPI is calculated, however, is easier said than done. There is widespread agreement that the index overstates the rate of increase in the average family's cost of living. There is considerably less agreement on whether the index should be changed. Some believe that the index is doing exactly what it was designed to do—measure the cost of a fixed market basket over time. Others believe that meddling with the CPI can become a convenient substitute for doing something about inflation, rather like beheading the messenger who brings the bad news. Most important, the millions of Americans whose wages or benefits are increased whenever the CPI goes up will not welcome changes that threaten to lower the index or slow its rate of increase. At present this group includes not only unionized workers with cost-of-living adjustments in their contracts; it also includes social security beneficiaries, food stamp recipients, and most federal pensioners. Put together, they make up a formidable lobby.

Other measures

Those who follow more specialized accounts of inflation will run into other terms as well.

The *Producer Price Index* (formerly the Wholesale Price Index) is similar to the CPI but measures goods sold at stages of production other than retail. The price of farm produce, steel, lumber, industrial chemicals, and so on shows up first here.

The *Gross National Product Implicit Price Deflator*—GNP deflator for short—is the measure of inflation often favored by economists. Every year the Commerce Department is faced with the task of measuring real GNP—output in constant dollars—as compared with nominal GNP. It solves this problem by breaking down GNP into hundreds of component parts and discounting ("deflating") current production figures by an appropriate price index. If it finds, for instance, that consumers spent $2.2 billion on color television sets, while the Labor Department says that the price of color TV sets has gone up 10 percent, it will determine that "real" production of color television sets is $2 billion. When all the parts are added up, the department will have two figures—one for GNP in current dollars, one for GNP in constant dollars. Figuring the percentage difference between the two gives the GNP deflator.

This measure too has its problems. In particular, it understates the effects of rising import prices. That's because imports are *subtracted* when GNP is added up; rising imports thus give you a smaller apparent GNP and a smaller increase over last year's GNP than you would otherwise get. In an OPEC-dominated world, this can be a serious disadvantage.

The *underlying inflation rate* is the least well-defined measure of inflation. At any given point, inflation may be fed by a variety of fortuitous or uncontrollable events—bad weather, say, or OPEC decisions to raise the price of oil. The notion of an underlying inflation rate is at its best an attempt by economists to remove all these "price shocks" from the calculations and see how bad inflation would be if the wage-price spiral were all we had to worry about. At worst, such calculations are used by administration spokespeople to make the "true" inflation rate seem less than it is. This approach has its ironies. Consumers faced with spiraling food and gasoline prices are told, in effect, that inflation wouldn't be so bad if it weren't for spiraling gas and food prices.

In general, particular measures of inflation don't make much difference. Over time, they tend to follow similar paths. And time is important, for any one index may vary considerably from one month to the next. (In January 1980, for example, the CPI was rising at an 18 percent annual rate; in July 1980 it stood still.) Frequently, attempts to find or use new measures of inflation reflect political desires to make inflation seem better or worse than it is. The Consumer Price Index undoubtedly overstates the inflation that most families experience; nevertheless it is a useful measure of how prices are changing from one period to the next. In any event, the best solution to inflation is not to worry about how it is measured but to do something about the rate at which prices go up

Source Notes

There are three reference books that are indispensable to anyone interested in digging up economic statistics:

The *Economic Report of the President* is issued annually. It includes a report to Congress from the President outlining his economic priorities, and a longer, more detailed report on the state of the economy by the President's Council of Economic Advisers. It also includes more than one hundred pages of statistical tables and is the handiest reference book for aggregate economic figures such as Gross National Product, unemployment rates, and changes in the Consumer Price Index. In many cases the tables go back fifty years.

The *Statistical Abstract of the United States* is issued every year by the Commerce Department. It is a much more comprehensive work than the *Economic Report of the President,* including both detailed economic statistics and statistics on dozens of other subjects.

Historical Statistics of the United States, Colonial Times to 1970 is a massive two-volume compilation of the same kind of statistics found in the *Statistical Abstract* for years past. In most cases, of course, the data relating to the eighteenth and nineteenth centuries are rough by today's standards; the sketchy statistics gathered at the time have had to be supplemented with reconstructions and estimates by present-day historians and statisticians. Still, the historical figures give a broad measure of how things have changed over the years.

In these notes, *Economic Report of the President* refers to the volume issued by Jimmy Carter's administration in early 1980; its tables, for the most part, run through 1979. *Statistical Abstract* refers to the *Statistical Abstract of the United States, 1979,* published in 1980. Its tables ordinarily run through 1978 and sometimes extend into 1979. All these works are available in most libraries. They can be purchased in the U.S. government bookstores to be found in many big cities, or through the Superintendent of Documents, Washington, D.C. 20402.

The "inflation rate" in this book is measured by changes in the Consumer Price Index (see Appendix). The Index and its various components can be found in the *Economic Report of the President,* p. 259ff. (back to 1929) or in the *Statistical Abstract,* p. 483ff. (back to 1950). Month-to-month changes for all the index's components are reported in greatest detail in the *Handbook of Labor Statistics,* issued every year by the U.S. Department of Labor's Bureau of Labor Statistics. Current index figures can be found in the Labor Department's monthly magazine, *Monthly Labor Review.* Historical data on the CPI, including a reconstructed index for the years before 1919, when the Labor Department first began gathering systematic price data, can be found in *Historical Statistics,* pp. 210–11.

In the text, single-year inflation rates for the years after World War II are the so-called December-to-December rates, measured from the end of one year to the end of the next. In all other cases, "inflation rate" refers to the average increase in the CPI during the course of the year. These two numbers differ significantly only when you're looking at what happened within a given year—for example, inflation may have increased rapidly toward the end of a year—not when you're considering what happened over a period of years.

Note: In the citations that follow, omission of an author's name means that the reference was not by-lined. Also, no page references are given for newspaper articles because pagination frequently changes from edition to edition. Full publishing data for a book are given only the first time the book appears in the notes.

Page

6 Opinion-poll lists: The *Newsweek* poll for February 1980, for example, showed that inflation was once again the number-one worry after being displaced briefly by "international problems." In response to the question "What do you think is the most important problem facing the country today?" roughly half of the poll's respondents cited inflation. See *Newsweek*, March 3, 1980, p. 27.

15 Coffee, record album, automobile, and gasoline prices culled from memory, from newspaper ads of the time, and from components of the Consumer Price Index. New-home prices: *Statistical Abstract*, p. 792; mortgage rates: *Statistical Abstract*, p. 542.

18 Average after-tax income: *Economic Report of the President*, p. 229. The government calculates this figure using the Commerce Department's "personal consumption expenditures deflator" as a measure of inflation (instead of the Consumer Price Index).

The price of eggs: A "typical worker" in this example means a factory worker. In 1935 factory employees made an average of 54¢ an hour (*Historical Statistics*, pp. 169–70); in 1980 the figure was just over $7.00 (*Monthly Labor Review*, August 1980, p. 76). The price of a small color TV set in 1980 is estimated at $300. In 1970, taking the "television set" price index as a guide, a similar set would have cost at least $290. (Average wages in manufacturing were then $3.36 an hour.) In reality the gap may be even greater; color television sets have almost certainly grown less expensive relative to black-and-white sets, yet the index lists them together.

20n. The "balance on merchandise trade," which measures imports compared to exports, was $–30.9 billion in 1977, $–33.8 billion in 1978, and $–29.5 billion in 1979 (*Survey of Current Business*, June 1980, p. 33). Gross national product in 1979 was approximately $2.5 trillion; in 1977 and 1978 it was nearer $2 trillion (*Economic Report of the President*, p. 203).

The "balance on current account" showed a small deficit in 1971, 1972, and 1979, and a somewhat larger deficit in 1977 and 1978.

20 Welfare benefits: Average monthly payments in families under the AFDC program rose from $190 in 1970 to $256 in 1978, an apparent increase of 35 percent. In the same period the Consumer Price Index rose 68 percent (*Statistical Abstract,* p. 352).

Single-parent families account for 19 percent of all families with children living at home, according to the Census Bureau's 1980 estimates, and 90 percent of all single-parent families are headed by a woman. The median income of female-headed families rose 67.6 percent between 1970 and 1978 (the last year for which complete figures are available) while the Consumer Price Index was rising 68.0 percent. See U.S. Bureau of the Census, Current Population Reports, Series P-60, *Money Income of Families and Persons in the United States,* 1970 and 1978.

Minimum wage rates: *Statistical Abstract,* p. 423.

Winners and losers: Industry-wide earnings figures (retail trade, etc.) are from the *Statistical Abstract,* p. 420. The figures on librarians, college professors, steelworkers, and other occupational categories are from Paul Blumberg, "White-Collar Status Panic," *The New Republic,* December 1, 1979, pp. 21–22. Vacuum-cleaner salesmen, Avon ladies, household workers, free-lance writers, and the cowboy all turn up in Edwin McDowell's story "The Big Pay Squeeze: Who Hurts Most," *The New York Times,* April 20, 1980.

21 The elderly: The median income of families headed by a person over sixty-five doubled between 1970 and 1978, for a real gain of nearly 20 percent. The average real gain in median income for all families over the same period was slightly over 6 percent. See Current Population Reports, Series P-60, 1970 and 1978. Note that family median-income figures do not show the same increase during the 1970s as the average after-tax income figures mentioned earlier. The disparity is accounted for mainly by the fact that average family size has decreased since 1970.

Old people living in poverty: *Statistical Abstract,* p. 464. The same point was made by Lester C. Thurow in

"A Government Program with Marks of Success," *The Boston Globe,* April 22, 1980.

Social security benefits account for nearly 40 percent of the total money income going to persons aged sixty-five and over, according to the Social Security Administration. In-kind benefits such as Medicare raise the fraction of total income accounted for by social security to at least half. Cf. Lester C. Thurow, *The Zero-Sum Society* (New York: Basic Books, 1980), p. 159.

Congress raised social security benefits 20 percent in 1972 and at the same time put in place the "machinery for automatic increases starting in 1975." It also raised benefits 11 percent in 1974 ("Social Security Recipients Will Collect 14.3% Increase in Benefits in July," *The New York Times,* April 23, 1980). Average monthly benefits paid to men under social security rose from $131 in 1970 to $292 in 1978, a real increase of 33 percent. For women the figures are $101 and $230, a gain of 35 percent (*Statistical Abstract,* p. 338).

Private pensions: In 1950, only 450,000 people were receiving benefits from private pension plans. By 1970 the figure had risen to 4.7 million, and by 1975 to over 7 million (*Statistical Abstract,* p. 340).

22 Quintiles: From Current Population Reports, Series P-60, 1978. Note that the figures in the text are for families; comparable figures for households of single or unrelated individuals are considerably lower and exhibit greater inequality.

Unionized workers: The gap between unionized workers' wages and nonunionized workers' wages has been growing since the early 1950s, though not in every year and not in every industry. See Daniel J. B. Mitchell, *Unions, Wages, and Inflation* (Washington: The Brookings Institution, 1980).

23 Inflation in other countries: Between 1969 and 1979, U.S. prices rose 101 percent. Over the same period, prices in Canada rose 105 percent; in Japan 137 percent; in France 136 percent; in Italy 219 percent; and in the

United Kingdom 236 percent. The West German inflation rate was only 63 percent (*Economic Report of the President,* p. 327; data extend through third quarter of 1979).

26 Stock prices: Standard & Poor's common index (500 stocks) in *Statistical Abstract,* p. 543. Bond prices: Standard & Poor's index of corporate AAA bonds in *Statistical Abstract,* p. 543.

Decline in stock prices: "Analysis of declining real stock prices by two MIT economists indicates that they are probably related to mistakes in how the financial community evaluates stocks during a period of inflation rather than to the effects of inflation on income flows" (Lester C. Thurow, *Zero-Sum Society,* p. 53. The reference being made is to Franco Modigliani and Richard A. Cohn, "Inflation, Rational Valuation, and the Market," *Financial Analysis Journal,* March/April 1979, p. 3).

27 Stock ownership: Slightly more than 25 million individuals aged twenty-one and over owned stock in 1975 (*Statistical Abstract,* p. 544). The adult population of the United States at the time was 130.8 million.

In 1972, the richest 1 percent of the population owned 15.1 percent of all real estate, 56.5 percent of corporate stock, 60.0 percent of bonds, 13.5 percent of cash, 52.7 percent of debt instruments (notes, mortgages, and so on), 7.0 percent of life insurance, 89.9 percent of trusts, and 9.8 percent of miscellaneous assets owned by individuals. All this added up to roughly a quarter of personal wealth (*Statistical Abstract,* p. 470).

Home prices: The median sales price of an existing home rose 112 percent between 1970 and 1978 (*Statistical Abstract,* p. 791), while average prices were rising 68 percent.

Greenspan citation: from Clyde H. Farnsworth, "Loan Shock: A 16½% Prime," *The New York Times,* February 24, 1980. Senator Cranston as quoted in Robert D.

Hershey, Jr., "Inflation at 13.3%: What is This Rapacious Thing?" *The New York Times*, February 3, 1980.

28 Profits: After-tax profits per dollar of sales for all manufacturing corporations rose from 4.0¢ in 1970 to 5.4¢ in 1978 (*Statistical Abstract*, p. 569).

29 Gains and losses: see, for example, Joseph J. Minarik, "Who Wins, Who Loses from Inflation?" *Challenge*, January/February 1979, pp. 26–31.

30 Lester C. Thurow quote: from "Our Standard of Living Has Not Fallen," *Challenge*, March/April 1980, p. 48.

Wage figures: The hourly wages are for "production or nonsupervisory workers on [private] nonagricultural payrolls" (*Monthly Labor Review*, April 1980, p. 81).

30n. Between 1970 and 1978, part-time workers increased from 14 to 15 percent of the labor force (*Statistical Abstract*, p. 397).

Paul Ryscavage as quoted in Christopher Conte, "The Baby Boom Muddies the Picture," *The Wall Street Journal*, March 27, 1980.

31 Fraction of the population working: The proportion of people considered "not in the labor force"—that is, not working and not looking for work—fell from 38.7 percent in 1970 to less than 36 percent in 1979 (*Statistical Abstract*, p. 394).

32 Israeli inflation rate: reported in *The New York Times*, January 16, 1980. The statistics about Ghana and Peru are from Robert Fuller, "Inflation: The Rising Cost of Living on a Small Planet" (Washington: Worldwatch Institute, Paper No. 34, January 1980), p. 12.

34 Nineteenth-century prices, as explained above, reflect a reconstructed price index (*Historical Statistics*, pp. 210–11). Though the numbers may not be exact the long-term trend is unmistakable. Twentieth-century figures (after World War I) reflect the modern Consumer Price Index.

38 The story of Henry P. Crowell and Quaker Oats, along

with much of the more general information on the emergence of large corporations, is taken from Alfred D. Chandler, Jr., *The Visible Hand: The Managerial Revolution in American Business* (Cambridge: The Belknap Press of Harvard University Press, 1977), p. 293ff. The historian describing the mill (quoted by Chandler) is Arthur E. Marquette, author of *Brands, Trademarks, and Good Will* (New York: McGraw-Hill, 1967).

Quaker Oats's size and rank: from "*Fortune*'s Directory of the 500 Largest Industrial Corporations," *Fortune,* May 5, 1980, p. 274ff. The three largest cereal companies, according to a report in *The Wall Street Journal,* account for 80 percent of the breakfast cereal sold in the United States and have been charged by the Federal Trade Commission with maintaining a "shared monopoly" (Lawrence Ingrassia, "Cereal Firms, FTC Still At It 4 Years Later," *The Wall Street Journal,* June 25, 1980).

39 Figures for 500 largest industrial firms calculated from *Fortune*'s Directory.

41 The account of the cigarette industry is compiled from the following sources: William Bennett, "The Cigarette Century," *Science 80,* September/October 1980, pp. 36–43; Alfred D. Chandler, Jr., *The Visible Hand,* pp. 249–50 and passim; "*Fortune*'s Directory of the 500 Largest Industrial Corporations"; Steve Lohr, "Reynolds Discontinuing Real 'Natural' Cigarettes," *The New York Times,* June 24, 1980; John Koten, "Tobacco Marketers' Success Formula: Make Cigarets in Smokers' Own Image," *The Wall Street Journal,* February 29, 1980; Steve Lohr, "Cigarette 'Tar Wars' Intensify," *The New York Times,* April 15, 1980; Richard Hodierne, "Tastes Like a Chemical Should," *The Boston Globe,* March 30, 1980.

43 Per capita cigarette consumption: *Statistical Abstract,* p. 816. Cigarette-industry profit figures: "*Business Week*'s Corporate Scoreboard: How 1,200 Companies Performed in 1979," *Business Week,* March 17, 1980, pp. 81–116.

44 Price-fixing cases: "Four Gypsum Concerns Settle Price

Case, Agreeing to Pay Taxes on $12.3 Million," *The Wall Street Journal,* March 4, 1980; "Five Firms Charged with Fixing Prices of Packaging Paper," *The Wall Street Journal,* February 29, 1980; Jeffrey H. Birnbaum, "Prospect is Waxing of 2 Crayon Firms Settling Price Case," *The Wall Street Journal,* February 29, 1980.

47 Robert R. Nathan quote: from "Imperfect Markets and Government Policy," *Society,* July/August 1979, p. 15. Price leadership: "U.S. Steel Corp. Follows Price Rise on Sheet Items," *The Wall Street Journal,* March 6, 1980; "Alcoa Lifts Prices of Ingot in U.S. 6 Cents a Pound," *The Wall Street Journal,* March 31, 1980; "GM Raises Auto Prices an Average 2.2%; Ford, Chrysler Are Expected to Follow," *The Wall Street Journal,* April 1, 1980; Reginald Stuart, "Chrysler, VW Raise Prices; Action Follows Other Producers," *The New York Times,* April 8, 1980.

48 Appliance industry: "An Appliance Boom That May Not Last," *Business Week,* March 10, 1980.

49 Chandler quote: *The Visible Hand,* p. 134.

50n. 1 Cf. Chandler, *The Visible Hand,* p. 171.

50 Chandler quote: *The Visible Hand,* pp. 316–17.

50n. 2 Cf. Chandler, *The Visible Hand,* p. 319.

50 Frederick Lewis Allen quote: from *The Big Change: America Transforms Itself, 1900–1950* (New York: Harper & Bros., 1952), p. 74.

51 On the airlines: Winston Williams, "Airlines Encounter Deregulation Snags," *The New York Times,* November 11, 1979; Winston Williams, "Ailing Airlines Blame C.A.B.," *The New York Times,* February 22, 1980; Winston Williams, "Ailing Airline Industry Engaged in a Rate War," *The New York Times,* March 15, 1980; Winston Williams, "Airlines Get Lottery Fever," *The New York Times,* April 15, 1980 (the quote is from this story); William M. Carley, "Losses Jolt Airlines as Fuel Costs Climb and Ticket Sales Drop," *The Wall Street*

Journal, April 23, 1980; "Now the Battling Airlines Try Mass Marketing," *Business Week,* April 28, 1980; Brenton Welling, "A Price War Aggravates the Airline Nosedive," *Business Week,* June 30, 1980.

On the auto industry: John R. White, "The Ford Style on Rebate: 'We Fish Where the Fish Are Biting,'" *The Boston Globe,* March 6, 1980; "GM Increases 1980 Car Prices an Average 1.6%—Similar Boosts Are Expected Soon by Rest of Industry Despite Deep Sales Slump," *The Wall Street Journal,* July 1, 1980. Note that this increase was in addition to the 2.2 percent rise referred to in the text.

52 Robert M. Solow quote: from "What We Know and Don't Know About Inflation," *Technology Review,* December 1978/January 1979, p. 42.

53 Joan Robinson quote: from "Solving the Stagflation Puzzle," *Challenge,* November/December 1979, p. 42.

Arthur Okun quote: from "The Invisible Handshake and the Inflationary Process," *Challenge,* January/February 1980, p. 7.

The price of sugar: "Sugar Price Rise Hurts Consumer," *The New York Times,* June 14, 1980.

Labor Department quote: from "Supply, Demand, and the 'Invisible Hand': Some Prices Still Fall," *The New York Times,* July 13, 1980.

54 On Kodak: "After Silver's Sharp Fall: High Hopes at Kodak," *Business Week,* April 14, 1980; What Goes Up Often Stays Up," *The New York Times,* April 20, 1980; "Kodak Cuts Prices as Much as 28%," *The New York Times,* May 6, 1980; "In Film, Silver Lining is a Cloud," *The New York Times,* August 11, 1980.

55 Firestone cutbacks: Iver Peterson, "Firestone Tire Plans to Close 6 Plants, Idling 7,265," *The New York Times,* March 20, 1980.

The Means memorandum is excerpted in Gardiner C.

Means, *The Corporate Revolution in America* (New York: The Crowell-Collier Press, 1967), pp. 77–100.

60n. Discount oil dealers: Charles Kenney, "Heating Oil Can Cost Less in Cash Deal," *The Boston Globe,* August 29, 1980.

63 Peter Meyer quote: from "Entangled Freedoms," *Harper's,* June 1980, p. 56.

Trucking profits: "Truckers Quietly Get Set for Deregulation," *Business Week,* March 24, 1980.

64 On the New York taxicab industry: "If the Cab Business Is So Bad . . ." *The New York Times* (editorial), March 4, 1980; David A. Andelman, "New York's Taxi Industry Thriving on Some Controversial Economics," *The New York Times,* March 13, 1980; "Hail Not the Taxi Deal," *The New York Times* (editorial), April 5, 1980.

Anesthesiologists, opticians, pharmacists: Michael Pertschuk, "An Inflation Paradox: Business Regulation of Business," *Challenge,* January/February 1979, pp. 57–58.

Lawyer advertising: Linda Greenhouse, "Lawyer Advertising Cutting Fees," *The New York Times,* August 3, 1980.

65 "Industry practices": Isadore Barmash, "Inquiries into Price Fixing: New U.S. Policy More Aggressive," *The New York Times,* September 24, 1980.

Rolf H. Wild quote: from *Management by Compulsion: The Corporate Urge to Grow* (Boston: Houghton Mifflin, 1978), p. 66.

66 Home prices: *Statistical Abstract,* pp. 791–92.

The tax example is calculated from the 1979 Form 1040.

Estimated $14 billion in uncollected revenue: *Statistical Abstract,* p. 261.

67 The specific information on housing in this section draws on the following sources: Paul Starr and Gosta Esping-Andersen, "Passive Intervention: How Government Accommodation of Powerful Private Interests Produces Inflation in Housing and Health Care," *Working Papers for a New Society,* July/August 1979, pp. 15–25; Robert J. Samuelson, "Inflation Has Found a Home," *National Journal,* March 10, 1979, p. 402; Brooks Jackson, "Costly Mortgages Spur Dire Predictions for Housing as Big Subsidies Are Sought," *The Wall Street Journal,* March 7, 1980; Sandy Graham, "Shocked Homeowners Have Trouble Selling; Some Change Tactics," *The Wall Street Journal,* March 21, 1980.

68 Starr and Esping-Andersen: from "Passive Intervention," pp. 21–22, 24.

Medicare spending: Robert Reinhold, "Two Reports Identify High Cost Patients," *The New York Times,* May 6, 1980.

70 Coffee prices: *Handbook of Labor Statistics,* pp. 434–35.

The general history of U.S. agricultural policy was recounted to me by Dr. Wayne Rasmussen of the U.S. Department of Agriculture.

On specific crops: Richard L. Hudson, "Dairymen Curdled by Moves to Decontrol Reconstituted Milk to Quiet Inflation," *The Wall Street Journal,* April 8, 1980; Seth S. King, "Dairy Prices Rising as Surpluses Mount," *The New York Times,* May 4, 1980; Seth S. King, "Dairy Aid Reviewed," *The New York Times,* June 5, 1980; "Dairy Farmer Diets Are a Bit Rich," *The New York Times* (editorial), June 23, 1980; Blaine Harden, "The Feudal World of King Tobacco," *The Boston Globe,* May 5, 1980; Mark Kramer, "The Ruination of the Tomato," *The Atlantic Monthly,* January 1980, pp. 72–77.

74 The account of farm economics before the Depression draws mainly on Lester V. Chandler, *America's Greatest Depression 1929–1941* (New York: Harper & Row, 1970), pp. 53–57. The quotation in the footnote on p. 74 is from p. 65 of this book.

75 New England fishing industry: Bruce A. Mohl, "At Port,

Supply vs. Demand," *The Boston Globe*, June 24, 1980.

78 Nineteenth-century wage rates: *Historical Statistics*, pp 164–65, 172.

The quotation is from Robert Hunter, *Poverty* (New York: Macmillan, 1904), cited in Frederick Lewis Allen, *The Big Change: America Transforms Itself, 1900–1950*, p. 59.

79n. Philip Taft, *Organized Labor in American History*, 1st ed. (New York: Harper & Row, 1964), p. 408.

79 Depression statistics: *Historical Statistics*, pp. 135, 169–70.

80 The account of Homestead and the Amalgamated comes largely from Philip Taft, *Organized Labor in American History*, pp. 136–45. It also draws on Katherine Stone, "The Origins of Job Structures in the Steel Industry," *Review of Radical Political Economics*, Summer 1974, pp. 113–73, esp. p. 121. The lengthy quote is from Taft, pp. 141–42.

83 The account of union organizing during the Depression draws primarily on Taft, pp. 411–537, and on William E. Leuchtenburg, *Franklin D. Roosevelt and the New Deal* (New York: Harper Colophon Books, 1963), pp. 95–117 and passim.

Leuchtenburg quote: *Franklin D. Roosevelt and the New Deal*, p. 239.

84 Leuchtenburg quote: *Franklin D. Roosevelt and the New Deal*, p. 107.

30-hour week: Leuchtenburg, p. 56.

85 Quote: from Leuchtenburg, p. 106. Union membership figures are from Taft, *Organized Labor in American History*, pp. 419–20.

Leuchtenburg quote: *Franklin D. Roosevelt and the New Deal*, p. 240.

86 Union membership figures: *Historical Statistics*, p. 178; *Statistical Abstract*, p. 427.

88 "Union Accord": *The New York Times,* August 18, 1980. According to the story, 6,000 unionized employees at Uniroyal, Inc., took the "highly unusual step of accepting a 12.9 percent pay reduction this year and a 6.5 percent cut in 1981."

89 Relief spending: *Historical Statistics,* pp. 1120, 1128.

The account of CWA, PWA, and the other agencies follows Leuchtenburg, *Franklin D. Roosevelt and the New Deal,* pp. 118–42. The quote is from p. 129.

90 A summary of modern income support programs can be found in F. Ray Marshall, Allan G. King, and Vernon M. Briggs, Jr., *Labor Economics: Wages, Employment, and Trade Unionism,* 4th ed. (Homewood, Ill.: Richard D. Irwin, Inc., 1980), pp. 455–85.

The figures on transfer payments are for 1979. They are from the *Economic Report of the President,* pp. 226–27, 289–90.

91 Men over sixty-five working: *Historical Statistics,* pp. 131–32; *Statistical Abstract,* p. 392.

92 William Green quote: cited in George Martin, *Madam Secretary: Frances Perkins* (Boston: Houghton Mifflin, 1976), p. 390.

Martin Dies quote: cited in Leuchtenburg, *Franklin D. Roosevelt and the New Deal,* p. 263.

Minimum-wage figures for the 1930s are from Martin, *Madam Secretary,* p. 392. Current figures are from *Statistical Abstract,* p. 423.

94 On wage variations among firms, see John T. Dunlop, "Wage Contours," in Michael J. Piore, ed., *Unemployment and Inflation: Institutionalist and Structuralist Views* (White Plains, N.Y.: M. E. Sharpe, Inc., 1979), pp. 63–74.

95 Wage contours: see Dunlop, "Wage Contours," in Piore, *Unemployment and Inflation.*

On nurses: Colman McCarthy, "Nursing Profession:

An Ailing Patient in Need of Attention," *The Boston Globe,* March 16, 1980; Loretta McLaughlin, "Nurses: Shortage or Rebellion?" *The Boston Globe,* June 16, 1980.

99 The account of the Depression draws on the following sources: Robert L. Heilbroner, *The Worldly Philosophers,* rev. ed. (New York: Simon & Schuster, 1961), p. 214ff; William E. Leuchtenburg, *Franklin D. Roosevelt and the New Deal,* passim; Lester V. Chandler, *America's Greatest Depression,* passim; *Historical Statistics of the United States,* passim. Heilbroner quote: *Worldly Philosophers,* p. 217.

Chandler quote: *America's Greatest Depression,* p. 45.
Hoovervilles: Leuchtenburg, pp. 2–3.

100 National Industrial Conference Board study: Chandler, p. 34.

Chandler quote: *America's Greatest Depression,* p. 51.

101 Hoover quote: cited in Susan Winslow, *Brother Can You Spare a Dime?* (New York: Paddington Press, 1976), p. 17.

102 The account of economic theory and the Depression draws on Heilbroner, *The Worldly Philosophers,* pp. 214ff; on John Kenneth Galbraith, *Money* (Boston: Houghton Mifflin, 1975), pp. 183–234; and on Robert Lekachman, *The Age of Keynes* (New York: Random House, 1961), passim.

103 The Fed's actions: Galbraith, *Money,* p. 185.
Federal spending: *Historical Statistics,* p. 1114.

104 Leuchtenburg quotes: *Franklin D. Roosevelt and the New Deal,* p. 249.

1974–75 slump: *Economic Report of the President,* p. 209 (GNP); *Handbook of Labor Statistics,* p. 213 (unemployment). 1919–21 slump: *Historical Statistics,* pp. 226, 126. Note that the text refers to drops in output over the course of a year, rather than the often-used "peak to trough" measure of a recession's severity. Yearly averages are a better measure of a downturn's seriousness, in my view, because they take into account how quickly the economy recovers from recession.

105 Government employment figures: *Historical Statistics,* p. 1102 (civilian employees); p. 1141 (military); p. 1104 (state and local employees). Current government employment figures are from the *Statistical Abstract,* pp. 277, 313, 373. Estimate of indirect government employment: Lester C. Thurow, *Zero-Sum Society,* p. 165.

106 Unemployment rates for occupational groups: *Statistical Abstract,* p. 407.

107 Figures on transfer payments: *Historical Statistics,* p. 1124; *Economic Report of the President,* p. 289.

Division of transfer payment "dollar": calculated from *Statistical Abstract,* p. 330.

109 National debt (dollar increase and proportion of GNP): *Statistical Abstract,* p. 254.

109n. The idea of "paying off the debt" is suggested in Robert L. Heilbroner and Lester C. Thurow, *The Economic Problem,* 5th ed. (Englewood Cliffs, N.J.: Prentice Hall, 1978), p. 469.

111 Budget surpluses: *Economic Report of the President,* p. 289. The years were 1960 and 1969. In addition, there were surpluses of less than a billion dollars in 1963 and 1965.

113 On the gold standard, see the entertaining pamphlet by Josephine Polomski O'Brien entitled *Gold.* It is published by the Federal Reserve Bank of Philadelphia and is available for free.

114 Metal dollars: According to a spokesperson for the Treasury Department, the "Susan B.'s" cost about 3¢ apiece to produce (including labor).

115 The account of panics draws heavily on John Kenneth Galbraith, *Money,* pp. 100–15; 183–97; and passim.

116 Bank failures: *Historical Statistics,* p. 1038.

117 On the Federal Deposit Insurance Corporation's recent activities: Richard F. Janssen, "Behind the Signs at the FDIC," *The Wall Street Journal*, April 28, 1980; "First Pennsylvania Bank Gets Assistance of $500 Million from FDIC, 22 Banks," *The Wall Street Journal*, April 29, 1980.

118 On the possibility of another "real depression," see Walter Heller, "Can There Be Another Crash?" *Challenge*, March/April 1980, pp. 31–36.

122 Productivity, real wage, and unemployment figures: *Economic Report of the President*, pp. 247, 244, 237.

123 Troop-level figures: *World Almanac*, p. 715. Defense spending figures: *Statistical Abstract*, p. 364; fiscal years ending June 30, veterans benefits excluded.

124 Budget deficits: Unified budget basis, fiscal years ending June 30.

125 Money supply: *Economic Report of the President*, p. 271.

Nixon quote: reported in Martin Mayer, *The Fate of the Dollar* (New York: Times Books, 1980), p. 171.

On the "wrong medicine" argument, see Gardiner C. Means, "Simultaneous Inflation and Unemployment: A Challenge to Theory and Policy," in John M. Blair, ed., *The Roots of Inflation* (New York: Burt Franklin & Co., 1975), pp. 17–19 and chart on p. 20.

126 The McCracken article (*Washington Post*, July 28, 1971) is quoted by John Kenneth Galbraith, *Money*, p. 288. The account of Nixon's New Economic Policy draws on Galbraith, pp. 286–301; on George P. Shultz and Kenneth W. Dam, *Economic Policy Behind the Headlines* (New York: W.W. Norton & Co., 1977), pp. 65–85 and passim; and on Robert Lekachman, *Inflation: The Permanent Problem of Boom and Bust* (New York: Vintage Books, 1973), pp. 21–30 and passim.

Chickens for broiling: Shultz and Dam, *Economic Policy*, p. 78.

127 Lekachman quote: *Inflation*, p. 28.

Galbraith quote: *Economics and the Public Purpose* (New York: New American Library, 1975), p. 190.

Shultz suggestion: Shultz and Dam, *Economic Policy*, pp. 68–69. The account of international finance draws on Shultz and Dam, pp. 109–31; on Galbraith, *Money*, pp. 293–301; on Robert Z. Aliber, *The International Money Game*, 2nd ed. (New York: Basic Books, 1976), passim; on Irving Friedman, *Inflation: A World-Wide Disaster* (Boston: Houghton Mifflin, 1973), pp. 237–53; and above all on Martin Mayer, *The Fate of the Dollar*, passim.

128 Nicholas von Hoffman quote: from "Passing the Buck," *New York Review of Books*, April 3, 1980, p. 16.

129 Paul M. Sweezy quote: from Harry Magdoff and Paul M. Sweezy, *The End of Prosperity: The American Economy in the 1970s* (New York: Monthly Review Press, 1977), p. 1.

Figures on foreign dollar reserves and gold supply: Aliber, *International Money Game*, p. 39.

132 Nixon quote: reported in Mayer, *The Fate of the Dollar*, p. 202. Aliber has Nixon calling it "the most important agreement in history," *International Money Game*, p. 45.

1970 exchange rates: *Statistical Abstract*, p. 915. 1980 exchange rates: *The New York Times*, October 1, 1980.

133 World money supply: Aliber, *International Money Game*, p. 23.

World commodity prices: Reuters index, cited by Mayer, *The Fate of the Dollar*, p. 209.

Martin Mayer quote: *The Fate of the Dollar*, p. 209.

Dan Morgan quote (and additional information on grain buying): Dan Morgan, *Merchants of Grain* (New York: Viking, 1979), pp. 156–58.

134 Adam Smith quote: from "Oil's No Problem," *Esquire*, April 1980, pp. 19–20.

135 Figures on oil use: from Steven A. Schneider, "Interna-

tional Rivalries and the Oil Price Revolution," Ph.D. Dissertation, University of California at Berkeley, 1980, chapter 4. This discussion of oil use and OPEC draws heavily on Schneider's work.

137 *Business Week,* quote: "How Price Tactics Feed Inflation," *Business Week,* March 10, 1980, p. 36.

Real interest rates: Tom Herman, "Even Today's Steep Interest Rates Appear Low if Taxes and Inflation Are Taken Into Account," *The Wall Street Journal,* April 3, 1980.

Business debt: Alfred L. Malabre, Jr., "Debt Grows at Same Pace as Postwar Economy, But Spurt in Private Borrowing Worries Some," *The Wall Street Journal,* February 26, 1980. See also *Business Week*'s special issue, "The New Debt Economy," October 16, 1978, p. 76ff.

Credit and mortgage figures: *Economic Report of the President,* pp. 280–82.

Money supply: *Economic Report of the President,* p. 271. The growth figure refers to M_3, a relatively broad measure of the money supply. Narrower measures–M_1, M_1+, and M_2, all since redefined by the Fed–grew somewhat more slowly.

138 On Eurodollars and other financial instruments, see Robert B. Zevin's newsletter, *U.S. Trends* (issued by the United States Trust Company's Boston office), Volume III, Number 4 (November 23, 1979). The growth of financial assets that are largely outside the Fed's control has led some analysts to conclude that the Fed can no longer effectively manage the money supply. ("Has the Fed Lost Hold of the Money Levers?" *Business Week* columnist Lewis B. Beman asked in the March 10, 1980, issue.) It also led President Carter to extend the Fed's jurisdiction–to include credit-card lending, money market funds, and the like–by invoking the Credit Control Act of 1969 (March 14, 1980).

Robert L. Heilbroner quote: from "Inflationary Capitalism," *The New Yorker,* October 8, 1979, p. 134.

142 Calvin Coolidge: "When people are out of work," the taciturn president is alleged to have said, "unemployment results."

Government regulation: Mark Green and Norman Waitzman, "A Challenge to Murray Weidenbaum," *The New York Times,* October 28, 1979; Murray Weidenbaum, "Mr. Weidenbaum Answers His Critics," *The New York Times,* November 4, 1979. See also Green and Waitzman, "Cost, Benefit, and Class," *Working Papers for a New Society,* May/June 1980, pp. 39–51.

142n. Nicholas A. Ashford quote: from "In Many Cases, Regulation Pays," *The New York Times,* June 15, 1980.

Detroit and small cars: "The automobile industry might be smarting further beneath the wave of economic Japanese and European imports had the environmentalists' call for fuel efficiency not helped force domestic changes in Detroit" (Anthony J. Parisi, "Utilities Have Cause to Thank Their Critics," *The New York Times,* September 7, 1980).

144 Minimum wages: The federal minimum was scheduled to reach $3.35 an hour on January 1, 1981, just as this book was going to press (*Statistical Abstract,* p. 423). The minimum wage fell from about 50 percent of average manufacturing wages in 1970 to about 45 percent in 1980.

Robert Gough and Robin Siegel: cited in Lester C. Thurow, *Zero-Sum Society,* p. 47.

145 Petroleum industry net income: *Statistical Abstract,* p. 607.

146 Oil imports rose from 811 million barrels in 1972 to 2,275 million barrels in 1978: *Statistical Abstract,* p. 206. They started to decline in 1980.

Robert L. Heilbroner quote: "The Inflation in Your Future," *The New York Review of Books,* May 1, 1980, p. 6.

147 Alfred L. Malabre, Jr. quote: from *America's Dilemma:*

Jobs vs. Prices (New York: Dodd, Mead & Co., 1978), p. 105.

148 Lloyd J. Dumas quote: from "Economic Conversion: Cutting the Defense Budget without Sacrificing Jobs," *Working Papers for a New Society*, May/June 1979, p. 52.

151 High-employment budget figures: *Economic Report of the President*, p. 50.

Arthur Schlesinger Jr. quote: from "Inflation: Symbolism vs. Reality," *The Wall Street Journal*, April 9, 1980.

Washington's role in the government sector: both Lester C. Thurow and Robert L. Heilbroner have made this point repeatedly. The figures for 1979 are from *Economic Report of the President*, pp. 288–89.

153 Milton Friedman: see, for example, Milton Friedman and Rose Friedman, *Free to Choose* (New York: Harcourt Brace Jovanovich, 1980), p. 257.

155n. See Martin Feldstein and Kathleen Feldstein, "The Fed Shifts Monetary Policy Aims," *Boston Globe*, July 8, 1980.

158n. Lester C. Thurow argument: *Zero-Sum Society*, pp. 62–63.

160 Administrative inflation: Gardiner C. Means, "Simultaneous Inflation and Unemployment," in Blair, ed., *The Roots of Inflation*, p. 11ff.

165 Figures on firm size refer to proprietorships, partnerships, and corporations (1975 data rounded upwards): *Statistical Abstract*, p. 555.

169 Martin and Kathleen Feldstein quote: from "Policy to Combat Inflation Gives Strength to Recession," *Boston Globe*, August 19, 1980.

Geoffrey H. Moore quote: from "A Truism: Recession Slows Inflation," *The New York Times*, November 18, 1979. Not everyone, it should be noted, accepts this "truism." Herewith a sample of article titles, all written by economists or business journalists:

"Recession Isn't Cure for Inflation, Study for Congress Says," *The Wall Street Journal*, April 28, 1980;
Michael K. Evans, "Recession Stalls Inflation But It's No Solution," *Boston Globe*, May 6, 1980;
Edward Cowan, "Can a Recession Slow Prices?" *The New York Times*, June 13, 1980.

172 The Fed and the Hunt brothers: "The Fed was so worried that the giant Hunt silver debacle could damage the commercial paper market, and thus the entire U.S.—indeed, international—financial system, that it was willing to endorse the billion-dollar underwriting of the Hunt brothers' enormous silver losses." *Business Week*, May 19, 1980.

Robert B. Zevin reference: from *U.S. Trends*, Volume IV, Number 1, February 22, 1980.

Hyman P. Minsky quote: from "The Federal Reserve: Between a Rock and a Hard Place," *Challenge*, May/June 1980, p. 35.

173 Auto prices: *Business Week*'s adjectives for the auto companies' price hikes were "nervy" and "aggressive." *Business Week*, August 18, 1980, p. 27.

Arthur Okun quote: cited in Edward Cowan, "Can a Recession Slow Prices?" *The New York Times*, June 13, 1980.

Council of Economic Advisers: from *Economic Report of the President*, p. 101.

174 *Wall Street Journal* quote: Alfred L. Malabre, Jr., "Shadows in the Promised Land," May 5, 1980.

174n. Lester C. Thurow quote: *Zero-Sum Society*, p. 65.

175 Peter Drucker quote: from Laurence J. Peter, *Peter's Quotations: Ideas for Our Time* (New York: Bantam Books, 1979), p. 470.

177 Economics profession: The most notable exception is, of course, John Kenneth Galbraith, and a cogent case for controls can be found in *Economics and the Public Purpose*, especially chapter 30, pp. 292–305. See also Galbraith's *A Theory of Price Control,* reissued in 1980 by Harvard University Press (Cambridge).

New York Times/CBS poll: reported in E. J. Dionne, Jr., "The People Want Controls," *The New York Times,* February 3, 1980. Shortly before, Yale economist James Tobin had written in the *Times,* "Mandatory controls are unthinkable now; only the people support them" ("Why the Fed's Cure Won't Work," *The New York Times,* November 11, 1979).

178 The debate on controls:

Shlomo Maital, "Inflation: It's Time for Controls," *The New York Times,* January 13, 1980;

Leonard Silk, "Uncertainty on Controls," *The New York Times,* February 22, 1980;

"Time for Controls?" *The New Republic* (editorial), February 23, 1980, pp. 5–9;

Leonard Silk, "Price Controls Gaining Friends," *The New York Times,* February 27, 1980;

Walter Heller, "The Case for Wage and Price Controls," *The Wall Street Journal,* February 27, 1980;

"Shock Treatment for Inflation," *Business Week* (editorial), March 3, 1980, p. 96;

Paul Samuelson, "The Case for Controls," *Newsweek,* March 3, 1980, p. 57.

178 (box) Sidney Weintraub offered a short account of his plan in "The Human Factor in Inflation," *The New York Times Magazine,* November 25, 1979, pp. 116–19ff. It is presented in greater detail in his book *Capitalism's Inflation and Unemployment Crisis* (Reading, Mass.: Addison-Wesley, 1978), pp. 121–63.

The New Republic reference is to the editorial "TIPsy over inflation" in the magazine's issue for March 15, 1980; Lester C. Thurow quote: *Zero-Sum Society,* p. 67.

180 Lid on a boiling kettle: Or, as *New York Times* writer Robert D. Hershey put it, "corking a whistling teapot instead of turning down the heat" ("Inflation at 13.3%: What Is This Rapacious Thing?" *The New York Times,* February 3, 1980).

186 England and Canada: The idea is from Paul Starr and Gosta Esping-Andersen, "Passive Intervention," pp. 24–25.

187 OPEC: Or, as Rutgers economist Alfred S. Eichner has proposed, the United States could pursue "an agreement between the major commodity-producing countries and the major commodity-consuming countries to stabilize the price of basic commodities (including oil)." "Combating Inflation," *The New York Times,* July 8, 1980.

APPENDIX

The Appendix draws on the following sources:

The Consumer Price Index: Concepts and Content Over the Years (Washington: Bureau of Labor Statistics, May 1978);

Measuring Price Changes: A Study of the Price Indexes, by William H. Wallace and William E. Cullison, 4th ed. (Richmond, Va.: Federal Reserve Bank of Richmond, April 1979);

Revising the Consumer Price Index (Washington: Bureau of Labor Statistics, 1978);

Revising the Consumer Price Index: A Brief Review of Methods (Washington: Bureau of Labor Statistics, 1976);

The Consumer Price Index Revision—1978 (Washington: Bureau of Labor Statistics, 1978);

Janet L. Norwood, "The Consumer Price Index Puzzle," *Challenge,* March/April 1980, pp. 41–45.

Index